Stress *and* Emotion
A New Synthesis

Richard S. Lazarus, PhD, obtained his BA in 1942 from the City College of New York. After military service in World War II, he returned to graduate school in 1946, obtained his doctorate at Pittsburgh in 1948, taught at Johns Hopkins and Clark Universities, then came to Berkeley in 1957, where he has remained.

Lazarus's research career at Johns Hopkins and Clark centered on New Look experiments on motivated individual differences in perception. Among other research topics such as perceptual defense and studies of projective methods, he did research on autonomic discrimination without awareness (which he and McCleary called "subception").

At Berkeley after forming the Berkeley Stress and Coping Project, he mounted efforts to generate a comprehensive theoretical framework for psychological stress and undertook much programmatic research based on these formulations, pioneering the use of motion picture films to generate stress reactions naturalistically in the laboratory. Later he shifted to field research and a systems theoretical point of view. His theoretical and research efforts contributed substantially to what has been called the "cognitive revolution" in psychology.

Lazarus has published over 200 scientific articles and 20 books, both monographs and textbooks in personality and clinical psychology. In 1966, *Psychological Stress and the Coping Process*, which is now considered a classic, appeared. In 1984, with Susan Folkman, he published *Stress, Appraisal, and Coping*, which continues to have world wide influence. In 1991, he published *Emotion and Adaptation*, which presents a cognitive-motivational-relational theory of the emotions.

Lazarus became a Guggenheim Fellow in 1969, and has received two Doctors Honoris Causa, one from the Johannes Gutenberg University in Mainz, Germany in 1988, and one from Haifa University in Israel in 1995. In 1989 he was awarded the Distinguished Scientific Contribution Award by the American Psychological Association, and the APA Division 38's award for Outstanding Contributions to Health Psychology. He also received an award from the California State Psychological Association for Distinguished Scientific Achievement in Psychology in 1984.

As of 1991, he became Professor Emeritus at Berkeley, in which status he has continued to write and publish research on stress, coping, and the emotions.

Stress *and* Emotion

A New Synthesis

Richard S. Lazarus, PhD

SPRINGER
PUBLISHING COMPANY

PAPERBACK

Springer Publishing Company, Inc.
11 West 42nd Street
New York, NY 10036

Cover design by Mimi Flow
Acquisitions Editor: Bill Tucker
Production Editor: Helen Song

09 / 5 4 3

New ISBN 0-8261-0261-1 (pbk.) © 2006 by Springer Publishing Company, Inc.

Library of Congress Cataloging-in-Publication Data

Lazarus, Richard S.
  Stress and emotion : a new synthesis / by Richard S. Lazarus.
          p.   cm.
      Includes bibliographical references and index.
      ISBN 0-8261-1250-1 (hardcover)
      1. Stress (Psychology). 2. Emotions. I. Title.

BF575.S75L315   1999
155.9'042—dc21   98-45782
                                                                                         CIP

Printed in the United States of America by King Printing Co., Inc.

This book is for curious students and professionals everywhere, but especially for my wife of 54 years, Bernice, whom I love; my beloved son and daughter, David and Nancy, and their impressive families. May they have just the right amount of stress in their lives and ample joy.

Contents

Contents

Figures and Tables

Foreword

Stress and Emotion: A New Synthesis provides a searching analysis of the premises and reasoning that underlie Richard Lazarus's ideas about emotion and stress, appraisal, and coping. The book is a treat to read. It has breadth, depth, and style. It challenges conventional notions about psychology in general, and emotion and stress in particular. It makes us think. Lazarus writes informally, as though he is having a conversation with the reader. It is, of course, a one-sided conversation, but as did I, the reader may find himself or herself making notes in the margins or even exclaiming out loud when there is a need to make the conversation more two-sided. Lazarus's enthusiasm for conceptualizing, systematizing, and trying to get things right is catching. His work is scholarly, but his scholarship is not dry. In commenting about the work of others, he lets us know what pleases him and what perplexes him and, in a very charming way, he also manages to let us know what pleases and perplexes him about his own work.

This is not a book a young psychologist, even a very talented one, could write. It reflects a lifetime of study and experience. The ideas about emotion and relational meaning had their roots in Lazarus's work of the 1950s and have been central to his work since the 1960s. Between then and now he has directed extensive programs of laboratory and field research, he has engaged in extensive exchanges with other researchers and scholars here and abroad, he has had graduate students who challenged the status quo, and throughout, he has constantly reflected upon the writings of others who think about similar problems. The presentation in this book reflects these experiences. The ideas are rich, clearly articulated, and they continue to be fresh.

Early in the volume Lazarus spins a fascinating epistemological history of mid-century psychology. This was the period when what we might call modern psychology, or as it is more commonly called today, behavioral science, emerged from the conflict between the psychoanalytic tradition and radical behaviorism. I was completely absorbed by this account. My interest could be attributed to the fact that I have always enjoyed history. But in this instance I attribute my interest to Lazarus's grasp of the epistemological issues, their historical context, their significance, and his easy style of telling us about it.

There is an interesting tension in this volume—the tension between theory and abstraction on the one hand, and the requirements of scientific research on the other. The 1990s have been a period of enormous intellectual activity for Lazarus. Most of his work in this period has been on the development of his theory of emotion. In this volume, he also addresses the requirements of research. He challenges the systems approach, which has been advocated in principle by a number of psychologists, but in practice is difficult to apply in research. Instead, Lazarus urges us to use emotion narratives to understand what is stressful for people, why, and how they cope. He presents his reasoning, and he starts us on the path. Many of us who do research on emotion, stress, and coping are drawn to narratives. This has been true in my own research program about coping in the context of AIDS-related caregiving and bereavement. The most exciting insights my colleagues and I have gained have been through the analysis of narratives. Quantitative measures help, but the gold is in people's stories. I am not surprised Lazarus is enthusiastic about the narrative approach. He is, at heart, a clinician. But it is good to see him encouraging researchers to use this technique.

Some might be tempted to call *Stress and Emotion: A New Synthesis* the capstone to Lazarus's work. His career has, after all, spanned nearly 50 years and he has been enormously productive in virtually every one of those years. But I think to call this book a capstone would be a misnomer. This book will generate new ideas and approaches for psychologists who want to study emotion and stress, and I fully expect that within a few months of its publication, Lazarus will look it over, appraise most of it favorably, and then decide there is still more to be said. And he, of course, will be the one to say it. May it be so!

SUSAN FOLKMAN
San Francisco
August, 1998

Preface

The book you are about to read is not, strictly speaking, a revision of *Stress, Appraisal, and Coping*, which Susan Folkman and I published in 1984, but a sequel to it. The earlier book is more than 15 years old and where it examines research and writings on a variety of topics, it does not, of course, cite publications later than 1984. However, it is still useful in many ways for students and mavens of stress and coping.

The fundamental reason for writing this sequel is my desire to pull together my late-life outlook about stress and emotion, which emphasizes appraisal, the coping process, and relational meaning as central to our understanding. This is a subject to which I have dedicated most of my professional life, and I want my present views and speculations to be portrayed and remembered accurately. To those familiar with my previous work, my outlook should have a familiar ring, but there is much that is new to justify another excursion into it which, I hope, will seem eminently worthwhile to old and new readers.

Given the proliferation of research and theory, there is almost no way of adequately reviewing all or even most of the new literature. I have, therefore, covered what I consider especially noteworthy and representative of today's research from my own perspective, especially if I think it moves our ideas about stress and emotion in a promising direction.

In the sequel, I examine the issues and ideas, sometimes difficult ones, that characterize this field and provide an up-to-date picture of my own outlook today. The book is designed to examine what we know and do not know about stress, emotion, and coping. Where I could, and without wanting to patronize knowledgeable readers, I have avoided jargon and striven for high readability, which means that those without much familiarity with this subject should be able to make sense out of all or most of what I have written.

The most important topical additions to this version are, first, an attempt to integrate the fields of stress and emotion, which have always belonged together but have traditionally been treated separately. Second, I have proposed that we move beyond a systems approach, which is probably not practical in today's research world, and turn to a narrative theoretical and research approach that I now believe is the most promising way to examine the dynamics of stress and emotion from both a variable-centered and person-centered perspective.

The book has its own structure and, more or less, goes its own way. It begins by presenting epistemological and metatheoretical fundamentals in Part I.

Part II deals with the physiological, social, and psychological levels of analysis, and gives an account of appraisal and coping in both stress and emotion theory and research, constructs I regard as the psychological essence of this field.

In Part III, I proceed to stress and trauma, chronic stress, posttraumatic stress disorders, crisis and its management, and stress and emotion in special groups, such as the aged, children and adolescents, and persons who are uprooted from their countries and have immigrated to others. These concerns of stress and emotion were not treated in the 1984 book because, at the time, they were not yet of widespread interest.

Part IV presents the arguments for and against emotion narratives as a research approach and describes vignettes of 15 emotions.

In Part V, which ends the book, there are discussions of the role of the emotional life in health and clinical interventions for emotional distress and dysfunction. I close the book with a wish list for a viable psychology of the future.

I am keen to express my thanks in more than a proforma way to Dr. Ursula Springer and her publishing staff, including Bill Tucker, the managing editor. They have been consistently encouraging, helpful, flexible, and easy to work with at every stage of the development of this book and my autobiography, which appeared in 1998. I also want to express great appreciation to Professor Susan Folkman, of the University of California at San Francisco, for agreeing to do a foreword for this book.

RICHARD S. LAZARUS

PART I

Philosophical Issues

Theorists and researchers should make their philosophical approach to science and their view of humanity known at the outset. This helps make their outlook, prejudices, and the theoretical and research approaches that inform their arguments in our contentious discipline clear to those who read their works. It could also defuse some of the arguments about models, theories, and research strategies, and improve communication.

In chapter 1, in keeping with this position, I discuss the epistemological and metatheoretical issues underlying my approach to stress and emotion to make my outlook clear from the start, and help the reader more readily understand what follows.

CHAPTER ONE

Epistemology and Metatheory

In all scientific disciplines, theories depend on working assumptions of all kinds, which are not subject to confirmation or disconfirmation, though they should be evaluated with respect to their internal logic, reasonableness, and fruitfulness. In psychological research and theory, especially in so-called postmodern science, and in an era characterized by a philosophy of deconstruction, it should be recognized that, implicitly or explicitly, we adopt an epistemological position about how we can know about ourselves and the world, and employ a metatheory about the nature of our being, without necessarily being explicit about it. It seems wise to begin this book by elaborating my own philosophical outlook, despite the rather abstract and sometimes forbidding quality of the words epistemology and metatheory.

Psychologists argue bitterly about all sorts of substantive issues, sometimes without recognizing the basic philosophical assumptions that fuel their arguments. It is important for scholarly researchers and theoreticians to make their ideological prejudices known at the outset, which is the purpose of this chapter.

Even scholars who are suspicious of theory—especially theory that, as in psychology, seldom permits deductive inferences that can make or break a particular system of thought—make all sorts of assumptions about the variables they choose to study because they cannot study everything that could be relevant. It would be better to refer to the hypotheses being tested in research as hunches or suppositions rather than tightly organized deductions. From this standpoint, the word "hypothesis" could be regarded as a scientific affectation, and it is often used merely to be in conformance with the academic scientific culture.

The important point, however, is that research needs always to be guided by ideas about how things work, even if they are not formally articulated as theory. And facts, to be of any value, need to be interpreted with respect to their implications for the human condition and how it works.

Epistemology and metatheory are properly a part of the philosophy of science. Psychology had just become a separate discipline of its own only a decade or so before World War II, having been part of philosophy in earlier days. One of the major rationalizations for this separation was that our field was, or should be, an experimental, laboratory science in the image of physics and biology.

From this standpoint, psychologists were enjoined to abandon what was referred to snidely, and with a holier-than-thou air, as armchair speculation. Psychology, it was said, should reject theoretical speculation in an effort to be scientific. But it went much too far in trying to demonstrate its scientific commitment and credentials, and still does with erroneous restrictions and shibboleths for which the field has been paying dearly for quite some time.

One of these shibboleths is the standard form of inference that depends on probabilistic tests of the statistical significance of observed differences in central tendencies that, for many decades, have been mandatory for reporting research. At long last, there is beginning to be debate about the significance test in psychological research, and its basis and utility (*see,* for example, a special section of *Psychological Science,* edited by Hunter [1997]).

In the 1950s, the field seemed to be on the verge of major changes in the epistemology and metatheory that had been dominant during the first half of the 20th century—namely, radical behaviorism, whose philosophical basis was the doctrine of positivism. The modifying adjective "radical" distinguishes extreme behaviorism from a softer kind that came into being later, and that was more compatible with the cognitive-mediational reasoning that began to emerge once again in the late 1950s and 1960s, but did not flower until the 1970s.

During the first 50 years or so of the century, psychology was most often defined as the study of behavior rather than mind. It had a love affair with the positivist commitment to operationism, which is a doctrine that seeks to define everything on the basis of information derived solely from our sense organs. Operationism recognized only positive facts and observable phenomena, and rejected inquiry into causes or ultimate origins. The mind was considered strictly private and undiscoverable by science. From this viewpoint, all scientific psychology could do was to link observable stimuli to observable responses in an effort to predict behavior. Ironically, even dyed-in-the-wool behaviorists were willing to talk about mind when it came to their personal experience, where it seemed useful in making sense of how we are as beings, but definitely not in the cause of their scientific work.

Although there had been earlier defections, just after World War II increasing numbers of psychologists were beginning to abandon the dogmas of behaviorism and positivism for a new outlook, referred to as value-expectancy theory or *cognitive mediation*. As will be seen shortly, this was not new to the 20th century at all but, except for the relatively brief period of behaviorism, had been the dominant view since the time of the ancient Greeks. In any case, a strict stimulus-response (S-R) psychology, which was the heir of behaviorism, was gradually being discarded in favor of a more complex stimulus-organism-response (S-O-R) way of thinking.

The O of S-O-R stands for organism, but it usually refers to thoughts that occur between an environmental stimulus display and the behavioral response, and these thoughts were said to have a causal influence on that response. Nevertheless, the O really should refer more broadly to mind because other processes, such as motivation, situational intentions, beliefs about self and world, and personal resources, to name some of the most important, also constitute the O in S-O-R psychology.

For some, cognitive mediation refers primarily to subjective meaning, an implication that still makes many psychologists uneasy. Actually, my own outlook, which centers on an individual's appraisal, is not a true phenomenology. I take the position that, on the whole, people perceive and respond to the realities of life more or less accurately—otherwise they could not survive and flourish. However, they also consider personal goals and beliefs in their perceptions and apperceptions, and to some extent we all live by illusion (Lazarus, 1983, 1985).

Not only do people want to perceive and appraise what happens realistically, but they also want to put events in the best light possible so as not to lose their sanguinity or hope. So the subjectivism you will see here, if this is what it should be called, is really a compromise—perhaps a better term would be a process of *negotiation*—between the objective conditions of life and what people wish or fear.

Anyway, awareness of the major changes in the outlook of psychology in the second half of the 20th century will help the reader understand and appreciate the approach to psychological stress, coping, and the emotions that is offered in this book. If the reader is to understand fully what happened when stress and emotion emerged as an important subtopic of modern psychology, it is important to have a firm grounding in the past and present outlook of the discipline. So let us begin our philosophical excursion with a brief look at recent history (Lazarus, 1998).

TRANSITION TO COGNITIVE MEDIATION

As pointed out by Kuhn (1970), who has examined scientific revolutions of the past, especially in physics, scientific research always depends on assumptions and theories about how things work, even if they are not made explicit. These assumptions guide what we pay attention to and explain. Theories are seldom abandoned on the basis of data alone, but it takes a new theory or metatheory that seems to do a better job.

Many social scientists, myself included, consider meanings and values to be at the center of human life and to represent the essence of stress, emotion, and adaptation. This requires making interpretive inferences from what we observe, which is the dominant psychological outlook of our times, though there is still substantial ambivalence about it.

To behaviorists and positivists, what has just been said will seem more like theology and metaphysics than science. Their restrictive view of psychological science has been, in the main, mostly abandoned, but many psychologists appear unable to move beyond the restrictive tenets of behaviorism. This conservativism greatly handicaps the study of individual differences, personal meaning, and how people construct it from their daily encounters. So, psychology today, which, on the basis of an inferiority complex, still seems desperate to be regarded as a laboratory science, continues to display a troubling degree of what could be called residual behaviorism.

Chapter 3 emphasizes individual differences as the main reason for adopting a subjective view of psychological stress and emotion. The most important sources of individual differences consist of inferred goals, beliefs, and personal resources, but they are very difficult to measure effectively merely by observing surface behavior in any given situation. To a considerable extent, we depend on introspection by persons about these psychological characteristics, which shall henceforth be referred to as *self-report,* as well as behavior, and measurements of bodily changes.

Self-reports are distrusted by many psychologists, especially by those with ultrascientific leanings, and sometimes not enough by others. From this standpoint, we should not ask people to tell us what they want or truly believe, and still call what we do science. We must acknowledge that self-reports can be an ambiguous source of information about the mind for several reasons, but few research psychologists make any real effort to increase the validity of self-reports by improving on the ways they are obtained (*see,* for example, Lazarus and others, 1995).

Nor are the other major sources of data—namely, observable behavior and bodily changes—any more reliable than self-report as bases of inference about mind and the interpretations we make to understand it. Much of the time, ironically, they are even less useful than self-reports, despite the standard prejudice of behavioristic psychologists about them. Instead of valuing our ability to communicate what we think and feel, an outmoded and unproductive ideology is allowed to decorticate people as objects of study by treating them as no more able to tell what is in their minds than any other "dumb" animal that lacks the capacity and speech to make observations.

Near the end of the period in which the behavioristic ideology was dominant, several illustrious figures in psychology, most of them in the subfields of personality, social, and clinical psychology, published maverick positions expanding a pinched S-R outlook into the broader, richer, and more forward looking S-O-R psychology we see today. A partial list in the United States would include Solomon Asch (1952), Harry Harlow (1953), Fritz Heider (1958), George Kelly (1955), David McClelland (1951), Gardner Murphy (1947/1966), Julian Rotter (1954), Mutzafer Sherif (1935), and Robert White (1959).

Notice that most of these mavericks did their most important work in the 1950s. They produced broad theories of mind and behavior, which were often frankly subjective, and opened the study of mind to a broad range of phenomena and processes not countenanced by radical behaviorism. This facilitated the development of subjective theories of stress, and more recently, theories of emotion that center on how people appraise the circumstances of their lives.

There were also some older generation figures who preceded and influenced this group of mavericks—for example, Gordon Allport (1937), Kurt Lewin (1935), Henry Murray (1938), and Edward Tolman (1932)—all of who's major works were published in the 1930s. To this list one could add many European figures, such as William Stern (1930), who had created a purely individual psychology, Gestalt psychologists, existentialists and phenomenologists, psychoanalytic thinkers, ethologists, and those adopting the verstehende movement, which could be interpreted as a psychology of meaning and understanding. Many of the European psychologists later migrated to the United States before and during the Nazi era and World War II.

In the United States, the New Look movement of the 1940s and 1950s (Bruner & Goodman, 1947) was also part of this revolt against the severely confining epistemology and metatheory of radical behaviorism. In sharp contrast with the traditional normative approach, the New Look emphasized individual differences in perception, an important subfield of psychology that had earlier focused on the study of how people in general perceived the world, and paid little or no attention to variations in motivation and beliefs among individuals and social groups.

New Look researchers recognized that individuals could deviate from the perceptual norm or standard without necessarily suffering from psychopathology. What we perceived was said to be the result of motivational, emotional, and ego-defensive processes, as well as what was present in the environmental stimulus display. This viewpoint, with which I resonate, gave a strong impetus to my own approach to stress and emotion.

If we look at what is happening in the social sciences as the 20th century comes to a close, there appears to be a strong trend to complain about methodological narrowness, which inhibits the growth of programmatic knowledge and understanding. This complaint suggests that the dissident positions of the previously cited mavericks have been, to a considerable extent, given lip-service. Psychology; indeed all of social science, is said by many to be presently in the doldrums.

No one has presented the case against methodological preciousness in the social sciences better, and in more hopeful terms, than Richard Jessor (1996, p. 3). Consider the following quote, which opens his recent remarks about this:

> Although still emerging from the thrall of positivism, social inquiry has for some time been undergoing a profound and searching reexamination of its purpose and its methods. Canonical prescriptions about the proper way of making science are increasingly being challenged, and a more catholic perspective on the quest for knowledge and understanding is gaining wider acceptance. The honorific status accorded particular research methods—the laboratory experiment, the large-sample survey—has less influence on working social scientists than before, and there is a growing commitment to methodological pluralism and more frequent reliance on the convergence of findings from multiple and diverse research procedures. This openness of the postpositivist climate in the final decades of the twentieth century has presented the social disciplines with the opportunity to think anew about what it is they are really after and how best to achieve those objectives.

Jessor then proceeds to criticize the shibboleths of social science, which seem to be based on remnants of behaviorism and positivism. He makes five valuable points, which are paraphrased subsequently:

First, there is widespread dissatisfaction with scientific accomplishment in psychology. Few people read scientific journals extensively today because little of what journals present supports systematic advances in our knowledge or will make much difference in the years to come. Few studies are replicated or are part of programmatic research. We are overloaded with input that seems to go nowhere, much of which is not very relevant to our daily lives.

There is also a terrible gap between the potential richness of what we and the great classical and modern literary writers say about mind and behavior, and what our research reveals. This discrepancy, especially between our own speculations and what we are able to study effectively, can be depressing for the ambitious researcher who is keen to make impressive discoveries that have value for our society. As a necessary corrective to the regressive forces in psychology, it is important to tackle issues with a broad spectrum of methods rather than limiting ourselves to one or two, say, the laboratory experiment or the large sample survey because we erroneously regard them as the scientific gold standard.

Second, too much research is a-contextual. Social scientists still venerate the search for general mechanisms that transcend context, which refers to the environmental settings in which mechanisms are said to occur and the kinds of persons that are being studied. The situational context makes a major difference in whether these mechanisms work, and in what way.

Third, there is still too much reluctance to take a *subjective* stance in our research and theories. We leave our inner life to be explored by the humanities. The reader who knows something of my past work might have expected me to approve this idea. I have often thought the great writers do a better job of describing people, their plights, and their inner lives than do most psychologists trying to be scientific. Such a statement will be regarded by many psychologists as heresy. The essence of my theory of stress and the emotions is the process of *appraisal,* which has to do with the way diverse persons construe the significance for their well-being of what is happening and what might be done about it, which refers to the coping process.

Fourth, the person is left out of much of the research on social behavior, ironically, even in the field of personality where individuality is of the essence (*see,* for example, Carlson, 1971; little seems to have changed since then). The importance of *interindividual differences* in the goals and beliefs that shape the personal meaning of our transactions with the environment is understated or ignored in much of psychological research in favor of sweeping normative statements about people in general. The same point can validly be made about *intraindividual differences*—that is, the study of changes in the same person's actions and reactions over time and across situations.

Fifth, too little research in psychology is longitudinal, which results in the failure to consider long-term developmental patterns and human life trajectories. A greater use of personal narratives and biography would be useful. They are a source of knowledge that has traditionally been anathema in those who argue for old-fashioned science with a capital S, but narratives seem to be coming into fashion. The maverick psychologists listed earlier helped to move psychology once again toward a doctrine of cognitive mediation. Many were concerned with the *meanings* that were constructed from a person's transactions with the environment, whether or not they used the M word.

The doctrine of cognitive mediation began to dominate psychological theory and metatheory in the 1970s. The change in outlook is often referred to as the *cognitive revolution,* though given the long history of cognitivism from ancient times through the middle ages, it could hardly be called a revolution, except when considered against the brief, aberrant period of radical behaviorism. Behaviorism could not last as a doctrine because it reduced the extraordinary human mind to the lowest common animal denominator and seriously oversimplified the adaptive behavior of even less advanced animals.

A quote from Bolles (1974, p. 14) captures the transition from behaviorism back to an earlier cognitivism:

> Originally, before psychology became an autonomous discipline [when it separated from philosophy], cognitive views of man prevailed. The early philosophers as well as the man of letters and the thoughtful layman all stressed man's rationality and explained his behavior in terms of ideas, perceptions and other intellectual activities. Then psychologists suffered that curious passion to be scientific. Thinking was merely a physical process going on the brain; perception was merely the result of certain neural inputs; man was reduced to a mass of S-R connections; and behavior was explained by a vast matrix containing nothing but S-R units. This was an appealingly simple system but it was soon found to be inadequate even for the explanation of animal behavior.

Before leaving this topic of the growing dissatisfaction of social scientists with the standard epistemology, a recent discussion of what Schneider (1998) refers to as romantic psychology should be mentioned. His courageous article in the *American Psychologist,* the house organ of the American Psychological Association, is titled with the colorful phrase "toward a science of the heart" (p. 277). The author questions the dominant view of psychology as a natural science, and argues that there is a long history of dissidence about this, though it has never had a dominant position. This is courageous because one can expect that, given the way most research psychologists think, the way our young students are brainwashed, and the extent of copycatism, his attempt to correct the balance will probably be derided. Schneider (1998, p. 277) puts this provocatively:

> Throughout its history, psychology has been the locus of debate concerning the proper nature of the study of mental life. All have not agreed on how psychology ought to achieve scientific status or even whether psychology is best conceived and designed as a science at all. If some believe this debate has never been significant or if they believe it is now over, this is only because of the attempted hegemony of the logical positivist view, the well-established view that psychology is to be a science modeled on the natural sciences, and that its applications would follow from the development of the physical sciences.

The author cites several historical theses to the contrary, including that of Wundt (1905) who is remembered as the founder of the first psychological laboratory, but who presented his volkenpsychology as including higher and more complex forms of thought. Schneider also cites Giorgi (1970) as suggesting that the main criticisms of psychology are that, in consequence of its natural science outlook, it not only lacks unity, but the subject matter is irrelevant to the most important human problems and the way we actually are as beings (*see also* Polkinghorne, 1988). This is a devastating criticism, but given the history of the field, it should be taken seriously. Conversely, Schneider's overall theme is, sensibly, not that we abandon natural and reductive science altogether, but that we should try to make it more relevant to our nature as biological and social creatures. We must make room for diverse approaches to the subject matter.

Nevertheless, psychologists who feel self-righteous about their scientific credentials need to examine other viewpoints found in the history of our field. Most such views emphasize the need for qualitative-descriptive research methodologies, and meaning structures that vary with the context of our lives as well as holistic or synthetic modes of thought. The most recent manifestations of these minority viewpoints, as identified by Schneider, include existential-humanistic, hermeneutical, narrative, semiotic, cultural, relational, transpersonal, phenomenological, and ecological psychologies. Quite a few of these are compatible with the doctrines espoused subsequently and throughout this book.

MY EPISTEMOLOGICAL AND METATHEORETICAL PRINCIPLES

Keeping the preceding preamble in mind, in the sections that follow, four main epistemological and metatheoretical issues are presented, on which my theory of stress and the emotions rests. Remember, the substance of stress and emotion is deferred until Part II, and here only some of the broader philosophical themes on which this substance rests are presented. The four issues include (a) the psychology of interaction, transaction, and relational meaning; (b) process and structure; (c) analysis and synthesis; and (d) systems theory.

INTERACTION, TRANSACTION, AND RELATIONAL MEANING

Instead of viewing mind and behavior as solely a response to an environmental stimulus display, it is more fruitful to view them in relational terms—that is, as the product of the interplay of two sets of variables, those in the immediate environment and those within the person. Although there is nothing really new in this position, it is widely honored in the breach.

One of the most serviceable ways of thinking in modern psychology has been to recognize the *interaction* of causal variables, as in statistics. Few psychologists today think in only terms of main effects. Rather, two variables interact to influence a third, and we recognize the recursive principle that not only does the environment affect the person, but the person also affects the environment.

However, although interaction is important, the meaning a person constructs from relationships with the environment operates at a higher level of abstraction than the concrete variables themselves. Therefore, in addition to interaction, we need to speak of transaction and relational meaning.

The concept of threat, for example, arises when a person with an important goal faces an environmental condition that endangers the attainment of that goal. This is a meaning a person constructs from the confluence of personality and environmental variables. We say, for example, that because the environmental conditions obstruct their goals and beliefs, such persons are threatened by psychological harm, which seems imminent or is, at least, a distinct possibility in the near future.

The *relational meaning* of threat is not inherent in the two sets of separate variables. It takes the conjoining of both by a mind that considers both the environmental conditions and properties of the person in making an appraisal of being threatened. In effect, threat results from these environmental conditions and the unique personal qualities an individual brings to the encounter. The person and environment interact, but it is the person who appraises what the situation signifies for personal well-being.

To distinguish this relational meaning from interaction per se, we might use the word *transaction* (Dewey & Bentley, 1949). Transaction adds the personal connotation of what is happening to the perceived event, just as the word, apperception, adds meaning to the word perception. To apperceive is to see through to the implications of what is perceived, and this meaning is made possible by the functional juxtaposition of a thinking, evaluating person and an environment, most often another person.

Nevertheless, because of confusion between what interaction and transaction are all about, it is better to use the term *relational meaning,* as it is construed by the person. The term *appraising,* which is the verb form of the noun "appraisal," refers to the evaluative process by which the relational meaning is constructed. I speak of constructed to point out that, although it depends partly on the environment, an appraisal also depends on how a person construes what is happening in that relationship.

The phrase relational meaning belongs to all of psychology, not just stress and emotion. It has the virtue of allowing us to understand why individual differences are ubiquitous in human thought, emotion, and action. Despite sharing much with other people and social groups, each of us also responds distinctively to the same environmental stimulus, especially when its meaning is ambiguous, as it is in much of social activity. On the basis of our unique relationship with that environment, we react as individual persons who differ in our most important goals, beliefs, and personal resources, these psychological characteristics having been forged from the interaction of different biological origins and developmental experiences.

Psychology needs to develop a new conceptual language. Instead of the traditional stimulus and response phraseology, which implies that the two terms are separable, we need a language of relationships. In any case, concern with individual differences and a language of relational meaning is, in my judgment, essential for progress in the field of psychological stress and emotion to occur. I shall have more to say about this in chapter 8, which presents a narrative approach to the emotions.

STRUCTURE AND PROCESS

A complete science must deal with both structure *and* process. Structure refers to the relatively stable arrangements of things, and process to what structures do and how they change. Two analogies can help us understand this distinction. They are the geological landscape wherein we live and the automobile engine, both of which are more or less familiar to most of us.

Throughout our lifetime, we expect to see landscapes as retaining basically the same contours over time—for example, mountains, seas, rivers, and even many man-made things, such as roads and buildings, although the latter are apt to be less permanent than the natural landscape. We would be shocked and alarmed if we looked out of our window one morning to find that the mountain we have always seen is missing. Despite changes of season and the different colors they bring, or the clouds that sometimes obscure the scene, the contours of the hills and valleys always look the same over a long period. This constancy continues year after year and may not noticeably change even over our lifetime. This is, of course, an example of *structure*.

Yet the constancy or stability, measured in eons, is only temporary. The familiar features of the landscape once did not exist and, in fact, are even now slowly changing, but too slowly to notice without careful measurement. Before the Sierra Nevada mountains, and the Coast Range where I live were thrust upward long ago as molten rock from beneath the surface of the earth, the fertile central valley of California was below sea level and under water.

Their rapid emergence in geological history, and the slow changes in them that are constantly occurring, are examples of *process*. They are the result of continuing erosion of the mountains by wind, the flow of rainwater down their slopes, rocks breaking off periodically, earthquakes, and volcanos that spew forth new rock, all representing a continuous process of change. In effect, structure implies stability and process implies change. You cannot have one without the other, as when the contours of the mountains create pathways for the flow of streams and rivers as water falls from the skies, and for the pattern of the wind. Structures and processes affect each other and are interdependent.

The same principle also applies to something as different from landscapes as an automobile engine. The engine parts constitute the structures, and the way they are connected and arranged makes possible the work—that is, the processes or functions—that the engine was designed for, which is to make the car go. To illustrate, fuel has to be converted into the movement of the drive wheels. Liquid gasoline is mixed with oxygen and turned into a gas when fed into the cylinders to be exploded by an electrically generated spark. The explosions convert the latent energy of the exploding gas into motion by forcing the pistons to move up and down rapidly in the cylinder walls. The up-and-down movement, in turn, must be transformed by structures called shafts and gears into the forward or backward rotation of the drive wheels.

Like the contours of the landscape, the engine as such lasts awhile, but eventually the parts wear out, and when the valves leak oil or fail to produce the proper compression, the engine must be repaired. When crucial parts of the structure break down and cannot be repaired, the car can no longer do the work for which it was designed. Here too, structure and process are interdependent, and we cannot understand an engine without referring to both.

The mind also works by means structures and processes, and our task as psychological scientists is to discover the principles that make it do so. Its structures and processes cannot be observed directly, as it can in the case of the landscape or an engine, but they must be inferred from the ways people and infrahuman animals function—that is, what they do and the conditions that affect it.

Thus, habits and action styles are structures because, after they have been acquired through learning, they remain more or less stable over time, some of them lasting as long as we live. Goal patterns and belief systems, learned earlier in life, are also structures—they are relatively stable over time. Along with environmental conditions, they influence decisions and shape our thoughts, emotions, and actions, which are processes that serve adaptation. To some extent, goals and beliefs are also capable of changing as life circumstances change. We know relatively little about how such change is brought about and to what extent particular person properties are capable of change or resisting it.

Psychology has had a tendency to emphasize structure more than process. What is stable, hence consistent over time, is easier to measure and deal with than action and change, which are evanescent. A good example is intelligence, which was once considered to be immutable, but is now seen as capable of modest changes. Our measurements of intelligence were once predicated on the assumption of stability, and tests were required to be reliable over time—that is, they were said to be a personality trait. If the test scores changed substantially in repeated measurement over time, the test was rejected as psychometrically inadequate.

If, however, we are interested in processes, such as appraisal and coping, which are by definition not so stable, this poses a dilemma for mental measurement because processes imply change, not stability. Stability and change are two sides of the same coin. The more stability a trait displays, the less it seems capable of change; the more it changes, the less stable or trait-like it is said to be.

We will see in later chapters that appraisal and coping, which are the basic theoretical constructs of stress and emotion, are sensitive to conditions of the environment and they vary with personality. Although they can be traits—some people seem always to be under stress or to cope with different stresses using a similar style—they also change from situation to situation and over time, in which case they must be regarded as processes. We do not want to obscure such change, and so new types of psychometric standards are needed to reflect this interest in process in contrast with structure.

Stress is concerned with unsatisfactory situations of life that we want to change for the better, and emotions come and go quickly with changes in circumstances. So these topics, along with psychological development and change over the life course, are especially compatible with a process emphasis (Lazarus, 1989a, & 1989b).

ANALYSIS AND SYNTHESIS

Analytic reduction is the attempt to explain phenomena at a higher level of analysis by reference to variables and processes at lower levels. The highest level for the physical and social world is the physical ecology of the world, the way a country functions, a culture, the social structure of that country or culture, and so forth. They are treated as the highest level because they are the broadest arrangements we can find in the world, encompassing all the diverse levels and subsystems within them, for example, the phenomena of mind and behavior, physiology, molecular biology, chemistry, and physics. Science is usually defined as the attempt to look for causes in the variables and processes of a lower, presumably more basic level, as when it tries to explain mind by reference to variables and processes in the brain.

Such efforts to explain in this way often go in the other direction, as when we try to explain physiological processes by reference to psychological ones, or psychological processes by reference to the sociological. This, of course, should not be called reduction because the direction is upward instead of downward, but its logic is similar.

My position on this approach to science is that, although it can be instructive and useful to relate different levels of analysis, none of these efforts at explanation works. The main reason for this is that the concepts at one level do not usually translate to other levels, and so what is being compared are apples and oranges, and they do not match. The notion that we are explaining in this way is an illusion, though it is widely employed.

Why do I say that the reasoning of analytic reduction is faulty? The most important answer is that psychology speaks of thoughts, goals, impulses, beliefs, defenses, emotions, appraisals, coping processes, and so forth, but these concepts are not found in neural processes as conceived by physiologists. And if we go down to the next lower level—for example, molecular biology, which deals with neurohumoral cellular processes—these too show even less of a match to those at higher levels of analysis, as in psychology or sociology. Thoughts are not found in microcellular processes in the brain but in what cells allow us to do. Mind is transcendent; it is dependent on biochemistry, and neural processes, to be sure, but they are not comparable events. And the brain depends on how we live our lives, for example, on the sugar and oxygen that we provide by our actions, and by living in the environment. The two are related, but explaining one by reference to the other is poor reasoning.

Having said that the study of the interdependencies of brain and mind can be instructive and important, let me assure the reader that I truly believe that the effort to explain one by the other is pernicious. Some physiological psychologists get this wrong, but others get it right. Thus, Allen Schore (1997,1998; *see also* 1994) has enthusiastically and effectively argued for the study of brain and mind while also eschewing explanation by reduction. For example, he writes (1997, p. 814) that

In Schore (1994), I document how a spectrum of sciences—from developmental, cognitive, physiological, and social psychology to psychobiology is currently detailing the neurochemical mechanisms that mediate affective functions, while psychophysiology is now systematically investigating the bidirectional transduction of psychological and physiological processes that underly mind-body relations. Recent advances in the new fields of "affective neuroscience (Panksepp, 1991) and "social neuroscience" (Cacioppo & Berntson, 1992), in conjunction with data from the more established area of "cognitive neuroscience" (Gazzaniga, 1995), are giving us a more detailed picture of the brain structural systems that mediate the psychological and, especially, the emotional phenomena that Freud began to describe in the Project [for a scientific psychology].

Discussing why Freud abandoned this project, Schore adds that

Freud thought that ultimately this psychoanalytic science could be rejoined to its biochemical and neurological origins, but that (a) the time was not right and (b) this rejoining would not be a simplistic "taking over" or "reductive explanation" of psychoanalytic knowledge in biochemical or neurophysiological terms.

Then, Schore (1997, p. 814) makes the following cautionary statement:

This work is providing important clues to the identification of psychic structure—psychoanalytic models of internal structural systems should not be reduced to neurobiology but should be compatible with current knowledge of brain structure.

And in a different article (Schore, 1998, p. 834):

Analysts might do well to heed the words of Arnold Modell (1993, p. 198):
All sciences are autonomous, yet must share concepts that lie across
their frontiers.

With respect to Schore's own research in developmental biology, it
is his view that the orbital prefrontal cerebral cortex keeps changing
with the infant's early experience, and, in turn, this changes the child's
sophistication about the significance of its transactions with the
social and physical environment. Herein lies the interdependency of
mind and brain as the child matures and learns how to adapt and
reacts emotionally. The psychological concepts he draws in this
analysis are not those of the past, but current ones, such as appraisal
and coping, showing his respect for the side of the equation that per-
tains to the mind and his focus on adaptation. About this Schore,
1998, p. 338) writes:

In other words, the establishment of an attachment bond of emotional
communication with the mother, the most important environmental
object in early infancy, enables the child to receive the mother's affective
appraisal of objects in the nonmaterial environment in late infancy. These
interactively transmitted, affectively charged external appraisals provide
the developing individual with the requisite experiences that ultimately
allow for the organization, in the second year, of brain networks that can
generate internal evaluations of the personal significance of what is happening in an encounter with the environment (Lazarus, 1991a) and can
elicit emotions to actual or expected changes in events that are important
to the individual (Frijda, 1988).

Sociology, anthropology, and political science deal with collectivities, such as social class, gender, political and economic institutions
and practices, cultures, and ethnic groups, but psychology deals with
individuals and their psychological relationships with each other as
well as with institutions. These differences in explanatory systems put
a major crimp in what I consider a fantasy of a unified science. We cannot explain what happens at one level of analysis by reference to the
concepts of another level.

The different sciences are also usually incomplete in a continuous
search for truth or understanding that is always changing over time. At
any point in our search, our knowledge is far from complete and often
inaccurate. Therefore, if we try to explain psychological processes by
reference to physiology, we are, in effect, trying to understand one set
of obscurities, how the mind works, on the basis of another set of obscurities, how the brain works, and we end up thinking we have explained

something by virtue of the neurological pathways they occupy in the brain, mistaking a label or a location for understanding.

My views about this are often seen as heretical, or absurd, by colleagues in several disciplines, though I do have substantial company among scholars who see this controversial issue as I do. Nevertheless, I am always amazed at what I see as the failure of first-rate scholars across fields to recognize the fundamental flaws in analytic reduction, especially when mind is reduced to brain.

Instead of arguing, as many physiologists and psychologists do, that we need a knowledge of the brain to develop a sound psychology, the better view is really the other way around. Without a good grasp of psychological functioning, physiology is nothing more than anatomy—that is, the structure of the brain, not its functioning, which is the business of physiology. To know how the brain functions requires that we know how the mind works, thereby turning the argument for reduction on its tail (*see* Lazarus, 1993, 1995; and Panksepp, 1993, for opposing views of this issue).

The form of analytic reduction that has been employed so successfully in science over the last few centuries is to seek the separate component causes of larger phenomenal units. These component causes, however, are each only a part of the larger unit. Although looking for causal variables is a very important aspect of science, if this were all the psychological science that is entailed, we would be distorting the phenomena of nature.

For example, analytic reduction runs the risk of treating the parts of the mind as independent entities, as if they were equivalent to the whole, as we so often do when we think of hereditary genes. Although genes seldom act alone, but usually interact with other genes as well as environmental variables in producing physical or psychological phenotypes, they are often, erroneously, given too much credit for the phenomena they influence.

In the psychology of emotion, this problem is reflected in the misleading idea that the functions of mind—namely, cognition, motivation, and emotion—are controlled by separate portions of the brain and, therefore, are independent of each other. The counterpoint is that in the normal course of events they are fused or interdependent (*see*, for example, Lazarus, 1984, 1997; and Zajonc, 1984 for opposing views of this issue). The separate components are organized into a larger unit, the system of the mind that, in turn, operates interdependently with the local physical and social environment, and is embedded in larger systems.

In a useful discussion of this problem of part-whole relationships, Shore (1996, pp. 322–323) has the following things to say about component and causal models in cultural anthropology, which applies equally to psychology:

> [We must] distinguish between "component models" and "causal models." A component model "characterizes all the potential behaviors that the component can manifest." A causal model represents the cause-and-effect relations between known attribute values and unknown values. It distinguishes the inputs and outputs from each component and "identifies which attributes cause component behavior and which attributes are caused by component rules."

Shore also points out that the problem of component analysis is prefigured by what has become known as Meno's paradox, in which one can name specific virtues but cannot define virtue in general. For example, the specific components of virtue do not tell us what virtue is as a general trait. Yet, this is the way we commonly try to define something—that is, by a list of its attributes. Still, as Socrates observed: How can you try to define something if you do not know what it is? The problem concerns the use of a list of components to define what the whole idea is, such as relational meaning (*see also* Mantovani, 1996).

To go a bit further with the issue of analysis and synthesis, it could reasonably be argued that there are no natural categories, but we construct them to make sense of what we see. If we are to understand complex phenomena, we must also synthesize the causal components we have isolated back into the original whole from which the components came, such as the mind, where they function interdependently. Mind, in turn, is part of a larger system, which includes the physical and social ecology of which it is a part (Lazarus, 1997).

Reductive analysis and the search for universal mechanisms has gained for science and society considerable control over our lives and the world in which we live. However, science is a larger enterprise that must draw on *both* analysis and synthesis (Dewey & Bentley, 1949) to be complete. Psychology usually overlooks this step in its obsession with reductive analysis and mechanism as a universal model of how things work.

For much of psychology, reductive science without extensive naturalistic description and multivariate research is apt to be a dead end. It might be good for the purpose of identifying causal variables, but it is not adequate for the task of comprehending the ubiquitous interindividual and intraindividual differences about which our field has long been so ambivalent. If we are truly interested in individuals in contrast with norms about people in general, which describe no person in particular and even misleads us about those norms because it is based on small population differences, we will need a changed epistemology and metatheory to guide our empirical research (*see* Lazarus, 1998; and in press).

One of John Dewey's illustrations of the importance of the larger field in which individual components operate is the cell. We constantly assume the cell is the basic building block of the body, implying, in effect, that all cells are essentially alike, yet we ignore how different they are depending on where in the organism they are located and function. Dewey argued that the appearance of cells and what they do depend greatly on the organs in which they are found. An in vivo cell in a human stomach acts in a different fashion from an in vitro cell in a Petrie dish, unconnected with other cells.

Nearly 60 years ago Paul Weiss (1939), an embryologist, did a series of experiments in which he transplanted neut embryo cells from one portion of the body to another. If they had continued to grow in their original location, they would have become skin and hair cells, but in the new location, they would have become the neut's eyes. What actually happened to these cells depended, however, on how early in the life of the organism they were transplanted. If they were grafted to the new location early enough, they grew into eye cells. However, if they were grafted later, they became skin or hair cells, as if their characteristics had been preordained by the original location, which made them resistant to the new environmental pressure to become eye cells.

Thus, the younger a cell is, the more plastic is its identity, which means it will take on the characteristics of the cellular environment in which it is found, whereas older cells must follow their original local destinies. The lesson this teaches is that a cell is not a basic building block for all tissues, but derives its ultimate characteristics contextually from where it is found in the body and from the kind of species in which it is found.

Applied to psychology, this challenges separatist premises in the search for the basic "atoms" of psychology—for example, that stimuli and responses, or perceptions and actions, are separate and independent behavioral building blocks, regardless of context. A holistic metatheory, which is illustrated by action theory (Frese & Sabini, 1985; chapters by Gallistel, von Hofsten, Neisser, and others), suggests that a stimulus is never independent of, and always implies, a response. By the same token, perception cannot be truly separated from, but always implies, an action. In other words, these components of behavior are always conjoined and function together as a gestalt or whole.

To understand complex phenomena properly, it is not enough to pursue the analytic, reductive search for causal components, and then to treat these components as if we have drawn up a full account of how things are and work. They are only functional components of a larger biological, psychological, or social field or system. As argued by the gestaltists, the whole cannot be understood by reference solely to its parts.

We must be able to move back and forth in our thinking between the two levels of abstraction, the component parts *and* the whole. One cannot properly be understood without the other. Dewey spoke of synthesis as distinguished from analysis. Later, in discussions of appraisal and emotion, the reader will be able to see this principle in action with respect to the emotions.

SYSTEMS THEORY

In recent years, linear S-R formulations in psychology have begun to be supplanted by what has been called *systems theory,* which some consider the scientific wave of the future. Linear thought suggests that antecedent variables affect mediators, such as goal striving and thought, which, in turn, influence consequent or outcome variables in a straight line flow. This type of model is really much too simple to reflect the complex events taking place in mind, emotion, and action, and the multiple directions of cause and effect. Most typically, the imagery is of a stimulus affecting a response as a still photo rather than a motion picture in which there is a continuous, multidirectional flow.

Systems theory takes a very different stance about mind, emotion, and action. First of all, it recognizes mind and behavior as subsystems operating within larger systems, usually viewed at different levels of analysis, for example, the socio-political level; the psychological level of the mind; the physiological level that centers on the brain, peripheral nerves, and hormonal substances; the microbiological level of cellular processes; and particle physics. One of the great ambitions that some regard as a futile hope is to have a unified science that maps the interconnections and interdependencies of each level.

Each subsystem of systems theory comprises many variables. Causal actions are reciprocal, and the same variable sometimes acts as an independent variable or cause, at other times as a mediator, and at still other times as a dependent variable or effect, though never at the same instant. Feedback loops make possible many different causal pathways, and many variables influence mind and behavior, including what a person anticipates in the future as well as what has happened in the past. It is in this sense that the reasoning of systems theory is no longer limited to linear processes. Each variable can play many roles, which offers the potential of enormously complex relationships in their influence on outcomes.

The implications of this way of thinking are profound. We must be open to diverse methodologies. No longer is it reasonable over the long term to seek single, or even a few causes, to understand the complex phenomena in which we are interested. This is what laboratory experiments and statistical modeling are capable of doing best. Instead, naturalistic, longitudinal research designs are especially suited to this psycho-social-biological complexity. Because each variable is apt to influence every other variable, often recursively, the use of complex models of psychological analysis is invited by system theoretical analysis.

Recently, however, I have become less sanguine about the prospect that a systems theory agenda can actually be accomplished and increasingly concerned about some of its metatheoretical and practical problems. This has led me to explore the possibilities inherent in a narrative approach to stress, emotion, and adaptation. The problems of systems theory in seeking an understanding of persons and their emotional lives, and the advantages of a narrative approach for unifying variable and person approaches, are discussed in chapter 8, where I examine where the science of a narrative psychology of the emotions might stand.

When all is said and done, I believe it will help the reader to bear in mind each of the four epistemological and metatheoretical issues and principles I have discussed in this chapter throughout the remainder of this book. They can be remembered as a series of contrasts—for example, *interaction versus transaction and relational meaning, structure versus process, analysis versus synthesis,* and *linear analysis versus systems theory.* These contrasts will appear repeatedly as we examine substantively the theory of stress and emotion, which begins in chapter 2.

Levels of Scientific Analysis

It is now time to turn to the different levels of scientific analysis of stress and the emotions. First, in chapter 2, I look at stress and emotion in general, argue for the unity of stress and emotion in adaptation, and then turn more narrowly to the physiological and social levels. In chapter 3, I come to psychological level of analysis—that is psychological stress. In chapters 4 and 5, I draw on the specific psychological constructs of appraisal and coping.

PART II

Levels of Scientific Analysis

Stress and Emotion

Never before has there been so much interest in stress, worldwide, among social and biological scientists, and on the part of
the general public. This interest extends to diverse clinical practitioners who apply scientific knowledge to help ameliorate emotional
distress, dysfunction, physical diseases, and social ills generated by
stress. Stress has become a household word, and we are flooded with
messages about how it can be prevented, eliminated, managed, or just
lived with. A major reason for the currently high profile that stress
research and theory has acquired is abundant evidence that it is
important for our social, physiological, and psychological health.

HOW STRESS BECAME A MAJOR
INTERDISCIPLINARY CONCEPT

It was not always this way. When I did my graduate work in psychology
in the late 1940s and took my first academic job, there was virtually no
public or scientific interest in stress. In the United States, the first professional stirrings arose in connection with World Wars I and II, especially the latter. It can legitimately be said that war is a likely impetus
for the exploration of stress, especially how it affects the well-being
and performance of soldiers.

Every country that maintains a fighting force needs to be concerned
with the fact that a substantial proportion of its soldiers develop
symptoms of stress, ranging from mild anxiety to severe and debilitating emotional distress and major mental disorder. Although some are
more vulnerable than others, the longer soldiers are exposed to battle
conditions, and the higher the casualties, the greater is the statistical
probability of emotional disorders. Thus, the relative incidence of

such disorders in combat airplane flight crews during night bombing is 12.0 when flying casualties occur after only 160 hours, and only 3.3 when they occur after 360 hours of flying during coastal reconnaissance. This incidence is only 1.1 in training when it takes 1,960 hours of flying to result in a casualty (Tomkins, 1989). These disorders not only impair or destroy the ability to fight, but also make soldiers miserable and sometimes unable to function at all.

During World War I, when Americans in France were experiencing very high casualties in trench warfare, shell shock, which is what battle-induced emotional breakdown was called in those days, was erroneously attributed to the effects on the brain of the terrible noise of exploding shells. In World War II, a psychological cause was recognized, which was a dramatic and important advance in our thinking, and combat-induced emotional disorders came to be called war neurosis or battle fatigue. A more recent expression for these and other stress-induced ailments is *posttraumatic stress disorder*, a term that originated following the Vietnam War.

Notice that the terms battle fatigue and posttraumatic stress disorder imply an external cause for the symptoms. Unlike war neurosis, these terms are less onerous to the victim because they do not connote personal responsibility for the trouble, with its implication of inadequacy and, therefore, blame. Regardless of terminology and related to the role of individual vulnerability, however, the bottom line is that the emotional problems are presumed to be the result of stress.

During and following World War II, it was mainly the military brass who were concerned about stress, and they hoped research would provide two kinds of practical information: First, how should men be selected for combat and what kind of person would be resistant to the stresses it inevitably creates? Second, how should people be trained to cope effectively with combat stress and its deleterious effects?

These important questions, and the thinking behind them, continued to be features of military psychology in the United States during the Korean and Vietnam Wars. Like previous wars, they were major research laboratories for the study of stress and coping, and helped fuel the growth of the stress industry. The answers required a basic knowledge about how stress works, which we did not yet have.

Simple answers were not forthcoming because of the complexities that result from individual differences in the conditions that arouse stress. A different approach was needed, and it became necessary to examine personality factors that influence individual vulnerability, and to study how diverse people cope with stress. As we shall see later and in the next chapter, psychological stress is neither solely in the environment itself or just the result of personality characteristics, but depends on a particular kind of person-environment relationship.

In the aftermath of World War II, something else also became evident. Stress became the province of everyone, not just soldiers. No one could escape stress, and all of us had to learn how to deal with it. Two reasons can be given for the expansion of interest from the military aspects of stress to its role in our routine daily existence.

First, modern war had become what is referred to as total war. Leaders of nations at war came to realize that the way to win was to make it impossible for an enemy to continue to fight, and the civilian population was just as important in this as the military. Civilians maintained the industrial machine needed to wage war. They were as much the enemy as the soldiers who were fighting.

Technologically advanced weapons carried by airplanes could also rain down terror on a population from the skies and made large-scale destruction and killing possible. This realization led to the sustained bombing of London by Nazi Germany for the purpose of destroying factories and commerce, and to kill or demoralize civilians who kept the allied war machine going. The besieged allies, the United States and Great Britain, quickly followed suit (most of Europe and quite a bit of Asia had already been overrun by the main Axis Powers, Germany and Japan). As we gained air superiority, we did the same to German and Japanese cities. Everyone had now become potential victims of war, and combat stress was no longer restricted to soldiers. The face of major war had changed forever.

Second, and even more important, it slowly dawned on us that stress was a problem in peacetime as well as wartime, and this awareness was the primary impetus for the extraordinary growth in the stress industry in the 1960s, 1970s, and beyond. Stress takes place at one's job, in one's home, and in school—in effect, anywhere people worked with each other or had close relationships as, for example, coworkers, family members, lovers, friends, students, and teachers. Stress became a topic of major importance in the social and biological sciences. Knowledge about it filtered down to the lay public via the media, though not always accurately, and interest was widespread.

What happened to the terminology designating the diverse phenomena of stress is also an interesting story in its own right. Even before the struggle to adapt to life was given the name "stress," its importance had been implicitly recognized by scholars and professional workers, if not the public at large. Sociologists, anthropologists, physiologists, psychologists, and social workers had previously used several divergent yet overlapping terms for the subject matter—for example, conflict, frustration, trauma, anomie, alienation, anxiety, depression, and emotional distress.

These concepts, which reflected the adaptational problems imposed by difficult conditions of life, were brought together under the rubric of stress. Stress became the dominant concept uniting them. As Cofer and Appley (1964) put it in a scholarly treatment of motivation, "It is as though, when the word stress came into vogue, each investigator, who had been working with a concept he felt was closely related, substituted the word stress and continued in his same line of investigation" (p. 449). Stress became the dominant term for uniting these concepts, and for identifying the causes and emotional consequences of the struggle to manage the pressures of daily living.

In a review of major self-help books on stress management, Roskies (1983, p. 542) presents an amusing and somewhat sardonic comment about the overkill involved in the public discovery of stress, as manifested in self-help books. She was not impressed with these books or the evidence about what they accomplished, writing:

> In recent years our traditional understanding of the causes of disease has been transformed by a powerful new concept: stress. From its humble origins as a laboratory term in the 1950s, stress has now become a short-hand symbol for explaining much of what ails us in the contemporary world, invoked to explain conditions as diverse as nail biting, smoking, homicide, suicide, cancer, and heart disease. From an anthropological perspective, stress serves the same purpose in modern society as ghosts and evil spirits did in former times, making sense of various misfortunes and illnesses that otherwise might remain simply random games of chance. . . .
>
> It would be un-American to accept a new cause for disease without seeking to cure or control it. Thus, it is not surprising that the ranks of self-help manuals have recently been joined by books devoted to teaching us how to manage stress. Among the array of do-it-yourself guides to increasing sexual pleasure, building the body beautiful, and unlocking hidden mental and emotional capacities is a new crop of manuals devoted to taming the killer stress.

As always in the field of psychology, in which we constantly seem to rediscover the wheel, ideas and the language used to express them can usually be traced to an earlier time. For example, Plato and Aristotle in Ancient Greece more than 2,000 years ago had important and provocative things to say about internal conflicts among thoughts, desires, and the emotions, which seem quite modern, but the word "stress" had not yet been invented.

The basic trilogy of mind began with Plato who, to oversimplify a bit, divided the mind—he called it the soul—into reason, appetite, and spirit. Today we label them cognition, motivation, and emotion. These mental faculties, as they are sometimes called—or better still, mental functions with reason regarded as the highest—are often in conflict. Aristotle followed in this tradition but added a very important idea in his book *Rhetoric* (Aristotle, 1941, Book II)—namely, that how one construes an event causes our emotional reaction to it.

He wrote, for example, that anger is the result of the subjective interpretation that we have been slighted by another, and this causes our desire for revenge. Thus, Aristotle treated cognition as in the service of emotion as well as its regulator. This treatment is, to my knowledge, the earliest version of what today we call cognitive mediation. I discuss this concept, and that of appraisal, which is the essence of such mediation, more fully in chapter 3.

The Ancient Greek tradition of conflict between reason and emotion (passion in those days) was borrowed and further amplified by a Roman scholar, teacher, and writer named Seneca, whose main interests centered on the control of anger and violence. Later, the social and personal need for rational control of our emotions became a centerpiece of the Roman Catholic Church in the Middle Ages, which wanted its flock to make moral choices in which animal instincts or passions—as emotions were called until modern times—were subordinated to reason and controlled by human will. In effect, the classicists saw reason and will as processes that could keep destructive emotions in check, making psychological conflict inevitable.

ORIGINS OF THE STRESS CONCEPT

As nearly as anyone can tell, the word "stress" was first used in a non-technical sense in the 14th century to refer to hardship, straits, adversity, or affliction (Lumsden, 1981). In the late 17th century, a prominent physicist-biologist, Robert Hooke (Hinkle, 1973), made a lasting contribution by formulating an engineering analysis of stress. He addressed the practical question of how man-made structures, such as bridges, should be designed to carry heavy loads without collapsing. They must resist buffeting by winds, earthquakes, and other natural forces capable of destroying them.

Hooke's analysis of the problem drew on three basic concepts, load, stress, and strain. *Load* refers to external forces, such as weight; *stress* is the area of the bridge's structure over which the load was applied; and *strain* is the deformation of the structure, produced by the interplay of load and stress. This analysis greatly influenced 20th-century models of stress, which drew on the idea of load as an external force exerted on a social, physiological, or psychological system. Load is analogous to an external stress stimulus, and strain is analogous to the stress response or reaction.

When these engineering ideas were applied to society, the body, and the mind of an individual, the basic concepts were relabeled and often used differently. Stress and strain were the main terms to survive. We now speak of a *stress stimulus* or stressor as the external input, and *stress response* or reaction as the output.

Strain is still used by physiologists to represent the stress-produced change in or deformation of the body. Sociologists, who focus on the social system, reverse the order of the terms, speaking instead of a strain in the social system, and stress reactions in the people who are part of that system. Whatever the terms used, however, in stress analysis there is almost always a stimulus—that is, an external event or stressor—and a response or reaction. As you will soon see, however, much more than input and output is needed to understand the stress process fully.

WHY IT IS USEFUL TO STUDY EMOTION
IN ADDITION TO STRESS

In the past, stress was viewed as a unidimensional concept—that is, as a continuum ranging from low to high, a concept superficially analogous to arousal or activation (Duffy, 1962). For a while, there was considerable interest in the concept of activation, which united a psychological dimension, ranging from sleepiness to alert excitement with a dimension of activity and inactivity in portions of the nervous system—specifically the brain stem and the autonomic nervous system.

However, there were two early attempts to divide stress into types, both of which have remained influential. In one, the distinguished physiologist, Hans Selye (1974) suggested two types: distress and eustress. *Distress* is the destructive type, illustrated by anger and aggression, and it is said to damage health. *Eustress* is the constructive type, illustrated by emotions associated with empathic concerns for others and positive striving that would benefit the community, and it is said to be compatible with or protective of good health. This important hypothesis remains vague and controversial and, despite its widespread appeal, has still not been adequately supported or refuted by empirical research.

In a second attempt, I drew a distinction among three types of psychological stress, harm/loss, threat, and challenge, and argued that the appraisals associated with each are different (Lazarus, 1966). *Harm/ loss* deals with damage or loss that has already taken place. *Threat* has to do with harm or loss that has not yet occurred, but is possible or likely in the near future. *Challenge* consists of the sensibility that, although difficulties stand in the way of gain, they can be overcome with verve, persistence, and self-confidence. Each is coped with differently, and has different psychophysiological and performance outcomes.

Despite these subdivisions of stress types, the typical idea of stress is much simpler than that of the emotions. Either as a single dimension, or with only a few functional categories, stress tells us relatively little about the details of a person's struggle to adapt. Emotion, conversely, includes at least 15 different varieties, greatly increasing the richness of what can be said about a person's adaptational struggle.

To digress briefly about the idea of several qualitatively different emotions, this approach is in contrast to the approach that earlier dominated the psychology of emotion in which emotion was reduced to a few independent dimensions, such as pleasantness-unpleasantness, excitement-relaxation, and positive-negative. I should mention in this context one of the recent pioneers of this field, Silvan S. Tomkins, whose two-volume work, *Affect, Imagery, and Consciousness*, Vol. 1: *The Positive Affects*, and Vol. 2: *The Negative Affects*, were both published by Springer (New York). Near the end of his life he added a third and fourth volume to the first two: Vol. 3: *Affect, Imagery, Consciousness: The Negative Affects, Anger and Fear* (1991); and Vol. 4, *Affect, Imagery, Consciousness: Cognition, Duplication, and Transformation of Information* (1992), both also published by Springer.

Tomkins was one of the earliest modern psychologists to take seriously the distinctiveness of several emotions of interest to the Ancient Greeks, Plato and Aristotle, and to adopt a *categorical* rather than dimensional approach. He emphasized surprise (startle), joy, anguish, anger, fear, and shame, and described their psychodynamics in some detail. He was an extraordinarily broad scholar who adopted a strongly evolutionary, genetic, physiology-of-the-brain approach, which differs substantially from cognitive-mediational theories of today. He also is known for having used the felicitous electronic metaphor for emotions as amplifiers of the cognitive activity that helped animals and persons to evaluate their adaptational encounters in helping them survive.

Tomkins was not particularly interested in the cognitive factors, such as appraisal, as an influence on the emotions, and was suspicious of the modern emphasis on this. The idea of cognitive mediation struck him as an overintellectualized way to make hot emotions cool and pallid, a position I argue against in chapter 4, where I offer a defense of appraisal theory.

His evolutionary-physiological focus led him to take the position that the pattern of facial expressions not only indicated automatically which "affect" (the word he used instead of "emotion" to refer to the psychological experience of the emotion) had been aroused but also was said to cause the affect, a stance not in accord with cognitive theorists and researchers. In any case, his emphasis on the face led him to be a mentor to two of the most active researchers today on facial expression and emotion: Carroll E. Izard and Paul Ekman.

But to return to my own categorical approach, my list of 15 emotions includes anger, envy, jealousy, anxiety, fright, guilt, shame, relief, hope, sadness, happiness, pride, love, gratitude, and compassion, and is at present one of the longest lists in the field. Each emotion tells us something different about how a person has appraised what is happening in an adaptational transaction and how that person is coping with it. In effect, each emotion has a different scenario or story about an ongoing relationship with the environment.

So, if we know what it means to experience each emotion—that is, the dramatic plot for each—then knowing the emotion being experienced provides a ready understanding of how it was brought about. This provides the advantage of substantial clinical insight about the dynamics of that person's adaptational life. We should not allow this potential gain to be forgotten in our research on stress by failing to consider the emotions involved in stress and adaptation.

To offer a few brief examples, anger is about being demeaned or slighted. Guilt is about a moral lapse. Hope is about a threat or a promise whose outcome is uncertain but could possibly be realized. Happiness is about attaining a goal one has been seeking or making significant progress in that direction. Compassion is about having empathy for someone else's plight—and so forth for the other emotions, whose psychodynamics are described in some detail in chapter 9.

There is another potential gain from knowing the emotion being experienced and the story it reveals about the person-environment relationship. If someone typically responds in many encounters with the same emotion, say, anger, anxiety, sadness, or happiness, we have captured a stable feature of this person's emotional life—that is, he or she is evidently disposed to be an angry, anxious, sad, or happy person, or perhaps more accurately, the person-environment relationship is a stable one. The emotional response in some degree can be said to transcend the situational context; we have discovered a personality

trait and have learned something structurally important about how
this person relates to the world.

THE UNITY OF STRESS AND EMOTION

One of the dilemmas of writing about stress is that this topic is interdependent with the field of emotion. When there is stress there are also
emotions—perhaps we could call them stress emotions—and the
reverse, although not always the case, often applies. That is, when
there are emotions, even positively toned ones, there is often stress
too but by no means always. Given this interdependence, the oddity is
that two separate literatures have developed, almost as if stress had
no bearing on the emotions, and the emotions had no bearing on
stress. Scholars and scientists concerned with stress and coping
research and theory tend not to know or cite emotion research and
theory, and vice versa.

This separation of fields is an absurdity, but it reflects the highly
fractionated nature of our discipline and social science in general.
People working in these fields specialize in increasingly narrow topics
and often remain parochial in outlook. This specialization probably
reflects the way stress and emotion were defined decades earlier and
the issues of greatest interest to psychologists. Stress was initially
regarded as a practical subject matter and emotion was treated as a
basic science conundrum in human and animal life, which needed to
be understood for its own sake. Today, however, the practical importance of the emotions in our psychological and physical well-being,
and in social functioning, is widely recognized.

During the 1950s and 1960s, several pioneers in stress theory and
research published important and forward-looking treatises on psychological stress and emotion. The interdisciplinary quality of the
stress concept is illustrated by the fields represented by these scientists. The only important fields not represented subsequently in the
examples cited in the next paragraph are anthropology and social
work, the latter being more akin to psychiatry as an applied field,
though professionals in both these fields have made important contributions to what we know about stress and emotion.

Two research-oriented psychiatrists, Grinker and Spiegel (1945)
studied the stresses of military combat; a social psychologist, Irving
Janis (1958) studied how a patient he was treating psychoanalytically
dealt with the stress of major surgery; a sociologist, David Mechanic
(1962/1978) carefully documented the stresses and coping processes

provoked in graduate students facing a career-threatening examination; a personality psychologist, Magda Arnold (1960) formulated the first programmatic statement of appraisal theory; and several clinical psychologists formulated approaches to treatment and prevention designed to help patients cope with stress more effectively (see chapter 11).

My first monograph on stress and coping (Lazarus, 1966) reviewed research and formulated a theory of psychological stress, which was based on the construct of *appraisal.* This theory drew frankly on a subjective approach, which relied on the idea that stress and emotion depend on how an individual evaluates (appraises) transactions with the environment.

In the process of formulating this theory, I also began to see that stress was an aspect of a larger set of issues that included the emotions. So I subsequently set about transforming the construct of appraisal to fit the emotions too (Lazarus, 1966, 1968; Lazarus, Averill, & Opton, 1970; Lazarus & Averill, 1972; Lazarus, Averill, & Opton, 1974; Lazarus, Coyne, & Folkman, 1982; Lazarus, Kanner, & Folkman, 1980). These efforts culminated in three later monographs on emotion and adaptation, (Lazarus, 1991; Lazarus & Folkman, 1984; and Lazarus & Lazarus, 1994), the latter being a lay-oriented version of emotion theory.

The interdependence of stress and emotion is the main reason I entitled the present book *Stress and the Emotions: A new synthesis.* One major theme is that we cannot sensibly treat stress and emotion as if they were separate fields without doing a great disservice to both. There are more communalities than divergences in the way these embodied states of mind are aroused, coped with, and how they affect psychological well-being, functioning, and somatic health.

It should be obvious that certain emotions—for example, anger, envy, jealousy, anxiety, fright, guilt, shame, and sadness—could be called *stress emotions,* because they usually arise from stressful, which refers to harmful, threatening, or challenging conditions. Although we think of many emotions as positively toned, because they arise from circumstances favorable to the attainment of important goals, they are often closely linked to harm or threat. For example, relief results from a harmful or threatening situation that has abated or disappeared; hope, more often than not, stems from a situation in which we must prepare for the worst while hoping for better.

Even happiness, pride, love, and gratitude, which are usually considered to be positive in tone, are frequently associated with stress. For example, though happy about something good that has happened, we may fear that the favorable conditions provoking our happiness will end, so we engage in coping efforts to prevent this from happening. Or we fear that when conditions of our life are very favorable, others will resent our good fortune and try to undermine it. And when pride is viewed by others as the result of having taken too much credit, say, for our success, that of our child, or someone we are identified with, or as a competitive putdown, we must either reject the social pressure or soft-peddle our pride. Our biblical language expresses this in the aphorisms: "Pride goeth before a fall," and "overweening pride."

Love, which is so often treated as a highly desirable emotional state, can be exceedingly stressful when it is unrequited, or if we think our lover is losing interest. When gratitude is grudging, or violates one's values, the social necessity of showing it may be stressful. And compassion can be aversive when we fail to control our emotional reaction to the suffering of others. All this makes a strong case that stress applies not only to the so-called stress emotions, but also to those that are positively toned and the relational conditions that surround them.

THE UNITY OF STRESS, EMOTION, AND COPING

Usually coping has been linked to stress rather than the emotions, and emotion theorists have either ignored it or treated it as separate from the emotion process. Coping is said, incorrectly, to come into focus after an emotion has been aroused to regulate it or deal with the conditions provoking it.

This is unfortunate because coping is an integral part of the process of emotional arousal. Judging the significance of what is happening always entails evaluating what might be done about it, which determines whether we react, say, with anxiety or anger. For example, when demeaned, viewing oneself as helpless favors anxiety and withdrawal, whereas having a sense of power over the outcome favors anger and aggression. Separating emotion from coping does a disservice to the integrity and complexity of the emotion process, which at every turn considers how we might cope.

We should view stress, emotion, and coping as existing in a part-whole relationship. Separating them is justified only for convenience of analysis because the separation distorts the phenomena as they appear in nature. The three concepts, stress, emotion, and coping, belong together and form a conceptual unit, with emotion being the superordinate concept because it includes stress and coping.

LEVELS OF STRESS ANALYSIS

Returning now to the stress process itself, to remain clear minded we must distinguish between the way different scientific disciplines treat it, thereby reflecting different levels of scientific analysis. Physiology is concerned with the body, especially the brain and its hormonal neuro-transmitters. Two other disciplines—sociology and its cousin, cultural anthropology—deal primarily with the society or sociocultural system. A fourth discipline, psychology, is concerned with individual mind and behavior.

In the following sections, I take up two of these levels of stress analysis, the sociocultural and the physiological levels; examine how they relate to each other; and review the distinctive variables essential to each. Psychological stress, which deals with the individual mind, and discusses appraisal and coping in detail, is reserved for chapter 3.

Sociocultural Level

The social structure has to do with the way society is organized—for example, into social classes, age, and gender—and how objective and subjective membership in these subgroups influence social meanings, values, social beliefs, attitudes, and actions, which are the major aspects of culture. Sociologists and cultural anthropologists are the main disciplines concerned with this level.

What connects the social structure and culture to stress is that certain conditions, such as sociocultural change, immigration, war, racism, natural disasters, and social crises, such as economic depressions, unemployment, poverty, social isolation, privation, and social anarchy, all breed stress reactions in individual persons and social groups, depending on their respective positions in the society. As I noted earlier, these sources of turmoil in the society are often referred to by sociologists as *social strains,* which produce *psychological stress* in individuals and collectivities or groups (Smelser, 1963).

In addition, social scientists of diverse interests, as well as clinical psychologists, psychiatrists, and social workers who draw on social science concepts in their efforts to help troubled individuals, also study natural and industrial disasters (Baker and Chapman, 1962; Lucas, 1969), common social sources of stress, such as school examinations (Mechanic, 1962/1978), family problems (Hetherington & Blechman, 1996), and organizational or job stress (Cooper & Payne, 1980; French, Caplan & Van Harrison, 1982; Kahn, Wolfe, Quinn, Snoek, & Rosenthal, 1964; and Perrewé, 1991).

In the 19th century, several seminal social thinkers, such as Max Weber, Emil Durkheim, and Karl Marx, who could be considered among the founding fathers of modern sociology, were concerned about social injustices and their role in producing alienation from society in large segments of the population. Durkheim (1893) wrote about the experience of anomie, which overlaps with alienation but refers specifically to the loss or lack of acceptable norms on which to predicate one's life in a troubled society. This is also a concern of anthropologists and psychologists, as in the problems presented by dislocation and immigration (Berry, 1997) and change within a culture (Shore, 1996).

All three founding fathers of sociology wrote about alienation from work and from society as a result of the industrial revolution and technological change. They observed that factory workers no longer could take responsibility for their product from start to finish, as once was true of artisans and guild workers in preindustrial society. Instead, they saw themselves as contributing only a small part to the total production process. Their only reward was economic, so they lost both a sense of efficacy, pride, and commitment to their work.

Anomie and alienation, regardless of the way they are brought about, are not only antithetical to the maintenance of a rule-based society, but they also play an important negative role in morale, personal motivation, identity, and social commitment. Other words for these states of mind are "powerlessness," "meaninglessness," "normlessness," "isolation," and "estrangement from the self," all of which have negative emotional consequences.

Sociological research has shown that when a community is undergoing strain, the incidence of social deviance and mental illness increases (as observed, for example, in a classic study by Hollingshead and Redlich, 1958). The connection is so strong that alcoholism, suicide, crime, and mental illness are widely regarded as symptoms of social decay, but these symptoms are most prevalent in people who are excluded from or have a marginal position in the social structure. This brings sociological concepts closer to psychology. An important difference between the concept of stress as found in sociology and psychology is that sociology focuses more on the social structure, whereas psychology attends more to the state of mind of individual persons and subgroups that the social system comprises.

Cultural anthropology, in many respects, mixes these two outlooks, but all the social sciences touch on both levels of analysis, even when it is centered mainly on a single level. Cultural anthropologists focus attention on diverse cultural values and meanings. Presumably, values and meanings are strongly influenced in childhood. The resultant values, goal commitments, and beliefs about self and world are perpetuated—though they can also change—when these children grow up. These variables influence what is stressful, and how stress emotions are coped with and expressed publicly.

The important point about levels of analysis is that sociological concerns with panic, riot, and fads and fashions (Smelser, 1963), and anthropological concerns with social meanings and cultural values, direct our attention to *collectivities*—that is, subgroups within the society—though attention must also be paid to the *individuals* who these collectivities comprise, which is the major domain of psychology. Similarly, suicide, crime, and mental illness can be viewed as both social and psychological phenomena, but the way they are understood at these different levels is not exactly the same.

Before proceeding, I should also offer a mild disclaimer about field differences and territoriality, which stereotype sociologists, anthropologists, and psychologists, often distorting what as individuals they are concerned with. When it comes to stress and emotion, it should be clear that considerable overlap exists among the several social science disciplines. The distinctions in levels of analysis between sociology, psychology, and cultural anthropology, therefore, get blurred because of the interdependence of social structure, culture, and individual lives.

This is illustrated by the fact that many cultural anthropologists today refer to themselves as cultural psychologists or psychological anthropologists and, along with sociologists, often sound much like psychologists and vice versa (White & Lutz, 1986). Blurring also occurs with certain metatheoretical outlooks within disciplines—for example, symbolic interactionism in sociology and appraisal theory and social constructionism in psychology—all of which are frankly subjective in their approach to social behavior and psychological processes.

We must not, however, allow these overlaps among social science disciplines to fool us about the main differences between the two levels of analysis—that is, that of the *society* and the *individual mind*, regardless of the discipline that deals with them. Concepts of stress and emotion are handled differently at these two levels of analysis. This difference applies also within psychology, within sociology, and within cultural anthropology, and helps account for many of the standard arguments within and between representatives of each field.

To concretize the level of analysis problem, consider two families and the individuals living within them. Imagine that one family is living in comparative harmony; the parents generally present a common front in dealings with their children. Another family, in contrast, suffers from much social strain in the form of marital conflict, anarchy, and resentment. Other social characteristics of these families also can converge or diverge—for example, how they make decisions, as in the contrast between authoritarian or democratic styles of parenting.

Social scientists need to recognize that descriptions of the two families as social systems do not necessarily characterize the states of mind of the individual children living within them, which points up the importance of paying attention to the problem of levels of analysis. We are likely to find some of the children of the authoritarian family secure, sociable, and accepting of others, and others who reject parental authority and are hostile and in trouble with the law. In the democratic family too, we are apt to find some children who reject parental authority or authority in general—as represented, for example, by teachers and police—and other children who are respectful of authority and comfortable with themselves.

The point is that social system differences between the two family environments apply to some extent to their individual children, but only in a probabilistic sense. Each individual child grows up with a distinctive temperament, unique values and goals, and particular styles of thinking. Although parents have an important influence on their children, the effect on any individual child is usually complex and variable both in kind and degree. Often we grossly overstate this influence. And often too, the effects of parenting can even work in a direction opposite to the parental pressure, as when the parents drink or smoke, but none of the children do, perhaps because they have become conscious of the bad example set by their parents, or are strongly influenced in this by the community, peers, and the media.

The important point is that children do not come out as carbon copies of their parents, and it is open to question whether parents should always be held responsible for their childrens' vices or receive credit for their virtues. The child's emotional pattern, which is affected by a combination of family, environmental, and individual personal variables—some of them genetic, some experiential, or both—cannot be explained by reference to the social structure in which they are living. Nor can we explain the social structure of the families by referring to the characteristics of the individual children. Any determinism imposed by family environments is a soft (i.e., loose) one.

This is also true of the coping process. The way a family as a whole copes with stress—that is, as a family culture—say, by denial and avoidance, or by vigilance, does not allow us to predict how any given individual within the family copes. And vice versa, we cannot identify the family coping pattern by reference to the coping of its individual members.

To make this statement more general, as in the issue of the different levels of analysis of mind and brain, the makeup and behavior of any given individual cannot be adequately explained by reference to the culture of a social system any more than the social system is explainable by reference to the individuals living within it. It is valuable to look at the interplay of both levels, but one cannot be reduced to the other. This epistemological point is constantly missed by many researchers who regularly fail to distinguish between what is happening at the social and individual levels.

THE PHYSIOLOGICAL LEVEL

Physical stressors have to do with the body's reaction to noxious physical conditions; the term noxious means harmful to living tissues. Major classes of noxious agents include injuries resulting from accidents; ingestion of harmful substances, such as alcohol, drugs, or medicines; invasion by microorganisms such as bacteria and viruses; and abnormal growths, such as cancers or malignancies that spread unchecked and, if not successfully treated, ultimately produce death by destroying vital organs. There are also special systemic failures we barely understand, examples being allergies and autoimmune diseases in which the immune system fails to distinguish between a foreign protein and one's own tissues, and attacks its own organs as if they were alien.

The 19th century scientist who made a major contribution to the physiology of stress was the French physiologist, Claude Bernard, who discovered that one of the liver's functions was to store sugar, which is essential to all biological and psychological functions. A pancreatic hormone, insulin, regulates how much sugar is stored in the liver, and how much is sent into the bloodstream to provide energy for the cells of the body. If the pancreas is unable to make and secrete insulin, diabetes occurs, which is fatal unless the right amount of the hormone is supplied from the outside. If too much insulin is secreted (sometimes as a result of a tumor of the eyelet cells of the pancreas), the opposite of diabetes occurs, leading to insufficient sugar in the blood and brain, attacks of mental confusion, and ultimately coma and death.

This discovery directed the attention of biological and social scientists to the concept of *homeostasis,* whereby a stable internal equilibrium of the body is maintained that is essential to survival. Just as the right amount of sugar must be available in the bloodstream and in the cells of the brain despite a lack of food, other bodily equilibria must also be maintained. For example, the body temperature must be kept within a narrow range regardless of the outside temperature—on the average, roughly around 98.6° F. Sufficient oxygen must also be provided to the cells of the brain for them to function, even when it is not in good supply in the environment, say, on very high mountains where the oxygen level of the atmosphere is low.

Claude Bernard did not contribute directly to stress and emotion, but his research and ideas paved the way for a complex and sophisticated modern view of adaptive processes, which facitate evolution-based survival. The danger from these processes, however, arises when we engage in adaptive actions, such as obtaining food, seeking shelter, putting on clothing against the cold, seeking shade to protect against the heat, and dealing with predators, which disrupt the homeostatic steady state.

Concretely, the danger is that the very struggle to adapt and survive, especially the last mentioned one, can severely impair the homeostatic steady state on which our lives depend. This became the central theme of the research and ideas of another distinguished physiologist, Walter Cannon (1932). Cannon focused his attention on dealing with predators, or what he called the "fight-or-flight" reaction, which is associated with the emotions of anger and fear. Bodily resources must be mobilized to sustain an attack or to flee from danger. This places considerable strain on the body's ability to maintain a stable internal environment. In effect, if prolonged and intense, anger and fear are physiologically stressful and carry the potential for bodily harm.

Following from both Bernard's and Cannon's work, the most important modern theory of physiological stress was formulated by Hans Selye (1956/1976). For the purpose of understanding physiological stress, grasping its connection with the psychology of stress and making sense of the role of stress emotions in health, it should help the reader to know at least the main outlines of Selye's most important ideas. His research and theoretical formulations provide chapter and verse about how the body responds when it must mobilize to cope with harms and threats to its integrity. He described an orchestrated neurochemical set of bodily defenses—referred to as the general adaptation syndrome (GAS)—which is brought to bear against noxious conditions or physical stressors.

The GAS consists of three stages. The first stage is the *alarm reaction*. A noxious agent initiates this elaborate neurohumoral process in defense of the living body. If the stress continues, the second stage, *resistance*, comes into play as the body is mobilized to defend itself. The injured tissues become inflamed, which helps isolate them from the rest of the body so the damage can be contained and dealt with without further harm. When the initial swelling has been relieved by antiinflammatory adrenocortical hormones, healing is facilitated. The stage of resistance is catabolic in action—that is, it draws on and uses up bodily resources rather than building or restoring them anabolically.

The third stage is that of *exhaustion*. If the stress is severe enough, or continues long enough, bodily resources begin to fail. Although the GAS helps us survive in the face of noxious environments, depletion of resources is the potential physiological cost of the defense, which is usually controlled because the syndrome does not often go beyond the second stage. However, if the struggle so weakens the organism that it can no longer sustain itself, it results in death.

Though initiated by a noxious agent, the GAS is actually set in motion by action of the pituitary gland, which is closely linked to the hypothalamus. The pituitary is a part of the brain that also serves as an endocrine gland. It manufactures and secretes a master hormone, ACTH which, when released, stimulates the adrenal glands to pour their hormones into the bloodstream. ACTH stands for adrenocorticotrophic hormone, which refers to the master hormone that initiates the secretion of adrenal hormones. Subsequently, I have underlined the first letter of each meaning unit to clarify the four letter acronym. "Adreno" stands for adrenal glands; "cortico" for the cortex or outer rind of the glands; "trophic," originating with the word tropism, for the stimulating agent; "hormone" for the biochemical substance—thus ACTH.

One set of adrenal hormones released by ACTH consists of corticosteroids, which are produced by the outer rind of each adrenal gland. The other set, influenced more by the autonomic nervous system, consists of two closely related catecholamines, adrenaline and noradrenaline, which are produced by the medulla or inner portion of each gland. In recent years, biochemists have discovered another group of hypothalamic hormones, the endorphins, which act on the mind and body like morphine and the opiates, producing euphoria and reducing pain. It might not be amiss to think of ACTH as the main biochemical initiator of the GAS defense against stress, and the endorphins as having the opposing effect of dampening the awareness of pain and stress, and the defense against it (see Figure 2.1).

The antagonistic action between hormones, as noted previously, is a property of many other physiological systems of the body, most notably, the nervous system. Stimulating one portion of the system increases arousal, whereas stimulating the other dampens it, making it possible for the internal environment to return to its preprogrammed equilibrial state. To see how this works, we need to know something about the human nervous system.

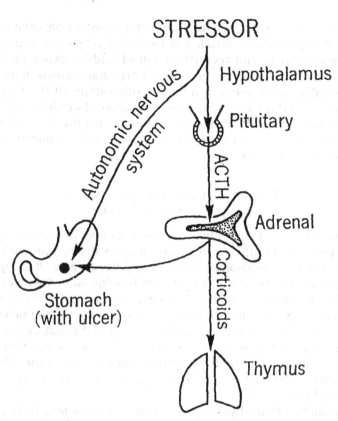

FIGURE 2.1   Principal pathways mediating the response to a stressor. From Selye, 1974, Figure 4, p. 42. Reprinted with permission of Lippincott-Raven.

The nervous system is divided into two major parts: the central nervous system (CNS) or brain, and the peripheral nervous system (PNS). The brain exerts substantial control over the striate muscles of the body that control voluntary or intentional action as well as the PNS which, in turn, is also divided into two subsystems. The voluntary nervous system, or somatic system, is controlled volitionally (by our will or intention), and the autonomic nervous system (ANS), which is sometimes called the involuntary nervous system, is not under volitional control. However, the ANS influences the action of hormones and has a profound effect on all the tissues of the body.

The ANS also has two branches. One consists of sympathetic nerves that arouse us, as when we react with a stress emotion. Its action on the body is largely catabolic—that is, it uses up bodily resources for energy and emergencies. The other, consisting of parasympathetic nerves, dampens this arousal, and facilitates relaxation and anabolic processes—that is, the reconstruction of bodily resources and the restoration of energy. As in the case of hormonal systems, here too we see the antagonism between different subsystems of the body—one that arouses and the other that dampens arousal—only in this case, it is the primary result of neural rather than biochemical action. Hormones and nerves control the body and mind in concert, overlapping greatly in their effects.

BLURRING THE PHYSIOLOGICAL AND PSYCHOLOGICAL LEVELS

Selye proposed that the initiator of the GAS may be psychological as well as physical. In other words, this complex defense process can be brought about by *psychological harms and threats* as well as by physically noxious agents. The idea that what is going on in the mind can do bodily harm is in no sense new. This was assumed by ancient philosophers and is also by modern medicine. One version is the proposal of Sir William Osler, a famous physician writing in the first decade of the 20th century, that a life of intense work and pleasure exposes people to chronic stress and strain and predisposes them to heart disease—an obvious forerunner of a related hypothesis about the type A personality (Hinkle, 1977).

The principle that physiological stress reactions may have psychological origins tends to obscure the distinction that needs to be drawn between physiological and psychological stressors. As in the contrast between social and psychological stress, physiological and psychological stress also operate at distinctly different levels of analysis, each of which draw on separate concepts and observations. When the cause of the physiological defense is psychological, the process leading to the GAS is indirect because a mind rather than some body process initiates or sustains it. Our analysis must then follow the principle of cognitive mediation.

This proposal that psychological and physiological events are separate and distinct—albeit two versions of the same process—points us toward some of the difficulties of distinguishing between physiologically and psychologically noxious agents. For example, exercise, a change in temperature and humidity, and other physical demands on the body will produce many of the same bodily changes that psychological stress and emotion will produce, such as elevated heart rate, blood pressure, respiration rate, and so forth.

If one wishes to attribute the physiological reaction to psychological causes, one must rule out physical causes, which is why, when psychological stress is studied in the laboratory, the physical conditions must be kept constant and the research subject relaxed and prevented from moving too much. These experimental controls eliminate or greatly reduce bodily changes that have a physical cause. The same potential confounding complicates the effort to attribute bodily diseases to psychological causation. I take this issue up more fully in chapter 10 on stress, emotion, and disease.

The confounding of physical and psychological causes imposes a tricky problem for Selye's concept of the GAS. If the environment is noxious, the animal or person usually senses the presence of a harm or threat. But it is possible that the two kinds of stress, physiological and psychological, have different consequences for the body, a possibility not foreseen by Selye.

Experimental monkeys that are being starved in a research study normally get very upset when it is feeding time and they see control monkeys being fed. If the temperature in their cage is rapidly increased, they perceive a clear danger to their well-being and become emotional even before the heat begins to cause significant physiological change. And if a human male is placed on a treadmill, in addition to being physiologically challenged, he is apt to become ego-involved in how he is doing and, therefore, threatened psychologically, especially if a female friend is present or there is an attractive female nurse monitoring the test. All this illustrates the confounding of physical and psychological stressors.

Mason, et al. (1976) reported a fascinating study designed to eliminate the confounding between the two levels of analysis. Primates were exposed to physical harms, such as heat, fasting, and physical exertion without being allowed to realize that there was any danger. The starved experimental monkeys were given nonnutritive placebos, which calmed them while the control monkeys were being fed. When the temperature was increased in their cage, it was done so gradually that they would not be alarmed. And a human male subject who was placed on the treadmill was never permitted to attain a treadmill speed at which his competitive ego would be engaged. In this way, the physical stressors were kept separate from the psychological stressors so that their effects could be studied without the contaminating psychological effects.

These researchers found that corticosteroid secretion is minimal or absent in the case of physical harms, but is strongly activated when an animal recognizes a harm or threat, resulting in a confounding of the two levels of causation. We need to realize that a threat is purely psychological because it is a potential harm that has not yet materialized, though it too can affect the body via the emotions, such as anxiety, which it produces. The physical stressors in their experiments did not, by and large, produce major corticosteriod secretion as Selye would have predicted, whereas the psychological stressors did. This suggests, ironically, that the corticosteroid response of the GAS could be a special product of psychological threat.

Consistent with this interpretation, there is also an old study by Symington et al. (1955), which suggests that unconsciousness eliminates the adrenal effects of physical stressors. As long as patients remained unconscious while they were dying of injury or disease, they showed a normal adrenal cortical level—that is, as assessed during autopsy, their corticosteroids were not elevated. In contrast, those who were conscious during the death process, and were presumably aware of what was happening, showed elevated adrenal cortical changes. It would seem, therefore, that some psychological awareness—akin to a conscious perception or appraisal—of the psychological significance of what is happening may be necessary to produce the adrenal cortical changes of the GAS.

In 1955, Selye was invited to speak to the American Psychological Association and he gave a lecture that helped communicate knowledge of and an interest in his theories among psychologists and stimulated added interest in psychological as well as physiological stress. The result of the increased interest generated for psychological stress has been quite remarkable. In a literature search, (Hobfoll, Schwarzer, & Chon (1996) found that over 29,000 research papers have been published on psychological stress and coping since 1984, not including relevant publications that did not include the key words "stress" or "coping."

However, Selye did not help us understand the way psychological stressors work, only how they affected the body. The most difficult problem for psychological stress theory is to specify what is psychologically noxious—that is, to identify the rules that make a psychological event stressful, thereby producing a stress reaction. We must examine this more closely in chapters 3 and 4, which provide a partial answer in terms of the process of appraisal.

Psychological Stress and Appraisal

Traditionally, there have been two main ways of defining psychological stress, one that focuses on the stimulus or provoking event—that is, the stressor—the other on the response or reaction—that is, the mental and bodily reaction generated by the stressor. Each turns out to be inadequate.

STIMULUS AND RESPONSE APPROACHES TO PSYCHOLOGICAL STRESS

If we define stress as an environmental stimulus, we need to consider what kind of event fits this definition. It is sensible to begin this discussion with a stimulus approach, then follow with a consideration of a response approach, although the two perspectives, as we shall see, really combine into one.

STIMULUS APPROACH

The Social Readjustment Rating Scale of Holmes and Rahe (1967) was one of the first modern stress measurement scales. It makes use of a distinctive scaling method, with a unique conceptualization. The approach was designed to identify common life changes (life events) on the basis of the amount of effort presumably needed to cope with them (see Dohrenwend & Dohrenwend, 1974, for a review and analysis). This scale illustrates a stimulus approach quite well (see Table 3.1).

The idea that something that happens in the environment—that is, a stimulus—which provokes stress reactions and the need to cope, is a natural and appealing way of thinking about psychological stress. We like to explain our disturbed emotional reactions by referring to the fact that we lost our job, failed an important exam, were insulted by

3.1 Social Readjustment Rating Scale

	Life event	Mean value
1	Death of spouse	100
2	Divorce	73
3	Marital separation	65
4	Jail term	63
5	Death of close family member	63
6	Personal injury or illness	53
7	Marriage	50
8	Fired at work	47
9	Marital reconciliation	45
10	Retirement	45
11	Change in health of family member	44
12	Pregnancy	40
13	Sex difficulties	39
14	Gain of new family member	39
15	Business readjustment	39
16	Change in financial state	38
17	Death of close friend	37
18	Change to different line of work	36
19	Change in number of arguments with spouse	35
20	Mortgage over $10,000	31
21	Foreclosure of mortgage or loan	30
22	Change in responsibilities at work	29
23	Son or daughter leaving home	29
24	Trouble with in-laws	29
25	Outstanding personal achievement	28
26	Wife begin or stop work	26
27	Begin or end school	26
28	Change in living conditions	25
29	Revision of personal habits	24
30	Trouble with boss	23
31	Change in work hours or conditions	20
32	Change in residence	20
33	Change in schools	20
34	Change in recreation	19
35	Change in church activities	19
36	Change in social activities	18
37	Mortgage or loan less than $10,000	17
38	Change in sleeping habits	16
39	Change in number of family get-togethers	15
40	Change in eating habits	15
41	Vacation	13
42	Christmas	12
43	Minor violations of the law	11

From Holmes & Rahe (1967), *Journal of Psychosomatic Research,* Vol. 11, Table 3, p. 216. Reprinted with permission from Elsevier Science.

someone, injured or placed in harm's way, and so on. To be able to point to harmful external events, such as a major loss, justifies our emotional distress, subsequent illness, or dysfunction, ignoring for the moment that, with some exceptions, most such events do not just happen to a passive person, but the victim has probably inadvertently contributed to them in some ways and may be coping with them successfully or unsuccessfully. Still, from a commonsensical standpoint, changes in one's life, especially defeats and losses, are psychological stressors for most people and illustrate a stimulus definition.

Samples of diverse types of persons from different countries were asked by Holmes and Rahe to rate how much readjustment each of several life events required. The results provided the basis for the rating scale. The highest rated event turned out to be death of a spouse, followed by divorce, marriage, and so on, ending with relatively low rated events, such as taking out a real estate mortgage (given inflation, the amount of the mortgage, which in the scale is listed as $10,000, now in the 1990s after a long period of inflation, seems almost absurd), trouble with in-laws, getting married, and going on a vacation.

The last two items point up the idea that positively toned events, such as a vacation, can also make significant adaptational demands. Indeed, anecdotally speaking, it is common for people who have traveled widely on vacation to fall ill with respiratory infections during or after returning home, presumably because the stress of travel increases vulnerability by weakening immune system competence.

When used clinically or in research to evaluate amount of stress, individuals are asked to indicate which life events on the list had occurred during the past year. A high score, which could result from several high life changes or a pileup events that make moderate adaptational demands, was said to predispose people to illness roughly 6 months to a year later. Research supported this presumption, which has been demonstrated in many studies. However, though statistically significant, which suggests that at least the basic principle is valid, the correlations between life events scores and illness typically fell within the .3 range or less, which improves prediction over chance by less than 10%, and is, therefore, too low to have practical value.

Although they did not favor the term *stress*, the original conception of Holmes and Rahe had been that any change, whether positive or negative, was stressful because change events make adaptational demands. However, subsequent research evidence suggested that negative events play a much greater role in illness than positive events.

For many years, there was great enthusiasm in health psychology for doing research on life events and illness. The enthusiasm has now waned considerably—partly because of limitations in the reasoning on which it was based and partly because of problems with all stimulus-centered approaches in an era of cognitive mediation—because of their failure to consider individual differences in appraisal and coping.

Another reason too about this loss of enthusiasm is that the original list of life events is incomplete—for example, there is no item for death of a child, and few of the items listed deal with the infirmities of old age or the problems of the very young. Other kinds of stressful experiences are also important but are not included in the list—for example, natural disasters, such as earthquakes, floods, or fires, and man-made disasters, such as war, uprooting, and immigration.

As we saw in chapter 2, the more cataclysmic the event, the more likely it is to generate psychological disturbances in its wake. Yet in the ordinary course of life, especially in middle-class communities, the really high scoring life events occur infrequently, and there may still be plenty of stress. Revised lists and rating procedures came into being later, which were designed to improve the original scale, but there is no perfect approach to the measurement of stressors. As will be seen shortly, one approach of the Berkeley Stress and Coping Project even emphasized seemingly minor daily hassles as sources of stress, which I will discuss shortly.

RESPONSE APPROACH

In contrast with a stimulus approach, stress is also frequently defined as the troubled reaction to stressful stimuli, which is a response definition of stress. We say we feel pressured, harmed, or threatened, or we feel disturbed, distressed, depressed, angry, anxious, sad, and so forth, which is what stress means in emotional response terms. Physiology and medicine tend to define stress as a response, such as a disturbed bodily or mental state, which reminds us of Selye's GAS (see chapter 2).

Aside from the fact that it is far too simple, this kind of reasoning is completely circular—it is, in other words, a tautology, in that it does not answer the question of what it is about the stimulus that produces the stress response. What is circular or tautological in its reasoning is that stress stimulus is defined mainly by the fact there is a stress response, and the stress response is, in turn, defined by referring back to the stimulus that presumably brought it about in the first place.

In effect, the stress stimulus was not defined independently of the observation of the stress response. No universal principle is offered in advance about the kind of stimulus that is noxious—that is, capable of producing a stress response in all or even most people, so we do not gain any real understanding of what is going on—only a vacuous label, which cannot be used to predict a stress response.

An S-R definition would be easier to justify if everyone responded to certain events, say, death of a spouse, in the same way—that is, with a commensurate degree of emotional distress, dysfunction, or illness. But even major events like this, which can be extremely stressful, do not affect everyone in the same way. Thus, death of a spouse is extremely traumatic for one person, but may be a welcome relief for another who has seen the spouse suffer greatly in an extended, traumatic period of dying and has shared in that suffering. Using an S-R approach without further specification of the rules leaves us unable to define what makes a stimulus a stressor.

The main problem with this approach to stress is that what makes the stimulus stressful depends to some extent on the characteristics of the person exposed to it, which would account for the ever-present individual differences. There is no better case for the need for a relational definition of stress than this dilemma—in effect, it takes both the stressful stimulus condition and a *vulnerable person* to generate a stress reaction. Putting the person into the equation is the only way to solve the dilemma. Let us, therefore, turn directly to individual differences in how people respond to the same stimulus. (for a dissenting view, *see* Hobfoll, Schwarzer, & Chon, K-K., 1996, who argue that stimulus-response research designs in the study of stress are more scientific because they are based on observation rather than subjective appraisals, and that despite the popularity of cognitive-mediational views, most research remains S-R in outlook).

INDIVIDUAL DIFFERENCES

Psychology has always been ambivalent about individual differences, largely because the task of science is viewed as a search for general laws that transcend the particular contexts in which they operate. Individual variations around a general law are commonly considered to be errors of measurement or a nuisance in the effort to identify general laws. We need to understand human variation if we are to deal effectively with individuals. No one has addressed this issue more perceptively than Kurt Lewin (1946, p. 794), who wrote:

> The problems of general laws and of individual differences frequently appear to be unrelated questions which follow somewhat opposite lines. Any prediction, however, presupposes a consideration of both types of questions; problems of individual differences and of general laws are

closely interwoven. A [scientific] law is expressed in an equation which relates certain variables. Individual differences have to be conceived of as various specific values which these variations have in a particular case. In other words, general laws and individual differences are merely two aspects of one problem; they are mutually dependent on each other and the study of one cannot proceed without the study of the other.

One might think the claim that certain stimulus conditions are stressful should provoke no logical or theoretical difficulty because, after all, certain events are much more likely than others to be psychologically noxious. They represent harms or threats to many or most people, so we tend to think of them as stressors. However, the degree and kind of stress response, even to singularly powerful stress conditions, are apt to vary from person to person, and these variations need to be understood. By the 1960s and 1970s, psychology appeared more ready than previously to make an assault on the problem of individual differences. Let us see what happens when we take the problem seriously.

The existence of substantial individual differences means that a stimulus alone is insufficient to define stress, as I have been arguing, because it begs the question of what makes a stimulus a stressor. To say that statistically some type of event has a high probability of resulting in a stress reaction does not really help much. If this were not true, it could not properly be called a stressor, but psychological noxiousness is not as easy to specify as physiological noxiousness.

If exceptions to the expectation of a disturbed reaction are common, or the variations in intensity and variety of the reactions are the rule, which they usually are, the stress response cannot be predicted with any precision or dependability and we cannot logically call the stimulus a stressor, except for certain people whose characteristics have not been specified. And as we move from major catastrophes to lesser ones, individual differences in the kind and degree of the stress reaction increase. Not being able to say why reactions to the so-called stress stimulus vary undermines the logic of calling that stimulus a stressor. To have a rule-based definition, we must identify the characteristics that make some people *vulnerable* to the stimulus as a stressor, and others not vulnerable, or less so.

Solid evidence of individual differences in response to so-called stressors abounds. Evidence was reported in an early experiment by Lazarus and Eriksen (1952) in which the threat of failure resulted in a marked increase in variability rather than an average increase or decrease in performance. In effect, some experimental subjects did much better following failure while others did much worse. It was as if the stress condition affected people by pushing the performance of some of them upward while pushing others downward (see Figure 3.1). As a result of this and later research, it became increasingly clear that reactions under stress cannot be predicted without reference to personality traits and processes that account for the individual differences in the ways people respond to a so-called stressful stimulus (*see also* Lazarus, Deese, & Osler, 1952, for an early review of this kind of research).

Incidentally, although Hooke, whose ideas were discussed in chapter 2, was a physical scientist, he was also interested in individual differences in the elasticity of metals, which is a factor in their resistance to strain. Various forms of iron provide an illustration. Cast iron is hard and brittle and breaks easily, whereas wrought iron is soft and malleable and bends without breaking. This physical difference provides a good metaphor for individual differences in resiliency under psychological stress, and the capacity of diverse individuals to resist becoming psychologically distressed and dysfunctional.

One could attempt to attribute such differences to variations in the stimulus conditions being faced. After all, no two situations are ever exactly alike. When we are demeaned in a social transaction, the details of this assaultive message are never the same twice. And if we face an uncertain threat—for example, when we are about to be interviewed for an important job, the next time this situation recurs there will be a different interviewer who has a different agenda, or we may feel more confident about dealing with it.

Nevertheless, the details are less important than the overall message when we react with, say, anger or anxiety. It is the meaning constructed by a person about what is happening that is crucial to the arousal of stress reactions. Many or most problems of human social relationships have happened to us before and probably will again. Often the new experience is fundamentally the same in the way we evaluate its significance for our personal well-being, despite differences in detail.

The psychological meaning a person constructs about an environmental event is the proximal cause of the stress reaction and the emotions it produces, which can be contrasted with a distal cause. The *proximal-distal* dimension refers to the ordering of various events in accordance with their personal relevance or psychological closeness—that is, their meaning for that person (Jessor, 1981). It is the personal significance of what is happening, which is the *proximal* cause of a stress reaction.

The term *distal*, in contrast, applies to large social categories, such as class and gender. It means, literally and figuratively, being far away

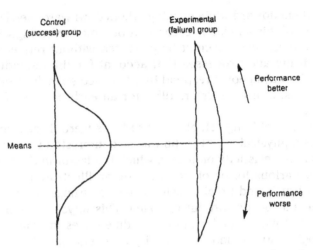

FIGURE 3.1   Individual differences in performance under stress. From
Lazarus & Eriksen (1952).

from the person or, more appropriately, from the person's concerns. A
broad social category, such as social class or gender, does not permit
us to say how the individual persons belonging within it will experience what happened. These distal variables do not convey the same
personal significance or meaning for every person in the social category,
though there may be an increased probability of shared meanings.
Women do not all react alike, any more than men do, and the same
could be said about people of the same age, poor people, or rich people. Such membership categories are too broad to predict the presence of the same values, goals, and beliefs. We need to know more to
know how the individual person thinks, feels, acts, and reacts. Stress
stimuli, such as life events and natural or man-made disasters are distal for the same reason. People react to them differently.

But there is another problem with major life events or environmental disasters as the basis for stress measurement, which I have not yet
addressed. Our daily lives are filled with experiences that are stressful
but rather than representing major life changes, as emphasized in the
Holmes and Rahe approach, many of these daily experiences arise
from chronic or recurrent conditions of our lives, some of them seemingly minor irritants or daily hassles.

In research by the Berkeley Stress and Coping Project during the
1980s, we referred to these conditions as *daily hassles* (Lazarus, 1984),
the seemingly little things that irritate and upset people, such as one's
dog throwing up on the living room rug, dealing with an inconsiderate

smoker, delays in the commute to work, having too many responsibilities, being lonely, having an argument with one's spouse, and so
on. These chronic or recurrent conditions are stressful too and sometimes they get out of hand. When a person endorses a hassle as having
occurred, that person has already interpreted the event as having stressful significance. Therefore, what happened is a proximal cause of
stress by virtue of its acknowledged relevance to that person's values,
goals, situational intentions, and beliefs.

Although daily hassles are far less dramatic than major life changes,
such as divorce and bereavement, and what constitutes a hassle varies
greatly from person to person, our research has suggested that, especially when they pile up or touch on special areas of *vulnerability* (Gruen,
Folkman, & Lazarus, 1989), they can be very stressful for some people
and very important for their subjective well-being and physical health
(DeLongis, Coyne, Dakof, Folkman, & Lazarus, 1982; Kanner, Coyne,
Schaefer, & Lazarus, 1981).

To make sense of this, we need to know about the variations in personality that influence the things to which people are vulnerable to
refine our conception of what makes them stressful. I shall list some of
these shortly. Some personality characteristics—for example, those
related to coping resources—have also been found to help people
resist the deleterious effects of stress. These include among others
one's sense of self-efficacy (Bandura, 1977, 1997), the ability to think con-
structively (Epstein & Meier, 1989), hardiness (Maddi & Kobasa, 1984;
Orr & Westman, 1990), hope (Snyder et al., 1991), learned resourcefulness (Rosenbaum, 1990), optimism (Scheier & Carver, 1987), and the
sense of coherence (Antonovsky, 1987).

So we must also draw on a relational approach in defining stress,
one that considers the person. When I said earlier that stress depends
not only on the environmental condition but also on what makes a person vulnerable to it, I was anticipating a relational approach, which is
described subsequently. This is only a partial solution to the problem
of individual differences, as will be seen when I discuss the concept of
appraisal and a subjective approach. It takes both a relational approach
and one that views what is happening through the eyes of the person,
to cope effectively with individual differences in the stress process.

RELATIONAL APPROACH TO STRESS

A relational way of thinking provides a second or third alternative to
stimulus and response definitions and the dilemma of individual

differences, depending on whether we separate the stimulus and response, or combine them into an S-R psychology. To separate them makes little sense because they are always conjoined. If we combine S and R, the relational approach becomes the second approach to stress.

A good way of thinking about stressful person-environment relationships is to examine the relative balance of forces between environmental demands and the person's psychological resources for dealing with them. A seesaw provides a good analogy, with environmental load on one side of the balance point or fulcrum and the person's resources on the other side. If the environmental load substantially exceeds the person's resources, a stressful relationship exists (see Figure 3.2).

Note how apt the seesaw analogy is for Hooke's concept of environmental load and strain. His is a truly relational view of stress because it involves a comparison of the relative weight of the load and the resistance of the physical object. In psychological stress, the comparison is between the power of the environmental demands to harm, threaten, or challenge, and the psychological resources of the person to manage these demands—in effect, depending on personal vulnerability or resistance to their stressful consequences.

If the person's resources are more or less equal to or exceed the demands (Figure 3.2a), we are dealing with a nonstress situation. However, in this case, an unexpected basis of stress may then arise— namely, lack of involvement and, therefore, boredom or tedium (see Figure 3.2b).

From the standpoint of this way of thinking, stress is particularly powerful when the individual must struggle with demands that cannot easily be met. Thus, anxiety, which is a stress emotion, is more likely to occur and will be stronger when a person has a poor regard for his or her own capacity to cope with the world effectively. This idea has been explored substantially by Bandura (1997) via his concept of self-efficacy. Greenberg et al. (1992), as well as others, have shown that self-esteem reduces anxiety in the face of a stressor, such as the anticipation of a painful electric shock.

If the ratio of demands to resources becomes too great (Figure 3.2c), we are no longer talking about high stress but trauma (see chapter 6 for a discussion of the difference). The person feels helpless to deal with the demands to which he or she is exposed, and this can result in feelings of panic, hopelessness, and depression.

We must be wary, however, not to take analogies, such as the seesaw, and the capacity of a bridge to bear a load, too literally for a consideration of psychological stress. They are useful in a didactic sense, but are often misleading when applied to physical, physiological, and

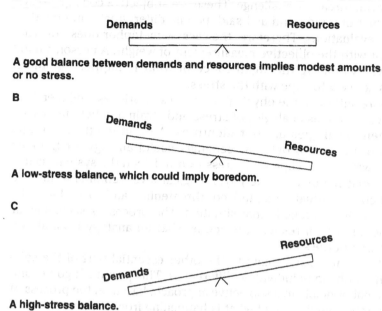

A

A good balance between demands and resources implies modest amounts of stress or no stress.

B

A low-stress balance, which could imply boredom.

C

A high-stress balance.

FIGURE 3.2   Seesaw analogy.

psychological stress. A major difference between physical stresses and those relevant to physiology and psychology has to do with the contrast between inanimate objects and living creatures. Another difference is the contrast between automatic physiological processes, such as homeostasis, and stress conditions in which an evaluating mind must interpret what is happening on the basis of personal values, goals, and beliefs.

Thus, in Hooke's engineering analysis of physical objects, load, stress, and strain refer to inanimate, mindless objects, such as a bridge or a piece of iron. When a bridge is deformed (strained) by an environmental load, it may sway freely within safe limits and resists coming apart and falling, but this resistance to stress is an automatic result of its physical construction and the building materials used, not any intention of a person's mind. And in physiological stress, the living body engages in automatic processes aimed at maintaining or restoring the internal equilibrium.

In psychological stress, however, a new complication is added, which has to do with an appraisal of psychological noxiousness—in other words, harm, threat, or challenge. These are subjective concepts—that is, a product of mind—and as I said, people differ greatly in how they make the evaluations. Therefore, the seesaw metaphor does not work as it might with the objective measurement of weight. A person's mind is at work evaluating the significance of what is happening, and it struggles actively to cope with the stress.

Therefore, although the physical properties of bridges, and metals in general, can serve as analogies of stress and strain and help us reason about them, analogies are not identities. And although the bodily defenses of the GAS provide a seemingly useful analogy for thinking about the way people cope with stress—both defend the system against assault—what happens at the psychological level requires a mind to judge whether a situation is, indeed, threatening, and to evaluate the available coping options in that situation. The processes seem similar or parallel in certain respects, which is what an analogy is all about, but they are not the same.

What I have just said points to the other essential part of the solution to the problem of individual differences. This part must go beyond the relational principle to a subjective approach, based on the process of appraising the significance of what is happening from the person's own perspective. When the person-environment relationship is combined with the subjective process of appraising, we speak of *relational meaning,* which is centered on the personal significance of that relationship.

The basic tenet of a relational approach is that stress and emotion express a particular kind of relationship between a person and the environment. For a relationship to be stressful, certain conditions must be met. The person must desire something from the environment—in effect, he or she wants to avoid certain outcomes as aversive, or to attain certain outcomes because they are congenial to the gratification of important goals and expectations. These are the relational meanings on which psychological stress is based. I must add that people differ greatly in their goals, beliefs about self and world, and personal resources, on which their expectations about the outcome depend.

A person is under stress only if what happens defeats or endangers important goal commitment and situational intentions, or violates highly valued expectations. The degree of stress is, in part, linked with how strong these goal commitments are, and partly with beliefs and the expectations they create, which can be realized or violated. A relational approach considers environmental *and* person characteristics, and their relative importance; the relational meaning gives us the other necessary part of the stress process, based on the subjective appraisals of the personal import of what is happening.

Reading what Vallacher and Nowak (1997) have recently written about relational approaches in what they call dynamical social psychology, one would think that such a view is old hat. They state (pp. 75–76):

> Indeed, it is hard to imagine how any situational factor or stimulus could influence interpersonal thought and behavior independently of the person's motives, goals, concerns and other internal mechanisms. In this regard, it has become quite commonplace for psychologists to note the importance of Person X Situation interactions in discussions of behavioral prediction.

They are right with respect to what should be the approach recognized by all of psychology—social psychology included. However, as indicated in chapter 1, interaction is not tantamount to relational meaning, and it is, indeed, also true that this kind of outlook was broached in mainline journals as early as the 1930s. Even today, however, few research studies go beyond lip service and take it seriously enough to design research with this in mind; moreover, psychologists touting science are still not comfortable with the concept of relational meaning and with subjective measurement as a source of data.

In chapter 2, I presented a brief history of and arguments for a cognitive-mediational-relational approach to stress and the emotions. The problems posed by individual differences create the necessity for this kind of approach. To appreciate this fully, we should examine the construct of appraisal in greater depth because it is the theoretical heart of psychological stress, and the emotions too, from the perspective of appraisal, coping, and relational meaning.

ANTECEDENT CONDITIONS OF APPRAISAL

Before we proceed further, let us examine the four substantive environmental variables that influence stress and emotion—namely, demands, constraints, opportunities, and culture—and the person variables that interact with them, which influence our reactions via the process of appraisal.

ENVIRONMENTAL VARIABLES

Demands

These consist of implicit or explicit pressures from the social environment to act in certain ways and manifest socially correct attitudes. There are multiple demands to conform to social conventions, to do what one's job entails, to excel, to love and be loved, to be thoughtful and kind, to be respected or admired, to take care of our children, to be concerned with the well-being of our families, to behave with consistency and integrity, and so forth. Many of these demands are later internalized, so it is often difficult to tell whether the primary pressure is external or internal.

These environmental demands, and the conflicts they can create with our inner goals and beliefs, are among the most obvious sources of psychological stress. How these demands and conflicts are coped with, and the emotions aroused by the struggle, influences our morale, social functioning, and physical well-being.

Constraints

Unlike social demands on people to act in prescribed ways, constraints define what people should *not* do, which are also backed up by punishment if violated. For example, a physical attack when we are angry is proscribed in most societies, but in almost all societies, there are occasions in which outright retaliatory aggression is accepted, and sometimes almost mandatory to preserve one's social and self-esteem.

I have always enjoyed English professor Jane Tomkins's description of the morality of violence as portrayed in American Western movies and illustrated in the movie *Shane*, which suggests unspoken rules of a complex texture and considerable subtlety. She writes about the justification of violence as follows (1989, pp. 33–34):

> The structure of this sequence [in the movie] reproduces itself in a thousand Western novels and movies. Its pattern never varies. The hero, provoked by insults, first verbal then physical, resists the urge to retaliate, proving his moral superiority to those who are taunting him. It is never the hero who taunts his adversary; if he does, it's only after he's been pushed "too far." And this, of course, is what always happens. The villains, whoever they may be, finally commit an act so atrocious that the hero *must* retaliate in kind. At this juncture, the point where provocation has gone too far, retaliatory violence becomes not simply justifiable but imperative: now we are made to feel that *not* to transgress the interdict against violence would be the transgression. The feeling of supreme righteousness in this instant is delicious and hardly to be distinguished from murderousness. I would almost say they are the same thing.

The rules about anger and aggression in our society tend to vary with social class and ethnicity. Thus, middle class values reject physical attack but accept it—even value it—as a matter of self-defense, and certain forms of verbal attack are also forbidden even when provoked.

Values about this are commonly inculcated in children by their parents (*see,* for example, Miller & Sperry, 1987). An attack should never exceed what is appropriate in light of the offense that generated it.

Among the most interesting social constraints are those that facilitate or interfere with the coping process. When we cope with stress in ways that violate social standards, say, of the community or the company for which we work, we may need to censor certain actions even though they would otherwise be personally useful. Whether the constraints pose a conflict depends on the fit between the needs of the individual and the values of the institution. They often add to ongoing stress and set limits to what we can do to cope. An institution that facilitates the ability of its personnel to cope is apt to be more highly valued than one that thwarts sound coping.

Consider, for example, a person whose job involves the stress of work overload, which can also interfere with responsibilities to the family, thereby adding to the overall stress. Normally, the best way to cope with overload is by eliminating responsibilities that are lowest in the hierarchy of importance. However, doing so may be viewed by the employee as risking the disapproval of the employer or supervisor. This impression may seem to threaten the worker's job, the likelihood of obtaining a promotion or raise, or merely the desire to be approved or admired at work. How to resolve it can be a serious dilemma.

Social constraints, such as these, may be viewed by a worker unrealistically. Even if the constraints are only imagined rather than real, workers may be unable to change the way they see things and, therefore, they may be unable to take action to relieve job stress because of the employment risks these actions seem to entail. They may be reluctant, for example, to ask for help from their employer or supervisor because they believe that doing so will put them in a bad light, or perhaps they think the supervisor is prejudiced against them. In such instances, the constraint is no longer external, though originally it was. It is now based on their own personal values or beliefs, and may stem from incorrect inferences about the way things are.

Opportunity

This is the third substantive environmental variable that influences the process of appraisal. It arises from fortunate timing but could also depend on the wisdom to recognize the opportunity. To take advantage of it often requires the right action at the right moment. We can sometimes facilitate the arrival or use of an opportunity by preparatory activity. We choose the most opportune social setting in which to live or work, or develop the necessary skills and knowledge—for example, by seeking an education in relevant subjects. In this way, a combination of luck and positioning oneself to take advantage of an opportunity combine fortuitously. This is an excellent example of the power of a relational analysis because it centers on both person and environment as essential components in forecasting a favorable adaptational outcome. But more of this later.

Culture

This is the subject matter of the field of cultural anthropology and cultural psychology. The role of cultural factors in emotion has become a very fashionable topic in the last decade or so, as illustrated by recent reviews and discussions, such as those of Lutz and White (1986); Kâgitçibasi and Berry (1989); Marcus and Kitayama (1991); Mesquita and Frijda (1992); Scherer, Wallbott, and Summerfield, 1986); and Shweder (1991).

There are also numerous specialized treatments of the topic of culture and emotion—for example, of the so-called self-conscious emotions, such as shame, guilt, embarrassment, and pride, whose strong cultural determinants are discussed in Tangney and Fischer's (1995) informative book with chapters by Kitayama, Markus, and Matsumoto, Wallbott and Scherer, Miyake and Yamazaki. Another topic of interest, cultural differences in individualism and collectivism, is reflected in a book edited by U. Kim, Triandis, Kâgitçibasi, Sang-Chin Choi, and Yoon (1994). The contrast between cultures that emphasize individualism (Western societies like the United States) and those emphasizing collectivism (Asian societies like Japan, Korea, and China) is a recurrent theme in much cross-cultural research. Because the sense of self (as independent versus interdependent) is said to differ in such societies, shame, guilt, pride, and anger are favorite targets as emotions for cross-cultural research.

Kitayama, Markus and Matsumoto's (1995) chapter in Tangney and Fischer's volume provides some of the rationale for the expectation of cultural differences. The author's (pp. 458–459) conclude

> Emotions are action-oriented, script-like structures that simultaneously respond both to the external situation and to internal sensations (Kitayama & Markus, 1994). Emotional experience is both constituted by and constitutive of social relationships. From this point of view, emotions should differ in accordance with one major dimension of the social content, namely, the assumption and practice of independence or of interdependence. We have argued and presented evidence that emotions in fact vary

in the degree either to which they engage or connect the self in ongoing relationships, and thereby promote the interdependence of the self with others (social engagement), or to which they disengage and separate the self from such relationships, and thereby promote the independence of the self from the relationships (social disengagement). We have suggested that "self-conscious" emotions and "other-conscious" emotions have remarkably divergent social functions along this social orientation dimension. We have also pointed out that taking this social dimension into account makes it possible to shed some new light on cross-culturally divergent organizations of emotional processes.

I don't challenge that there are important cultural differences that affect stress, coping, and emotion in individuals growing up in these societies, but I believe the relatively thin (in my opinion) data have been interpreted with too much sanguinity by the protagonists of cultural differences in emotion. Most of the data seems to restate the cultural values of countries and ethnic groups. Much of it is based on reports by people who may be just restating their culture's formal values rather than portraying the actual dynamics of their stressful and emotional transactions.

In addition, though typically the cultural differences reported are statistically significant, they are modest in size, there being great overlaps between the distributions of research subjects in the cultures being compared, though these overlaps are not usually reported. Even if the interpretations of such differences are correct, this tends to exaggerate their actual scope and the in-depth participation of the people being studied.

There are also substantial studies, for example, by Mauro, Sato, and Tucker (1992), that obtained essentially negative results comparing appraisal dimensions and emotions among four national groups, Hong Kong, Japan, The People's Republic of China, and the United States. They found little in the way of differences among the groups, though there were a few that dealt with the appraisal variables of control, responsibility, and anticipated effort.

Although the authors began the research with the expectation of finding clear cultural differences in the emotion process, they seem convinced of the opposing position, which emphasizes human universals in the psychological processes that arouse diverse emotions, as analyzed in appraisal theory. Because it depended on superficial questionnaires, this study, like many others, was not ideally designed to provide in-depth answers about which we can be confident.

Some of my reservations about the typical interpretations of cross-cultural research findings have been published recently (Lazarus,

1997). There I expressed the concern that cultural psychologists and anthropologists treat culture as a monolithic concept, as if everyone growing up and living within the same culture subscribes to the same values and beliefs, or shares common emotional and coping processes. The United States—along with many other countries throughout the world—is multi-ethnic; it contains diverse ethnic or subcultural groups, which makes it difficult to say authoritatively how Americans as a people think and react emotionally to similar events.

We are in danger of repeating the mistake of the recent past when the concept of "national character" in the 1940s and 1950s—that there was a distinctive German, American, or Japanese personality—was criticized and later abandoned as overstated and circular. There was no way to tell whether what was being described was the external cultural environment, or a culture that was internalized by the personalities of the population living there (see Kelman, 1961; also House, 1981, on how social structure becomes a part of the personalities of its people). However, the socially correct position today is to appreciate and preserve cultural and ethnic differences in outlook.

The concept of multiethnic and multicultural societies may even apply to some extent to Asian countries like Korea, Japan, and China, at least more than has been generally assumed. I have recently been impressed by evidence of major variations among the people of Japan on the basis of the existence of large, deviant religious cults. I am thinking here of the Aum Shinri Kyo (Supreme Truth) and the Soka Gakkai (Value Creating Society), two Japanese cults, which have recently gained the attention of the American media. And there is growing crime and deviance in Japan, where it was once uncommon.

The Aum Shinri Kyo, which killed many Japanese in a Tokyo subway using a powerful nerve gas, has been described as having the crazy mission of building an army, equipped with Russian tanks and biological weapons, for an eventual Armageddon, which would follow a war between Japan and the United States.

The Soka Gakkai seems to be an even more powerful and wealthy religious cult, according to our news sources. It has been active in Japan for decades, has its own political party, and claims 8,000,000 members in Japan and 300,000 in the United States. Even if these figures are too high, this group seems to be much larger than Aum Shinri Kyo, and to have a set of values and beliefs quite different from the rest of the population.

I mention these groups because their size and presence in Japan suggests that Japanese culture is not as monolithic as we have tended to assume. This challenges the notion that most people in Japan think and feel more or less alike and in accordance with common values and beliefs, which is what cultural psychologists have emphasized (*see,* for example, Kitayama and Masuda, 1995; Marcus and Kitayama, 1991; and Shweder and LeVine, 1984.

In an *Annual Review of Psychology* chapter, Bond and Smith (1996, p. 227) gave voice to this kind of challenge in writing:

> Researchers infer that because culture X has certain values, individuals within that culture will share those values. This is an assumption the authors deem invalid on the basis of "growing cultural heterogeneity both of nations and of smaller social systems within them."

Another complication is that even within a society, demands are often honored in the breach, often with evident social hypocrisy—that is, when what is said is contrary to what is done or felt. Upholding moral standards in specific adaptational transactions is not always a simple choice but involves weighing several conflicting values. Some persons make naive judgments about such matters and others more sophisticated ones. Or they set extremely high standards for themselves despite the social hypocrisies and value complexities they perceive. Still others are very clear about what they can get away with, and do so without the need for self-justification, unless directly threatened about what they have done.

To a considerable extent, social order and civility depend on the willingness of people to act in accordance with the demands and constraints of the social system. This is not always enough to ensure obedience. The way societies commonly deal with infractions of custom and law is by punishment. Such punishments can be mild or severe, depending on societal values and customs, which can change over time. They include disapproval, preventing the person who violates the rules from enjoying the fruits of social interaction, or more serious punishments, such as being ostracized, imprisoned, or put to death. For those who disobey the law, there is the constant threat of discovery and punishment, which is an added source of chronic stress.

An alternative approach does not assume that all people within the culture have the same basic beliefs, values, goals, and ways of coping. To the extent that the people of a culture are heterogeneous rather than homogeneous, one could identify discrete groups that share common outlooks of certain kinds and assess the contributions of these outlooks to their tendency to react to social transactions with this or that emotion, or to select particular coping strategies. I think this approach would be superior to making assumptions about how individuals think, act, and feel on the sole basis of membership in a particular culture.

Along this same line of thought, I also believe that species-based human universals are underemphasized by culturists today (Brown, 1991; Shore, 1996; and Tooby & Cosmides, 1990). In my view, the basic relational meanings that underlie each of the 15 emotions I emphasize in my theory are universal and found in all cultures, though the specifics of the arousal of each emotion could differ as a result of differences in the appraisal of provocative events, which, in turn, arise from shared cultural outlooks or divergent individual goal hierarchies and beliefs (Lazarus, 1991, 1995). This position is clearly controversial.

On this point, I note in passing that Kâgitçibasi and Berry (1989), writing about cross-cultural psychology, observed three trends in current research, first, an emphasis on individualism versus collectivism; second, an effort to develop an appropriate psychology within cultures that have not generated their own brands of psychology; and third, the search for cultural universals, though I would refer to the latter as a search for biological universals or what is common to humankind across cultures.

Shore (1996, p. 8), a cultural anthropologist, points out that

> Anthropologists have come to question the degree to which we can assume culture to be shared within a community in the face of competing interest groups and politically positioned individuals.

Shore recognizes that a key issue in anthropology is how the normative culture, which is an environmental set of conditions, gets transmitted to and internalized by individuals within that culture. We also belong to and have social intercourse with numerous groups, which complicates how we manage societal demands, constraints, and opportunities, and reconcile them with our personal goals and beliefs. The social system rarely speaks with a single voice, and what is a demand in one segment of society or in a situation may not be in another.

I read with interest and admiration the interesting volume, based on an international conference in Seoul, Korea, on the topic of individualism and collectivism, which was edited by U. Kim et al. (1994). I was gratified to see that many of the authors of the individual chapters raised serious questions about the simplistic nature of this dichotomy at both the cultural level and at the individual level. They recognized that cultures could differ in their emphasis on one or the other, as could individuals within a culture, but disavowed the notion that individualistic values and collectivist values were incompatible.

These two opposing values could well be in conflict in any individual, be expressed or not depending on the situational context, with one or the other being more important to the individual, even in a culture that leaned in the opposite direction. I would add that, for such individuals, the emotional outcome should reflect the particular person-environment relationship represented in their social transactions, sometimes even more than the cultural outlook, though superficially most individuals would comply, at least superficially, with cultural dictates (for a different view and research findings about cultural differences in individualism and collectivism, however, *see* Dunahoo, Hobfoll, Monnier, Hulsizer, & Johnson, 1998).

Many years ago I was fascinated by anthropologist Ruth Benedict's (Maslow, 1964) now almost forgotten concept of synergy, which refers to the extent to which the institutions of a culture make it possible for the individual to provide simultaneously for his or her own advantage and that of the group. School grades and exams in the United States are the antithesis of synergy because grading on the curve is a zero sum game in which everyone competes with everyone else, and only so many *A*s are given. If your neighbor receives an *A*, there is less chance statistically that you will receive an *A*.

Benedict also argued that low-synergy cultures were highly aggressive, and high-synergy cultures were more benign interpersonally, and provided some evidence of this in the diverse Indian cultures of the American Southwest. This is a far more sophisticated position than the either-or cultural dichotomy between individualism and collectivism so characteristic of earlier research.

My own proposal about biological universals and sociocultural variability in the arousal and regulation of the emotions draws on an "if-then" analysis, which, in brief, goes something like this (for a more detailed discussion, see pages 191–194 of Lazarus, 1991): If a person appraises his or her relationship to the environment in a particular way, then a specific emotion, which is tied to the appraisal, will usually follow unless the appraisal is changed by cognitive coping processes. And if two individuals make the same appraisal, then they will experience the same emotion, regardless of the actual circumstances. I view this as a psychobiological principle. The biological universal here is that a particular relational meaning leads to a particular emotion, and each emotion has its own relational meaning, or core relational theme, as I refer to this meaning (*see also* Reisenzein, in press, for a genetically focused version of this idea).

Conversely, variations among cultures, and among the individuals living in it are the result of differences in the way a culture views human relationships. Thus, what is an offense might be defined differently by different peoples, and this will lead to diverse emotional reactions from one culture to another. The relational meaning of situations that provoke anger—that is, being demeaned or slighted—is always the same regardless of culture, but the definition of slight could differ, even among a goodly number of individuals who grew up in that society. The essence of an emotion is how human relationships are appraised. I view this as the psychosocial or variability principle.

In any case, the four environmental factors I have dealt with previously—namely, demands, constraints, opportunities, and culture, in combination with person variables, operate together as important potential influences on the appraisal of harm/loss, threat, and challenge, the coping process, and the emotions that result from them. Cultural variables are environmental factors, with only the potential of shaping emotions; for the potential to become a reality in any individual, the cultural values and meanings must be internalized and become a part of that individual's goals and beliefs. Otherwise, what we have is mere public compliance rather than commitment (Kelman, 1961).

The psychological consequences of environmental variables are also moderated by a number of formal—as distinguished from substantive content—properties of situations relevant to appraisal, for example, the predictability of events, temporal factors, such as the imminence of a harm, their duration, and the timing of events in the life cycle, which implies that what is harmful or beneficial at one point in life might not be at another, and ambiguity about what will happen and what might be done to prepare for and control it. I have given little attention to these except for imminence and the time relations.

PERSON VARIABLES

It is now time to consider the person variables with which the environmental variables interact. Three kinds of person variables are especially important in shaping appraisal—namely, goals and goal hierarchies, beliefs about self and world, and personal resources, which a person brings into transactions with the environment.

Goals and Goal Hierarchies

Motivational traits are crucial in stress and in all emotions. Without a goal at stake, there is no potential for stress or emotion. Emotions are the result of how we appraise or evaluate the fate of one's goals in adaptational transactions, and in life in general. Negatively toned or stress emotions arise from goal thwarting or delay, and positively toned emotions from making progress toward goal gratification. A complication is that more than one goal is often implicated in an adaptational transaction, and they may be in conflict with each other, so a decision must be made about which goals are most and least important in any given situation.

The preceding statement points to the importance of a person's goal hierarchy in the emotional life. The hierarchy of what we value most and least, along with the probabilities and costs of trying to actualize them in a given transaction, determines the choice of goals that a person will go for in any given transaction, and which emotions are aroused by the outcome. We must ask how a person feels about the goal that is the loser in the goal competition—for example, whether that person is threatened more by the achievement implications of what is happening or by the implications for social affiliation. The answer is important if we are to understand or predict the emotional outcome.

Beliefs About Self and World

These have to do with how we conceive ourselves and our place in the environment. They shape our expectations about what is likely to happen in an encounter; what we hope for and fear; and, therefore, what our anticipatory and outcome emotions are likely to be. We must consider our chances of mastering the transaction and having a positive outcome, what we have to do to attain the goal, and what price we must pay for success and failure. Our appraisals constantly deal with these kinds of questions.

Personal Resources

Person variables influence what we are able and unable to do as we seek to gratify needs, attain goals, and cope with the stresses produced by demands, constraints, and opportunities. They are closely related to what in the women's movement today is spoken of as empowerment, based on one's resources.

Personal resources include intelligence, money, social skills, education, supportive family and friends, physical attractiveness, health and energy, sanguinity, and so on. We are born with many of them and others are achieved by sustained effort. But regardless of their origins, they greatly influence the chances of adaptational success.

For better or worse, personal resources are apt to become stable personality traits, which makes them less amenable to change when we want to help people cope better. Many of them cannot readily be changed early enough in life to make a difference. People who have them are lucky; people who do not have them face handicaps in a competitive society. If we are to capitalize on knowledge of the coping process, we must learn what works and does not work in stressful encounters because the prospects of changing unproductive coping behavior into more productive ones are probably greater than trying to change personal liabilities into resources.

To think clearly about this, it would be useful to know the characteristics that can be changed in people in general, and in specific individuals, how to do so, and the characteristics that are refractory to change. So far, this is one of the major riddles of psychology. The dilemma is illustrated by the relative failure of modern industrial and postindustrial societies to deal with indigenous poverty or failure in education, at work, or in adaptation in general in large segments of society.

ORIGINS OF THE APPRAISAL CONSTRUCT

I first began to think programmatically about individual differences in psychological stress in the early 1950s when I was doing research sponsored by the military on the effects of stress on skilled performance. It was then I became convinced that the main source of variation in the arousal of stress and how it affects human functioning is the way an individual evaluates subjectively the personal significance of what is happening.

In my early explorations, I was impressed by a monograph written by two research-oriented psychiatrists, Grinker and Spiegel (1945), about how flight crews dealt with the constant stress of air war. As far as I know, they were the first to refer to appraisal in a technical sense, though the term was employed in their book casually and only once, if I remember correctly. They wrote:

> The emotional reaction aroused by a threat of loss is at first an undifferentiated combination of fear and anger, subjectively felt as increased tension, alertness or awareness of danger. The whole organism is keyed up for trouble, a process whose physiological components have been well studied. Fear and anger are still undifferentiated, or at least mixed, as long as it is not known what action can be taken in the face of the threatened loss. If the loss can be averted, or the threat dealt with in active ways by being driven off or destroyed, aggressive activity accompanied by anger is called forth. This *appraisal* of the situation requires mental activity involving judgment, discrimination and choice of activity, based largely on past experience. (p. 122; italics added)

It seemed to me then, and still does now, that Grinker and Spiegel's monograph contains most of the important elements of a theory of stress and emotion. Their reference to action that can be taken in the face of threat implies that the coping process also shapes the emotions that are aroused. Their approach was subjective in that it depended on how people construed what was happening to them and their options for coping. Their analysis strongly influenced the way I came to think about stress and the emotions.

I could see then that stress had to do with the personal meaning of what was happening to the person who, in combat, was in imminent danger of being killed. However, what could be done to cope with this stress was constrained by the inability to evade the danger without debilitating guilt or shame about letting one's buddies down, being accused of cowardice, or otherwise being punished by the military system. Here was an intractable conflict that forced them to depend on somewhat primitive intrapsychic forms of coping, such as denial, avoidance, detachment, and magical thinking.

In an article reviewing and interpreting individual differences in stress research, my colleagues and I wrote (Lazarus, Deese, & Osler, 1952, p. 294) that: "The situation will be more or less stressful for the individual members of the group, and it is likely that differences in the *meaning of the situation* [italics added] will appear in [their] performance."

My intention to implicate personal meaning, in the form of individual differences in goals and beliefs in the stress process, was expressed many times in my writings in the 1950s. In each previous and following instance, the italicized phrase in quotations from my writing implicates, often quite explicitly, the role of motivation, personal meaning, and a relational analysis. For example, in Lazarus, Deese, and Osler (1952, p. 295), we wrote that "Stress occurs when a particular situation threatens the *attainment of some goal*" (italics added).

The relational emphasis can also be found in Lazarus and Baker (1956a, p. 23). There we offered the thought that stress and emotion depends on "the degree of *relevance of the situation to the motive state*" (italics added), which is a statement about relationship. And individual differences in the subjective evaluation of the encounter was again mentioned in another article by Lazarus and Baker (1956b, p. 267), in which we wrote that "Relatively few studies have attempted to define stress in terms of internal psychological processes which may *vary from individual to individual* and which determine the *subject's definition of the situation* (italics added)."

Unfortunately, however, in my early accounts, I made the same mistake as William James in his discussions of the direction of causation of emotion and action. We both used the term *perception* rather than *appraisal.* In Lazarus and Baker (1956a, p. 22), for example, we stated that "Psychological stress occurs when a situation is *perceived* as thwarting or as potentially thwarting to some motive state (italics added), thus resulting in affective arousal and in the elicitation of *regulative processes* aimed at the management of the affect" (italics added).

These statements, in addition to suggesting an appraisal-like interpretation of the situation, also point to motivational and coping factors in the stress process and intimate that stress always represents a particular kind of relationship between person and environment. The expression, "regulative processes," is another way to speak of the concept of coping.

The term *perception* is ambiguous in that it does not necessarily connote an evaluation of the personal significance of what is happening for well-being. The term *apperception* would have been more apt because it implies thinking through events to their implications. Although William James's theoretical opponent, John Dewey (1894), was later quite clear on this score, James failed to articulate the idea that perception could mean more than merely the registration of the facts.

At that time, I was influenced by the New Look movement, illustrated by the work of Jerome Bruner (Bruner & Goodman, 1947), whose concept of perception had a much broader set of referents than in its classical usage. It implied, for example, the operation of goals and beliefs—in effect, the *personal meaning* of what was being perceived. This is exactly what I had in mind by the term perception—namely, that the way persons construe events depends on variations in goals and beliefs.

Influenced by Magda Arnold's (1960) impressive monograph on emotion and personality, I referred to this as *appraisal* for the first time in Lazarus (1964), and Speisman, Lazarus, Mordkoff, and Davison (1964). Appraisal, much more clearly than perception, connotes an evaluation of the personal significance of what is happening. As far as I know, Arnold was the first person to make a programmatic case for a cognitive-mediational approach to the emotions, with appraisal as its central construct.

Appraisal soon became the centerpiece of my theory of psychological stress (Lazarus, 1966). At the time of that monograph, the subject matter of stress had little, if any, cachet as a topic in psychology, though this was to change greatly in the 1970s. Janis's first work on stress (1951), and his later work on the threat of surgery (1958), had not yet achieved notice as classics, as they were considered to be later. Mechanic's (1962/1978) study of students under stress took until the 1970s to gain the importance it would ultimately come to have. Before the 1970s, psychology was just getting ready to think in terms of cognitive mediation. As usual, timing is everything.

The same could be said of the emotions, a topic that burgeoned during the 1980s and beyond. There were important efforts before the 1960s, most of them, however, without a cognitive and motivational focus, except for Leeper's (1948) and McReynolds's (1956) treatments of emotion, and the philosophers whose writings were included in a book on emotion edited by Calhoun and Solomon (1984).

Let us now examine the construct of appraisal and consider how it operates. The premise of appraisal theory is that people (and nonhuman animals too) are constantly evaluating their relationships with the environment with respect to their implications for well-being. I first take up the role of appraisal in stress theory, then in emotion theory, though the two areas of concern need ultimately to be combined because they really belong together conceptually and in practice.

APPRAISING AND APPRAISAL IN STRESS THEORY

Before proceeding, a seldom-made but useful distinction should be made about appraisal-related terminology. The noun form, *appraisal,* should be used for the evaluative product, and the verb form, *appraising,* for the act of making the evaluation. This has the advantage of emphasizing appraising as a set of cognitive actions, a process performed by an individual who may or may not have been conscious of doing it.

This distinction was implied in a target article (Lazarus, 1995) I published in a journal devoted to debates about current issues among social scientists. One commentator criticized my usage for not having been consistent throughout the article, but this should not detract from the value of the distinction. McAdams (1996) has made a parallel distinction with respect to the concept of self. He referred to the process by which a person constructs selfhood developmentally with the gerund "selfing," and the product of this construction with the noun "self."

There are two kinds of appraising: primary and secondary. Although they always work interdependently, it is best to discuss them separately.

PRIMARY APPRAISING AND APPRAISAL

Primary appraising has to do with whether or not what is happening is *relevant* to one's values, goal commitments, beliefs about self and world, and situational intentions. Values and beliefs are apt to be weaker factors as influences on actions or reactions than goal commitments because we can have values without ever acting on them. We may think, for example, that it is good to have wealth, but not worth making a major commitment to obtain it. The term *goal commitment,* conversely, implies that a person will strive hard to attain the goal, despite discouragement or adversity.

The important principle here is that, if there is no goal commitment, there is nothing of adaptational importance at stake in an encounter to arouse a stress reaction. Without a stake in one's well-being in any given transaction, stress and its emotions will not occur. The person goes about attending to routine matters until there is an indication that something of greater adaptational importance is occurring, in which case it will interrupt the routine because of its potential for harm/loss, threat, or challenge (Mandler, 1984).

What questions do we ask in primary appraising in any transaction? Fundamental is the question of whether anything is at stake—in effect, we ask: "Do I have a goal at stake, or are any of my core values engaged or threatened? And if there is a stake, what might the outcome be?" If the answer to the fundamental primary appraisal question is no—in other words, we don't consider the transaction to be relevant to our well-being—there is nothing further in the encounter to explore; in effect, there will be no stress.

If, conversely, we make the appraisal that what is occurring is a condition of stress, the transactional alternatives are harm/loss, threat, or challenge. *Harm/loss* consists of damage that has already occurred. *Threat* consists of the possibility of such damage in the future. *Challenge* is somewhat like Selye's eustress in that people who feel challenged enthusiastically pit themselves against obstacles, feel expansive—even joyous—about the struggle that will ensue. Performers of all sorts, whether musicians, entertainers, actors, or public speakers love the liberating effects of challenge and hate the constricting effects of threat.

SECONDARY APPRAISING AND APPRAISAL

Secondary appraising refers to a cognitive-evaluative process that is focused on what can be done about a stressful person-environment relationship, especially when there has been a primary appraisal of harm, threat, or challenge. Such an appraisal, which is nothing more than an evaluation of coping options, is not actually coping but is most often the cognitive underpinning for coping. Still, if it is part of an active search for information and meaning on which to predicate action, it is not inappropriate to refer to it as coping too. The issue of what to call it is ambiguous, and as I have noted many times in my writing, appraising and coping are often difficult to distinguish empirically.

Because threat and challenge are focused on the future, we are usually in a state of uncertainty because we have no clear idea about what will actually happen. Threat and challenge can both occur in the same situation or in a continuing relationship, though one or the other usually dominates. In some situations, we are more threatened than challenged, and in other situations, the reverse may be true.

The more confident we are of our capacity to overcome obstacles and dangers, the more likely we are to be challenged rather than threatened and vice versa, a sense of inadequacy promotes threat. Because confidence in ourselves varies greatly among different people, individuals differ in whether they are more prone to experience threat or challenge. We can think of this tendency as a personality trait and a concept like self-efficacy (Bandura, 1982, 1997) applies.

But situations vary greatly in whether they pull for threat or challenge. Some clearly impose too much of a demand on a person's resources to lead to challenge, and they are likely to be threatening, whereas other situations provide much latitude for available skills and persistence, and so encourage challenge rather than threat. The substantive contents of environmental variables influencing an appraisal consist of situational demands, constraints, and opportunities of which the individual is cognizant. The formal environmental variables that do so consist of situational dimensions, such as novelty-familiarity; predictability-unpredictability; clarity of meaning-ambiguity; and temporal factors, such as imminence, timing, and duration. These variables can moderate the effect of content variables that influence appraisal.

To speculate about this further, I suggest that strong familiarity, predictability, and clarity favor challenge; imminence, bad timing (when there are many other stresses), and long duration favor threat. Nevertheless, and consistent with a relational view of stress, in any transaction both the environmental circumstances and person variables combine in determining whether there will be a threat or challenge appraisal.

By the 1960s, my research interests centered firmly on how appraisal and coping worked in the stress process. Coping can reduce stress reactions, sometimes by actions that change the actual relationship between a person and the environment (problem-focused coping), and sometimes merely by changing the meaning of that relationship (emotion-focused coping). I also used the term *cognitive coping* to express this idea that coping can influence stress and emotion merely by a *reappraisal* of the person-environment relationship. Originally thinking of these processes as ego defenses, I later came to see that they are best viewed generically as forms of appraisal and reappraisal, and not necessarily as self-deceptions, though they could be defensive in any given instance.

Increasingly, however, I could also see that conceptually appraisal and coping go hand in hand and overlap, which results in uncertainty about whether, in any given instance, a stress-related thought or action is an appraisal, a coping process, or both. The uncertainty stems from the fact that cognitive coping (like an ego defense) is basically a reappraisal, which is difficult to distinguish from the original appraisal, except for its history. Not many have examined this problem fully, but see Troop (1998), who addresses the dilemma with considerable care, sophistication, and wit. Given this ambiguity, the answer about which process is occurring must always be based on a full exploration of what is going on in the mind of a particular individual and the context in which the transaction arises.

The qualifying adjective, "secondary," is not intended to connote a process of less importance, but suggests only that primary appraising is an evaluation of whether what is happening is worthy of attention and mobilization. Conversely, secondary appraising is focused on what can be done to cope. So the differences between them are not about timing but the contents of the appraisal. Primary appraising does not necessarily come first nor does it operate independently of secondary appraising, and there is an active interplay on the part of both. The distinctly different contents of each type of appraisal alone justifies treating them separately when being discussed. However, in practice and research they should each be regarded as parts of a common process.

In any stressful transaction, we must evaluate coping options, and decide which ones to choose and how to set them in motion. The questions addressed vary with the circumstances, but they have to do with issues such as: "Do I need to act? When should I act? What can be done? Is it feasible? Which option is best? Am I capable of doing it? What are its costs and benefits? Do the costs exceed the damage, and might it be better not to act? What might be the consequences of each alternative type of response, say, acting or not acting? Decisions about coping actions are not usually etched in stone and must often be changed in accordance with the flow of events, though some are unchangeable once we go beyond a given decision point.

The previous questions have been posed in very general terms, but further details about the transaction are required to make a realistic decision about what to think and do (Janis & Mann, 1977). Because conditions vary greatly, each type of stress, for example, harm/loss, threat, or challenge, contains its own particular issues requiring decision and action. Therefore, for effective analysis, broad categories of stress, such as these, must be narrowed to more specific stressful conditions—for example, bereavement, a life-threatening illness, a terminal illness, a rejection, a minor or serious slight, a job opportunity, and so on. As you will see later, the emotional response to these conditions is apt to differ, though individual differences always remain substantial.

Depending on what is found in research dealing with coping and emotion, even the preceding details, which label the stressful plight of the person, might have to be made still more narrow. Different versions of bereavement or illness—for example, how the person died—have psychologically relevant properties that could influence what can be done to cope and the emotion experienced. Just as individual persons must often take these small details into account in their own appraisal and coping efforts, the scientific study of appraising and coping must consider them too in the search for workable principles, and the same could apply in clinical efforts to help people cope more effectively.

The broadest categories of stress analysis, such as harm/loss, threat, and challenge, which I presented as separate types of stress, are apt to be conjoined in the same transaction and, therefore, should be separated for only convenience of analysis. For example, harm appraisals, which have to do with the past, also have implications for the future and, therefore, usually contain elements of threat as well. Challenge appraisals too may include elements of threat. Although threat appraisals tend to be subordinated to challenge when one's state of mind is sanguine about our resources to affect the desired outcome, this can quickly change depending on shifting fortunes, in which case threat then might predominate over challenge.

Whether or not the terms threat and challenge are used, as opposed to, say, a sense of mastery or control over events, a tremendous amount of research since 1984 has supported the basics of what this cognitive mediational, appraisal-centered theory of stress and coping has proposed. To review the studies individually would require too much space, and be tedious for both the reader and me, so I make use of a mere list here. Please forgive the following long dull list, but these studies of appraisal make useful contributions to research on appraisal theory and will be valuable for others who are interested in pursuing the problem. The list, which is organized alphabetically, also suggests substantial research interest in primary and secondary appraisal:

Abella & Heslin (1989); Babrow, Kasch, and Ford (in press), who make a useful analysis of ambiguity or uncertainty in appraisal and emphasize that information and meaning are not the same; Bombadier,

D'Amico, & Jordan (1990); Chang (1998); Croyle (in press); a programmatic series by Dewe that deals with work stress (1987, 1989, 1991a, 1991b, 1992a, 1992b, 1992c); Hemenover & Dienstbier (1996a, 1996b); Jacobson (1987); Landreville, Dubé, Lalande, & Alain (1994); Landreville & Vezina (1994); Larsson (1989); Larsson, Kempe, & Starrin (1988); Lavellee & Campbell (1995); Law, Logan, & Baron (1994); Levine (1996); Locke and Taylor (1990); Long, Kahn, & Schutz (1992); Nyamathi, Wayment, & Dunkel-Schetter (1993); Parkes (1984); Paterson & Neufeld (1987); Peeters, Buunk, & Schaufeli (1995); Peeters, Schaufeli, & Buunk (1995); Repetti (1987), Sellers (1995); Solomon, Mikulincer, & Hobfoll (1987); Terry (1994); Terry, Tonge, & Callan (1995); a programmatic series by Tomaka & Blascovich, as in Tomaka & Blascovich (1994), Tomaka, Blascovich, Kibler, & Ernst (1997), Tomaka, Blascovich, Kelsey, & Leitten (1993), Turner, Clancy, & Vitaliano (1987); and Vitaliano, Russo, & Maiuro (1987). This research, much of it dealing with work and study situations, and physical illness and chronic pain, supports the importance of appraisal in a wide variety of sources of stress.

We must also think of this research in terms of the concept of coping, which is developed in greater detail in chapter 5. I make the assumption (*see also* Lazarus & Folkman, 1984) that good coping consists more often than not of selecting the best coping process for a particular situation, the criterion being the fit between what one does, the requirements of the conditions being faced, and one's individual needs. It also consists of being able quickly to abandon a strategy that is failing and shifting flexibly to another. The quality of the appraisal is critical for good coping. The ability and willingness of the person to sustain a coping strategy against even unfavorable conditions until it has been given a good try, is also important. Given the complexities and ambiguities of social life, and the coping process, good coping is not something to take lightly. Undoubtedly, it often depends on a considerable amount of good luck.

For a long time, I greatly valued the epigrammatic quality of the serenity prayer of Alcoholics Anonymous, which is more about secondary appraisal than coping:

God grant me the courage to change what can be changed, the serenity to accept what cannot be changed, and the wisdom to know the difference.

When all is said and done, and given the difficulties of making a sound judgment about what will work or not, the wisdom of these words offers mainly a broad philosophical guide. It does not provide concrete help with the details of each specific case or stressful transaction.

How Appraisals are Constructed

Magda Arnold (1960) viewed appraising as instantaneous rather than deliberate. She wrote (p. 172):

> The appraisal that arouses an emotion is not abstract; it is not the result of reflection. It is immediate and undeliberate. If we see somebody stab at our eye with his finger, we avoid the threat instantly, even though we may know that he does not intend to hurt or even to touch us. Before we can make such an instant response, we must have estimated somehow that the stabbing finger could hurt. Since the movement is immediate, unwitting, or even contrary to our better knowledge, this appraisal of possible harm must be similarly immediate.

When I first wrote about appraising (Lazarus, 1966), I thought Arnold had underemphasized the complexity of the judgment that is often called for in garden-variety emotions. I still do, though I am now more impressed with the instantaneity of much appraising, even complex and abstract ones. Appraisals are commonly based on many subtle cues in the environment, what has been learned from previous experience, and a host of personality variables, such as goals, situational intentions, and personal resources and liabilities. All this provides a basis for a decision about how to respond, so you can see how complicated the process could be.

In this light, the speed of many or most appraisals is remarkable, and we know little about how they actually work. Reisenzein (in press) has recently speculated about the cognitive processes involved. There must be considerable simultaneity in the process of scanning for such sources of information, if that is what we do. I am inclined to believe we have the necessary information at the tips of our fingers, as it were, perhaps as tacit knowledge about ourselves and our environment, so scanning in the computer sense is not always necessary, or even likely in most instances.

When Arnold wrote her monograph, psychology was just beginning to think in terms of stepwise information processing. So my own treatment of appraising was more abstract than Arnold's, more conscious and deliberate. Although the expression was redundant, I used the term *cognitive appraisal* to emphasize the complex, judgmental process that must be involved.

One of the remarkable changes that has taken place in psychology since then is the attitude toward and interest in unconscious processes. In the 1950s, psychology had been nihilistic about the ability of our science to deal with the unconscious mind (*see*, for example, Eriksen,

1960, 1962). As applied to cognitive mediation in the field of stress and emotion, the question at that time was whether an appraisal can be unconscious. The issue of whether unconscious processes are smart or dumb—the latter presumably involving primitive and wishful thinking, as Freud suggested, is still being debated (e.g., a special 1992 *American Psychologist* journal section, edited by Elizabeth F. Loftus, which included brief articles by Erdelyi, Greenwald; Kihlstrom, Barnhardt, and Tataryn; Lewicki, Hill, and Czyzewska; Loftus & Klinger; and Merikle).

In the 1980s and 1990s, an explosion of interest occurred in what was unconscious, and what this meant, and the most common answer to the question today of whether an appraisal can be unconscious is a resounding yes. It is widely assumed that we often make appraisals without awareness of the complex factors involved in the judgment. However, neither instantaneity nor the unconscious map closely onto each other or require simple or primitive types of thought (Lazarus and commentators, 1995).

This explosion of interest, and research too, has tended to center on what might be called the *cognitive unconscious,* which has to do with matters to which we attend or fail to attend and the influences of these events and ideas on thought, feeling, and action. Recent articles and books by Bargh (1990), Bowers (1987), Brewin (1989), Brody (1987), Buck (1985), Epstein (1990), Kihlstrom (1987, 1990), LeDoux (1989), Leventhal (1984), Shepard (1984), Uleman and Bargh (1989), and others attest to this renewed interest. We can also look back to related positions by Merleau-Ponty (1962) about the embodiment of thought and Polanyi's (1966) discussion of tacit knowledge and that of Reber (1993) more recently.

I conclude that there are two main contrasting ways an appraisal can come about. First, the process of appraising can be deliberate and largely conscious. Second, it can be intuitive, automatic, and unconscious. The distinction is important because the circumstances of appraising vary greatly. Sometimes an appraisal requires a slow, deliberate search for information on which to predicate how we should react, especially about what can be done to cope with one's predicament. At other times, a very rapid appraisal is called for.

I have also come to the conclusion that in the garden variety of emotional transactions, including those that are stressful, rapid or instantaneous appraising usually applies. By the time we are adult, most of the scenarios resulting in an emotion are repetitions of the basic human dilemmas of living, which most of us have already experienced, often more than once, such as triumph, attainment of a goal, loss, disappointment, uncertain threat, violating a moral stricture, being insulted or subtly demeaned, and so forth—see the core relational themes in chapter 4. This repetition is not likely to be identical to the previous versions in detail, but its basic significance or relational meaning remains the same.

Therefore, we do not have to proceed through the whole of the appraisal process to make a rapid evaluation, de novo, each time we appraise. If we have had previous experience with the same kind of relational problem, a minimal cue can provoke the stress reaction and its associated coping process without the need for reflection or new learning. I once referred to this principle as the short-circuiting of threat (Lazarus, & Alfert, 1964; Opton, Rankin, Nomikos, & Lazarus, 1965).

There is, however, another kind of unconsciousness, which is the result of ego-defense processes as emphasized by psychoanalysis. This is often referred to as the "dynamic unconscious" (Erdelyi, 1985). Far less attention is being given today to this kind of unconsciousness compared with the so-called cognitive unconscious. In a monographic treatment of the emotions (Lazarus, 1991), I took note of the distinction between unconscious appraisals, based either on "casual inattentiveness" or "defensive reappraisal" (Lazarus and commentators, 1995). In Lazarus & Folkman, (1984) we also spoke of defensive reappraisal.

It is important to examine the ways unconscious appraisals that result from ego-defensive processes differ from appraisals that are the result of inattention. As I see it, the main difference is that, compared with the dynamic unconscious, unconscious thought contents resulting from inattention can be made conscious fairly easily by drawing attention to the relevant situation in which they occurred. Defensive reappraisals, however, should be more difficult to make conscious because of the strong motivation not to confront them. Because the person does not wish to be exposed to threatening ideas, the exclusion is deliberate—that is, it is employed as a means of coping with the threat. Awareness would defeat the purpose of the coping maneuver.

An inference is that there may be two conflicting appraisals at the same time, one that is conscious and, therefore, capable of being readily reported, and another at a deeper level that cannot easily be acknowledged. Thus, the statements: "I am not angry," or "I am not scared" must have unconscious counterparts, such as "I am angry," or "I am scared," the latter expressing the unwillingness to face proscribed deeper motives that lie behind these emotions.

From the standpoint of an appraisal, the mental contents produced by ego-defense distorts what a person can tell us about the meaning of a transaction with the environment. This makes the task of assessing how the person is appraising the transaction very difficult because what is reported cannot be accepted at face value. This is also a good reason why psychology is reluctant to accept the idea of unconscious appraisals. It makes the task of learning the truth of what is in the mind a challenge.

Nevertheless, the problem presented to the researcher or clinician, although difficult to overcome methodologically, is not refractory to solution. Skilled clinicians, and laypersons good at making inferences about the implications of common social behaviors, use contradictions of several kinds to alert themselves to defensive distortions in self-reported appraisals (Lazarus and commentators, 1995).

One such contradiction is between what a person says at one moment, and what is said at another. A second is between what is said, and contrary behavioral and physiological evidence, such as gestures, evidence of discomfort, physical flushing or paling, and willful acts that belie what is being said. A third contradiction is between what is said and the most likely normative response to the provocative situation. Clinically, we use the fact that most people would be angered or made fearful in the same situation to second guess the person who denies it.

However, in many cases, we would be wrong because the individual in question may have a different perspective on the events of interest. In research, a comparable strategy would be the use of multiple levels of data—that is, self-report, actions, and evidence of emotions from bodily changes, from which to draw inferences about what is in the mind of research subjects.

Although the recognition that self-report can be distorted does not provide information we can count on about what a person truly thinks, wants, or feels, it does suggest the need for a continuing search for evidence to confirm one or another interpretation. It should be possible to get a clearer picture of these dynamics with appropriate research or sustained clinical attention to the alternative possibilities.

Self-report is often viewed too negatively by psychologists as a flawed source of information about personal meanings, but the negative opinion is not fully justified because little or no effort is being made to maximize its accuracy and minimize the sources of error. Nor are the problems any less daunting with the use of physiological and behavioral data. The problems inherent in self-report need not defeat our search for valid understanding unless we give up on the effort to check and recheck the inferences derived by employing multiple data sources. Casually constructed questionnaires, such as those used in survey research, are particularly vulnerable if we want to examine in depth what people want, think, and feel, and their appraisals in adaptationally relevant transactions.

Having discussed the role of appraising in psychological stress, we are now ready to examine this process in the emotions. The basic appraisal ideas remain viable, but they must be expanded to handle 15 different emotions rather than merely harm, threat, and challenge, which are fundamental types of stress (see chapter 4).

Emotions and Appraisal

Having discussed appraising and appraisal in psychological stress in chapter 3, we turn to the same cognitive processes and contents, only now it is directed to the emotions, remembering, however, that stress and emotions are conjoined. This means, in effect, that we must expand our treatment of appraising and appraisal to the emotions that are usually regarded as positively toned, such as relief, happiness/joy, pride, and love as well as the stress emotions.

APPRAISING AND APPRAISAL IN THE EMOTIONS

One bit of foolishness in the way people in Western society, including many of its scholars, think about the emotions is that they are irrational. We constantly pit emotion against reason, as if these two psychological functions were always in opposition. Our culture says that "it was our emotions that made us act foolishly, or made us follow unwise political policies." We say, "Emotions got the better of me; they made me abandon reason." We think that emotions are a form of craziness and that they fail to follow logical rules.

If this were true, then we might have no hope of understanding them. Emotions would be unpredictable, not subject to scientific analysis. However, this notion could not be farther from the truth. Although it is correct to say that we employ reason to keep destructive emotions from getting out of control, and that emotion and reason are often in conflict, the arousal of emotion actually depends on reason and follows clear rules. The scientific problem is to identify what these rules are. Let us examine more closely the idea that emotions are irrational and dispel what is false in it.

RATIONALITY OF THE EMOTIONS

Emotions are the product of reason in that they flow from how we appraise what is happening in our lives. In effect, the way we evaluate an event determines how we react emotionally. This is what it means to speak of cognitive mediation. Despite the great appeal that blaming human foolishness on our emotions has had since ancient Greek times, emotions follow an *implacable logic*, as long as we view them from the standpoint of an individual's premises about self and world even when they are not realistic. Given our traditional way of thinking about this through the ages, the argument I make below about joining of emotion and reason, and the implacable logic of the emotions, is probably a hard sell.

Economists think of rationality as making decisions that maximize self-interest, and much of psychology seems to have accepted this way of thinking. One problem with it is that to be rational requires that we know what our self-interests are, and often we cannot say or are incorrect in our presumptions about this.

Another problem is that this way of defining rationality venerates self-interest against all other important human values, such as sharing our bounty with others, sacrificing for our children, manifesting loyalty even when it might endanger us, being concerned with fairness, justice, and compassion—in other words, the very values that are so often patronized in a capitalistic society by denigrating them as idealistic, values that should be hallmarks of civilization. Would we want to say that greed is rational, whereas idealism is irrational? And if there were such a world, would we really want to live in it? Self-interest can be greatly overdone, and it has consistently produced great wealth, power, and fame for the few and extensive worldwide misery for the many.

It is foolish to act consistently against our best interests, though people often do this. For example, in a fit of anger we attack powerful and threatening others, or alienate those whom we love with angry and cutting assaults. It is also unwise and counterproductive not to appraise danger when it occurs, or to appraise it when it does not exist, though people often do both. Clearly it is foolish to behave as I have described, but does this mean we are being irrational?

To my way of thinking, this is the wrong question. We should be asking about what it is that truly accounts for human folly, not the relatively infrequent occasions when it can be blamed on emotions that impair reasoning in transactions in which we have a major personal stake. We engage in folly, not so much because we think illogically, but because we have appraised events in a particular way, most often based on unwise or inaccurate assumptions, motives, and beliefs.

Much of the time, these assumptions result in emotions that are inappropriate to the realities of the situation we are facing. And there can be little doubt that as individuals and as a society, we often act unwisely or, as historian Barbara Tuchman calls it, the march of folly. Yet being unwise is not the same thing as being irrational. We have many goals, not one, and actions based on powerful situational intentions often end up defeating the attainment of other goals that we also deem important. But it is our brand of *reason* that has failed us, not our emotions. Emotions mainly reflect what we think we want, and how we believe we should try to attain it, and much of the time, our choices are, indeed, unwise.

There are two reasons why the emotion process can get in the way of reason, though both are usually combined into a single failing and reinforce each other. One is that our attention has been distracted or misdirected, as when the heat of intense emotion momentarily overpowers our ability to reason. The second is that we lack the capacity to control our impulses, to think before we act, as when we fail to inhibit going after short-term goals that defeat us in the long term. It may be foolish to allow one goal to completely thwart another goal of nearly equal importance, though one must often choose. Perhaps this could be called irrational, but I have reservations about this because calling something irrational does not help us understand what is actually happening.

Let us explore why such a label does not help us much in understanding a person we regard as crazy, or in more professional terms, psychotic. If we are convinced people are out to harm us, it would be reasonable to feel frightened or angry. Referring to this as paranoia—a mental condition that involves delusions of persecution or grandeur—indicates disordered thinking, but does not tell us why such a person displays or experiences fear rather than anger, anger rather than fear, guilt, shame, or whatever.

To know why the particular emotion occurs, it is necessary to view things from the vantage point of the paranoid person's own immediate perspective. To understand, we must get inside the mind of the person, as it were, and gain a clear notion of what made that person act in such a counterproductive fashion. Simply labeling it as delusional will not enable us to do this.

All of us make many foolish assumptions about the world, which program us to experience unrealistic emotions in our daily lives. Calling them irrational denigrates another person's reasoning without clarifying what that other person is up to. Once the nature of the inaccurate premise that has been made about our own life and those who are important to us becomes known, our feelings can readily be explained. These feelings follow from that premise, however erroneous it might be. Once we grasp what that premise is, there is a sensible logic to the emotions that flow from it.

Elsewhere (Lazarus & Lazarus,1994), the common causes of erroneous judgments that affect our emotions were identified. I have condensed them into five here. They help us understand what happens when we act foolishly without using the vague, pejorative word "irrational."

One common cause consists of *disorders* that involve damage to the brain, as in senility, psychoses, and mental retardation. Persons with these disorders, when severe, are usually unable to reason adequately, which means that often their emotions have inadequate foundations in social and physical reality. Nevertheless, as I said earlier, what we need to know is why they react with the emotions they do, which vary greatly from person to person and situation to situation. Psychotics or brain-injured people do not necessarily have the same emotional patterns. Merely to point to their disability supplies only a portion of the answer—that is, why their emotions are deviant—but not the kinds of emotions they show in particular social contexts.

A second cause is *lack of knowledge* about the situation in which we have a personal stake. With an opaqueness similar to the distortion that results from ego defense, genuine ignorance can distort our relationship with the environment, leading to emotions that make sense from only the standpoint of what we believe is true. For example, physicians once drew blood from sick people by means of leeches on the erroneous premise that it offered the hope of curing or alleviating sickness. From the perspective of what was known in those days, this procedure was not so much irrational—it had its own rationale, suitable to the ideas of the times—but given what we know today, it was simply ignorant and erroneous.

A more poignant example is that, knowing nothing about microorganisms as causes of disease, physicians in the 19th century carried germs unknowingly from autopsies of cadavers they had recently been dissecting to the wombs of women delivering babies, thereby spreading a deadly disease called childbed fever. It was ignorance, not emotion or irrationality, which led them to engage in actions that today we would abhor.

But we had better not be too arrogant in touting what we think we know today. The political humor in this warning is portrayed in Woody Allen's film, *Sleeper.* After sleeping for many decades, as in the celebrated fictional legend of Rip Van Winkle, the main character of the story, on awakening, discovers a new doctrinal world; instead of avoiding saturated fats in our diet, a "postmodern" belief has been acquired that it is healthy to eat fats. This, of course, is an ironically humorous put-down of modern scientific medicine, which will probably change many times over with the acquisition of new knowledge, or the realization that previous recommendations were in error. Truth and knowledge are always relative and timebound.

A third cause of inappropriate emotion and action is that we have not paid attention to the right things in our social relationships. In most relationships, there is too much to consider, and we must decide what is important and what is not, which may force us to make hasty, often incorrect guesses. Our attention may also have been intentionally misdirected, as when magicians fool us with their slight of hand or manipulations trying to sell us something we do not need. We may also judge that another person is lying on the basis of faulty assumptions about how to distinguish a lie from the truth (Ekman, 1985, 1992), and we unwisely put our trust in those who are concealing their real motives.

Fourth, when we attempt to cope effectively with a personal crisis, such as a life-threatening disease, we may be unable to face the truth and, therefore, engage in *denial*. We should feel anxious and act accordingly, but sell ourselves on the idea that the illness is temporary and minor and that we will soon get better. The defense leads us to make erroneous judgments and, thereby, to experience emotions and act inappropriately with respect what is needed to prolong our life. It is important, however, to qualify this statement somewhat because denial can help preserve our morale and is only harmful when it prevents us from doing what is essential. But it is not harmful when we cannot to do anything constructive to improve our situation (Lazarus, 1983).

Fifth, when we make errors in judgment, it is often the result of *ambiguity* about what is going on rather than irrationality. Most of our social relationships are filled with uncertainty about what other people think, want, intend, and feel, and it is easy to make an incorrect judgment. We see malevolence where it does not exist, or good intentions where there is venality or evil, and this leads us to react with an emotion that deviates from reality. The cause lies in inadequate information and judgment, not emotion, which merely reflects that judgment.

MY COGNITIVE-MOTIVATIONAL-RELATIONAL THEORY OF EMOTIONS

Appraisal theory provides a set of propositions about what one must think to feel a given emotion. If the theory is sound, it should make it possible to make a good guess about what a person has been thinking from what that person is feeling, and vice versa we should be able to predict the emotional reaction if we know beforehand what that person is thinking, and the environmental conditions he or she is facing. This is the implacable logic of which I spoke. Such a stance gives us considerable power over our emotions—knowledge is power—because the theory provides the rules of appraisal lying behind each emotion. The following analysis is based on this premise and offers a propositional understanding of how the emotions work.

What was said about appraising and psychological stress in chapter 3 must now be applied to the emotions. We must expand our analysis from harm/loss, threat, and challenge by adding a fourth type of appraisal—namely, *benefit,* which allows us to encompass positively toned emotions as well as the negatively toned ones that flow from stress.

As in the case of psychological stress, emotion is tied to person variables, such as personal values, goals, goal hierarchies, belief systems, and personal resources as well as social (environmental) events of importance (see chapter 3). These person variables, in conjunction with environmental variables, shape the appraisals on which each emotion rests. What changes as we shift our attention from stress to the emotions are the person-environment relationships and relational meanings, which must be added to our analysis of appraisal.

In the 1980s, several emotion theorists with a cognitive-mediational perspective sought to analyze what a person must think to feel one or another of the various emotions. Those who identified appraisal components include Conway & Bekerian (1987); Dalkvist & Rollenhagen (1989); de Rivera (1977); Frijda (1986); Lazarus (1966, 1991); Oatley & Johnson-Laird (1987); Ortony, Clore, & Collins (1988); Reisenzein & Hofmann (1993); Roseman (1984), Scherer (1984); Smith & Ellsworth (1985); and Solomon (1976), to mention the most active and visible during this period.

In addition to those psychologists who proposed lists of appraisals that shape each of several emotions, Weiner (1986) presented an attribution theory of emotion, which also falls within the cognitive-mediational framework but at a more abstract level. The attributional dimensions explored by Weiner include locus of causality, stability, controllability, intentionality, and globality. Most of them represent what I would consider distal, cold knowledge (Lazarus & Smith, 1988) rather than proximal, hot or emotional appraisals. For example, locus of causality usually has to do with who is considered responsible for a harm/loss or threat, but it is a cool, distanced causal attribution, whereas blame is an appraisal that carries immediate emotional heat.

Despite important differences in detail, there is remarkable agreement among appraisal and attribution theorists about what a person must think to react with, say, anxiety, or any other emotion. The appraisal variables common to cognitive-mediational theories include pleasantness—though I regard this as a response variable rather than a pre-emotional appraisal (Lazarus, 1991)—having a goal at stake, locus of responsibility, or what some treat as accountability, legitimacy, and controllability. There has been a flurry of research to evaluate the role of these appraisal variables in the emotions. My own list of appraisal components contains the same general categories I employed in stress analysis—namely, primary and secondary appraisal.

PRIMARY APPRAISING AND APPRAISAL

The three primary appraisal components are goal relevance, goal congruence, and type of ego involvement.

Goal relevance is fundamental to whether a transaction is viewed by a person as relevant to well-being. In effect, there is no emotion without there being a goal at stake, just as there is no stress.

Goal congruence or incongruence refers to whether the conditions of a transaction facilitate or thwart what the person wants. In plain English, if conditions are favorable, a positively toned emotion is likely to be aroused. If they thwart what the person wants, a negatively toned emotion is apt to follow.

Type of ego involvement has to do with the role of diverse goals in shaping an emotion—for example, self & social-esteem, moral values, ego ideals, meanings and ideas, the well-being of other persons, and life goals (see Table 4.1). Thus, pride and anger are consequences of the desire to preserve or enhance self & social-esteem; anxiety depends on an uncertain threat that has existential implications having to do one's identity, and life and death; guilt depends on moral values, and shame on ego ideals, and so on.

Many modern writers about emotion, including most appraisal theorists, have recognized that goals are important in the arousal of stress and an emotion (e.g., Stein , Liwag, & Wade, 1996). Not much attention has been paid, however, to the role of goals in shaping the qualitative content or category of an emotion, and I believe it is more important than has been acknowledged. In Table 4.1, I take the unusual position in emotion theory of trying to link particular emotions, such as anger, anxiety, guilt, shame, and so on, to the fate of particular goals, as in the previous paragraph.

TABLE 4.1 Types of Ego Involvement[a]

Social and self-esteem
Moral values
Ego ideals
Meanings and ideas
Other persons and their well-being
Life goals

[a] Ego involvements refer to commitments, which might be thought of as goals that fall within the rubric of what we usually mean by ego identity.
From Lazarus (1991), *Emotion and Adaptation*, Table 3.2, p. 102. Copyright by Oxford University Press. Reprinted with permission.

SECONDARY APPRAISING AND APPRAISAL

In stress theory, secondary appraisal has to do with options for coping. The same applies to the emotions. Particularly with respect to the choice of an emotion, a person must evaluate three basic issues—namely, blame or credit for an outcome, coping potential, and future expectations, which I believe are better thought of as fitting within secondary rather than primary appraisal, though this could be debated.

Both *blame* and *credit* require a judgment about who or what is responsible for a harm, threat, challenge, or benefit. This judgment, however, can easily be cool and detached. To assess responsibility is to make an assessment that has the cognitive status of information; to assess blame or credit, however, is to make a hot or emotional appraisal—if we blame we become angry; if we accept credit we feel pride, which is positively toned.

Two additional bits of knowledge influence the judgment of blame or credit. One is that the outcome of the transaction is the result of an action that was under the control of the provocateur or perpetrator, as the law enforcement profession refers to this role. If what happened could not have been avoided, it is more difficult to attribute blame or credit. The other appraisal issue is the attribution of malevolence or intentionality, which greatly increases the tendency to assign blame or credit. Even when no one is evidently responsible, frustrated people often look for someone or some institution to blame, a process traditionally labeled as scapegoating.

Coping potential arises from the personal conviction that we can or cannot act successfully to ameliorate or eliminate a harm or threat, or bring to fruition a challenge or benefit.

Future expectations may be positive or negative—for example, that the troubled person-environment relationship will change for the better or worse.

As is true of all appraisal theories, the diverse appraisal components shape which of 15 emotions will occur in a transaction. Each emotion involves a different appraisal pattern. I give brief summaries of the relational meanings for each emotion below.

CORE RELATIONAL THEMES FOR EACH EMOTION

Recalling my discussion in chapter 1 of reductive analysis and synthesis, the examination of separate appraisal components is usually conducted at too elemental a level of analysis to be sufficient for a full understanding of the emotions. Each appraisal component is a partial meaning rather than a complete one with respect to the emotion involved.

I say this because, in searching for elemental causal appraisal components, we run the risk of losing the forest for the trees—that is, we usually fail to search for or synthesize the components into the whole phenomenon. And by focusing on the component parts of an appraisal, they are often then treated as if they were the whole. The partial meanings must be combined to produce the total gestalt—in other words, the emotional phenomenon as it occurs in nature, the most important feature of which is its relational meaning.

This is why I have cast my own brief descriptions of the emotions globally as core relational themes rather than merely giving a list of separate appraisal components, which all appraisal theories, except mine, have tended to do. The core relational theme for each emotion expresses a synthesis of the whole relational meaning underlying each emotion. Whether or not appraisal theorists agree with the content of my core relational themes, I believe this principle of part-whole relationships remains more important than any minor disagreements about the specific appraisal components for each emotion.

Some appraisal theorists, such as Scherer (1984), argue that a person must examine each appraisal component sequentially, asking and answering, as it were, a series of separate meaningful questions. In my view this cannot be the way appraisal works in nature, especially when it occurs rapidly (perhaps even instantaneously).

For a very fast emotional reaction to occur, a person cannot spend much time asking and answering separate appraisal-focused questions, but must rapidly synthesize the necessary bits of meaning as a unitary whole. Most appraisal theories are good at distinguishing the separate components of meaning on which the emotion rests but do not address how they are synthesized into the relational meaning appropriate to the prescribed emotion.

I am saying, in other words, that the examination of the process of appraising must be taken to a higher level of abstraction—namely, the core relational theme for each emotion. There is no contradiction between having separate appraisal components and core relational themes and combining them into a more complex thought. Two different but closely related levels of abstraction are then provided, the separate partial meanings, and the synthesized relational meaning, which defines and describes the emotion itself.

Each emotion has its own core relational theme, which is a shorthand summary of the global relational meaning. In Table 4.2 I have presented what I believe is a reasonable list of core relational themes for each of the 15 emotions in my cognitive-motivational-relational theory.

CRITIQUE AND DEFENSE OF APPRAISAL THEORY

With the sharp change in the dominant outlook of psychology from militant behaviorism to cognitive mediation, it should be no surprise that vigorous disagreements would exist among psychologists about the merits of appraisal theory. The debates between Zajonc (1980, 1984) and myself (Lazarus, 1982, 1984a, 1991b) are illustrative (*see also* Lazarus, in press; 1998).

A critique of appraisal theory was recently published by Parkinson and Manstead (1992), though without any rebuttal from an appraisal theorist. Because of their temperate but vigorous attempt to come to terms with how appraisal relates to emotions, it would be useful here to articulate the substance of any disagreements between us. I use this opportunity to present my own rebuttal.

I should note at the outset that the issues are more than substantive in that they reflect contrasting epistemologies and metatheories. Recalling what I said about this in chapter 1, epistemological differences have to do with prescriptions and proscriptions about how knowledge about the world is won, and they reflect the nature of science and how it is defined. Metatheory has to do with assumptions we make about the nature of human and animal minds (Lazarus, 1998).

The discussion by Parkinson and Manstead is of particular interest, and I think a bit odd because, with the exception of one major point, despite its attempt to offer a critique of my appraisal theory, it seems to accept most of what I have argued about the role of appraisal in stress and emotion. At the same time, it snipes a bit—as those feeling obliged to defend science often do—about a so-called common sense

TABLE 4.2   Core Relational Themes for Each Emotion

Anger   A demeaning offense against me and mine.

Anxiety   Facing uncertain, existential threat.

Fright   An immediate, concrete, and overwhelming physical danger.

Guilt   Having transgressed a moral imperative.

Shame   Failing to live up to an ego ideal.

Sadness   Having experienced an irrevocable loss.

Envy   Wanting what someone else has.

Jealousy   Resenting a third party for loss or threat to another's affection or favor.

Disgust   Taking in or being too close to an indigestible object or idea (metaphorically speaking).

Happiness   Making reasonable progress toward the realization of a goal.

Pride   Enhancement of one's ego identity by taking credit for a valued object or achievement, either one's own or that of someone or group with whom we identify.

Relief   A distressing goal-incongruent condition that has changed for the better or gone away.

Hope   Fearing the worst but yearning for better.

Love   Desiring or participating in affection, usually but not necessarily reciprocated.

Gratitude   Appreciation for an altruistic gift that provides personal benefit.

Compassion   Being moved by another's suffering and wanting to help.

Aesthetic experiences   Emotions aroused by these experiences can be any of the above; there is no specific plot.

From Lazarus (1991). *Emotion and Adaptation,* Table 3.4, p. 122. Copyright by Oxford University Press. Reprinted with permission.

approach to the mind, which tends to be denigrated. This is an issue I addressed in Lazarus (1995).

In any case, Parkinson and Manstead say (1992, pp. 138–139):

> We will also accept Lazarus's definition of emotion as necessarily involving an evaluative relationship to some intentional object, a recognition of its personal meaning. We feel that this accurately captures the idea of emotion contained in common sense, allowing our theoretical reflections to map onto the measurement of the implicit concept via subjective self-report.

The authors then add to the preceding statement, writing (p. 139) about the one point of disagreement:

> We only really take issue with Lazarus on the question of whether cognitive appraisal is the only route to the apprehension of the personal meaning of objective events or relationships.

These two statements, especially the preceding sentence, astonished me, because here they seem to be saying that the only substantive disagreement between us is whether appraisal is a *necessary factor* rather than merely a sufficient factor in the emotion process. This seems to me to go a long way toward greatly narrowing the substantive disagreement.

As I have said before (Lazarus, 1995), if the empirical case were to be substantial that emotions could be aroused without cognitive mediation, I would comfortably accept that position. However, as the evidence now stands, it would not be my preferred position, because I see no reason to accept it.

A reasonable argument could be made that there are biologically determined emotional reactions to a limited set of stimuli—for example, music and social signals that, especially in infants or young babies and infra-human animals, might contain inherent emotional meanings. This can be observed, for example, in reactions to maternal approval and disapproval, though learning is difficult to rule out in such instances. The phenomenon of looming is sometimes cited in this connection— that is, when a stimulus rapidly approaches our eyes, we react with automatic defenses against it even when we know the person responsible intends us no harm (*see* Campos, Mumme, Kermoian, & Campos, 1944 on functionalism, and the concept of affordances described by Gibson, 1966; and Baron & Boudreau, 1987). Nevertheless, I don't think the empirical case is strong enough or applies widely enough to emotional phenomena to force me to abandon my predilection for a single, meaning-centered approach as the prime, if perhaps not only, cognitive-mediational conceptualization.

The empirical evidence on either side is weak or nonexistent, because of the total confounding of appraisal and neurophysiological processes that might be produced by drugs or music, or whatever, and I am not convinced the case for an independent type of causation—that is, in the absence of cognitive mediation—can be made for methodological reasons. On the premise of the desirability of parsimony, one principle about how emotion is aroused should be better than two, assuming that principle effectively covers the ground. Thus far, I believe it does.

Those who criticize appraisal theory must obtain evidence of the work of neurophysiological, or some other direct kind of causation, which is independent of appraisal, just as they urge the progenitors of appraisal theory to support their arguments with more and better evidence for regarding it as the "only route to the apprehension of the personal meaning of affective events or relationships," as Parkinson and Manstead put it previously.

Much of their critique is centered on the allegation that evidence for the role of appraisal is weak, but they cite little evidence on the other side, which is a double standard if I ever saw one. The authors' citation of research is also very selective. For example, they fail to refer to many studies, such as one by Shaver, Schwartz, Kirson, and O'Conner (1987), whose research narratives about the emotions and their antecedents, including appraisal, provide considerable support for many of the factors being studied today in research on appraisal, despite its dependence on self-report data.

They argue that we have failed to make the empirical case that appraisals precede the emotion (the reader should also *see* Lazarus, and commentators, 1995, for a discussion of the time relations between appraisal and emotion). I admit the difficulties involved in separating appraisal and emotion empirically and accept that the temporal separation has not been made, any more than thought can be unconfounded from any other suspected cause, such as drugs, music, or neurophysiological processes that might be presumed by some to be even more proximal.

The separation of an appraisal from emotion depends on there being a time gap, which would be impossible to show if the emotional response to an appraisal is, indeed, instantaneous. Even if there was a small time gap, little or no room is left to treat them as separate variables, which would be necessary to prove the causal link. I am not sure how to solve the problem, and I once suggested microanalytic methods of research to do it (Lazarus, 1995) (but *see* Reisenzein, 1995, about a preponderance of evidence).

Parkinson and Manstead point to a much more serious problem than this, however, writing (p. 133) that

> respondents in the dimensions of appraisal studies probably reported their representations of emotion rather than directly reading out their own ongoing experiences.

In other words, they are saying that explanations given for emotions occur after the fact and may represent rationalizations of their emotions, which is certainly a possibility, though it is only a logical possibility with no empirical support of which I am aware.

If we take Aristotle seriously, there are at least two kinds of causality, each with very different consequences for how we might understand phenomena (White, 1990). In philosophical jargon, one kind is called *synthetic causation,* which approaches the problem from the standpoint of a traditional cause-and-effect analysis—that is, it is necessary to show that certain antecedent variables result in the reaction, as in John Stewart Mill's cannons of experimentation (1949; first published in 1843).

The second kind of causality is called *logical or analytic causality*. In this case, one variable logically implies another without any necessary causal ascription. In other words, an appraisal implies a particular emotion, but it is also an integral aspect of that emotion. Therefore, there would be no point in considering an appraisal as an antecedent cause of an emotion because it and the emotion are part and parcel of the same phenomenon.

In his review, Shweder (1991) makes this point clearly and criticizes my attempt to treat appraisal as a causal variable in the synthetic sense. He implies that I want to have my cake and eat it too when I draw on both ways of thinking. I am reluctant to drop the synthetic variety out of the conviction that traditional cause-and-effect science has had substantial success in improving our lives. However, this approach is incomplete in the way it tries to understand the phenomena of our lives (see chapter 1), because it limits itself to part processes and never gets us back to complete phenomena (we could also speak of systems), as they appear in nature.

Parkinson and Manstead also press for laboratory proof of the causal relationship, as seems standard in modern psychology. However, I have long been doubtful about experimental proof of anything, though data can provide important confirmation of our ideas. Psychologists who seek such proof often overstate its viability as science, and need to recognize its tentativeness and fallibility (Lazarus, 1998). The idea of proof is fundamentally flawed, which is not to say that evidence should not be sought, because science must not depend on mere faith. Theories are not normally discarded on the basis of specific evidence, but they must be superseded as the intellectual climate, or zeitgeist, changes (Kuhn, 1970).

The traditional epistemology of modern psychology is outdated. Parkinson and Manstead fail to see that a theory, even one that is not proved, may be the most encompassing and useful way to think about a phenomenon and, as such, should not be readily attacked unless one finds a more effective alternative (Reisenzein, 1995). Psychology has long been uncomfortable with theory, but it is important to find the most accurate and all-encompassing theoretical understanding we can construct. Although much more could be said, I think it better to rest my defense of appraisal theory on the basis of what I have already said.

I would like to end this chapter by asking what a person would be like who had no emotions. Dreikurs (1967, p. 207) provides an interesting and revealing answer:

We may easily discover the purpose of emotions when we try to visualize a person who has no emotions. His thinking ability could provide him with much information. He could figure out what he should do, but never would be certain as to what is right and wrong in a complicated situation. He would not be able to take a definite stand, to act with force, with conviction, because complete objectivity is not inducive to forceful actions. This requires a strong personal bias, an elimination of certain factors which logically may contradict opposing factors. Such a person would be cold, almost inhuman. He could not experience any association which would make him biased and one-sided in his perspectives. He could not want anything very much and could not go after it. In short, he would be a completely ineffectual as a human being.

To this I would add that a person with no emotions would not be a flesh-and-blood biological creature but a machine. I say this to undermine the impression that people get sometimes about a theory that emphasizes reason, which is that an ideal human would be one who thinks rather than feels. Emotions are not appraisals, but a complex organized system consisting of thoughts, beliefs, motives, meanings, subjective bodily experiences, and physiological states, all of which arise from our struggles to survive and flourish by understanding the world in which we live. Dreikur's analysis is an important corrective to a way of thinking that erroneously treats reason as cold without considering the emotional heat that is generated by having a personal stake in a transactional outcome.

It is *not* that we have two minds—one emotional and one of reason— as Goleman (1995, p. 8) has recently but unwisely put it when he wrote that "In a very real sense, we have two minds, one that thinks and one that feels." Nonsense. We have one mind, and it contains both thought and feeling. Passion and reason combine as one in our mind. Only when we are at war with ourselves do they diverge, but this is pathology not a healthy state. They are both parts of the whole, each a subsystem embedded in an integrated, larger system. There is nothing more human than our reason *and* our emotions. We are probably the most emotional creature on the earth as a result of the complexity and subtlety of our thought, our mind's and body's role in adaptation, and our dependency on other people, all of which are relevant to survival and how we flourish as individuals and a species.

CHAPTER FIVE

Coping

Permit me to begin my first formal discussion of coping by recapitulating four themes I developed in earlier chapters about the importance of coping and the unity of stress, appraisal, coping, and emotion. This will summarize ideas that serve as a reminder of what I would like the reader to bear in mind.

First, the importance of the coping process in emotion has been generally underestimated because the emphasis has been on appraisal. Many emotion theories, although not being unfriendly to the concept of coping, really ignore the coping process. My position is that, in addition to appraisal, coping is an essential aspect of the emotion process and the emotional life.

Second, traditionally coping and emotion are typically treated as separate entities, coping being said to follow a stressful transaction and the arousal of an emotion. I believe it would be better to treat coping as an integral part of a conceptual unit—namely, the emotion process. Emotion is a superordinate system that includes motivation (an individual's goals), appraisal, stress, emotion, and coping as component parts. It distorts nature to break the emotion process into its component parts and then fail to see their interdependence and put them back together.

Third, coping is involved in the emotion process from the start to the finish. Secondary appraisal, which prepares the way for coping, is an important factor even in the arousal stage because it affects a person's understanding of the nature of the adaptational encounter that is being faced, especially the available coping options and any constraints against them. Coping, along with appraisal is, in effect, a mediator of the emotional reaction (*see* Folkman & Lazarus, 1988a, 1988c). The constructs—motivation, appraisal, coping, stress, and emotion— are conjoined in nature, and should be separated for only the purpose of analysis and discourse.

Fourth, the traditional division into positively and negatively toned emotions, if taken too literally, leads to distortions of the emotion process. For example, it is easy to assign coping to only the stress emotions, such as anxiety, anger, guilt, shame, sadness, envy, jealousy, and disgust. Yet not infrequently, the so-called positively toned emotions involve harms and threats, which require coping.

COPING HISTORY

Coping has to do with the way people manage life conditions that are stressful. To some extent, stress and coping could be said to be reciprocals of each other. When coping is ineffective, the level of stress is high; however, when coping is effective, the level of stress is apt to be low. One must be conservative in offering this as a principle, however, because effective copers probably extend themselves more than ineffective ones, so they create more potential stress for themselves but can usually handle it. In any case, coping is an essential feature of stress *and* emotional reactions, and if we do not give major attention to how it works, we will fail to understand the constant struggle to adapt to troubling chronic stresses and those produced by changing life conditions.

Scientific interest in coping was, at first, slow to develop, but this began to change in the 1970s, and coping research and theory then expanded rapidly thereafter. Four recent books attest to the growing maturation of the field of coping—Aldwin (1994) dealing with developmental issues; Gottlieb (1997ab), which deals with chronic stress; Eckenrode & Gore (1990), which deals with social stress; and a handbook edited by Zeidner and Endler (1996), which ambitiously tries to cover the field.

In a foreword to the handbook, Carver (1996, p. xi) wrote that "The vast majority of the work done in this area has occurred within the past two decades." A recent literature search, reported in a chapter in the handbook by Costa, Somerfield, and McCrae (1996), identified 113 articles on coping in 1974, 183 in 1980, and 639 in 1984, a high level of interest that has been growing ever since, though quantity does not testify to its quality (*see,* for example, Somerfield and commentaries, 1997).

Although the term *coping* was not much used before the 1970s, the basic idea is certainly not new, as is evident in the modern history of clinical psychology and psychiatry, which emphasized the psychoanalytic concept of ego defense. I view ego defense as falling within the broader rubric of coping, a convention that seems to have become widely accepted. The Freudian view of defense was process centered, but ironically, it inspired mainly trait-centered efforts at measurement—for example, the contrasting coping styles of repression and sensitization.

The reason for the trait emphasis is interesting in its own right because it has to do with treatment strategies of clinical psychology and psychiatry. Cognitive therapists, for example, consider chronic adaptational failures to be the result of stable pathogenic ways of thinking (Lazarus, 1989b). It is, therefore, reasonable to assume that these ways of thinking must be changed in treatment if the troubled person is to function better.

Ego psychologists, such as Karl Menninger (1954) and Norma Haan (1969), viewed coping and defense as reflecting a hierarchy of health and pathology. Coping was said to be the most mature way of dealing with stress or trauma. Defenses were regarded as neurotic or psychotic efforts to adapt because they departed significantly from reality (*see* Parker & Endler, 1996, for a recent historical overview, as well as Lazarus, 1966, 1993 a b; and Lazarus & Folkman, 1984). Early on, coping was generally conceived of as a structural or personality characteristic (i.e., a consistent trait or style for dealing with stress).

One of my main contributions to research and thought on coping is a *process* formulation (e.g., Lazarus & Folkman, 1984), which is justified because stress refers to an unsatisfactory life situation that the person wants to change; besides, to be efficacious, coping must be sensitive to changing relational demands.

Still, as I said in chapter 1, the two ways of thinking, process and structure, are both essential to a proper understanding of coping. They address different questions, trait focusing on structure or stability, process on flux or change (Lazarus, 1993a), but these properties represent two sides of the same coin. Let us examine the contrasts between trait/style and process approaches.

COPING AS TRAIT OR STYLE

There are three ways to view coping from the trait/style perspective. One is merely to describe coping patterns that seem habitual—that is, we discover they have some degree of stability by correlating coping thoughts and actions in the same persons over time or across conditions. This is an a-theoretical approach to structure because a coping trait is defined empirically by its stability or consistency over time and conditions. In this usage, traits and styles are not different from each other, both being defined empirically as actions that are characteristic of the individual (Lazarus, 1998c).

A second approach is to derive from theory the personality dispositions or traits that might influence stable coping action patterns. In effect, such a disposition, say, a goal or belief, leads to the formation of a stable style of coping over time and across transactions. Dispositions can be shown consistently to shape coping thoughts and actions, which can then be referred to as styles that to some extent transcend the environmental conditions being faced. In this approach, the two represent different types of constructs. This kind of trait approach usually leads to low or at best modest interindividual and intraindividual correlations.

A third, and I believe the most sophisticated and promising approach, is advocated by Wright and Mischel (1987) and several other like-minded theorists, and is sometimes identified as a *conditional trait approach*. From this perspective, certain environmental conditions are said to be made *functionally equivalent* by a trait, such as a goal commitment or belief. The trait must be shown empirically to shape the reaction under certain kinds of environmental conditions—namely, those that it makes relevant and salient for the person-environment relationship.

The evidence for this approach comes from validating predictions of a coping style by its correlations under these conditions. Thus, achievement goals should only influence achievement strivings in those contexts in which these strivings are subjectively defined as relevant to goals that are high in the person's goal hierarchy (McClelland, Atkinson, Clark, & Lowell, 1953).

I prefer not to adopt a purely empirical, ad hoc approach, in which coping thoughts and actions are found to be correlated from one occasion to another, and which describes alternative 1 indicated earlier. Within a trait frame of reference, dispositional variables influence the choice of coping strategies either in general (alternative 2), or in particular environmental contexts (alternative 3) that are predictable from trait theory. Instead, I favor the causal frame of reference in alternative 3, in which we try to identify personality dispositions that affect coping thoughts and actions, based on the principle of functionally equivalent environmental conditions.

What are some of the personality dispositions or traits that influence coping styles? In Chapter 3, I suggested three—namely, goals and goal hierarchies, beliefs about self and world, and personal resources. Resources include intelligence, education, money, social skills, a supportive family and friends, physical attractiveness, health and energy, and favorable ways of thinking, such as optimism.

As developed more fully in chapter 8, a systems view of stress, emotion, and coping is, of necessity, multivariate. This means that, although we can undertake a trait-centered research approach to the factors influencing coping style with one or two antecedent variables, it is incumbent on the researcher-theorist to include as many such variables as possible if we want to identify the pathways leading to important coping styles. No variable acts alone, but each interacts with other variables in the system, and contributes to coping theory by defining the relevant or salient environmental and personality factors—in effect, what a system is all about.

The history of research on coping styles goes back to earlier ideas in the 1930s about expressive styles, and in the 1950s about cognitive styles and controls. Allow me to trace the outlines of this work, which led to the coping typologies or dimensions employed in present-day research.

The first modern work on cognitive styles of which I am aware was the research of Allport and Vernon (1933) on expressive movements, which are usually distinguished from instrumental actions in which there is a goal-forged explicit intent, though the difference between expressive and instrumental is often ambiguous and difficult to define. These authors studied the tempo of a person's actions (e.g., slow or brisk walking movements), degree of emphasis in writing (e.g., bearing down hard on a pencil or using light pressure), and expansiveness (e.g., use of writing space, as in large and free-flowing or small, cramped letters).

Modest consistency was observed in expressive movements over time and under diverse conditions, which suggested that they were, indeed, styles. And if there were expressive styles, there might also be cognitive styles, which would be even more useful to study because they have to do with the habitual ways people think about and handle their adaptational transactions.

In the heyday of Freudian influence of the 1950s and 1960s, several other researcher-theorists, mostly psychoanalytic ego-psychologists, took up research on cognitive styles. Among the most visible were Gardner, Holzman, Klein, Linton, & Spence (1959). Their research subjects performed a variety of cognitive tasks on which consistent styles of thinking and perceiving were noted. Led by George Klein, this group's most celebrated findings dealt with a cognitive style referred to as "leveling versus sharpening" (Holzman & Gardner, 1959), which became the basis for a long-term research project. Leveling is the tendency to overlook perceptual differences among objects and events; a person with this style views things in terms of sameness or similarity. The opposing style, sharpening, emphasizes making distinctions among objects and events.

The practical clinical value of this contrast is the hypothesis that levelers would favor the defense mechanism of repression whereas sharpeners would prefer intellectualization (or distancing) for dealing with threat. Findings supported this intriguing link between cognitive styles and ego defenses, which has encouraged considerable research by diverse psychologists over many decades. Klein (1958, 1964) speculated that it was the motivating properties of ego defense that fueled the development of cognitive styles, which he viewed as automatized extensions of efforts to defend against threat. However, the direction he proposed for the relationship between cognitive style and defense could go either way, or both ways, and this has remained an open question that was never really settled.

Meanwhile, another research group headed by Herman A. Witkin (Witkin, Lewis, Machover, Meissner, & Wapner, 1954) took a different tack. A laboratory situation was devised in an effort to differentiate people who were perceptually dependent on cues from the outside environment from those who depended on cues from their own body. Seated in a chair in a darkened room, subjects judged the tilt of a luminous vertical rod set in a luminous frame. The chair was tilted to a variety of positions, sometimes in the same direction as the rod, sometimes different.

The room was pitch black, so the subjects had to depend on either kinesthetic cues (feeling their muscles acting against gravity) in judging when the rod was upright, or on visual cues. Those who favored visual cues were called "field dependent"; those who favored kinesthetic cues were called "body dependent." These opposing tendencies were observed to be stable. Therefore, it was reasonable to call them cognitive styles, which in further research were shown to be correlated with certain personality traits including ego defenses.

A later research group, also organized by Witkin, expanded the original perceptual styles into a much broader dimension (Witkin, 1965; Witkin, Dyk, Faterson, Goodenough, & Karp, 1962) and referred to as "psychological differentiation." This construct was defined as the tendency to be analytical (body dependent) or, alternatively, global (field dependent) in the perception of objects and events.

There was also considerable interest in how stable ego defenses were and how they manifest themselves in daily life. An undergraduate student of mine at Johns Hopkins and I performed an experiment (Lazarus & Longo, 1953) demonstrating that the tendency to defend in contrasting ways against two kinds of threat, performance failure and a painful electric shock, was a stable personality trait. Those who remembered their successes better than their failures were more likely to recall verbal stimuli that had been followed by an electric shock better than verbal stimuli never associated with shock. These opposing tendencies seemed analogous to the ubiquitous defensive dichotomy between repression and sensitization, sometimes alternatively referred to as avoidance and vigilance, which have somewhat different or additional connotations.

Lazarus, Eriksen and Fonda (1951) also demonstrated that clinical outpatients, diagnosed as suffering from conversion reactions, were less likely to hear threatening sentences compared with neutral ones than those diagnosed as obsessive-compulsives, who heard more of the threatening sentences than neutral ones. In the experiment, the sentences were made difficult to hear by masking them on the tape recording with a white noise, leading average subjects to be capable of reporting about only 50 percent of what was played into their ears. As predicted from psychoanalytic concepts of ego defense, conversion patients presumably employed repressive defenses (or avoidance), whereas the obsessive-compulsives seemed to prefer intellectualizing defenses (or vigilance) as a method of coping.

Others too continued to focus their research on analogous defensive styles, though sometimes labeled and conceptualized differently. For example, Goldstein (1959, 1973) used the language of coping and avoiding, concepts that have a substantial overlap with Byrne's (1964) measure of repression-sensitization, which has been used more extensively in research on defensive styles than any other measure. Much later, Miller (1987) used the language of monitoring and blunting and presented a distinctive theoretical rationale.

In the continuing research over the years on repression-sensitization as cognitive or defensive styles, there has been much concern with whether low trait anxiety, which is usually a correlate of the repressive style, represents a person's actual state of mind or is defensive. The problem is how to determine whether what is labeled as a repressive style reflects a defense process or is merely a way of presenting oneself socially. If it is the latter, then a high score for repression only makes such persons appear to be psychologically sound (low anxiety) when, in reality, they are hiding the truth about their distress and dysfunction (Hock, Krohne, & Kaiser, 1996; Weinberger, Schwartz, & Davidson, 1979; Shedler, Mayman, & Manis, 1993, 1994).

These measurement issues, and others, such as whether cognitive styles, such as repression-sensitization, should be regarded as a dimension or a dichotomous typology, have plagued research on cognitive styles, and are still being debated. Thus, some of the work of Krohne's research group in Mainz, Germany (e.g., Krohne 1978, 1993,

1996) is devoted to these issues. Krohne and Egloff (in press) have designed the "Mainz Coping Inventory (Mainz is the city where their base of operations, The Johannes-Gutenberg University, is located) to deal psychometrically with these issues. A recent article by Hock, Krohne, and Kaiser (1996) provides a first-class review of this work, which also deals with personality variables that influence these coping styles, and are used to predict physical health and subjective well-being.

Research on coping (or defensive) styles, which had been examined much earlier by George Klein, Herman Witkin, and others in the 1950s and 1960s under the theoretical rubric of psychoanalytic ego-psychology, has shown remarkable vitality and staying power over the years. This approach to coping, however, presents some serious limitations, which I discuss subsequently.

LIMITATIONS OF THE TRAIT/STYLE APPROACH

One important limitation of the trait/style approach is that it reduces coping to a contrast between two extremely broad opposing styles. It oversimplifies the extremely rich and varied kinds of coping thoughts, actions, and strategies people employ under stress, which are the hall-mark of a process approach.

Second, the coping styles approach has ignored goal-oriented intentions and integrative strategies that could be defined as motivated, which people use in dealing with harm, threat, and challenge (Laux & Weber, 1991; Weber & Laux, 1993). These limitations apply whether one views repression-sensitization (or use other, related terms, such as avoidance-vigilance or monitoring-blunting) as a dichotomy or a dimension.

A third limitation is that coping styles usually ignore the very large middle portion of the style distribution (an exception is found in Goldstein's, 1959, 1973, research). In other words, and especially when it is viewed as a dimension, a style's predictive power is based on a small minority of subjects at either end of the distribution, so that the middle group does not contribute to the outcome variance.

This dependence on the distributional extremes invites the criticism that people falling at the extremes of these two defensive styles—namely, avoidance-repression and vigilance-sensitization—can be presumed to be neurotically rigid in their approach to coping. In all likelihood, an efficacious approach to coping depends on being flexible. In other words, the best coping should be responsive to the requirements of the stressful conditions being faced, which makes it process centered.

A fourth limitation of the trait/style approach is that the differences in the effects on adaptational outcomes of contrasting coping dispositions, although statistically significant, are invariably modest in discriminative power. This means not only that the amount of variance predicted by these styles must also be modest, but those opting for this approach to coping wind up having to make too much of too little.

In saying this, I am not advocating an unqualified contextual outlook, but rather a relational meaning approach that is not simply mechanistic, one that is predicated on both the environmental situation and the personality of the individual. This would be compatible with the third alternative to trait theory I spoke of earlier in which personality traits identify environmental variables that are functionally equivalent.

To move in this direction, we must make very thorough assessments of threat because one always copes with something in particular. We must learn to describe in detail how people cope, what they cope with, and the goal-oriented relational meanings underlying their choice of coping, considering individual variations. This is the obverse of what is done from the perspective of coping styles.

Those whose research emphasizes the dispositional or trait/style approach rarely assess to what extent the coping style that is said to result from the trait is representative of the way a person actually copes in different contexts and at various times. This may be the most important limitation of the trait/style approach to coping. My own research (Cohen and Lazarus, 1973) has already demonstrated that there is little or no relationship between a trait measure and a process measure of coping. To their credit, recent research by Krohne, Slangen, and Kleemann (1996) and by Kohlmann (1993), has confirmed that the degree of relationship is modest at best, which makes it difficult to argue that coping styles have much to do with the way people cope with specific threats in particular situations.

About this, Krohne et al. (1996, p. 328) present a mixed conclusion when they write:

> On the whole, our results confirm the important role of dispositional coping variables in the prediction of presurgical anxiety and perioperative adaptation.

However, immediately after on the same page they make the very significant qualification that:

> It is apparent, however, that actual coping behaviors bear no one-to-one relationship with coping dispositions thus clarifying the need to take patient's actual behavior in the perioperative situation into consideration when predicting adaptation and planning interventions.

Kohlmann (1993) is even less sanguine about coping style measurement. He writes in three separate comments:

> Of special interest is that in both studies a majority of subjects adopted a flexible way of coping across a range of different situations. That is, they changed the coping behavior according to the changing situational demands. (p. 119)
>
> These coping styles proved almost unrelated to patterns of actual coping behavior and aggregated measures of behavioral and cognitive coping. (p. 120)
>
> The results presented show that we are still a long way from being able to make accurate predictions for patterns of coping behavior on the basis of coping style. (p. 121)

My complaint is not with the style concept itself, but the kind of measurement that has become fashionable for it, and the failure to relate these styles to what people actually do from a process standpoint. The excessive breadth of coping styles, ironically, leads to an excessive narrowness in the range of coping thoughts and actions captured in research. It seems to me that we should not place our reliance on a single overbroad dichotomy or dimension, but on a variety of styles that could describe and integrate the myriad coping thoughts and acts used for real-life harms, threats, and challenges, and the relational meanings on which they are based. Motivational traits and situational intentions seem to provide a good organizing framework for a new brand of coping styles. But this calls for extensive description of what people do to cope before dichotomizing or dimensionalizing these data into styles.

Instead of focusing on a single-style contrast, we might also gain by using a (P) correlational analysis techniques to group people on the basis of whatever organizing strategies we find them consistently using over time and across occasions. We need to retain a sense of the forest (organized coping strategies) without losing sight of the individual trees (coping thoughts and acts). I believe we need to attack the coping style problem with more creativity than is now being employed.

COPING AS A PROCESS

Lazarus and Folkman (1984, p. 141) offer the following process view of coping: "We define coping as constantly changing cognitive and behavioral efforts to manage specific external and/or internal demands that are appraised as taxing or exceeding the resources of the person." To say this more simply, coping is the effort to manage psychological stress. A process approach to coping contains three main themes.

No Universally Effective or Ineffective Coping Strategy Exists

Coping must be measured separately from its outcomes, so that the effectiveness of each coping strategy can be properly evaluated. Efficacy depends on the type of person, the type of threat, the stage of the stressful encounter, and the outcome modality—that is, subjective well-being, social functioning, or somatic health. Because the focus is on flux or change over time and diverse life conditions, a process formulation is also inherently contextual.

Thus, denial, which was once thought to be harmful and signify pathology, can be beneficial under certain circumstances. This can be illustrated with diseases of several kinds, which are especially stressful when life threatening or handicapping (*see also* Maes, Leventhal, and de Ridder, 1996, for a recent review of research on coping with chronic diseases).

In a heart attack, denial is dangerous if it occurs while the person is deciding whether or not to seek medical help. This is a period in the heart attack when the person is most vulnerable, and delay in treatment as a result of denial can be deadly. Conversely, denial is useful during hospitalization because it is an antidote to so-called cardiac neuroses, a syndrome in which the patient is inordinately fearful of dying suddenly. This fear increases stress and prevents the patient from engaging in activity that would facilitate recovery. But denial again becomes dangerous when the patient returns home and must reestablish normal life activities. The danger at this clinical stage is that denial will lead the patient to take on too much, including stressful work and too much recreational pressure, which may have contributed to the cardiovascular disease in the first place.

There is also much research (Lazarus, 1983) suggesting that denial is useful in elective surgery (*see* Cohen & Lazarus, 1973), even showing faster healing of wounded tissues (George, Scott, Turner, & Gregg, 1980; *see also* Marucha, Kiecolt-Glaser, & Faragehi, 1998) but counterproductive in other diseases, such as asthma (Staudenmeyer et al., 1979). All this suggests that we need to understand when denial, and other forms of coping, are beneficial or harmful.

The explanatory principle I favor is that, when nothing can be done to alter the illness, or prevent further harm, denial can be beneficial. However, when denial, or just illusion, which could be considered a healthier form of denial, prevents necessary adaptive action, it is likely to be harmful (Lazarus, 1983, 1985; for an information-processing and automatic approach to denial, *see* Ben-Zur, in press).

Consider another illness, prostate cancer, which is common in older men. The idea that one has a dangerous cancer provides an ever-present stressful background of life and death, and functional concerns, which potentiate several specific threats. There is, for example, the threat posed by having to make a decision about how to treat the disease—especially in light of the conflicting judgments about what to do by physicians. The same can be said for breast cancer.

Another threat concerns the periodic need for many years, even after radical surgery, to determine whether cancer cells are still present or have spread to other organs. After successful surgery, there may be a period of low anxiety until the patient is again examined for medical evidence about the current status of the cancer. This period of low anxiety is the result of having survived surgery and, perhaps, good news from the pathology report. It could also be the result of coping by avoidance or distancing because all the patient can really do at this stage is wait, and vigilance and high anxiety would serve no useful purpose at such a time. However, as the time for a medical examination nears, avoidance or distancing are no longer likely to be effective, and anxiety will increase. If there is evidence of a recurrence or spread of the cancer, the patient is forced to cope in new ways to deal with the changed set of life-threatening options. This applies to breast cancer too.

Still another threat is uncertainty about what to tell others, such as acquaintances, friends, and loved ones about one's situation. Avoidance and silence are frequent coping strategies. A contrasting strategy is to tell everyone, or selected persons, such as acquaintances, friends, and loved ones, the truth about what is happening in an effort to gain social support as well as to be honest and open in such relationships.

When radical prostatic surgery is appropriate, two other powerful threats are always involved even after recovery from the surgery—namely, incontinence and sexual impotence. These consequences of surgery are common, with impotence resulting most frequently in men older than age 70, even if their ability to obtain and hold an erection was never before in question. A new erectile medication, Viagra, can evidently help many men suffering from this condition, though the percentage of failures, which is highest among those who have had radical prostatectomy, remains a problem.

Impotence is mostly a private matter. Incontinence, however, is even more devastating because of the urinary pads that are required, which can reduce self-esteem and social esteem by interfering with social relationships and travel. Women often note that urinary leakage is common at this age, even without evident disease, as many female-oriented television advertisements attest to these days.

Collective coping has, for a long time and in much of the world, involved the maintenance of silence about prostate cancer, a disease that, like breast cancer, was considered a social embarrassment. In some societies, physicians are still reluctant to inform patients that they have a dangerous or terminal illness. The result was that few men and their loved ones knew much about the disease, and most were ill prepared to deal with it. This secrecy is rapidly diminishing in post-modern societies, with the useful result that more and more men and their loved ones now have the understanding necessary to cope more effectively with the serious threats and frustrations the disease imposes.

The threats I mentioned, and the coping processes they generate, apply to any potentially fatal or disabling disease. Consider the following example, which involves two other diseases. In the first, an unmarried woman of 35 with multiple sclerosis must decide whether or not to announce to the men she is dating that she has a progressive, debilitating ailment. Not to do so would be unfair to them, but being open about it might chase them away and, therefore, be unfair to the woman with the disease.

In the case of breast cancer, men with whom a woman might be intimate might, without forewarning, experience distress at the discovery that the woman has lost one or both breasts, and flee the relationship. What is the woman's best coping strategy? Should she tell them in advance? How should this be evaluated? These are difficult questions for patients who must face these decisions, as well as for coping researchers who wish to explore the way people handle such dilemmas and identify what works best. (See also discussion of HIV/AIDS on p. 125 and on pp. 149–155.)

It is not valid to assume that the way an individual copes with one threat will be the same as that chosen for a different threat. The evidence, in fact, tells us otherwise. A *key principle* is that the choice of coping strategy will usually vary with the adaptational significance and requirements of each threat and its status as a disease, which will change over time.

COPING THOUGHTS AND ACTIONS SHOULD BE DESCRIBED IN DETAIL

To study the coping process requires that we describe what the person is thinking and doing at each stage, and the context in which it occurs.

In the late 1970s and 1980s, my colleagues and I, as well as several others in the United States and Europe, developed measurement scales and research designs for this purpose. Folkman and I (Folkman & Lazarus, 1988b), and our colleagues on the Berkeley Stress and Coping Project, developed a questionnaire/interview approach to coping measurement. It was called the "Ways of Coping Questionnaire-Interview," which soon was among the most widely used approach in both the United States, Europe, Scandinavia, the Middle East, South America, and Asia, (see Table 5.1), having been translated into many languages. It is a factor analyzed set of coping items with subscales that identify eight coping factors: confrontive coping, distancing, self-controlling, seeking social support, accepting responsibility, escape-avoidance, planful problem solving, and positive reappraisal. Others have found fewer factors, or have organized and labeled them differently. However, the main substance of what we have found continues to hold up and be useful.

Research on the coping process requires an intraindividual research design, nested within interindividual comparisons, in which the same individuals are studied in different contexts and at different times. Several individuals must be compared to avoid dependence on a single case. It is the only way to observe how much change and stability is found in what is happening within any individual across conditions and over time. The best generic research design for this kind of research is *longitudinal.*

MAJOR FUNCTIONS OF COPING

Two major functions are referred to as problem and emotion focused, which were first discussed in Folkman & Lazarus (1980), which is based on Folkman's dissertation. With respect to the *problem-focused* function, a person obtains information about what to do and mobilizes actions for the purpose of changing the reality of the troubled person-environment relationship. The coping actions may be directed at either the self or the environment. To illustrate, someone who has cancer must seek the opinions of different medical specialists about what treatment to select and which surgeon is the best available. This approach seems to illustrate the problem-focused coping function.

The *emotion-focused* function is aimed at regulating the emotions tied to the stress situation—for example, by avoiding thinking about the threat or reappraising it—without changing the realities of the stressful situation. To again illustrate, patients may approach their illness vigilantly or with avoidance. However, after the decision has been

TABLE 5.1   Factors and Sample Items from the Ways of Coping Questionnaire

Factor

1. Confrontive coping
   46. Stood my ground and fought for what I wanted.
   7. Tried to get the person responsible to change his or her mind.
   17. I expressed anger to the person(s) who caused the problem.
2. Distancing
   44. Made light of the situation; refused to get too serious about it.
   41. Didn't let it get to me; refused to think about it too much.
   21. Tried to forget the whole thing.
3. Self-controlling
   14. I tried to keep my feelings to myself.
   43. Kept others from knowing how bad things were.
   35. I tried not to act too hastily or follow my first hunch.
4. Seeking social support
   8. Talked to someone to find out more about the situation.
   31. Talked to someone who could do something concrete about the problem.
   42. I asked a relative or friend I respected for advice.
5. Accepting responsibility
   9. Criticized or lectured myself.
   29. Realized I brought the problem on myself.
   51. I made a promise to myself that things would be different next time.
6. Escape-avoidance
   58. Wished that the situation would go away or somehow be over with.
   11. Hoped a miracle would happen.
   40. Avoided being with people in general.
7. Planful problem solving
   49. I knew what had to be done, so I doubled my efforts to make things work.
   26. I made a plan of action and followed it.
   39. Changed something so things would turn out all right.
8. Positive reappraisal
   23. Changed or grew as a person in a good way.
   30. I came out of the experience better than when I went in.
   36. Found new faith.

From Folkman and Lazarus (1988b).

made about treatment, say, to opt for surgery, and there is nothing further they can do, an effort may then be made to distance themselves emotionally from the potential dangers that lie ahead. They may also reassure themselves that the right course of action has been chosen, and the best available surgeon secured. Janis (1968) referred to this way of justifying a commitment as bolstering. These patterns of thought and action seem to illustrate the emotion-focused coping function.

When we *reappraise* a threat, we alter our emotions by constructing a new relational meaning of the stressful encounter. Though at first patients may be anxious at the discovery of an illness, they can reassure themselves that all the medical tests point to a cancer that is localized; and because it has not yet spread, they are good candidates for surgery. These reappraisals are capable of reducing some of the anxiety attendant on the discovery of the life-threatening illness.

Reappraising is an effective way to cope with a stressful situation, perhaps one of the most effective. However, it is sometimes difficult to distinguish from an ego defense, such as denial. When the personal meaning of what is happening fits the evidence, it is not an ego defense, but one of the most durable and powerful ways of controlling destructive emotions.

For example, if our spouse offends us in word or deed, instead of retaliating in order to repair a wounded self-esteem we might recognize that, being under great stress, the spouse cannot realistically be held responsible for the attack. Given the stress, the offending action was probably not under his or her full control, so the basic intention should not be viewed as malevolent. A reappraisal of this kind makes it possible to empathize with one's partner's plight and helps us excuse the unfortunate outburst. Viewed as a form of coping, it defuses the anger that would ordinarily be felt. One hopes our spouse would do the same for us when we behave badly under pressure.

Reappraising an attack in this way is easier said than done. A vulnerable self-esteem makes it even more difficult than ordinarily because we are apt to be unduly sensitive to any sign of having been slighted or demeaned, so we too readily get aroused to anger and have a strong urge to repair our wounds by retaliating. But when such a reappraisal works, it illustrates the power of this form of cognitive coping to influence emotions. Remember, emotion-focused coping is a way of thinking that changes the relational meaning of the social transaction, though not the actual person-environment relationship.

LIMITATIONS OF THE PROCESS APPROACH

You will not be surprised that I see fewer limitations to the process approach to coping than the trait/style approach—after all, I have favored it consistently for many years. Before indicating the major limitation, however, allow me to note that in Lazarus (1993a), the question was raised about whether a coping process approach, which uses repeated measures to focus on the flux of coping, can be converted into a trait/type approach merely by asking questions about coping thoughts and acts in a trait format.

The question was prompted by publications of research that did exactly this, using the Ways of Coping Questionnaire-Interview in a way it was not intended. Although we developed the approach as a way of getting at the coping process, others have used it as a trait/type measure by asking how a person usually copes rather than with a particular threat that had actually been experienced. The problem with this is that the attempt to transform process into trait measurement promotes a vague response related more to the way a person might prefer to cope, influenced in all likelihood by what is socially desirable or ideal rather than how that person actually coped. The need to assess what was actually thought and done in a stressful encounter prompted our emphasis on particular threats (Somerfield, 1997).

The major limitation to the process approach is anything but trivial. It runs the danger of being too contextual at the expense of the big picture, the overall, coordinated strategies a person employs in dealing with life, the personality variables that produce this coordination, life goals and outlooks that make a person go forward in a steady adaptational direction, at least for a time, rather than merely reacting passively to the momentary pressures of immediate conditions. This narrowness of viewpoint is not inherent in a process formulation, but it is a real danger, as indicated in three common misunderstandings, which I discuss following the next section about generalizations from our, as well as others', research on coping.

MAJOR RESEARCH GENERALIZATIONS ABOUT COPING

Having reviewed the main theoretical and metatheoretical concepts of my approach to stress and coping, I now offer five empirical generalizations, which flow from the research of the Berkeley Stress and Coping Project during the 1980s. During that period, my colleagues and I embarked on a research program designed to tackle the process of coping by combined intraindividual and interindividual research designs (Lazarus & Folkman, 1984). The following generalizations were also reported in Lazarus & Folkman (1987) in a journal not widely read outside of Europe, so I repeat them here.

Many other laboratories have provided much supporting evidence of the validity and utility of our model of stress and coping over the years since accounts of our research were published. The evidence was often obtained using multivariate causal modeling techniques, though, regrettably, most of them were cross-sectional rather than longitudinal in research design.

As in my treatment of research on primary and secondary appraisal in chapter 4, to spell out each study separately would take too much space and be boring for the reader. So I will merely list international studies published after 1984 that I think make a useful contribution, acknowledging that my selection is biased by my particular theoretical perspective. I was influenced by the fact that many of the studies I cite drew substantially on the Lazarus-Folkman theoretical approach to coping, though I don't restrict myself completely to such studies.

The volume of research on coping is awesome. I hope I will be forgiven for neglecting significant studies. I cited some of these in Lazarus (1990), including studies by Larsson (1989), Larsson, Kempe, and Starrin (1988), and one by Oates (1988) that employed a longitudinal research design. Examples are presented subsequently of more recent research in this vein—that is, since 1984. They are organized alphabetically within certain broad content categories, many of which include studies that overlap in content.

One major category consists of studies of *coping with various kinds of illness* and physiological effects related to health, for example, studies or analyses by Ahlström (1994); Cohen, Reese, Kaplan, & Riggio (1986); Crocker, & Bouffard (1990); Croyle, Sun, & Louie (1993); Dunkel-Schetter, Feinstein, Taylor, & Falke (1992); Felton & Revenson (1984); Fleishman & Fogel (1994); Florian, Mikulincer, & Taubman (1995); Hallberg & Carlsson (1991); Heim (1991; Heim, Augustiny, Blaser, Bürki, Kühne, Rothenbühler, Schaffner, & Valach (1987); Heim, Augustiny, Schaffner, & Valach, 1993; Holahan, Moos, Holahan, & Brennan (1995); Manne, Sabblioni, Bovbjerg (1994); Manne & Sandler (1984); Noojin & Wallander (1997); Stanton & Snider (1993); Stanton, Tennen, Affleck, & Mendola (1992); and Van Heck, Vingerhoets, & Van Hout (1991). For those readers especially interested in coping with cancer, the research by Heim and his associates, listed above, is in my judgment particularly substantial.

Another category involves coping and diverse aspects of mental health. Studies relevant to this include Aldwin & Revenson (1987); Ceslowitz (1989); Jerusalem & Schwarzer (1989); Moos, Brennan, Fondacara, & Moos (1990); Nolen-Hoeksema & Morrow (1991); Schuldberg, Karwacki, & Burns (1996); Vitaliano, DeWolfe, Maiuro, Russo, & Katon (1990); Wells & Matthews (1994); and Zautra & Wrabetz (1991).

A special category includes studies of the casualties of war, such as Fairbank, Hansen, & Fitterling (1991); Florian, Mikulincer, & Taubman

(1995); Solomon, Mikulincer, & Avitzur (1988); Weisenberg, Schwarzwald, Waysman, Solomon, & Klingman (1993); and Zeidner & Ben-Zur (1994). There are many other studies performed by Israeli psychologists that I have not listed here, except for the above.

Among studies I have encountered, a relatively small category concerns work stress, such as Hamilton, Hoffman, Broman, & Rauma (1993); Jacobson (1987); and Kühlmann (1990), which are somewhat representative of many more I have not cited.

At this point, it becomes inefficient to identify particular categories, each of which consist of only a few studies. Therefore, I will cope with this problem by grouping many studies of very diverse contents, which include such issues as measurement, methodology, antecedent and consequent correlates, and a variety of issues of interest to afficionados of coping, such as alcoholism, depression, aging, social support, academic performance, warfare and imprisonment, appraisal, work stress and unemployment, the self-concept, coping effectiveness, alcoholism, the immune process, athletic competition, and negative life events.

Included in this large, complex, and amorphous category are articles by Auerbach (1989); Bramsen, Bleiker, Mattanja, Triemstra, Van Rossum, & Van Der Ploeg (1995); Deary, Blenkin, Agius, Endler, Zealley, & Wood (1996); De Ridder (1995); Edwards & Trimble (1992); Holahan & Moos (1987); Langston (1994); Martelli, Auerbach, Alexander, & Mercuri (1987); Masel, Terry, & Gribble (1996); McCrae & Costa (1986); Olff, Brosschot, Godaert, Benschop, Ballieux, Heijnen, de Smet, & Ursin (1995); Peeters, Buunk, & Schaufeli (1995); Pruchno & Resch (1989); Seiffge-Krenke (1995); Sellers (1995); Tait & Silver (1989); Terry, Tonge, & Callan (1995); Tomaka, Blascovich, Kelsey, & Leitten, 1993); Westman & Shirom (1995); and Wolf, Heller, Camp, & Faucett (1995).

A considerable proportion of this research employed the Folkman & Lazarus (1988b) Ways of Coping Questionnaire-Interview. The five empirical generalizations, all of which have been replicated numerous times by ourselves and others, follows.

COPING FACTORS USED IN DIVERSE
STRESSFUL ENCOUNTERS

In any single stressful encounter, on the average, people use almost all coping strategies available to them—that is, more than seven out of eight factorially identified types (Folkman & Lazarus, 1980), though given individuals may prefer certain particular strategies. One explanation for this is that stressful encounters are complex, and it takes time for people under given conditions of stress to explore alternative coping strategies. In effect, there is some trial and error in the selection of coping thoughts and actions, depending on what seems useful at the time.

Another reason is that every complex stressful encounter contains numerous psychological facets, such as the goal at stake or the threat to that goal, and each of the coping strategies may be tied in a loose fashion to particular facets. Not enough of the right kind of research has been done to clarify these ideas.

COPING AS TRAIT AND PROCESS

Some coping strategies are tied to personality variables, whereas others are tied to the social context. The Berkeley Stress and Coping Project examined five different stressful encounters reported by 100 subjects over a period of 5 months, one such encounter each month. The major strategies of coping, derived from factor analyses, varied in how consistent or variable they were across different stressful encounters (Folkman, Lazarus, Dunkel-Schetter, DeLongis, & Gruen, 1986; Folkman, Lazarus, Gruen, & DeLongis, 1986).

Based on autocorrelations across the five encounters, we found that certain coping strategies, such as positive reappraisal, showed significant but modest within-subject consistency from encounter to encounter. In other words, if positive reappraisal was employed by a person in one encounter, it was likely that person would use it again in another encounter. However, other coping strategies, such as seeking social support, were very inconsistent across different encounters. That is, if a person sought social support in one encounter, there was little likelihood that person would use it again.

COPING AS A PROCESS

As I indicated earlier in my discussion of coping with life-threatening or disabling diseases, coping strategies change from one time to another as the encounter unfolds or from one encounter to another, which is an empirical definition of what is meant by a process. To get at this kind of process, we studied such changes in a college exam (Folkman & Lazarus, 1985).

Psychologically speaking, like many other stressful encounters, an exam is not a unitary event, but its stressful demands extend over a series of stages, each connected to the formal testing arrangements specified by the instructor. The typical stages of an exam consist of a period of warning, a waiting period before the grades are announced, and another period after students learn how they did. There is also a confrontational stage in which the exam is taken, but it is not practical to study this directly because students would not cooperate while they are working on an exam whose outcome is important.

We found that the emotions experienced and the coping strategies reported varied with the stage at which the strategies occurred. For example, seeking information and social support were frequently drawn on after the warning, but their frequency dropped sharply in later stages. During the waiting period after the exam, distancing was frequently employed but not during the period after grades had been announced because students who did poorly would mobilize to cope with the bad news.

These collective patterns of coping make good sense because they display a good fit with the adaptational requirements of each stage. In the period after the warning, distancing is a poor strategy because it interferes with the mobilization needed to obtain information and study effectively to improve one's chances. However, after the exam has been taken, distancing is useful because no amount of mobilization, with its emotional arousal, could influence the outcome at this stage.

You can see that, if we had treated the exam as a single stressful encounter, and coping had been combined and summarized without regard to the stages of the encounter, the results would have been meaningless. Even worse, there would have been distortions in our understanding of the actual processes of coping. Few studies of stress and coping take this process principle seriously enough, but when they do they have replicated our findings (*see,* for example, Smith & Ellsworth, 1987).

SECONDARY APPRAISAL AND COPING

When conditions of stress are appraised as changeable—that is, when they are viewed as falling within the person's control—problem-focused coping predominates. However, when the conditions are appraised as unchangeable, emotion-focused coping predominates (Folkman, 1984; Folkman, Lazarus, Dunkel-Schetter, DeLongis, & Gruen, 1986); Folkman, Lazarus, Gruen, & DeLongis; Lazarus & Folkman, 1987). This finding links secondary appraisal, which has to do with the options for coping, with the choice of coping strategy.

COPING AS A MEDIATOR

Coping is a powerful mediator of the emotional outcome of a stressful encounter. It is not a moderator because the coping process arises *de novo* from the transaction between the person and the environment—that is, it is not present as a personality disposition before the encounter occurs.

Our research has shown that the emotional state at the beginning of the stressful encounter changes by the end of the encounter, the direction of this change depending on the coping strategy employed (Folkman & Lazarus, 1988; Folkman, Lazarus, Dunkel-Schetter, DeLongis, & Gruen, 1986). For example, planful problem solving and positive reappraisal led to changes in emotion from negative to positive, while confrontive coping and distancing led to emotional changes in the opposite direction. One weakness of this research is that it did not use a prospective research design. However, our finding was replicated prospectively in another laboratory (Bolger, 1990).

We must be wary about generalizing too easily about the efficacy of coping strategies from one or a few limited research findings for two reasons: First, most, though not all, of the research linking coping to particular emotional outcomes depends entirely on self-report data, which increases the possibility that the results confounded coping process and outcome measures. This is one of the vexing methodological problems of a cognitive-mediational theory (Lazarus, 1995), and it has led to inconclusive debates about confounding (see the debate between Dohrenwend, Dohrenwend, Dodson, & Shrout, 1984; and Lazarus, DeLongis, Folkman, & Gruen, 1985).

Second, as I said, our evidence suggests that a coping strategy, such as distancing, may be beneficial under certain conditions, as when nothing can be done to affect an outcome, and all one can do is wait. However, it may be harmful under other conditions, as when the person must mobilize to confront and change what is happening. To know the details of this contextual theme requires that the same coping strategy be observed under diverse conditions likely to influence its efficacy.

Allow me to restate the point in a more general way: The efficacy of any coping strategy depends on its continuing fit with the situational demands and opportunities provided by the environmental conditions being faced as well as the outcome criteria employed to evaluate it. My use of the qualifying word "continuing" expresses the idea that as conditions change, a prior way of coping may become obsolete and need to be changed to fit the new person-environment relationship.

MISUNDERSTANDINGS ABOUT THE COPING PROCESS

I close my account of coping with some misunderstandings about how coping should be understood, which have been indigenous to the field for years. They are the result, I believe, of the tendency of psychology to analyze mind and behavior in a reductive fashion by searching for antecedent causal variables, but failing to resynthesize them into a phenomenal whole. This infects our ideas about coping and how we measure it, and leads to serious misunderstandings about how coping works in nature. Here I limit myself to two main misunderstandings: (a) regarding coping functions as discrete action types; and (b) divorcing coping from the personality of the coper (Lazarus, 1993ab; 1997).

REGARDING COPING FUNCTIONS AS DISCRETE ACTION TYPES

The way I have spoken about problem-focused and emotion-focused coping invites certain errors, or bad habits of thought, about the distinction between problem-and emotion-focused coping. This distinction, which has been widely endorsed in the field of coping measurement and research, leads to their treatment as discrete action types, which is an oversimple and too literal conception of the way coping works. You might have wondered a bit earlier when I was describing problem- and emotion-focused coping why I said that the examples I used seem to illustrate the two coping functions. The qualifying word "seem" suggests some doubt about these categories. Let me indicate some of the sources of confusion.

There are two main errors. One is that when we allow ourselves to slip into the language of action types, we often end up speaking as if it is easy to decide which thought or action belongs in the problem- or emotion-focused category. On the surface, some coping factors, such as confrontive coping and planful problem solving, seem to represent the problem-focused function, whereas others, such as distancing, escape-avoidance, and positive reappraisal, seem to represent emotion-focused coping.

Yet if a person takes a diazepam pill before an exam because of distressing and disabling test anxiety, a little thought will show that this act serves both functions, not just one. Although the emotion and its physiological sequelae, such as excessive arousal, dry mouth, trembling, and intrusive thoughts about failing, will be reduced, performance is also improved because these symptoms will now interfere less with the performance. The coper's intentions are often consciously to achieve both goals. We should have learned by now that the same act may have more than one function and usually does.

A second error is that we wind up contrasting the two functions, problem and emotion focused, pitting one against the other and even trying to determine which is the more useful. In a culture centered on control over the environment, it is easy to come to the erroneous conclusion—which is common in the coping research literature—that problem-focused coping is always or usually a more useful strategy.

There is evidence that, under certain circumstances, emotionfocused coping can be detrimental to health and well-being (*see,* for example, Collins, Baum, & Singer, 1983; and Solomon, Mikulincer, and Flum, 1988; *see* Strentz & Auerbach,1988, for additional observations). In the Collins et al. study, for example, people who continued to struggle to change conditions that could not be changed, thus relying rigidly on problem-focused coping, were far more troubled over the long haul than those who accepted the reality and relied more on emotionfocused coping (*see also* McQueeney, Stanton, & Sigmon, 1997 for a limited review). Although it makes sense to ask which coping strategies produce the best adaptational outcomes under this or that set of conditions, this question fails to recognize that in virtually all stressful encounters, the person draws on both functions.

The key point is that in nature the two functions of coping are seldom if ever separated. Both are essential parts of the total coping effort, and ideally, each facilitates the other. It is the fit between thinking and action—that is, the balance between them and the environmental realities—which makes coping efficacious or not. However seductive it may seem, coping functions and strategies should never be thought of in either-or terms, but as a complex of interconnected thoughts and actions aimed at improving the troubled relationship with the environment. Coping also depends on an appraisal process that seeks the most serviceable meaning available in the situation, one that supports realistic actions while also viewing that situation in the most favorable way possible.

Divorcing Coping from the Personality of the Coper

Questionnaires designed to measure coping are not usually constructed to assess personality variables, which are important influences on coping. This deprives research on coping of the most important factor in stress, emotion, and coping, which is the relational meaning an individual constructs from an adaptational transaction. As I have said several times, this meaning depends on personality variables, such as goal commitments, beliefs about self and world, and personal resources.

I have often cited research by Laux and Weber (1991; *see also* Weber & Laux, 1993) as bearing on the personal meaning inherent in stressful relationships. This research examined married couples in anger- and anxiety-arousing interchanges. Their research suggests that if the main threat in an argument is appraised by one or both partners as the dissolution of the marriage, the expression of anger is apt to be inhibited in favor of efforts to save the relationship. In contrast, if that threat is a wounded self-esteem, then the preferred coping strategy is likely to be escalation of anger and retaliation to repair the psychic damage.

The situational intentions generated in the transaction depended on the personal significance, or relational meaning, of the transaction. This implies that to understand the choice of coping strategy, one must go beyond the superficial measurement of coping and identify these meanings, which, in turn, depend on the personalities of the participants.

Research by Folkman, Chesney, and Christopher-Richards (1994) makes a similar point using observations of how caregivers of partners dying of AIDS coped with the stresses of caregiving. Rather than the superficial stressors of such care, which were unending and unnerving, certain meanings had primary importance in shaping the coping process. Not only did the caregiver face the loss of the relationship when his lover died, because he either had the HIV virus too, or was a high risk to contract it, he could also visualize his own dim future in the form of a similarly inexorable and ugly death. He then had to face the uncertainty of whether, when his own time came, someone would care for him as he was now caring for his partner.

The conclusion to draw from this is that, to understand the relational meanings underlying the coping process, its measurement by superficial questionnaires should be supplemented with in-depth interviews designed to get at the personality variables involved and how the individual appraises what is happening (*see also* Folkman, 1997; and Stein, Folkman, Trabasso, & Christopher-Richards, 1997, for examples of research that follow this principle).

PART III

Research Applications

Having justified the connection between stress and emotion, and the reason for subsuming stress under the emotions, we are ready to turn to stress and trauma in chapter 6, including work and family stress, chronic stress, post-traumatic stress disorders, and crisis theory and management. In chapter 7, I discuss stress and coping in three special groups: those who are aging, children and adolescents, and immigrants.

CHAPTER SIX

Stress and Trauma

T his chapter introduces several stress-related topics, such as stress at work and in the family (and the spillover between them), chronic stress, posttraumatic stress disorders, and crisis theory and management. To help in understanding these special topics, I begin by first examining the differences between stress and trauma.

STRESS AND TRAUMA

In garden-variety stress, the person is able to cope without falling apart or developing serious symptoms of adaptational struggle. The person is "whelmed," so to speak, but not "overwhelmed," but this is always a matter of degree. When people are traumatized, however, they are overwhelmed, which means being unable to function without substantial help, possibly only temporarily, though the dysfunction could continue indefinitely.

My theoretical views mandate that the essence of trauma is that crucial *meanings* have been undermined. These meanings have to do with feelings of unworthiness, the belief that one is not loved or cared about, and perhaps among the most important, people who are traumatized no longer believe they are able to manifest any control over their lives. The fundamental meanings that once sustained traumatized persons—in effect, their very reason for living—have not been just threatened or challenged, as in most stressful transactions, but severely damaged or destroyed by the traumatic event. If we care about our traumatized friends or loved ones, we hope that the damage is only temporary and that they will succeed in the struggle to restore their psychological integrity.

What I said previously implies that trauma always involves existential issues, which provide the basis for individual differences in the appraisal of what has happened and its implications for the future. I submit that in the absence of an appraisal-focused conceptualization, the large and ubiquitous variations in the response to traumatic events cannot be adequately understood.

This is not to challenge that the more severe is the power of such events to harm, the higher is the proportion of people exposed to them who react with symptoms of mental dysfunction. I have already documented this point in chapter 2, where I discussed stress and military combat. When the threat of personal harm is substantial, the probability of major stress reactions and psychopathology increases. However, this is only a statistical relationship; the increased probability of serious symptomatology applies only to people who succumb, which is rarely even most of those exposed to the traumatizing circumstances (McFarlane, 1995). Individual differences remain a potent factor in the psychodynamics of stress.

Emphasizing the subjective appraisal of the person-environment relationship, as I do, only means that the severity of the environmental demands is not the sole influence on the adaptational consequences of events; person variables are equally important. How severe the reaction will be also depends on the details of the event and the coping processes that are generated. The issues surrounding stress and trauma are by no means simple or straightforward. I begin this chapter with the more garden-variety of stress that occurs in the context of work and family and proceed to chronic stress before turning to traumatic stress disorder and crisis and its management.

WORK AND FAMILY STRESS

Work stress (also called job and occupational stress) is a topic that normally falls within organizational psychology, which overlaps substantially with social psychology. There is also much interest in work stress on the part of clinical psychologists, who deal with its individual fallout. Family stress has had an independent identity for many years (Croog, 1970, which is now out of date; later in this chapter, I cite more up-to-date research to be found in Eckenrode and Gore, 1990; and Gottlieb, 1977a). In modern terms, work stress and family stress are said to interact substantially.

WORK AND FAMILY STRESS IN THE RECENT PAST

Research on work stress in the last two decades has centered on the conditions of the work environment that produce stress reactions and the personality variables that are important in this—see for example, Kahn, Wolfe, Quinn, Snoek, and Rosenthal (1964) on role conflict and ambiguity in one's job, and a series of books edited by Cooper and Kasl, such as Cooper & Payne (1991), Corlett and Richardson (1981), and French, Caplan, & Van Harrison (1982).

By focusing mainly on the arrangement of work in industry and, to a lesser extent, on personality variables as separate sources of work stress, the inner workings of the stress process itself have been overlooked in much past research. These inner workings have to do with the nature of ongoing stressful encounters between person and environment—usually involving interpersonal conflicts—and the coping processes arising from such encounters, which influence stress levels from moment to moment and across diverse encounters.

In Lazarus (1991c), which has been reprinted several times, I took the heretical position that industry needed to adopt a transactional, or relational meaning-centered approach, with an emphasis on interpersonal processes, the contexts in which they occur, and individual differences. Although it is possible to rearrange the pattern of institutional work to reduce stress, and to be selective about who one hires, older approaches do not deal effectively with the problem of work stress.

What is needed is to see working persons as struggling with multiple demands that tax or exceed their individual resources, which change with the various aspects of work. It is the misfit between the individual worker and the diverse demands they face on the job that are most important. An approach that is directed at changing only the work environment *or* the person rather than trying to change the daily work transactions of particular kinds of persons is not likely to succeed.

Though seemingly cost-efficient in the short run, the standard approach may not even be practical because what may be good for one worker is not necessarily good for another. What must be excepted from this statement, however, are extremely destructive and demeaning work environments, which are an abomination and should be closed down. These are probably atypical, special cases, and not garden-variety work settings, though they, again, seem to be on the increase.

My article was criticized, though mildly and on different bases by several psychologists who generally seemed familiar with and appreciative of my relational meaning emphasis (*see* Brief & George; Harris; Barone; all in the same book edited by Perewé, 1991). Some thought I was too centered on individuals. Others thought I failed to provide an adequate basis for identifying the sources of stress at work. And still others thought I had not sufficiently appreciated research that, to them, seemed to adopt a systems framework, which in those days I was still advocating.

With respect to the arguably excessive cost of an individual differences framework, a rejoinder could be that a more broadly based and, therefore, more efficient solution might be created by grouping individuals on the basis of common personality characteristics, such as personal goal hierarchies and beliefs; this is often referred to as (P) factor analysis, and sometimes as cluster analysis. It requires considering the work conditions that would create the best person-environment fit for each group. Then we would be dealing with people who shared common stressful relationships in their work environment rather than individuals who had divergent personal agendas.

The problem is that we do not yet know enough to do this well because there has been little research on such (P-based) groupings and the evaluation of the person-environment fit. One must also remember that such a fit might be poor for some aspects of a person's job but not others, which greatly complicates the idea of fit, and forces us to look at it as a process rather than a stable general arrangement.

A MORE CONTEXTUAL OUTLOOK TOWARD WORK AND FAMILY STRESS

A new approach has begun to creep into research and theory on job stress with the advent of two important insights. The first is that work cannot be isolated from other aspects of a person's life. In effect, the total context of a person's life always serves as an important background against which work stress operates as the figure in a figure-ground relationship. If we do not take the total life context of workers into account, including family life, goals, and the personal meanings they see in their family as well as working life (Locke & Taylor, 1990), we will fail fully to understand the stress and emotions they experience.

Two excellent recent books typify this new outlook and focus on the *spillover* between work and family stress, one by Eckenrode and Gore (1990), and the other by Gottlieb (1997). I draw on both these sources in this chapter because I believe they reflect constructive recent research developments. These books also reflect the second theme, which is a corollary of the first, that work and family stress interact, family being the background for work stress, and work the background for family stress.

Work and family create the two most important sources of daily stress in modern adult life. In today's world, where both husbands and wives often work and also accept responsibility for homemaking and raising the children, this is especially true. It is surprising that it has taken so long to recognize the contextual theme of a figure-ground relationship for these sources of stress. Eckenrode and Gore (1990, p. 215) articulate this point nicely when they write:

> The motivating principle and main lesson learned from this book is that stress processes are best understood when placed within the context of significant roles that people occupy, in this case work and family. A sensitivity to context is not new to the field of stress research, and the benefits of studying human behavior as embedded in multiple and interacting environments have been eloquently discussed by writers commenting on disciplines such as developmental psychology (e.g., Bronfenbrenner, 1986).

Stress and how it is handled depends on numerous distal and proximal variables, such as gender identities, functional relationships between husband and wife, and the conditions of work in which each is engaged. In effect, there is a *spillover* of stresses, a term given to the interplay of work and family stress. Perhaps the most important contribution of this excellent and revealing but slender volume, which consists of a series of research reports and analyses by very thoughtful and creative scholars and researchers, is expressed in a second quote below from Eckenrode and Gore's (1990, p. 217) discussion:

> Many of these chapters set forth a research agenda that takes us closer and closer to the daily lives of the persons we wish to study, for example, by using intensive interviews or daily diary methods. These more intensive, microanalytic approaches to stress research have begun to provide us with partial answers to questions regarding the psychological and social . . . processes that may underlie the effects of stress observed previously in less intensive sample surveys. These approaches also begin to specify the reasons for individual differences in reactivity to what objectively seem to be equivalent stressors.

I have been asserting the virtues of looking more closely at what people actually do under diverse conditions—that is, the proximal variables of the stress process (see chapter 3)—which, in many of the studies reported in Eckenrode and Gore's book, are examined by means of ipsative-normative research designs, the same individuals being studied over time and conditions.

As I see it, Eckenrode and Gore's book, with chapters written by an impressive collection of research scholars who eschew the methodological preciousness so often touted by behaviorists and operationists, breathes fresh air into the stultifying patterns of much past research on coping. The traditional science-centered analytic perspective separates the variables rather than focusing on their interdependency, and fails to resynthesizing the component variables and processes into the whole phenomena (or system) we see in nature.

Allow me to illustrate some of the newer research on work and family stress, and coping processes used in these central life contexts, by selectively describing two chapters of this book, one by Robert S. Weiss, the other by Leonard I. Pearlin & Mary E. McCall. Both focus on the social support given by homemaking wives to their working husbands. My purpose is to illustrate the microanalytic and proximal flavor of this research, not to offer detailed portraits.

However, the central theme of both these chapters is *social support,* a concept that came into being and became prominent in health circles during the 1970s and 1980s. Therefore, I should digress briefly to say something about this important topic, which is closely intertwined with stress, coping, and emotion, as background before turning to the research itself.

PSYCHOLOGY OF SOCIAL SUPPORT

Early ground-breaking articles on this topic include those of Cassel (1976), Cobb (1976), Kaplan, Cassel, & Gore (1977), Nuckolls et al. (1972), Berkman & Syme (1979), and Thoits (1982), who has provided a useful review of research. The earliest research, pioneered mostly by social epidemiologists, emphasized a person's social network. This is essentially an environmentalistic way of thinking about how much social support is available to people, and how it can facilitate health.

It soon became evident, however, that this was not about psychological processes. Besides, social relationships could have both positive and negative psychological effects, even leading to disappointments about the quality and quantity of the support people gave in the face of a personal life crisis. In consequence, later research emphasized social support as a psychological issue having to do with coping (Thoits, 1986)—having support depended on an effort to cultivate social relationships and to draw on them under stress. Given the many sensitive interpersonal issues involved—for example, whether the supporting person is a professional worker, a spouse, relative, or friend, and the diverse problems of recipients—those in a position to provide social support need to know how to give it in a way that is truly efficacious, and the recipient needs to know how to accept it gracefully.

Illustrative of these later psychological concerns about social support are numerous researches and analyses, illustrated by recent publications by Bolger, Foster, Vinokur, & Ng (1996); Brewin, MacCarthy, & Furnham (1989); Manne, Taylor, Dougherty, & Kemeny (1997); Wortman

& Lehman (1985); and an especially useful series of nine journal articles on the psychological process involved in social support edited by
Heller (1986). The volume of research in this field over the last several
decades has continued to be very large.

Let us consider more closely the issue of when attempts at giving
support are helpful or hurtful. Professors are often in the position of
wanting to help students facing stressful doctoral oral exams, which
could affect these students' professional futures. In such orals, the student is quizzed by up to five inquisitors—I use this term advisedly
because this is the way students often see them—often renowned
experts in their field, whose formal task is to determine whether the
student knows enough to be advanced to candidacy or awarded a
doctorate. A typical impulse on the part of the professor is to give
reassurance to such students by telling them that they are smart and
knowledgeable. Although this reassurance is well-intended, and
sounds like a sensible way to lower the stress level, which the professor knows can seriously impair the student's performance, this
encouragement often has the opposite effect of adding to the student's
anxiety about the exam.

How could this be? In one of the earliest studies involving students
and social support, Mechanic (1962/1978) reported, for example, on
students' wives who would give similar reassurances to their husbands with the message that there is really nothing to worry about. A
typical statement might be: "You've taken exams before and have done
well. I expect you to pass with flying colors."

Why isn't this apt to be helpful to the student husband? In the first
place, whatever the reality, the student is worried sick about the exam,
and the wife's statement challenges the legitimacy of his feelings.
Despite the reality of his anxiety, the wife's statement leaves him feeling misunderstood. He knows he is very anxious and that he may have
good reason for concern about the exam.

Second, the attempt at reassurance puts even more pressure on him
than there was before. To expect him to pass with flying colors means
that, if he doesn't, his wife, and probably his professor who gave him
the same message, will be disappointed in him. And they will both
have learned that he is not as good a student as advertised. So, as he
goes into the exam, even if he expects to pass, he still worries about his
reputation, and the possibility of failing cannot be totally disregarded.
Even highly successful people assume they have been lucky, feel fraudu-
lent, and assume their vaunted abilities have been overestimated.

What would be supportive in such a situation? Professors could tell
such students that they do not take the exam very seriously because,

as a result of exam stress they have found that some of their best students had trouble with it, whereas some of their poorest passed with flying colors. All the pressure cannot be eliminated, but knowing professors or wives understand what they are experiencing and its potentially negative effects on performance. That they will still have a high regard for the students regardless of how they do should help.

The wife too, if she were not disingenuous, should have said something like: "I understand your anxiety, and I'm worried too. But we've always managed before in a crisis, and if it doesn't go well, we'll manage this time too. Just do the best you can." In this way, she would have validated her student husband's feelings, shared them, and given valid encouragement that even in the face of the worst outcome they would manage somehow. And best of all, such a statement would not add to the pressure the student is already experiencing.

The point is that good intentions are not enough. One needs to give support with skill and sensitivity for it to be appreciated not merely for trying to help but for providing practical help beyond what might be expected. In light of these ideas about efficacious and inefficacious social support, let us return to the two chapters on spillover between work and family stress, and the social support sought by and given to men facing job stress by their wives.

WEISS'S RESEARCH

Weiss (1990) studied 75 men, aged 35 to 55, who were managers and administrators, married to wives whose work was homemaking and child care, and these men were the sole breadwinners in the family. They were interviewed at least three times for about 2 hours, 2 weeks apart. A subsample of 20 wives was also interviewed separately, and each once again with their husbands.

They were asked to talk about their emotional commitment to various sectors of their lives, including aims, gratifications, stressors, and social supports. Weiss wanted to throw light on exemplary and concrete critical incidents involving work stress that spilled over into family life. The main findings are portrayed subsequently as general observational and inferential statements, buttressed occasionally by quotes.

Men mostly believed that they should not bring home their stress from work because this would suggest they have been unable to meet the challenges of their job. Work is their responsibility, and they would fail the marital partnership by not being able to control their work stress. They are reluctant to seek their wives' help or advice, but try to manage stress by compartmentalizing it to the extent this is possible.

They try to keep their work stress from their wives because they believe their wives are unable to deal with it without getting upset; this would only add to their stress. Weiss regards compartmentalization as a fragile defense because it does not work.

The predominant outlook of the husbands is, in effect, to leave their worries behind when they leave the office. Although they may talk to their wives about work, especially their successes, they have little to say about their failures; they want to display competence to their wives rather than ineptitude. The respect and admiration husbands obtain from their wives helps to give them confidence and to believe in themselves more fully.

Ironically, many of the men also think that despite efforts to conceal work stress, it is nevertheless visible to their wives and children. They are right. Sensing what is happening, the wives are apt to feel that their husbands do not wish to talk with them about work; wives would prefer to be talked with rather than to. They feel it is patronizing and demeaning to be expected to provide unquestioning support, as though they were not a real partner in the marital relationship. In some cases, they insisted that the husband tell them about their workday despite their reluctance to do so, but this often makes matters worse.

With respect to the kinds of social support men seek from their wives, Weiss writes the following interesting comment:

> We might specify our concepts of support as help in the achievement of goals, whatever these might be, and help in the maintenance of the morale necessary to the achievement of goals. The very structure of marriage, the opportunity it provides men to perform as husbands and householders, provides support. That men are doing well in their roles is validated by the acknowledgement of how much they are doing by their wives and children. For none of these benefits do men need to talk with their wives about their situations. Men's wives are supportive just by managing the homes they share with the men, caring for their children and, not least important, looking after the men themselves. One point of the marital partnership is that its existence establishes that at least one other person is committed to what has become a shared enterprise. For men, their wives' shopping and cooking and cleaning not only are logistic services that free the men's time for work, but are also reminders that although the men are the figures out front, there are others who care about them, are invested in them and whom they represent. They can count on their wives, and they can feel that their wives count on them in all these ways.

When the men feel stressed at work, they would like their wives to accept the fact that they are burdened, tolerate their withdrawal and their work preoccupation, avoid adding more stressful demands by asking troubling questions, and not become anxious or irritated. This would help the husbands feel supported, even if it were done grudgingly, as long as the embarrassing problems are not discussed. Weiss writes (p. 37):

> The marital partner is indeed men's primary source of support, but this sometimes gives rise to paradoxical behaviors. To protect their wives as supportive figures, men may attempt to dissimulate the extent to which they are under stress. Asking for help—which men may do under situations of extreme stress—is itself injurious. But to gain help while not asking for it can require from their wives a high level of understanding and forbearance.

If and when the stress becomes severe and the husbands need help, which is evident in their increased distance from their children and their disturbed sleep at night, they may talk with their wives about their problems. However, there is often an unverbalized understanding that, when the men leave the bed quietly in the middle of the night so as not to disturb the wife and go into the kitchen, the wife might then rouse herself and join him, not to discuss his problems but to provide companionship and, in that form, reassurance about her continuing support.

Other husbands, and some wives too, deal with such problems by what Weiss calls dismissive problem solving. For example, the husband asks his wife to listen to his options, suggests advantages and disadvantages of each, and urges his wife to choose among them. The wife in these instances feels she has not been understood.

What is most striking overall about this research are the in-depth, proximal observations of how these married couples respond to each other in their husband's struggle with work stress, the attitudes and feelings that sustain these marital transactions, and their impact on the emotional states of both marital partners when work stress spills over into family life. Such spillover undoubtedly also goes in the other direction from family to work, but this aspect of the issue was not studied.

PEARLIN AND MCCALL'S RESEARCH

The chapter by Pearlin and McCall (1990) used a similar sample to that of Weiss. It also deals with comparable microprocessing issues, and adds importantly to the observations made by Weiss, without in any important way contradicting what he suggests is going on with respect to marital support. Their sample consisted of 25 couples, 20 to 50 years of age and older, and as in Weiss's sample, the husbands are the sole breadwinners. Wives and husbands were interviewed separately about work and family stress and marital support. About this support, the authors write:

> The social and interactional character of support may be observed in virtually all relationships in which individuals are engaged. Nevertheless, for several reasons the support process is revealed with particular clarity in marriage . . . [because] it is usually a more continuous relationship than most others, despite its brittleness. And it is usually more inclusive than most, encompassing over time a vast array of shared experiences that enhance sensitivity and understanding between the marital pair. Moreover, it is characteristically marked by intimacy and trust, attributes that can make it a bountiful source of emotional support. (1990, p. 40)

Pearlin and McCall identify four stages in the support processes they observed: The first is *revelation-recognition*. Here, the support giver or donor, in this case the wife, comes to recognize the emotional distress of her husband at work. There follows an *appraisal* in which the potential support donor makes a judgment about the legitimacy of the problem and its amenability to change. Once the problem is evaluated as warranting support, decisions are made about the *forms of support* that should be given and how they should be sequenced. Finally, the *outcomes of the support* become evident—for example, the extent to which the wife's actions are actually supportive or contributes to spousal conflict. These stages are reviewed subsequently in this order.

With respect to what is observed in the stage of revelation-recognition, Pearlin and McCall reinforce Weiss's (1990) findings. One reason husbands withhold information about their stress at work is that they believe their spouse does not want to hear about their problems, which could be true because the wife may resent the husband's consuming involvement in his work and the housekeeping demands this imposes on her. Another reason is that the husbands believe, often in the light of past experience, that the attempt at support will be inappropriate because the wife does not understand what is going on in his work setting. He will have to reject her advice, thereby risking conflict with her. Still other men avoid revealing work problems to prevent an unwanted emotional reaction, in which case he will have to deal with stress at home as well as at work. An additional reason is the concern that the stress reaction will be judged negatively and weaken the wife's esteem for her husband.

The result is that in most cases the wife does not gain the information about her husband's stress at work from what her husband tells her but in other ways. Again confirming and expanding on Weiss, the authors comment that despite husbands' efforts to conceal stress at work, wives usually recognize the emotional distress of their partner. Although they do not understand the details, they sense that something is wrong. The husband may become less talkative, spend more time watching television, be more distant, more irritable, less patient, all of which are clues to his emotional state. One is reminded here of efforts by medical doctors and families to conceal the presence of an incurable cancer, which may be tantamount to an imminent death; these efforts usually fail to fool patients, who sense that they are declining and near death. The strategy of concealment rarely succeeds for very long.

The wife has several options, one of which is to wait until the partner is ready to talk. In this highly charged atmosphere, the authors observe that it takes little to trigger a confrontation about the problem, and sometimes a blowup forces them to address what has been bothering them.

With respect to the appraisal stage and process, Pearlin and McCall suggest that, although it can involve other judgments, the dominant issue is apt to be legitimation—that is, whether the spouse at work has good reason for his distress and, therefore, deserves special spousal attention and support. The answer is usually based on the perceived fit between the problem and the emotional distress. If the distress seems out of proportion to the problem, the response is often advice to the husband not to be so bothered or to stop making a mountain out of a molehill. But the wife may try to give support anyway because the presence of distress, in itself, legitimizes the need.

Occasions where the wife withholds support often have to do with problems of reciprocity; for example, feeling exploited in the marital relationship breeds resentment even when the wife understands her husband's distress. Or she may be struggling with a problem at home, say, with the children, which seems to have a greater priority for her attention. There may also be a problem of support burnout because the problem of the husband seems chronic or recurrent, or he seems regularly to provoke recurrences.

As to forms of marital support and their outcomes, if by her actions the wife contributes to a clarification of the meaning of the problem— for example, the reasons why the husband is so troubled about what is happening at work—this clarification can be very helpful. However, giving advice is usually risky and often not helpful; even when it is sound, the advice often comes to recipients at a time when they are not ready or able to use it, though it might be appropriate at another time.

I have already illustrated the failure of well-intentioned efforts at support giving with the work of Mechanic (1962/1978) on how spouses react to student examination stress. Pearlin and McCall add additional substance to the important question of when the effort is supportive. In the couples they studied, the wife may try to protect the husband by not adding additional pressures in the home, and this alone may have supportive value. Or she might provide diversions from the husband's coping struggle by getting his mind off his troubles or encouraging pleasant social diversions. What works or does not work is, to some extent, an individual matter for both donor and recipient.

METHODOLOGICAL ISSUES

With respect to the methodology of this research, Pearlin and McCall (1990, p. 58) write:

> . . . small scale, intensive qualitative studies often enable the researcher to observe phenomena in depth. There is no doubt that the flexibility and probing character of such research allows one to pursue the hint of something important and to amplify it in a manner not permitted by more structured inquiries. But although it may lead to some riches, it leads away from others. Specifically, it is very difficult to conduct a comparative analysis of these data. Thus we cannot be sure what kinds of people under what kinds of conditions are likely to engage in what kinds of supportive behaviors. By way of example, we are unable to analyze how occupational states, family size, and the employment of wives may interact in shaping support processes.

The methodological concern that microanalytic research overlooks the macroanalytic, distal variables, such as gender, ethnicity, age, socioeconomic variables, different family patterns, such as when the wife is working or seeking a career, should be examined with care. For a long time, I have been advocating a research approach to stress and coping that uses small, nonrepresentative samples to make it possible to obtain repeated measurements on the same individuals over time and across conditions, while recognizing this limitation (Lazarus, 1981, 1990, 1998). The problem is especially important for those who prefer this research style.

Many readers, especially younger ones, may have already thought that the sample studied by both Weiss and Pearlin and McCall is an old-fashioned one consisting of sexist men, whose values are about protecting women and manifesting their old-fashioned macho stereotypes, a pattern that denigrates women and their role in marriage. This limitation does not belie the reality of the patterns shown by these particular couples and their stress and coping processes. However, one cannot generalize from a limited sample to others, say, families in which men and women are both employed, which seems to be the dominant pattern today. To do so, one would need to compare this sample with those of a similar age and work level whose husbands and wives both work.

These sampling problems, echoed by all researchers whose work I have been exploring, can be overcome by repeating the same kind of study with other small samples, selected on the basis of important comparative distal or proximal characteristics. One cannot do everything in a single study designed microanalytically. If, as I do, one eschews large sample, epidemiological research with large representative samples because it tends to be superficial, then I agree that appropriate generalizations require the systematic use of additional samples.

I am convinced that staying at the microsocial, proximal level of analysis offers a better prospect of obtaining ecologically valid and practical knowledge about stress, emotion, and coping processes in stressful social relationships. But investigators must be free to choose which approach they want to use, proximal or distal, just as it is appropriate to ask which approach provides more useful information and in-depth insights.

There is an even more serious problem with the methodology described here, which should be addressed directly. The greatest source of unease about many of the best and most interesting studies described in Eckenrode and Gore's book on work and family stress, and Gottlieb's book on chronic stress, is that the data were obtained after the transactions in question. This leaves the possibility that the informants failed correctly to remember what actually happened, were dissimulating, or could not identity the real provocations and reasons for what they did and said. This is the same point Parkinson and Manstead (1992) made in their critique of appraisal theory, to which I gave a rebuttal in chapter 4.

To deal with this problem, investigators must, at the very least, remain independent as observers and make sophisticated interpretative inferences about what is going on. These particular researchers are experienced and thoughtful, and I tend to have confidence in their professional and intellectual integrity, which is essential for this kind of research. I note too the convergence in the findings and interpretations of both studies, that of Weiss, and of Pearlin and McCall, which adds importantly to our confidence that they are on target.

I also believe that participant observation is more suitable for the problems being tackled than the mechanical procedures of the laboratory experiment, which have their own particular methodological problems (*see*, for example, an account of my reasons for abandoning the laboratory in stress, emotion, and coping research in Lazarus, 1998a). Still, it always remains to be demonstrated how the problem was handled.

These studies are reminiscent of Erving Goffman's (1959, 1971) distinctive examinations of social rituals as a participant observer. I always found his observations and interpretations to ring true—no proof, of course, but convincing nevertheless. Large-scale epidemiological data give us measurement statistics that are too abstract for a meaningful feel of the transactions in which we are interested. What is missing from such findings, which usually deal with distal variables, are individual stories, which our minds can easily understand, and with which we can generally resonate.

The preceding methodological problem may be overstated, but it is difficult to defend such research against the distinct possibility that the participants merely thought up justifications of their actions and reactions after the fact, without being aware of other, perhaps more valid, explanations of the processes that might actually have occurred. I know of no completely satisfactory way to second guess the criticism as long as the subject participants are reporting what happened and how they felt after the fact. Most other methods of studying the same process are just as prone to inaccuracies, or even more so. Yet the advantages of this kind of research may outweigh the disadvantages.

For example, in epidemiological studies, one misses a careful accounting of individual variations because it is unlikely that all or even many of the men and women studied closely fit the normative portrait. Such an accounting would be useful in obtaining a balanced picture of what is happening to the people in the study. The weakness of epidemiological studies is that they fail to provide a microanalytic portrait of the stress and coping process. If this kind of portrait is what we want, we need to do smaller-scale, in-depth research about interpersonal events and their psychological impact, and face up to the methodological problems, while trying to use other methods as checks on the inferences made.

In this kind of research, it would certainly be useful to study the process as it is happening before your eyes, as when married couples are brought into the laboratory to engage in an argument, which can then be videotaped and discussed immediately after. But there are problems with this kind of data gathering too, including the potential for artificiality when the argument is created in the laboratory by the researcher.

Another antidote to the danger of misreading the data is to use multiple measurement sources to evaluate the generality of the descriptions and conclusions drawn, though this has its problems too, as is pointed out later. To mention the most important without elaboration here, each response measure is sensitive to different antecedents, which produces naturally low correlations among them. There is no perfect solution if what one wants is absolute proof.

Before leaving the topic of the spillover of work and family stress, something brief might be said about the subject matter of job burnout, a stress arena that has generated a substantial literature of its own, and that was pioneered and elaborated on much earlier by Maslach (1982), and others, such as Pines, Aronson, with Kaffry (1981). This aspect of stress has also been tackled from the standpoint of spillover from husband to wife and wife to husband, which connects it with the marital studies of work and family stress.

Recent research by Westman and Etzion (1995) is illustrative, though they prefer the term *crossover* to spillover and used questionnaires rather than in-depth interviews to study the problem. They found that job burnout in military couples in Israel, on the part of either the husband or wife, strongly affects the other spouse. The subjective sense of control over their job stress on the part of one of the marital partners was also found to be a resistance resource that benefitted the other partner. Related research (e.g., Etzion, Eden, & Lapidot (1998) has shown that being away temporarily from job stress tends to relieve burnout, whether this is the result of vacation or some other activity, such as reserve service, even when this activity is quite demanding.

This extension from the topic of burnout at work to the marital relationship reflects the growing recognition among researchers and theorists that job stress has wide effects on people within the stressed person's social network. Even more important, to understand it fully, the phenomenon needs to be considered in the wider context of a person's life.

CHRONIC STRESS

In recent years, there has been a growing appreciation on the part of stress theorists and researchers that important differences exist between acute stress and chronic stress. *Chronic stress* arises from harmful or threatening, but stable, conditions of life, and from the stressful roles people continually fulfill at work and in the family. *Acute stress,* conversely, is provoked by time-limited, major or minor events that are harmful or threatening at a particular moment in life or for a relatively brief period. A qualification is needed, however, that stressful events, especially if they are major, often create many new sources of daily or chronic stress in their wake, making the distinction between acute and chronic somewhat more fuzzy than its protagonists might be willing to recognize.

Be that as it may, one notable manifestation of the growing importance of chronic stress is an impressive book of research-oriented chapters edited by Benjamin H. Gottlieb (1997a), which is mostly centered on the coping process. This is the same Gottlieb cited earlier. Most of the research chapters in Gottlieb's book, written by a substantial and creative group of contributors, approach chronic stress from the vantage point of a transactional or relational, meaning-centered analysis. They describe studies making intensive, microanalytic examinations of diverse kinds of chronic stress in mostly dyadic situations.

The research described in Gottlieb's book is subject to the same methodological virtues and limitations mentioned in connection with Eckenrode & Gore's book on work and family stress, and I would respond to them in the same way. I sampled a few of the following chapters to illustrate especially important principles, both substantive and methodological. I apologize to those I do not cite for my selectivity and to those whose work I must treat in a more cursory fashion than it deserves.

In his introductory chapter, Gottlieb (1997b, p. 3) suggests that coping with chronic stress is a long overdue subject. He writes in his opening paragraph:

> Compared to the voluminous literature that examines responses to acute or short-term stressful events and transitions that have clearly documented time spans, the behavioral and emotional regulatory processes that unfold in circumstances of unremitting demand have been understudied. For example, how do people deal with the ongoing threat of neighborhood violence or crime? How do family members come to terms with and learn to manage the long-term disability that results from spinal cord injury or the uncertainty that arises in the wake of a heart attack or stroke? Are there certain psychological devices that assist recently divorced partners to preserve or restore their sense of self-worth? Are there daily routines and patterns of social interaction that help people maintain their equilibrium in the face of persistent life strains that involve balancing multiple and frequently conflicting social roles?

Gottlieb (1997, p. 4) also quotes Wheaton (1994, p. 82), one of the chapter authors, who defines chronic stress as

> problems and issues that are so regular in the enactment of daily roles and activities, that they behave as if they are continuous for the individual.

From this perspective, stress includes the minor hassles of daily life as well as major catastrophes. Defining stress solely in terms of major life events is simply not an adequate strategy for throwing light on how people cope with stress. There has been considerable interest of late in the daily monitoring of a person's hassle-related thoughts and feelings.

In agreement with Gottlieb and Wheaton about the importance of recurrent and chronic stress, one of the enterprises of the Berkeley Stress and Coping Project in the 1980s was to contrast major life events with *daily hassles,* which refer to the seemingly minor, though sometimes very disturbing, daily annoyances of life that can impair morale, social functioning, and health. We found, surprisingly, that daily hassles were even more important factors in negative health outcomes than major life events (Kanner, Coyne, Schaefer, & Lazarus, 1981; Lazarus, 1981; Lazarus, 1984b).

In our effort to explain this seeming anomaly, we pointed out that to a considerable extent major life events, such as death of a spouse or divorce, affect morale, social functioning, and health by disrupting and changing the daily grind of stress, adding new demands and frustrations—hence, new sources of daily hassles, many of them recurrent or chronic. Two of the reasons for major loss—namely, death and divorce—overlap substantially in their consequences for daily hassles. However, they can also result in quite different effects too. There is a world of difference, for example, in the psychological reactions created by the desertion of divorce and the loss resulting from death of a spouse. Each produces different psychological sources of stress that serve as recurrent or chronic new adaptational requirements and the coping processes they require.

With respect to overlaps in both death of a spouse and divorce, the bereaved person must now struggle with many common new stressful experiences, such as loneliness, dating, caring for children, the need to learn how to manage money, service or repair the car, and so forth. With respect to differences, however, the person who is left alone as a result of divorce must cope with a sense of failure in the marriage and continue to deal with the divorced partner, who may still be living in the same community, and to deal with postdivorce problems of child custody and financial matters. Although the deceased spouse is also physically absent, the sense of failure is not important unless the marriage had been very rocky and there is no continuing stressful social contact.

Gottlieb points out that coping changes over time, so it must be sampled at different points of chronic stress to obtain a clear picture of the coping process. We do not need special markers of stress, which are so clearly provided by major life events to alert us to such change.

He observes, for example (p. 12), that

> Differences in respondents' ratings of the stressfulness of a given event may signify differences in their ability to absorb its impact [by] routinely and naturally deploying their resources. Reports of modest or no stress may be due to the respondent's ability to take the demand in stride [by] adopting certain attitudes, engaging in certain daily routines, and affiliating with particular people. Some individuals may possess the skills and resources to smoothly integrate adversity, whereas others may experience continuous disruption and distress.

In effect, in studying stress and coping, we must sample reactions to demands even during periods when they are being handled smoothly and without great evidence of emotional distress. This suggests that coping should not be exclusively defined in terms of the resolution of the stress. Chronic sources of stress, as in long-term ailments, such as heart disease or arthritis, must often be lived with and managed rather than resolved. As noted in the chapter by Aldwin & Brustrom (1997, p. 95)

> [Since it is unlikely that the stress situation will be resolved], Folkman and Lazarus (1980) carefully included the phrase "manage stress" in their definition of coping.

The point is that coping may not be capable of terminating the stress, but the person can often manage it, which includes tolerating or accepting the stress and distress.

Aldwin and Brustrom (1997) also identify three primary problems with current models of chronic stress. These are, first, that there are no studies systematically attempting to show how coping with chronic stress might differ from coping with acute stress. Second, how people develop strategies for managing chronic stresses, such as poverty, aging, and chronic illness, has not been studied or clearly outlined. And third, much of chronic stress is interpersonal, and social support may provide vital feedback to persons experiencing social difficulties about how serious the problem is, and the appropriateness of their reactions. Thoits' (1986) useful speculations about this have not yet been much exploited in studies of coping with chronic stress.

Like Gottlieb (1997) and Pearlin & McCall (1997), O'Brien and DeLongis (1997) emphasize the interpersonal, dyadic side of chronic stress in their chapter. Not surprisingly, they point out that coping with chronic stress can increase interpersonal conflict or tension, as when one partner's coping process hinders the coping efforts of the other, or affects the other person's well-being negatively. Here, the authors are addressing the interesting problem of mismatches between spouses or lovers, and also the social constraints on coping, both very important issues.

They also examine a novel feature of interpersonal coping, which they call "empathic coping," consisting of an effort to form and maintain strong social bonds. This kind of coping is said to contain several dimensions—for example, efforts to take the role of other persons and to view things as others see them; vicariously experiencing others' feelings and concerns; trying to interpret others' verbal and nonverbal communication in an effort to understand their thoughts and feelings; making efforts to respond sensitively to others; and trying to express caring and understanding in an accepting and nonjudgmental way.

These dimensions should remind us of earlier discussions of successful and unsuccessful social support when graduate students were threatened by exams that could determine their professional fate after several years of intense personal investment. This kind of naturalistic research effort revealed previously overlooked ways of coping that have a major impact on social and personal adaptation in interpersonal relationships.

Repetti and Wood (1997) also view coping with stress in families as largely an interpersonal process. They focus on both unintended and unnoticed processes, which consist of the small, often subtle, changes in social behavior and interpersonal relationships that provide important social cues about stressful experiences. The authors suggest that many chronic stresses are not readily noticed, yet often require special coping efforts. They remain largely unacknowledged by those who use them but influence the coping processes of other family members. For example, the parents of a chronically ill child may attempt to cope with their own emotional distress and feelings of guilt by unknowingly giving preferential treatment to the ill child, producing unintended effects on the other family members, including siblings. They sum up their research by writing (p. 208):

> [Our research] illustrates how coping with chronic stress [can be] an interpersonal process. Although the involvement of other family members may not be deliberate, it appears that children are affected by, and help to shape, parent's responses to at least one type of chronic stressor.

Cignac and Gottlieb (1997) provide an elaborate and useful chapter that offers a set of diverse kinds of coping. They concentrate on the stresses of caring for a demented relative, such as Alzheimer's patients. Their list of coping strategies, with definitions for each, greatly expands the contrast between problem-and emotion-focused coping, and the Folkman-Lazarus (1988b) analysis of the results of the Ways of Coping scales in which eight coping strategies were identified by means of factor analysis. Their list, with its set of definitions and examples is presented for its didactic value in Table 6.1. Table 6.2 examines appraisal types, as viewed by Cignac and Gottlieb (1997), and their coping efficacy.

I have previously cited as important and unique Susan Folkman's research with several collaborators on stress and coping as experienced by caregivers of partners dying of AIDS. Their chapter (Folkman, Moskowitz, Ozer, & Park (1997) makes a useful contribution by offering a detailed look at the coding employed to describe and evaluate what can be learned from recurrent interviews conducted over an extended time, including reactions to the caregivers' ultimate bereavement.

Some of their findings, however, are particularly relevant to concepts, such as hope, hopelessness, despair, and depression, and provide the best evidence to date for the idea that hope is best viewed as a coping process or, perhaps more accurately, as a consequence of coping, though the evidence is indirect because hope was not measured directly. The authors take the novel position that meaningful positive events can be a way of avoiding decompensation and maintaining hope and sanguinity under protracted and severe conditions of chronic stress. In effect, emphasizing, or making positive events happen, rather than waiting passively for them to happen, is an important strategy of coping in its own right.

Little could be done to stem the tide of a disease that grows steadily more incapacitating until it leads to death (the study was undertaken before the advent of newer drugs that today provide hope of slowing the deadly progression). The demands on caregivers, as their partner's death approached, became increasingly more debilitating and unrelenting, both physically and mentally. Not only must they face the depressing knowledge that soon they must lose their loved one, but in many instances the caregivers, especially those who have the HIV virus, will probably proceed down the same terrible path, perhaps without a partner to dedicate himself to their care.

Depression is a common psychological consequence of this traumatic situation. Caregivers showed high depression scores on the Center for Epidemiological Studies Depression Scale, CES-D (Radloff, 1977), a widely used test with an average depression score for the general population of 9. The caregivers' average score was 17.8. Surprisingly, despite their dysphoria, caregivers are able from time to time to experience positive emotional events, or what the Berkeley Stress and Coping Project referred to as *uplifts,* which might be considered the opposite of hassles. To those who assume that depression leads to an

TABLE 6.1 Definitions of Classes of Coping

Making meaning	Caregivers remind themselves that their relative's behavior is attributable to the disease from which he/she suffers and is not a result of the type of person he/she is
Acceptance	Caregivers accept or strive to accept their relative's disease/behavior and/or the necessity of their continued involvement in caregiving
Positive framing	Caregivers focus on positive aspects and/or minimize the negative repercussions of caregiving
Wishful thinking	Caregivers wish the course of the disease and/or their caregiving responsibilities would change
Avoidance/escape	Caregivers physically withdraw from caregiving for short periods of time and/or cognitively avoid thinking about their caregiving responsibilities
Vigilance	Caregivers are continuously watchful of their relative and/or are mentally preoccupied with thoughts about their relative
Emotional expression	Caregivers cope by expressing their emotions openly
Emotional inhibition	Caregivers cope by inhibiting their emotions and/or admonish themselves not to express their emotions
Optimistic future expectancies	Caregivers are optimistic or hopeful regarding their ability to manage their caregiving responsibilities in the future
Pessimistic future expectancies	Caregivers are pessimistic regarding their ability to manage their caregiving responsibilities in the future and/or fear that they will suffer a similar fate as their relative
Humor	Caregivers tease or joke with their relative when he/she exhibits dementia symptoms

TABLE 6.1   Definitions of Classes of Coping *(Continued)*

Help-seeking	Caregivers seek practical and/or emotional support from others
Verbal symptom management	Caregivers manage their relative's behavior with a range of verbal strategies such as explanations, changing the subject, reassuring and calming their relative, making requests, and instructing their relative
Behavioral symptom management	Caregivers manage their relative's behavior with a range of behavioral strategies such as assisting their relative with tasks, interrupting behavior with distracting activities, rearranging the environment, and taking over tasks and decisions

From Cignac & Gottlieb (1997), pp. 249–251. Copyright by the American Psychological Association. Reprinted with permission of Plenum Publishing Corp.

inability to experience positive emotions, this finding will come as a surprise. Positive and negative feelings are increasingly recognized as quite independent of each other.

At the time the Folkman et al study was begun, little was known about how people in similar circumstances sustain themselves psychologically and prevent decompensation into psychopathology. Much earlier than this AIDS study, Lazarus, Kanner, & Folkman (1980), of the Berkeley Stress and Coping Project, had proposed that positively toned occurrences could help in the process of coping with stress in three ways: (a) by serving as *breathers* (as in vacations, siestas, or coffee breaks), (b) as *sustainers* that could motivate a person under stress to continue to cope, and (c) as *restorers* that replenish personal resources and facilitate the development of new ones (*see also* the recent research of Caputo, Rudolph, & Morgan, 1998, which shows a beneficial relationship between positive life events and blood pressure in the context of stressful life events).

Although the focus of Folkman et al.'s research was on the stressful features of being a caregiver, fortunately, efforts were also made to measure positive events as well as negative ones, an assessment encouraged early on by the caregiver participants in the research. There was an average of six such events per caregiver and all but one caregiver reported a positive, meaningful event at each opportunity.

TABLE 6.2   Types of Appraisals of Coping Efficacy

Appraisal type	Definition and examples
Efficacious coping outcomes	Appraisals of successful coping outcomes; e.g., "I found this [letting the behavior play out] is the best thing." "I've tried everything but [changing the subject] seems to work."
Nonefficacious coping outcomes	Appraisals of unsuccessful coping outcomes; e.g., "Overnight she'll forget what we talked about and then it might start over again." "But it don't do no good. Tell her to shut up, you might as well try throwing gas on a fire. Just put[s] her in gear."
No coping options	Appraisals that nothing further can be done to manage the stressor's demands; e.g., "She has the problem and there isn't anything I can do to change it." "I just give up."
Control appraisals	Appraisals that respondents are exercising influence over the stress and their emotions; e.g., "There's quite a few things that I do to, uh, control myself and that there." "I'm fortunate enough to be able to control any upset feelings."
No control appraisals	Appraisals that respondents are unable to influence the stressor or control their emotions; e.g., "It's a situation that I can't control and I think that's probably what frustrates me. Most situations I can control!'" "Most of the time, it's [caregiver's anger] very difficult to keep it in."
Less stressor reactivity	Appraisals that the respondent is able to tolerate the stressor; e.g., "I think I'm . . . probably sensitive to a point, but now I'm so used to it that it's just water off a duck's back." "I think it may be because I've just got up . . . and I'm feeling pretty good and I've got lots of patience."
More stressor reactivity	Appraisals that the respondent is unable to tolerate the stressor; e.g., "I get more upset than I did. You think you'd get used to it, but I'm never going to get used to that." "I can't get used to a person staring out a window that was so active. It's just mind-boggling. Really, It's just like a hundred percent change in her and I just can't get used to it."

152

TABLE 6.2   Types of Appraisals of Coping Efficacy *(Continued)*

Appraisal type	Definition and examples
Depletion of energy	Appraisals of diminished energy; e.g., "I didn't know what it was at first but . . . trying to cope with it all, it's tiring me out." "It's when I feel less equipped to deal with it, if you know what I mean. It's a struggle then, and I'm tired and I'm not able to struggle."
Improved ability to cope	Appraisals of improvements in coping; e.g., "I cope much better now. In the past, I would lose my own temper. I don't do that anymore. My coping skills are better now that I'm aware of some of the symptoms that are here now or that will come in the future." "But I have discovered that I can now manage the stress of a bad mood in much more constructive a manner than I used to."
Coping self-criticism	Appraisals of one's shortcomings in coping; e.g., "You know you're thinking maybe you've done something wrong. you sit here and you think 'oh, geez, I should have been . . . been more sympathetic and then maybe the rest of the day would have been . . . would have had a better day myself.'"
Means/ends insights	Appraisals of the relationship between coping efforts and their outcomes; e.g., "If I can get the right thing . . . changing the subject and getting on the right subject [then] he'll forget what he's doing and then he's all right." "I'd really think twice about it [expressing anger] because I might hurt his feelings. I don't want him upset."
Strategic planning	Appraisals of the costs and benefits entailed in different coping efforts; e.g., regarding mother's confusion: "I remind myself to watch what I do next time in a similar circumstance . . . to not go into a lot of detail with my notes and that I talk to myself to remember." "Explain it to her or show her even though I know that she's not going to remember it. I feel a little better in that probably, that's the way of not having an outburst over something."

From Cignac & Gotlieb (1997), pp. 250–251. Copyright by the American Psychological Association. Reprinted with permission of Plenum Publishing Corp.

Nine types of positive events were reported, 35% of which were social, 18% entertainment, 15% conversational, and 12% work related. Folkman et al. also note that 75% of the positive events involved other people, and most did not include the caregiver's partner. In the main, the most frequent source of positive meaning was feeling connected to others and having a respite from caregiving.

About the need for positive events or uplifts, Folkman et al. (1997, p. 308) write:

> People who are infected with HIV are also faced with an ongoing threat to their own health and well-being. Depressive mood of the participants in this study was severe and persistent. Nevertheless, in the face of extreme and chronic stress, these men were able to report events that were meaningful and in most cases positive. In fact, not only were they able to report the events, but they also requested that the positive aspects of their lives be included in the interviews. At the very least, the findings indicate that individuals who are experiencing chronic stress in one part of their lives can—and even appear to need to—experience positive meaning in other aspects of their lives.

Now I come to the most important finding with respect to the idea that positive events (and hope) are aspects of coping—that is, they often result from an active search for surcease from unrelenting stress. About half the positive events were initiated by the caregivers. In other words, they did not wait passively for good things to happen but did things to bring them about. How do we know this?

The researchers drew a contrast between spontaneously happening positive events versus planned events, which means taking an ordinary event that was, in itself, affectively neutral, and infusing it with positive meaning. When the Folkman group coded these events and tested whether a given event was classified as one or the other, they found between 85% and 90% agreement on the part of the raters (see Folkman, et al. 1997, p. 300).

What is more, positive events initiated by themselves were more likely to produce positive feelings than positive events that occurred naturally, without the caregivers' intervention. It is as if traumatic conditions push the person to draw on the coping strategy of *positive reappraisal,* which is one of the 8 coping factors on the Ways of Coping Questionnaire/Interview.

In the Folkman et al. data, the endorsement of positive reappraisal as one of the coping strategies caregivers used was associated with evidence of positive mood, along with the background mood of chronic depression. (For additional sources on this research, see Folkman, 1997; Folkman, Chesney, Collette, Boccellari, & Cooke, 1996; and Folkman

& Stein, 1996.) Folkman et al. also report that caregivers often suggested that they felt more cared about and competent in consequence of experiencing the positive event. Thus, Folkman et al. (1997, p. 311) suggest:

> The very act of generating positive events may in itself also have a palliative effect. It diverts attention from what is stressful and makes individuals more aware of the positive aspects of their lives.

Although I think this conclusion is sound, the main problem with it is that the connection between hope and coping is an inference made without the actual measurement of hope as a state of mind. These researchers report considerable evidence that the caregivers generated positive experiences, but hope remains to be integrated empirically into the coping process (*see*, for example, Lazarus, in press, on hope and despair). This relationship is an important issue that has both practical and theoretical significance.

Many of the chapters in Gottlieb's book clearly highlight powerful and overlapping themes—for example, the value of in-depth, microanalytic research strategies that draw on a subjective, appraisal-centered theoretical approach. Important themes include an interest in the goals of the coping process, an interpersonal focus, change as well as stability, and the efficacy of coping. These research chapters provide a useful correction from the triviality of so much of recent research on coping.

POSTTRAUMATIC STRESS DISORDER

Although the concept of trauma and traumatic neuroses has long been a part of psychiatry (Kardiner, 1941), at the time of the publication of *Stress, Appraisal, and Coping* (Lazarus & Folkman, 1984), posttraumatic stress disorders (PTSDs) had not yet gained much attention in stress research and clinical practice, so we did not discuss the topic. It was not until the Vietnam War ended and veterans began reporting these disorders that major attention began to be given to the concept.

The dominant presumption had been that stress disorders, which could involve severe, even psychotic-like symptoms, were the result of a personal adaptational failure—hence, the term *traumatic neurosis*. PTSD shifted the onus for such symptoms from inner conflicts to events in the environment. The syndrome first appeared in the American Psychiatric Association *Diagnostic and Statistical Manual of Mental Disorders* (DSM) in 1980, after which it came into its own as a major clinical entity.

The DSM is used by both psychiatrists and clinical psychologists to help identify clinical disorders and provide diagnostic criteria. This manual, widely used in our fee-for-service health industry, has lost considerable credibility because of the unwise proliferation of disorders. It was as though practicing professionals were mainly interested in justifying payment for their therapies by insurance or managed care businesses, so much so that it has now become the butt of media satire.

This overextension of what is meant by psychopathology was clearly a self-serving financial and political maneuver, whether or not it makes any sense from a scientific viewpoint. Nevertheless, I empathize with the dilemma of the clinician whom I cannot blame for a society that idealizes individualistic greed. This puts practicing clinical psychologists, especially, under particular pressure to make a living in a system in which the needs of the patient become secondary to making a good living.

Because it begins with the prefix "post," PTSD has often been interpreted as being a delayed clinical syndrome as opposed to an immediate reaction to a traumatic encounter. The usual implication of such delays when they occur is that circumstances or coping processes, such as denial, or efforts to prevent the appearance of disturbed reactions, prevent the disorder from showing up immediately during or just after the traumatic encounter, but will usually emerge later.

Because a significant delay of symptoms is probably not typical, the qualifying prefix "post" should be used to suggest that only the disturbed emotions and psychological dysfunctions came after, and are the result of, the traumatizing experience. Conversely, an increase in the clinical symptoms of PTSD has been reported recently among aging veterans of Vietnam, who did not complain of the disorder at the time. Although other explanations of the sudden appearance of symptoms so many years later are possible—for example, they may be encouraged by other problems that focus the patient's attention on a widely referred to disorder—the question of delay of PTSD symptoms must remain open until more information is forthcoming.

Now, 15 years after the 1984 book appeared, there is a thriving industry of research, theory, and treatment, which should be addressed in this sequel (see, for example, Brewin, Dalgleish, & Joseph, 1996; and Nolen-Hoeksema & Morrow, 1991). Several books on the topic have also been written, two of the most useful being Peterson, Prout, and Schwarz (1991), and Kleber, Figley, and Gersons (1995).

In 1992, I gave an invited address about PTSD from my own theoretical standpoint to the International Society for Traumatic Stress Studies. I discussed how we should understand PTSD. The three main themes below illustrate the main ideas I presented at that time, as follows: (a) PTSD is always dependent on, and best understood, in terms of the person-environment relationship; (b) It is also dependent on relational meanings and the emotions displayed provide important insights about the adaptational process; and (c) the coping process is an essential element in whether there will be PTSD and how serious it is clinically. Allow me to elaborate on them.

1. Consistent with what was said in earlier chapters of this book, posttraumatic stress disorders must be understood relationally. In other words, what traumatized the person is not merely the environmental event but is also a result of personality characteristics that made that person especially vulnerable to the event.

The *DSM* III-R (1987, pp. 250–251) contains the conceptual basis of a diagnosis of PTSD. Notice that it defines trauma entirely as an environmental condition:

> The individual has experienced an event that is outside the range of usual human experience and that would be markedly distressing to almost anyone, e.g., serious threat to one's life or physical integrity; serious threat or harm to one's children, spouse, or other close relatives or friends; sudden destruction of one's home or community; or seeing another person who has been, is being (or has recently been) seriously injured or killed as the result of an accident or physical violence.

What this definition appears to do, unfortunately, is to moot individual differences as a factor in PTSD, though they always play a role in vulnerability to being traumatized, and in those who develop the symptoms. It does this by exaggerating the role of the traumatic environmental condition at the expense of an individual's vulnerability, an approach clearly motivated by the desire not to blame victims and to avoid the excessive focus on the failings of the person. This is a laudable social intention—that is, to modify the stultifying psychiatric tradition of always seeing the person as blameworthy for the traumatic reaction, which is what neurotic implies.

However, this intention goes much too far in that the research data clearly show that only a modest proportion of the people exposed to such conditions develop symptoms of the disorder (McFarlane, 1995). Relatively weak harms and threats may create major emotional disturbances and dysfunctions in many people, and very powerful stressors may not faze others who manage to cope with them effectively. In effect, major individual differences are always the rule. If this point is denied by professionals for whatever reasons, then we are back to a simplistic environmentalism or an inadequate S-R psychology. For a scathing critique of the *DSM,* see Albee (1998). The *DSM*-IV, however, softens this definition considerably—a step in the right direction—as can be seen in its statement of the diagnostic criteria for PTSD in Table 6.3.

TABLE 6.3 Diagnostic Criteria for (309.81) Post-Traumatic Stress Disorder

A. The person has been exposed to a traumatic event in which both of the following were present:
  (1) the person experienced, witnessed, or was confronted with an event or events that involved actual or threatened death or serious injury, or a threat to the physical integrity of self or others
  (2) the person's response involved intense fear, helplessness, or horror. **Note:** In children, this may be expressed instead by disorganized or agitated behavior
B. The traumatic event is persistently reexperienced in one (or more) of the following ways:
  (1) recurrent and intrusive distressing recollections of the event, including images, thoughts, or perceptions. **Note:** In young children, repetitive play may occur in which themes or aspects of the trauma are expressed.
  (2) recurrent distressing dreams of the event. **Note:** In children, there may be frightening dreams without recognizable content.
  (3) acting or feeling as if the traumatic event were recurring (includes a sense of reliving the experience, illusions, hallucinations, and dissociative flashback episodes, including those that occur on awakening or when intoxicated). **Note:** In young children, trauma-specific reenactment may occur.
  (4) intense psychological distress at exposure to internal or external cues that symbolize or resemble an aspect of the traumatic event
  (5) physiological reactivity on exposure to internal or external cues that symbolize or resemble an aspect of the traumatic event
C. Persistent avoidance of stimuli associated with the trauma and numbing of general responsiveness (not present before the trauma), as indicated by three (or more) of the following:
  (1) efforts to avoid thoughts, feelings, or conversations associated with the trauma
  (2) efforts to avoid activities, places, or people that arouse recollections of the trauma
  (3) inability to recall an important aspect of the trauma
  (4) markedly diminished interest or participation in significant activities
  (5) feeling of detachment or estrangement from others
  (6) restricted range of affect (e.g., unable to have loving feelings)
  (7) sense of a foreshortened future (e.g., does not expect to have a career, marriage, children, or a normal life span)
D. Persistent symptoms of increased arousal (not present before the trauma), as indicated by two (or more) of the following:
  (1) difficulty falling or staying asleep
  (2) irritability or outbursts of anger
  (3) difficulty concentrating
  (4) hypervigilance
  (5) exaggerated startle response

TABLE 6.3 Diagnostic Criteria for (309.81) Post-Traumatic Stress Disorder
(Continued)

E. Duration of the disturbance (symptoms in Criteria B, C, and D) is more than 1 month.
F. The disturbance causes clinically significant distress or impairment in social, occupational, or other important areas of functioning.

Specify if:
  Acute: if duration of symptoms is less than 3 months
  Chronic: if duration of symptoms is 3 months or more
Specify if:
  With Delayed Onset: if onset of symptoms is at least 6 months after the stressor

From the *Diagnostic and Statistical Manual of Mental Disorders, Fourth Edition.* Copyright © 1994 by American Psychiatric Association. Reprinted with permission.

Although it is fictional, consider the operatic plight of Don José in *Carmen,* and Cho-cho San in *Madame Butterfly.* It takes two, not one, to produce these tragedies—the foolish victim and the seducer. In *Carmen,* the seducer is the cigarette girl, and the main victim is the Spanish soldier who falls in love with her and behaves foolishly. In *Madame Butterfly,* the seducer is the American sailor, Lt. Pinkerton, and the victim is the young Japanese woman whom he marries and then deserts. In this tragedy, she leads with her chin in not fully understanding the reality of her situation.

One difficulty with these fictional stories is not that they fail to be believable—real life is full of similar tragedies. The problem is that they smack too much of psychopathology—that is, the vulnerability of one of the parties as an explanation—to serve persuasively in advancing the larger and more important theme of person-environment relationship. The question that must always be asked is: What is it about the person that contributes to victimization when experiencing a harsh environmental event?

In explaining what happened, it is always tempting to say of the victim: "He or she is sick." This is really no explanation, and the assumption that most, if not all, victims bring on disaster because of mental illness, is also not correct (see the discussion of rationality in chapter 5). So the basic rule is always the same. Trauma, just like the more garden-variety of stresses, can never be adequately defined as an external event. To be traumatized depends on the specifics of the connection between the event and the person who is responding to it—in other words, on the person-environment relationship.

2. Rather than blaming the concrete environmental conditions as the sole cause, posttraumatic stress disorders call for acknowledgment of two further principles: First, the main sources of trauma are the *meanings* a person constructs about what has happened; and second, the emotions of this disorder, which have been underemphasized in typical analyses, flow from these meanings and play a key role (*see also* Janoff-Bulman, 1989, 1992; Silver, Boon, & Stones, 1983; and Silver & Wortman, 1980, for similar approaches to the underlying meanings inherent in trauma).

In keeping with the emphasis on the undermined relational meanings of the traumatic experience as the basis of PTSD, the emotions produced by the trauma at different periods of the struggle to cope with the trauma provide the person and psychotherapist with clues about what these meanings are. They also reflect how the person has been coping with the trauma during and after its occurrence.

In accordance with the core relational themes I presented earlier, and similar to the way grieving works, which is a process of trying to restore one's integrity and verve after the loss, each emotion carries its own message about the personal significance of the trauma. Anger refers to damage to one's self-esteem. Anxiety refers to the existential threat of death and nonbeing. Sadness implies an irrevocable loss, though it may continue to be struggled against for a time in grief until it has been accepted. Depression communicates a sense of helplessness and hopelessness. Guilt signifies an immoral act or thought committed by the person in the traumatizing event, though it could also reflect the problem of survivor guilt. Shame indicates a failure to have lived up to one's ego ideals. Hope suggests the wish to restore one's integrity and function—and so forth for the other emotions.

An effective approach to PTSD requires that we examine the *flow of emotions,* and the thoughts and images associated with them, which has often been ignored or widely underemphasized in the literature about trauma. These emotions tell us much about the ongoing and ultimate success or failure of the traumatized person's effort to cope with what happened, the meanings entailed by it, and the struggle to restore integrity.

3. Flowing from this latter point, the third theme emphasizes the role of *coping* in posttraumatic stress disorder. One of the most influential approaches to the PTSD syndrome that centers on what happens to the coping process over the course of the disturbed reaction to trauma comes from the clinical observations of Horowitz (1976, 1989), and his theoretical speculations about them. Leaving aside the traumatic event itself, Horowitz describes two contrasting coping processes: denial, and intrusive thoughts and images.

These processes typically alternate with each other, depending on the stage of the disorder. It is not clear what accounts for the shifts from one to the other. A sensible interpretation is that the oscillation reflects a fluctuating attempt to construct appropriate meanings from a terrible and complex traumatic event. The event has threatened or undermined meanings about one's life that had been constructed before the traumatic experience, which previously worked and now seem problematic. This creates the need to evolve new, more functional ways of understanding what has happened.

The *denial* stage, which most commonly begins right after the trauma, is characterized by a kind of psychic numbing in which the mind seems inactive, unresponsive, and unable to mount significant volitional activity, and which can be interpreted as an attempt to avoid thinking about what happened. This is followed by *intrusive* thoughts and images, which can be interpreted as a process of reexperiencing the trauma, as if the sufferer is trying somehow to reintegrate the unthinkable into a previous psychological structure, perhaps without realizing this functional need.

The traumatized person seems to be unable to control these thoughts and images, which Horowitz refers to as unbidden—that is, they occur even though the person tries to avoid or deny them (Krupnick & Horowitz, 1981). The emotions experienced in the intrusive stage include rage, sadness, anxiety resulting from the sudden awareness of major vulnerability, guilt and shame about the person's role in the disaster, fears that cannot be quelled, and recurrent, distressing dreams. Except for sadness, which involves giving up the effort to restore what has been lost and accepting it, these are the emotions of a struggle against the permanence of the loss, which is similar to what occurs in grief.

One practical implication of the oscillation between denial and intrusive thoughts is that if the therapeutic strategy does not consider the present state of mind of the patient—that is, whether the person is engaged in denial or experiencing intrusive thoughts and images, the therapeutic intervention may fail (*see also* Martelli, Auerbach, Alexander, & Mercuri, 1987, for empirical support for this principle). The reason given for the failure is that it falls on a mind that is deaf to its objectives, just as advice may fall on deaf ears when it is given at an inappropriate psychological moment.

My writings are not well represented in the PTSD literature, perhaps because the earlier book (Lazarus & Folkman, 1984) made no mention of the syndrome. Yet cognitive-mediational concepts consistent with appraisal theory—for example, as represented in the writings of Mardi Horowitz, who also emphasizes appraisal and meaning and draws on the concept of coping without using the term—emerge as among the most influential and widely adopted formulations (*see also* Brewin, Dalgleish, & Joseph, 1996, for a somewhat different approach to PTSD).

CRISIS AND ITS MANAGEMENT

In addition to the contrast between trauma and stress, another word, "crisis," should be distinguished from garden-variety stress states. Although there is considerable overlap, in post-traumatic stress disorders the emphasis is placed on the traumatic environmental event when it should be on the person-environment relationship. Crisis theory, conversely, focuses on the response—that is, changes and processes within the person that arise as a result of a catastrophic event. Attention is directed toward the reorganization of the personality structure, which is necessitated by the struggle to cope with a crises. The disturbances generated by the crisis have demonstrated that the previous structure is not equal to the task of managing life without this personality reorganization.

A recent revision of an earlier edition of Slaikeu (1984) offers a clear account of crisis theory, its history, and strategies of therapeutic intervention. Slaikeu points out that Gerald Caplan (1964) was one of the main progenitors of crisis theory. Caplan drew on Erikson's (1950/1963) influential neo-analytic approach to lifelong psychological development as a series of stages representing transitions to new, more advanced levels of psychological organization. There is usually a struggle, sometimes a traumatic one, at each of the eight points of transition, beginning in infancy and ending with old age.

Even before Caplan's writings, interest in crisis management had begun to emerge with the clinical reports and interpretations of Eric Lindemann (1944), a noted psychiatrist, after the Coconut Grove nightclub fire in Boston on November 28, 1942, which killed 493 people. Lindemann's work centered on the "grief work" (his term) of the survivors and relatives of those who died. Lindemann succeeded in bringing together community resources to provide short-term clinical help for people suffering similar tragedies. Crisis intervention, in a great variety of forms, is now a standard feature of clinical psychology and psychiatry.

The basic premise is that a life crisis, whether as developmental pressures to make a transition from one psychic stage to another, or to deal with a traumatic event, can be a turning point in life. The person can either advance or regress, depending on how the crisis is managed. Slaikeu (1984, p. ix) writes:

Very few people avoid crises altogether. Adult life, whether neurotic or normal, healthy or ill, optimistic or pessimistic in outlook, is a function of how we have weathered earlier crises, whether these be changing schools, surviving the divorce of parents, dealing with life-threatening illness, or surviving the loss of a first love.

It is a time when "Everything is on the line," so to speak. Previous means of coping and managing problems break down in the face of new threats and challenges. The potential for good or bad outcomes lies in the disorganization and disequilibrium of crisis. A wealth of clinical data suggest that some form of reorganization will begin in a matter of weeks after the onset of crisis.

Like post-traumatic stress disorders, which call for professional intervention to facilitate effective coping, crisis management by clinical professionals is an effort to prevent further psychic regression and to set the person on a reconstructive course, a process often referred to as *secondary prevention.* Secondary prevention means that clinical help is given after a trauma or crisis has occurred, but before a serious worsening of the person's state of mind. Its premise is that such worsening might prevent a necessary reorganization of the personality.

In other words, professional intervention after a crisis has actually occurred must be distinguished from *primary prevention,* which occurs before a crisis has occurred. Table 6.4 outlines the professional features of crisis intervention while simultaneously comparing three kinds of prevention: primary, secondary, and tertiary.

As in the case of PTSD, the typical clinical approach to crisis management centers on the struggle to construct a functional meaning that permits continuity with the previous psychological structure as well as providing a workable transition to a new structure that would facilitate better functioning. An approach to stress that focuses on appraisal, relational meaning, emotion, and coping is compatible with the way crisis intervention has been conceived, and Slaikeu's account substantially draws on a cognitive mediational theoretical formulation.

TABLE 6.4   Crisis Intervention: Primary, Secondary, and Tertiary Prevention

	Primary prevention	Secondary prevention	Tertiary prevention
Goal	Reduce incidence of mental disorders; Enhance human growth and development through the life cycle.	Reduce debilitating effects of life crises; Facilitate growth through crisis experience.	Repair damage done by unresolved life crises, that is, treat mental/emotional disorders.
Techniques/strategies	Public education, public policy changes re: environmental stressors; Teaching problem-solving skills to children.	Crisis Intervention: Psychological First Aid; Crisis Therapy.	Long-term psychotherapy, retraining, medication, rehabilitation.
Target population	All human beings, with special attention to high risk groups.	Victims of crisis experiences and their families.	Patients, psychiatric casualties.
Timing	Before crisis events occur.	Immediately after crisis event.	Years after crisis event.
Helpers/community systems	Government (legislative, judicial, executive branches); schools; churches/synagogues; mass media.	Frontline practitioners (attorneys, clergy, teachers physicians, nurses, police, etc.); Families/social networks; Psychotherapists and counselors.	Health and mental health practitioners in hospitals and outpatient clinics.

From Slaikeu (1984), *Crisis Intervention*, Table 1.1, p. 10. Copyright ©1984 by Allyn & Bacon. Reprinted by permission.

Stress, Emotion, and Coping in Special Groups

The topics to be presented in this chapter cover stress, emotion, and coping in three particular kinds of persons: those who are aging, children and adolescents, and immigrants. Because of the factors of youth, age, and the special problems of being dislocated and, therefore, choosing or being forced to immigrate to a new society, each collectivity, which refers to a group of people who do not know each other, has certain characteristics that justify giving it special attention from both a theoretical and practical standpoint. Let us look first at aging and old persons.

AGING AND THE AGED

Three current books on aging should be mentioned at the outset, one on coping from a developmental perspective by Aldwin (1994); another on emotion and aging by Magai & McFadden (1996); and a third on clinical geropsychology, edited by an international consortium of four editors, Nordhus (Norway), VandenBos (USA), Berg (Sweden), and Fromholt (Denmark). The last mentioned book discusses research and theory on stress, emotions, and coping in aging. My discussion below draws substantially on my own contribution to that book (Lazarus, 1998).

My main thesis about aging is that, as people grow old, the probability of important losses of function increases, but the aging process remains highly *individual*. Cross-sectional research, which dominates the field, reveals only very modest differences among people whose chronological age is, say, 65, 75, and 85 years, or older and, whatever function is being measured, the overlap between the distributions of these age cohorts is very large. Comparative research on aging leaves two questions open—namely, how important and representative any observed age differences are, and whether they are a result of age or cohort differences—that is, the period in which each age group grew up—but more of this problem later.

Scientific knowledge tends to be defined normatively, following the epidemiological tradition of searching for causal variables that affect health, morale, and social functioning rather than as detailed descriptions of phenomena of interest. Aging is no exception. Because age-related differences in function late in life, though often obvious, can be quite modest and ephemeral, most of this research fails to describe adequately the variations among people at these age levels, and the timing of age-based losses. This research almost never gives as much attention to individual variations as it does to trying to identify normative or average patterns, which turns out to be all but useless as descriptions of the way it is for individuals.

DEVELOPMENTAL EXPLANATIONS OF AGING— A MAJOR LOGICAL ERROR

The developmental approach to childhood assumes a progression from infancy to adulthood, beginning with a relatively primitive mental status in utero or at birth, and proceeding toward an advanced and complex mental status at adulthood. To say this differently, the changes proceed from a less organized condition of mind toward increasing structure and function.

It is unsound, therefore, to interpret even the typical changes of aging in developmental terms because they do not reflect an increase in structure and function. Whenever and however they occur, to view the changes as developmental is to undermine the precise meaning of the concept of development as the progression of structure and function. This leads to a degraded definition of development as *any* change, regardless of its structural or functional significance. Regression, yes; this is the enemy of old age—but development, no.

Our understanding of chronological age differences in stress, emotion, and coping is, I believe, misled by developmental explanations, as if the changes in old age are inevitable and predictable, presumably preempted by heredity or maturation. There is no doubt that the statistical probability of losses in social, psychological, and health functions increases with age. But, if the size of the average age effect is modest or small, as the evidence suggests it is, the probabilities cannot be applied dependably to individuals because the extent and quality of these age-based losses vary greatly from person to person.

Moreover, what occurs as these changes occur is usually a coping effort to prevent regression—that is, to preserve endangered functions in the face of increasing physical and mental losses. Much of coping with aging consists of efforts to retard or compensate for the ultimate and inevitable loss of structure and function, and to actualize some goal commitments while abandoning others as no longer realistic. In other words, older persons try to cope by compensating as much as possible for the downward spiral toward increasing entropy and the inevitable approach of death.

Saying this does not mean that new, creative functions cannot emerge in old age, fueled, in part, by efforts to cope with the stressful demands imposed by losses. However, the process of coping with aging is a holding action designed to actualize viable personal values and goals. Old age also includes the potential for increased wisdom, though we still do not know how best to characterize and measure it.

A viable sense of past, present, and future is essential if we wish to have a satisfying old age. Living totally in the past, even if it was glorious, is not enough to sustain us when there is no longer the possibility of an encore. The present, and the immediate future, are what count. Otherwise, later life is likely to seem empty, a matter of just amusing oneself while waiting for death.

Because the precise forms and times of the appearance of structural and functional losses vary greatly from individual to individual, significant psychological changes are, therefore, not inevitable. This can be true even close to the point of death, especially when it comes relatively early, as in people who work or socialize effectively until the end. Some people experience far fewer losses in function but die suddenly from some rapidly deteriorating ailment, a death that seems premature to everyone, like dying in the saddle, so to speak. For any individual between the ages of 65 and 90 years or older, statistical averages do not necessarily provide an adequate description of their functional status.

METHODOLOGICAL PROBLEMS OF AGING RESEARCH

Because most of aging research is, unfortunately, cross-sectional, it suffers from the likelihood that observed chronological age differences could be the result of cohort effects. This makes it impossible to say whether it is aging that makes for these differences or merely the fact that the participants in the research grew up at different historical moments—for example, World War II, the Great Depression of the 1930s, the period of postwar economic expansion, or the 1960s to the 1980s.

Therefore, these cohorts have acquired different ways of thinking and reacting, forged by the distinctive experiences and values characteristic of their times.

Research some years ago by Elder (1974) demonstrated clearly the power of the outlook of the times on different cohorts. He studied two cohorts of children in the University of California at Berkeley Institute of Human Development in the Berkeley-Oakland region. The older cohort had grown up during the Great Depression of the 1930s, the younger cohort during World War II. The findings showed that they had very different sets of values, goals, and life patterns, which had been strongly influenced by their distinctive childhood-family experiences. The differences could not be attributed to the age difference but were best explained by reference to the societal period in which they had their formative experiences.

Perhaps it is not amiss to add that my wife and I, who were both born in 1922 and experienced the economic threats and struggles of the depression during the 1930s, share a common anxiety about money and poverty, deal with money frugally even though we are relatively affluent, and find that other couples of our times often have like-minded attitudes and values. Cohort effects are, indeed, strong influences on some of our most important psychological characteristics.

Given the shortage of longitudinal research, clinical geropsychologists are not being provided with the knowledge that would be appropriate for providing professional assistance to those with problems of morale and functional losses associated with aging. It is of the utmost importance to understand the variations in the state of mind of elderly persons, their patterns of adaptation, how such persons cope with stress in their lives, and what can be done to improve their outlook and ways of living—but more about this later.

Two cross-sectional studies, one of my own on stress and coping in aging, which was published by Folkman, Lazarus, Pimley, & Novacek (1987) as part of the Berkeley Stress and Coping Project, and one by Carstensen, Graff, Levenson, and Gottman (1996), illustrate this methodological problem. Folkman et al. (1987) compared two cohorts of 100 men and women, one between 35 and 45 years of age, the other between 65 and 75. The participants in the research were assessed once a month over a 12-month period with respect to their coping patterns as measured by the Ways of Coping Questionnaire/Interview (Folkman & Lazarus, 1988), and their sources of stress as measured by the Hassles Scale (Lazarus & Folkman, 1989), but the comparison between the two cohorts was cross-sectional—that is, all the data were collected at the same time rather than longitudinally.

Some modest but statistically significant differences were found in the patterns of stress and coping. For example, on the average, the younger cohort reported using more confrontive coping, more planful problem solving, and sought more social support for major stresses than the older cohort, which reported more distancing (and humor), accepting more responsibility for what had gone wrong, and more positive reappraisals. Gender effects were minor and mostly the result of role differences in work and family life, which replicates an earlier study by Folkman and Lazarus (1980).

The differences in coping between the two age cohorts seemed to fit their respective sources of stress, which, although overlapping, were not the same. The younger cohort reported more daily hassles in the domains of finance, work, personal life, family, and friends. The older cohort reported more hassles dealing with the environment, social issues, home maintenance, and health.

The second study published by Carstensen et al. (1996) is particularly interesting because of its unusual methodology of directly observing people with marital conflicts in a laboratory setting. Each couple discussed the events of the day for 15 minutes, then returned individually to review videotapes of their conversations, which had been rated for emotions and coping by observers. Stress and coping patterns were compared as a function of age.

The marital problems of older couples were judged by observers to be less severe than middle-aged couples. Younger couples disagreed more than the older couples about children, money, religion, and recreation. Older couples enjoyed talking about children and grandchildren, doing things together, dreaming about family life, and taking vacations together, more than the younger ones. They also appeared to regulate their emotions better as evidenced by lower levels of anger, disgust, belligerence, and whining. There were no gender differences between the two cohorts, though wives in both expressed more positively and negatively toned emotions than their husbands. Husbands tended to stonewall—that is, they refused to talk about conflicts—more than their wives did.

The findings of both studies seem to be relevant to aging, but the observed age differences are uninterpretable because the research designs of both were cross-sectional. No one can say whether the differences in stress and coping were the result of growing older or when each cohort grew up. In addition, the differences, although statistically significant, were not large enough to adequately characterize individuals from the two chronological age groups.

The main virtue of cross-sectional comparisons of chronological ages is that it makes possible the identification of variables that might influence the aging process. But if we really want to document differences that are based on the aging process, the only sure way is to do longitudinal research in which the same persons are studied over time and comparisons made of changes as they grow older. However, because of its high cost in resources and time, this kind of research is uncommon.

If, conversely, we want to study the effects of the emotional life on health and illness, such as cancer and heart disease, long-term longitudinal studies are necessary because the effects are very slow to develop, perhaps as many as 20 years or more. But for other kinds of research questions, such as the changing psychodynamics of the emotion process, which may take place very rapidly, the process of emotional arousal, its unfolding, and the coping process must be studied longitudinally over brief time frames rather than over long periods.

The key point to remember is that duration is not what defines longitudinal research. If the research design is intraindividual and prospective, it meets the fundamental criterion of a longitudinal study, which is to look at the same people over time, whether the period is long or short.

Two additional methodological problems are common in aging research (*see* Lazarus, 1996, and Lazarus, 1998b). First, researchers often use extremely diverse approaches to observation and measurement, such as projective tests, in-depth or superficial interviews like those used clinically, and superficial questionnaire measures. Frequently too, different variables are employed to study stress, emotion, and coping.

Multiple measures are useful in the same study when they are compared on the same persons. However, when they are used in separate studies with different samples, chaos is created in the search for valid generalizations about aging because the psychological significance of these variables differ, and the studies cannot validly be compared unless the data are transformed statistically, as in Block's (1961) Q-sort methodology.

Second, the tendency to report age differences solely as central tendencies is inappropriate when there are small but statistically significant mean differences. When little or no documentation is provided about individual or subgroup variations, the importance and implications of these small differences are apt to be overstated. The large overlap among the age-related means (averages) being compared is typically ignored in the research report because it seems to denigrate the importance of the differences, further distorting what is said about the characteristics of any given chronological age.

In effect, the statistical significance of the difference provides an inappropriate license to draw all sorts of conclusions blithely about differences between older and younger people, as if they reflected what most people are like at each chronological age. If the ubiquitous individual differences typically found in psychological research on aging were given as much attention as normative differences, there would be more utility to chronological age comparisons, even cross-sectional ones.

As a research strategy, grouping people on the basis of shared sources of stress and patterns of coping into clusters, using correlational analysis, would have more value, but this has not often been done programmatically. An inductive effort to organize descriptions of coping and the emotional life might then yield more insight into the most frequent problems of aging, and how they are coped with, than is presently achieved by the use of averages when making age-based comparisons.

What Is Lacking in Aging Research

The environments in which old persons live are increasingly being designed to maximize functioning and reduce the danger of injury by the use of walkers and canes, safety bars in the bathroom, making transportation available to and from markets, and providing the delivery of food and medicine from stores when ordered by phone. Just as ramps accommodate the needs of the handicapped person, these environmental designs make it possible for many older people to function autonomously who might otherwise need considerable care.

So much for changing the environmental conditions of aging. Let us now consider what the aging person does to cope with increasing mental and physical limitations. With respect to such coping efforts, the distinguished psychologist, B. F. Skinner (1983), wrote a charming article describing how, well into the 80s in age, he compensated for increasing memory problems. He told of hanging his umbrella on the doorknob the moment the thought of the likelihood of rain occurred to him, so he would not forget it when he went to his office.

Older persons joke[1] about the fact that they cannot remember the name of a public figure who they can clearly see in their mind's eye. What

---

[1] Two amusing jokes are told, usually by elderly people, most of whom cannot see, hear, or remember as well as when they were young (also presented in Lazarus, 1996).

A husband and his wife were arguing about which one of them is more hard of hearing. The husband insisted that his wife is; without telling her, he puts her to the test. First he stands 15 feet from the kitchen while she is busy making dinner and yells at the top of his voice, "What's for dinner?" No answer comes back. Then he stands 10 feet away from her and again yells the same question. No answer. On his third try, at 5 feet from the kitchen, he shouts the same question. At this point the wife answers, "For God's sake, I'm telling you for the third time, steak and potatoes."

The second joke is about two old men playing golf. One is about to make his drive from the tee, and says to his partner, "I don't see so well, so please watch where the ball goes." He hits the ball and turns to his partner, saying, "Did you see where it went?" The partner responds ingenuously, "Yes, I saw it, but I can't for the life of me remember where it is."

could not be recalled is not forgotten, though it cannot always be retrieved when wanted, but it suddenly pops into our heads at unexpected moments. The aged also experience the tendency to lose the thread of what we wanted to say just a few moments ago. A solution is to interrupt unpolitely so that the point can be made before it is forgotten.

To cope with short-term memory losses, elderly professors like me write the names of people they want to cite on their lecture notes, so they will not be embarrassed by forgetting them when needed. When writing articles, they often take much extra time to search for the name and reference of a person they want to cite, although when they were young this information would instantly come to mind.

However, despite the well-known deficits of aging, the extent of the loss, the age at which they appear, the strategies for dealing with them, the emotions connected with them, and the situations in which they arise are remarkably variable. This point about individual differences also applies to the other inevitable problems of growing old, including one's psychological outlook about death and dying.

SUCCESSFUL AND UNSUCCESSFUL AGING

The position I have articulated previously overlaps substantially with the view of aging presented recently by Baltes and Baltes (1990). To my way of thinking, these research scholars breathe a valuable dose of fresh air into a research field that has all but stagnated. For them, successful aging requires the acquisition of attitudes and coping processes that permit an aging person to remain independent, productive, and socially active for as long as possible, despite increasing deficits. Basically, they are talking about *coping* with aging, though they do not use this term. Below I quote from Baltes and Carstensen (1996, p. 399), who make some of the points I made earlier, and in Lazarus (1998b).

> We suggest that understanding the processes *(sic)* that people use to reach their goals under increasing limitations in resources, be they social, psychological, or biological, will lead to additional insights and progress in the field. The proposed model defines success as the attainment of goals, which can differ widely among people and can be measured against diverse standards and norms. The three processes identified in the model—namely, selection, compensation and optimization—in concert, provide a way to conceptualize the strategies older people use to age well even in the face of loss. We cannot predict what any given individual's successful ageing will look like until we know the domains of functioning and goals that individual considers important, personally meaningful, and in which he or she feels competent.

The study of aging requires that we catalog the coping strategies old people use. We must examine how these strategies work, and how well they affect morale, social functioning, and somatic health. The person variables that influence these adaptational outcomes, such as skills, resources and liabilities, energy level, available social supports, and the environmental conditions that interact with these variables, should also be important features of psychological research on aging.

We might, for example, study older persons who are still productive, whether or not they are officially retired. Such a research project could identify the problems being faced and explore in depth how they are coped with—in effect, providing a more formal version of Skinner's (1983) personal account. Such a study requires a comparison group with comparable demographics, but it could identify those who are or are not functioning adequately, and those who still work at something useful, whether for income or not. For this kind of study to be representative of older persons, and to include the important variables, a researcher might select people from different fields and types of activities.

Another type of study could group together for further study those who share similar health problems, such as Parkinson's disease, heart disease, arthritis, or myasthenia gravis. However, groupings based solely on diseases are suspect because similar bodily ailments, such as heart disease and cancer do not necessarily impose similar psychological demands on the people who suffer from them. Much can still be learned, however, about the relationship between a given ailment and the psychological stresses, emotions, and coping processes that are generated, and variations within each ailment (*see also* Aldwin, 1994).

In-depth studies of sources of difficulty in sustaining productive engagement during later life, and patterns of coping with these problems, have seldom been performed, but could be very useful for understanding aging. This kind of research would have to be designed longitudinally and identify when the problems began and when and why people stopped being engaged in productive effort.

We should not merely try to demonstrate what older people can or cannot do, though this would be useful, but we should also direct attention to persons who cannot seem to establish productive commitments that make some contribution to the community. My argument is not based on economics or a concern about the gross national product but on the psychological implications of being engaged in productive work for the aging individual. We would want to learn which failures— if that is what they are—might be ameliorated by teaching older persons to cope more effectively with the demands and opportunities of an active life.

Some of the most difficult coping problems of aging are existential ones, which are characterized by a lack of motivation to seek a satisfying commitment to a constructive activity. In younger persons, we already know that existential neuroses are very discouraging, both to the patient and to the clinician seeking to provide help. Because these persons understand that they should be striving toward some goal, but lack the motivation to do so, they will often say things like, "Tell me how to be engaged," or "how can I get motivated?" They know that they should have sustaining interests and activities to make for positive morale but are unable to initiate them. Unfortunately, it is all but impossible to impose motivation from the outside.

Emotional problems of aging that stem from functional losses, or lack of suitable coping processes, may be easier to manage clinically and be a more satisfying challenge for the clinician than motivational deficits. In any case, greater knowledge about how diverse individuals are coping successfully, or unsuccessfully, with problems of aging could make the provision of successful clinical assistance more likely.

CHILDREN AND ADOLESCENTS

As in the case of aging, there are sound reasons for giving special consideration to stress, emotion, and coping in children and adolescents. One is the obvious prospect that these processes differ during various periods of psychological development, especially if one were to compare very young infants, toddlers, school-age children, preadolescents, and adolescents—in other words, the whole gamut of early development, which is seldom studied with respect to stress and coping.

Cognitive and motivational processes change over the course of development, and appraisal theory suggests that stress, emotion, and coping are dependent on both cognitive and motivational processes. Therefore, there ought to be major developmental differences to consider, both formally, and with respect to the content of what people at different stages know about life and social relationships.

Interest in the developmental sources of stress and the coping processes in preadolescence and adolescence seems to be growing, but the field has not yet gained the maturity observed in the study of cognitive processes in emotion. Interest in the problems of children and families is illustrated by a series of articles in a special issue of the

American Psychologist, edited by E. Mavis Hetherington (1998), which deal with applications of developmental science.

These articles examine what are said to be important factors in adaptational disturbances in children, such as stress and socioeconomic disadvantage. I found what was presented there substantively thin and problematic, even somewhat politicized, and came away greatly confused about what is truly known about these problems (*see also* Hetherington & Blechman, 1996, about which I have the same criticism).

When it comes to this time of life, whether we should expect robust differences in patterns of coping and emotions between children of various ages, and adults, and what these differences might be, is not clear. In addition to developmental theory, a practical concern with measurement is also relevant. If we study children, especially very young ones, or even subteens, our assessment procedures must be suitable to their cognitive and social capabilities and outlook. The measurement procedures should be made meaningful to the special concerns of different age groups to motivate them to participate in such research wholeheartedly.

It might turn out that age differences, especially if we exclude young babies and toddlers who are unable to communicate verbally or are limited in this respect, might be meagre or ephemeral, as seems to be the case in aging because individual differences can overpower average age differences, though this could depend on the age ranges compared. Many research scholars (Ekman & Davidson, 1994; Lazarus, 1991a; Lewis & Haviland, 1993; Stein, Leventhal, & Trabasso, 1990; and Tangney & Fischer, 1995) have discussed emotions and early development from the standpoint of appraisal theory. I shall limit myself here to recent stress research with mostly preadolescents and adolescents.

In a review of empirical research on late childhood and adolescents, Compas (1987) organized the field into seven areas of research: attachment and separation during infancy; social support; interpersonal problem solving; coping in the context of school and achievement; Type A and B behavior; coping styles, such as repression and sensitization (or monitoring and blunting); and resilience or invulnerability to stress. Some of these areas now seem very dated, I touch on each of them below briefly.

Research on *attachment and separation* is usually based on the Ainsworth (1979) testing procedures, referred to as the "strange situation," in which the child is separated from the parent and then returned so that its emotional and coping reaction to reunion with the parent can then be assessed. This widely used procedure derives from the influential theoretical writings of John Bowlby (1969, 1973, and 1980), which is centered on attachment, separation, and loss. The child's reaction has been found to be fairly consistent over many years, and has been used with substantial success to predict interpersonal relations, emotional pattern, temperament, and coping in later life. Because of this success, and the basic concepts involved, this type of research has become very fashionable in recent years.

As a spin-off from this, the developmental importance of *social bonds* has made the topic of social support a major focus of research in health psychology. Conceptualizations based on adult data have been applied directly to children and adolescents without an examination of possible age differences, probably because peer influences and parental support have always been assumed to be of special importance in childhood. Recent work has confirmed the importance of supportive social connections for stress management and efficacious coping in childhood and adolescence as well as in adults. More complex and difficult to pin down is the problem of what is supportive and nonsupportive, which I discussed in chapter 6 on marital relationships in adults experiencing spillover from work stress to family life.

Cognitive problem solving in interpersonal contexts has been the main research and theoretical province of Spivack and Shure (1982, 1985). They examined how children and adolescents recognize they have a problem in social adaptation, how they examine it, and how problem-solving skills are acquired and subsequently influence social adaptation. These research scholars have proposed that, as complex cognitive processes develop, they become especially important to children at about 8 to 10 years of age.

The relevant components of problem solving in social adaptation include the ability to generate alternative solutions, have a sensitivity to social problems, understand the consequences of one's social actions, and develop means-ends ways of thinking and the ability to change in the face of such problems. As observed by Compas, it is not clear whether effective cognitive problem solving makes a difference in the way young persons cope with stress, although logically it should, and evidence suggests it is important in general adaptation. The relevance of cognitive problem-solving skills is also supported by D'Zurilla's work (1986; *see also* D'Zurilla & Goldfried, 1971, and D'Zurilla & Nezu, 1982), whose interests lie in the use of problem-solving training in cognitive therapy with adults.

The research of Carol S. Dweck and her colleagues (Dweck & Licht, 1980; Dweck & Wortman, 1982) in the context of *school achievement* has revealed a useful distinction between the academic functioning of mastery-oriented and helpless children. The topic is also relevant to self-esteem, which has been a very popular current topic in professional, lay thinking, and populist politics, though much overstated and misunderstood (*see,* for example, Greenberg et al., 1992). These researchers view coping as efforts to minimize stress and maximize performance, and center their attention on effective and ineffective coping in school achievement.

Effective copers—in effect, those oriented toward mastery—sustain high levels of motivation and persistence, and under the stress of failure increase their concentration and display enhanced rather than impaired performance. They are better at coping with failure than helpless children, presumably because they focus their attention on problem-solving and task-relevant information that facilitates performance rather than making causal attributions for their failures, which seem largely irrelevant to performance.

This theme overlaps with some of the ideas of Spivak and Shure, and also connects with Nolen-Hoeksema's (1991) research on rumination and depression, which I mentioned in the section on aging (for other studies along these lines, *see also* Nolen-Hoeksema & Morrow, 1991; Nolen-Hoeksema, Parker, & Larson, 1994; and Rusting & Nolen-Hoeksema, 1998). It is also relevant to what has been observed about test anxiety and academic performance (*see,* for example, Covington & Omelich, 1987; Liebert & Morris, 1967; Spielberger, Gorsuch, & Lushene, 1970; and my discussion of this topic in Lazarus, 1991).

Type A, a topic that was alive and well when Compas did his review in 1987, is no longer taken very seriously as an issue in stress and health (heart disease), though it has not been completely abandoned (*see,* for example, Ben-Zur & Wardi, 1994, on decision making and Type A behavior). Current views have emphasized hostility and its management in place of time pressure, and hopelessness emphasized in research recently discussed by Jenkins (1996), which I cited in chapter 11. I shall, therefore, say no more about it here.

Repression-sensitization (*see* Krohne, 1993, 1996; Krohne & Rogner, 1982; and the closely related concept of monitoring-blunting of Miller, 1981) has to do with coping styles. Krohne is a major figure in this kind of research. With his research group, he has been struggling with several unresolved methodological and conceptual issues of concern to trait psychologists (*see,* for example, Lazarus, 1993, and in press, on the distinction between coping style and process, and the state and trait-state perspectives, and in chapter 5 where I discuss this at length).

Few studies of coping style have been performed with children. One of the themes in research of this sort has to do with the developmental origins of a style and its stability over the life span. One thinks here, among others, of the work of Murphy and colleagues (Murphy & Associates, 1962, and Murphy & Moriarty, 1976) who observed infantile behavioral patterns that were associated with later defensive styles, Miller and Swanson's (1960) research reports on the origins of defense, and Loevinger's (1976) pioneering theory and research on ego-development stages.

The final major area of research dealt with in Compas's (1987) review, and possibly the most important, concerns resilience or *invulnerability* to stress in children. This has been the province of Norman Garmezy (1983) and Michael Rutter (1980), who have jointly published on the subject (*see also* Garmezy and Rutter,1983; and Haggerty, Sherrod, Garmezy, & Rutter, 1996). Their shared interest lies mainly in the factors predisposing children to be at risk for psychopathology and, the converse, invulnerability to stress. These researchers have given much attention to the personality characteristics that make for resistance to, or protection against, the deleterious effects of stress.

Notice that the concept of resiliency or its opposite, vulnerability, is said to depend on environmental variables and what I called personal resources (as well as its converse, personal liabilities) in chapter 3. You may remember that I listed environmental variables influencing appraisal as demands, constraints, and opportunities, and person variables as goals, goal hierarchies, and personal resources, such as intelligence, money, social skills, education, supportive family and friends, physical attractiveness, health and energy, and sanguinity.

Many of these personal resources (e.g., attractiveness and intelligence) are often considered more or less inborn, or at least relatively fixed, even though modestly changeable under certain conditions. Others (such as social skills and education) are more likely to be developed by sustained effort. I do not want to make the mistake of making too rigid a distinction between nature and nurture, yet one implication of what I have implied earlier is clearly controversial. This has to do with the possibility of changing personal resources (or liabilities).

To the extent that personal resources seem to be relatively fixed, especially by adulthood, we must, therefore, wonder whether they can be altered by means of clinical or educational efforts. How, for example, might we improve intelligence significantly, especially when the child is already near adulthood? What can we do about physical attractiveness, the absence of wealth, the right ethnicity or race, or family and friends? These challenges seem daunting. In contrast, I have always thought that teaching ineffective persons how to *cope* better might have a better prospect than trying to change relatively fixed personal resources or liabilities.

Whether I am right or not with respect to these personal resources, knowing what is malleable and what is not is an important issue. I see this as one of the problems of Garmezy and Rutter's approach to stress and coping. The implication of the concepts of resiliency or invulnerability is that what is important in psychopathology and health is not necessarily amenable to change. Conversely, if the adaptational-emotional problems have to do with faulty coping, clinicians could consider ways of teaching their patients to cope more effectively.

The bottom line in all this is whether we know enough about what works or does not work to consider trying to teach people how to cope better, or even whether coping is teachable. Given what little we seem to know, I am sure this issue would provoke strong debate among psychologists, but the question could provide an important research agenda for the future.

Compas (1987) closes his review and analysis of coping in childhood and adolescence with a brief discussion of future research needs. He suggests that there is a need for comprehensive measures of coping at these age levels, and he has pioneered an approach to the measurement of stress and coping in adolescents (Compas, Davis, Forsythe, & Wagner, 1987; Compas, Malcarne, & Fondacaro,1988). As we shall see subsequently, others have also tackled this problem. Compas suggests that prospective, longitudinal studies be mounted to clarify how coping resources, styles, and behaviors change or remain stable in development, a proposal with which I firmly agree.

Some very recent European research on stress and coping has focused on children and adolescents, though the observations of developmental changes within this broad age group remain modest. There is little in the way of true developmental comparisons within this broad age grouping. This is an important lack, but there is evidence of growing interest.

One of the few research scholars to address age differences in stress and coping is Inge Seiffge-Krenke (1995) whose detailed and nicely written monograph on *Stress, Coping, and Relationships in Adolescence* describes seven studies, mostly cross-sectional, but also with some repeated measurement strategies, of stress and coping in preadolescents and adolescents from the age of 12 to 19 years of age. Sieffge-Krenke states that she was strongly influenced by both Compas's work and my own work with Folkman.

Basic to these investigations is a Problem Questionnaire of her own construction, which covers 64 minor stressors. Coping was measured by means of interviews in which 20 relatively concrete coping strategies were examined across eight minor stressors that are found in a school setting, centering on teachers, parents, peers, romantic relationships, leisure time, self, and future. The list was used by Seiffge-Krenke as a guide for interviews. Other measures focused on interpersonal relationships, an assessment of the perceived family climate, and a content analysis of diary entries. In addition to interviews, other diverse assessment methods were employed in these studies, such as interviews, questionnaires, surveys, and content analyses.

This is the most ambitious and thorough international investigation in this area I have seen, encompassing 2,176 German adolescents, and more than 1,000 adolescents from Israel, Finland, and the United States. It dealt with the stressors adolescents report, their coping strategies and styles, appraisals, parental and peer influences, benefits and costs of relationships with parents, peers, and friends, coping successes and failures, and comparisons over time and across distal variables, such as age and gender. The amount of detail reported in this book is prodigious and difficult to assimilate. Because there is too much to cover in a limited space, my strategy here, as in previous discussions, is to select and comment on some of the most provocative findings and conclusions, and to note what I consider limitations.

Many adolescent stressors were perceived by these young persons as threatening and rather unpleasant. Seiffge-Krenke identified 10 events or conditions of life that had been named by her adolescent participants regardless of age and gender, which are spoken of as universal, though widespread might be a more accurate term. These are arguments with teachers, quarrels with parents, peer problems (such as disagreements, communication difficulties, feelings of being left out and ignored), poor grades, humiliation, experience of being in love, lonely, dissatisfaction with one's own appearance and behavior, and political events bearing on their future. Concern about the future, Seiffge-Krenke states, is present in different age cohorts despite great changes in living conditions over the past 30 to 40 years, and she argues that one can say that what is experienced as stressful has remained constant.

With respect to coping, the author reports a factor analysis of the 20 coping strategies that revealed two functional coping styles, which she labeled *active* and *internal coping,* and one dysfunctional style, which she labeled *withdrawal.* The designation of dysfunctional, based on the observation that the problem at hand was not solved immediately, troubles me because the reader does not know what actually went on during what was called withdrawal; after all, some problems might be allowed to fester for a while to evaluate what is needed and mount a better long-term solution. In addition, only two or three coping factors in a population this large and diverse surprised me greatly.

The author's analysis provides substantial support for the Lazarus-Folkman (Lazarus, 1966; 1981; Lazarus & Folkman, 1984, 1987) appraisal and coping-centered theoretical approach to psychological stress. With respect to the relationships between appraisal and coping, she writes (Seiffge-Krenke, 1995, p. 229) that

Coping processes cannot simply be labeled as inherently good or bad; rather the specific context has to be considered. . . . Thus, situational and contextual variables, as well as social norms and conventions, were much more influential [in the outcome of coping] than a "coping trait."

After doing a thorough and accurate job of describing the Lazarus model, the author also writes (Seiffge-Krenke, 1995, p. 65):

In analyzing the coping process, we found impressive evidence for the validity of the Lazarus model. Different stages of appraisal and coping could be exemplified and the importance of event parameters and appraisal for subsequent coping was demonstrated. The majority of the named events were assessed as being mildly stressful. This corresponded exactly to our intention of studying the manner in which adolescents cope with minor events or daily hassles as understood by Lazarus (*see* Kanner et al., 1981). Primary appraisal was usually followed by an initial reaction, in which confusion, first cognitive coping efforts, and impulses to act played a role. In secondary appraisal, very accurate estimates of the coping resources, the scope of action and the predictions about success were made. The prevailing negative appraisal of these minor events reported by the adolescents was somewhat surprising as were the numerous obstacles, barriers, and the limited changes brought about by coping.

Drawing on her extensive data, and from a developmental standpoint, Seiffge-Krenke considers the age of 15 to be a turning point in the use of coping strategies and social resources. Early adolescents reported the most stress, which fits the prior observations of B. Hamburg (1974) who considered early adolescence to be an especially stressful time. At about age 15 in Seiffge-Krenke's data, adolescence seems to be marked by (pp. 221–222):

the development of cognitive processes from simple, concrete, and more self-centered thinking to complex, abstract, and relational thinking. Early adolescents who operate at an earlier level of social cognitive maturity are, for example, unlikely to differentiate between sources of support. They are less able to recognize links between current behavior and long-range outcomes and they are possibly more motivated by self-centered needs. In contrast, late adolescents, having already reached a more mature social cognitive level, select social support strictly in accordance to the problem at hand, consider current options more often, think about the future consequences of their actions, and reflect about their position with respect to the perspectives of others.

What I missed most in this impressive research report is an in-depth examination of particular individuals' coping process, the kind of microanalytic, transactional description I strongly favored in the books by Eckenrode & Gore (1990), and Gottlieb (1997a), with their clear and dramatic narrative descriptions of the stress and coping process. For my taste, Seiffge-Krenke's approach consists of too much abstract, statistical, survey-oriented summaries and not enough proximal narratives, which could connect different individuals with the stressful environment with which they are coping. The data for this kind of analysis must be in hand, but the author does not present it in narrative form, which leaves the reader with masses of observations and generalizations that are difficult to integrate without concrete case material, and that could portray the children's actual transactions with the problems of their age.

What I think happened is that the environmental events and the children's responses have been separated, which follows the analytic penchant of scientific psychology, and so we do not get a feel for transactions and processes, despite the author's favorable take on these concepts. The human mind understands and finds stories more interesting and revealing. Nevertheless, this is an important book that provides rich fare. I know of no empirical source as extensive and detailed in documentation. Seiffge-Krenke makes much use of it in her thoughtful analyses of the implications of what she has found.

Another monograph addressing coping with serious illness in children—that is, life-threatening cancers and aplastic anemia—has recently been published by Pretzlik (1997) as a European-style doctoral thesis (which is far more demanding in effort and time as a rule than those in the U.S.). She reports six studies, which also draw substantially on the Lazarus-Folkman (1984, 1987) transactional and process approach.

A coping checklist designed for children, referred to as the *Kidcope Checklist,* is also presented. It contains items in response to contextual questions about stressful events, such as: "Did you try to forget it (distraction), stay on your own (social withdrawal), or try to see the good side of things (cognitive restructuring)? These questions appear to impose little or no strain on the cognitive capabilities at the ages of these children.

Five of the studies were conducted in hospitals, where 53 children from 7 to 16 years of age, and their parents, were studied. A variety of research methods was employed, including observation during the medical procedure of drawing blood, a questionnaire on the children's' perception of competence and self-worth, and a semistructured interview about coping strategies. Parents' coping and the social environment of the family were examined by means of a coping health inventory and a family environment scale.

The research results, surprisingly, seemed quite meagre and unremarkable to me for such potentially rich human tragedies as children with life-threatening or debilitating diseases. The findings suggest, for example, that coping in the children is linked to their life situation—that is, their everyday-life difficulties and the illness-related treatment. But how else could it be? Robust differences in sex, age, experience with illness, and self-esteem were not found. Children who rated themselves as more distressed during the blood test showed more distress in general. Despite the fact that the blood test was a routine procedure, children who took an active interest in it displayed less distress and had higher self-esteem than those who showed no interest.

Coping processes that were used for school stresses were different from those used for illness-related stresses, supporting the contextual view that strategies of coping depend on the particular harms and threats to which people are exposed. Relationships were also found between the way parents coped with their child's illness, the social climate of the family, and the way the children coped.

In one study, 10 coping strategies and their perceived helpfulness produced three main, but to me virtually incoherent, clusters of coping: (a) self-criticism and blaming others; (b) cognitive restructuring, distraction, and resignation; and wishful thinking, (c) social withdrawal, problem solving, emotional regulation, and social support. This latter group was less often employed in the blood drawing stress than other stresses, presumably because the children knew that having a blood test helps the doctors who are trying to help them. In another study, a negative relationship between stress behavior and age was found, younger children showing more distress than older children.

All told, even the author considers the major findings of the study sparse, though she pointed out that the family was an important element in the coping of these children (*see* Compas, Worsham, & Ey, (1992). Children valued the presence of the family, with fathers playing an important role, possibly because, as Pretzlik suggests, they did not have to put on a brave face with their parents.

Although the work is impressive because of the demands it makes on the researcher, the report reinforces my view, expressed in chapter 6 about work and family stress, and in my comments on Seiffge-Krenke's research, that microanalytic narratives of personal transactions throw more light on the stress and coping process than large-scale survey-oriented research, which lack the human touch. We must be brainwashing our young research scholars to believe that stories about transactions do not constitute science, and that scientific studies require only cold, statistical facts rather than a carefully analyzed description of what happens in real life (*see* Lazarus, 1998a, for a critique of psychology's epistemology and metatheory). Why can't we have both?

To take the large view of this research on young people, including the Seiffge-Krenke report, little narrative description is presented to give the reader an intimate sense of the personal dramas each child and parent is struggling with. When data are aggregated statistically, in the absence of transactional descriptions, we are in danger of losing the trees for the forest, and it is a struggle to assimilate the dynamic human significance of what is going on. Despite an outlook that professes to be transactional, I found little that is actually transactional (relational), or meaning-centered, in these accounts. The methodology of research should flow from, and be compatible with, the researcher's epistemological and metatheoretical outlook which, in these cases, need to be broader than what characterizes too much of today's psychological research.

STRESS OF UPROOTING, RELOCATION, AND IMMIGRATION

A major source of stress is having to emigrate from one society and culture and immigrate to another, whether involuntarily—as in the tragedy of slavery, the dislocation of wars, and genocide—or a voluntary decision to seek a better life. There has never been a time in the world when so many people from so many societies have been uprooted from their places of origin, either to live as stateless pariahs, or to struggle in a new country with a different language and culture, trying to make a better life for themselves.

Interest in immigration was substantial in the United States in the late 19th and early 20th centuries when waves of often destitute immigrants flowed from Europe. People often forget that the United States is mostly a product of immigration, early on from Europe. Except for a modest degree of social science research on immigration, it has only been in recent years that research and theoretical interest, has burgeoned. Now, even in France, Germany, and Denmark as well as the United States and other countries, immigration has aroused widespread political strife, which is the result of mistaken racial, ethnic, and religious assumptions and mostly false economic concerns, in which immigrants are pitted against the indigenous population.

I might comment briefly on a recent experience I had in Aarhus, Denmark, whose population, much to my surprise, is in an uproar over an immigrant group. If I can trust the translation of the newspaper article based on an interview with me as a visiting expert on stress, the immigrant group consists of 2nd generation Palestinians who have resettled in the small city of Aarhus. In the eyes of natives they are being funded generously, even more generously than many native citizens who are economically deprived and have deep roots in the country. This perception has created great resentment toward the immigrants, and some violence in what has for a long time (since the Viking days) been a peaceful and socially responsible society.

In my conversation with the Danish reporter who wrote the newspaper article, I suggested that this is a worldwide problem, typically built on envy and misunderstanding, as in the case of Latinos, hispanics and Asians in Texas and California. In my article, I suggested that it would be better to facilitate the adaptational struggles of immigrants, most of whom will in time not need help. I did not stay in Denmark long enough to learn how readers reacted to my comments.

Comments, such as mine, are apt to be taken as gratuitous and risky by the indigenous population because visitors do not share the actual social circumstances surrounding immigration. It's a bit like American Jews giving advice to Israelis about how to deal with the Palestinians. The Israelis are the ones who must live with the outcome of any given policy, not the advice givers. My experience in Denmark provides an all-too-common example of the prejudice and hostility that so commonly develops between immigrants and the native population, which is usually counterproductive because the strife damages the morale and integrity of both groups and impairs the ability of immigrants to make it in the society—a truly no-win situation all around.

The theoretical and practical issues of stress, emotion, and coping, and the problems of acculturation associated with this struggle to adapt to a new country, are so rich and important psychologically, and so filled with stress and distress, that there is beginning to be considerable professional and research interest in them. Until recently, there was only a modest volume of research in this area, and bibliographies were somewhat limited. I know of two such bibliographies, published by the National Institute of Mental Health, one on coping and adaptation by Coelho and Irving (1981), the other on mental health and social change by Coelho (1972). Though increasingly out of date, they remain a valuable source for those who want to explore this literature.

As might be expected when scholars get involved in a topic that had hitherto been unrecognized or understudied, new works, books, and controversies begin to appear. I have been influenced by the seminal work of John Berry, at Queen's University in Ontario, Canada, whose writings on the subject have generated considerable attention for at least a decade including a recent target article on immigration, acculturation, and adaptation (Berry, 1997), and a set of commentaries by several visible scholars including one by me (Lazarus, 1997).

Berry (1997) observes that the long-term psychological consequences of the struggle to acculturate are very variable. These consequences depend on social and personality attributes that were operative in the society of origin where the immigrant settles as well as what happened before and is going on during the acculturation process.

Berry emphasizes *psychological acculturation.* This refers to psychological changes and eventual adaptational outcomes—for example, psychological, sociocultural, and economic—which are brought about by the struggle of the immigrant to adapt to the concerns of the whole society and their own too. The relational aspects of Berry's analysis are illustrated by the theme that coping strategies and their adaptational outcomes result from how both groups, the immigrants and the indigenous population, perceive and react to each other.

Societies can become culturally plural or multicultural as a result of immigration, including both dominant and nondominant or minority groups. "Assimilation," however, represents only one of four ways of acculturation; Berry does not much like the word assimilation, which usually means taking on the characteristics of the dominant group and seeking daily interaction with it, as in the melting pot concept. Immigrants tend to be pressured to assimilate—that is, to be like everyone else in the dominant group, but often they remain viewed by the dominant group as different, strange, or undesirable. They often choose, sometimes perforce, other acculturation strategies.

These other strategies or ways of coping include *separation,* in which immigrants seek to maintain their original culture and avoid daily interaction; *integration,* in which immigrants try to maintain some degree of the original cultural integrity while seeking to participate as an integral part of the dominant social group; and *marginalization,* in which immigrants have little possibility or interest in preserving their own culture or having regular relations with persons from the dominant group. Because immigrants are often deliberately excluded, it might be better not to refer to marginalization as a coping strategy—it is probably seldom chosen voluntarily.

The evidence, Berry suggests, shows that integration is usually the most successful of the coping strategies and, not surprisingly, marginalization the least successful—that is, it is most linked with evidence of emotional distress and dysfunction or psychopathology. The term, however, as I said earlier, seems to confound strategy and outcome. Assimilation and separation produce intermediate adaptational results.

Figure 7.1 shows Berry's ambitious framework for viewing acculturation research. In this figure, we can see a highly complex systems view of acculturation, in which there are group variables; individual variables; stable person and social structures existing before immigration; those formed afterward in the new society; and ongoing psychological processes of adaptation, such as appraisal and coping.

I have two problems with Berry's analysis. One is that it subordinates many structures and processes—for example, those involved in stress and coping—to the rubric of acculturation. This suggests that what best characterizes the struggle of the person who relocates to another society is the task of acculturation. Berry acknowledges that immigrants and nonimmigrants experience much stress and cope with it apart from the problem of acculturation. Stress is a part of life everywhere. Some stress in immigration has to do with acculturation, but I suspect that much of it is of a different order.

My second concern is that Berry's system of variables is both too complicated to study, and too abstract—that is, too removed from the day-to-day struggles of living experienced by immigrants and other unassimilated groups in the larger society. I am pleased that Berry has included the basics of stress, emotion, and coping theory in his framework. I am bothered by the absence of a microanalytic, narrative sense of the adaptational struggle these relocating persons and their families experience in their daily lives, as I was with Seiffge-Krenke's and Pretzlik's accounts of their research. Berry's analysis too, is not transactional enough for me.

Nevertheless, Berry's framework is remarkable—I am awed by its thoroughness, metatheory, and scholarship—but I wonder who will be able to mount research from the perspective of this framework, except as an extremely incomplete patchwork, and whether research can encompass enough of the total system of variables to create a working understanding of the immigrant's struggle. I guess this remains to be seen. Though it is a tour de force, which could guide investigators in important ways, I believe it suffers from the same defects I found in the systems approach of Somerfield and Commentators (1997), which I criticized in chapter 8, criticisms that have led me subsequently to espouse a narrative approach to stress and emotions.

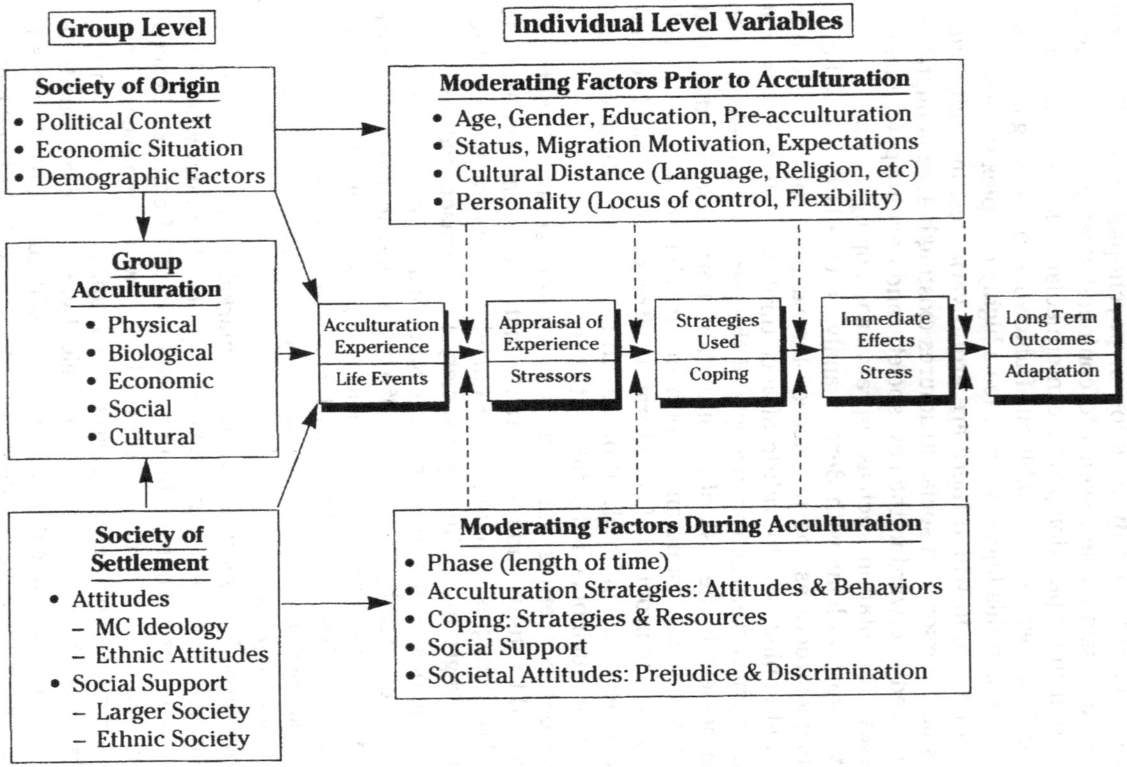
Group Level
Individual Level Variables
Society of Origin
• Political Context
• Economic Situation
• Demographic Factors
Moderating Factors Prior to Acculturation
• Age, Gender, Education, Pre-acculturation
• Status, Migration Motivation, Expectations
• Cultural Distance (Language, Religion, etc)
• Personality (Locus of control, Flexibility)
Group Acculturation
• Physical
• Biological
• Economic
• Social
• Cultural
Acculturation Experience
Life Events
Appraisal of Experience
Stressors
Strategies Used
Coping
Immediate Effects
Stress
Long Term Outcomes
Adaptation
Society of Settlement
• Attitudes
– MC Ideology
– Ethnic Attitudes
• Social Support
– Larger Society
– Ethnic Society
Moderating Factors During Acculturation
• Phase (length of time)
• Acculturation Strategies: Attitudes & Behaviors
• Coping: Strategies & Resources
• Social Support
• Societal Attitudes: Prejudice & Discrimination

FIGURE 7.1 **A framework for acculturation research. From Berry (1997), *Applied Psychology: An International Review, 46*, p. 15. Copyright © 1997 by International Association of Applied Psychology. Reprinted by permission.**

In addition, a major book that is focused on ethnicity, immigration and psychopathology—the most recent I have seen, and one of the first with a strong psychological orientation—has been published by Al-Issa and Tousignant (1997). This book looks at research on the problems of Southeast Asian refugees in Canada; immigrants to Quebec; Latinos, African Americans and Jamaicans in the United States; the Hutterites and East Germans; North Africans in France; Turkish immigrants in Belgium; the Aborigines of Canada; Maoris of New Zealand; Jews within and outside of Israel; and gypsies in Europe. This should give the reader some idea of the scope of this monograph, and of the immigration problems of today.

PART IV

Narrative Viewpoint

Having justified the connection between stress and emotion, and portrayed these topics in special collectivities, it is appropriate to go beyond a systems analysis. This means to examine how the emotions might be explored by means of a narrative approach, which can substitute for a systems theory research approach. This is done in chapter 8. In chapter 9, scenarios for each of the 15 emotions are presented from the narrative perspective—that is, as distinctive dramatic stories.

CHAPTER EIGHT

Emotion Narratives: A Radical
New Research Approach

In Lazarus and Folkman (1984), we dealt mainly with psychological stress, with only a single chapter devoted to emotion from a cognitive-motivational-relational perspective. When I started the present book, I was convinced that psychological stress and emotion should be portrayed categorically rather than dimensionally and studied as a system of interrelated variables that includes not only harm, threat, and challenge—that is, the stress emotions—but would also include emotions that are usually referred to as positively toned.

However, partly as a result of a recent experience I had as a commentator on an interesting and challenging article by Somerfield and Commentators (1997), who presented a systems theory model of stress and coping for applied research, I have developed a new viewpoint about the best research strategy for the emotions. Somerfield's presentation was a target article that attracted comments by fourteen active research scholars, many of them well known. He summarizes his basic thesis in the abstract for his article:

> Contemporary conceptual models of stress and coping are intricate systems formulations that depict adaptation as a dynamic, interactional process. The inherent complexity of these models presents conceptual and methodological challenges that make testing a complete model difficult. This article makes the case for a more microanalytic strategy for applied coping research that, by centering attention and available resources on selected high-frequency, high-stress problems, permits more conceptually sophisticated and clinically informative analyses. (p. 133)

My own comments were largely supportive of Somerfield's view that stress and coping must be approached in a holistic way as a system of many variables and processes. I did, however, have some reservations about his main recommendation—namely, that research be concentrated on a single, well-defined stressor, such as cancer. Other commentators addressed the same point, while indicating substantial support for the basic systems research premise.

Confusion is created by trying to compare coping in people who are struggling with many different kinds of stress, which makes it sensible to suggest that coping comparisons be restricted to the same kind of stress. There is also much data showing that coping varies when it must deal with diverse harms/losses, threats, and challenges. Each type of stress creates distinctive demands, constraints, and opportunities and, therefore, cannot be approached effectively by a common coping strategy. It is sound to say, as Somerfield does, that concentrating on a single stressful event or set of transactions would reduce the confusion resulting from this dependence of coping on the kind of stress being faced.

However, this solution is probably impractical because major and complex medical illnesses, and even the various cancers, have distinctly different psychological ramifications. Many of the demands, constraints, and resources involved in each particular illness, or even each type of cancer, are distinctive and call for different coping processes. This makes it important to compare appraisal and coping processes across illnesses, whether in the same study or as several overlapping research projects.

Thus, having as we do a separate National Institute of Health for each major illness, such as heart disease, cancer, and so on, makes it difficult to learn in what ways the psychological impact of one illness overlaps and differs from that of other illnesses. Not only does Somerfield's proposal of selecting a single disease fail to solve the problem of enabling us to compare coping within common sources of psychological stress, but it adds a further problem of narrowing too much the scope of the inquiry. Over the course of writing for publication my comments on Somerfield's proposal, and as a result of later ruminations, I began to have increasing doubts about a systems research approach as a solution to psychology's current doldrums.

My second reservation concerns the viability of a systems theory research approach, regardless of how it is organized. Although I view systems research as an idealized way of thinking about and doing research from a traditional scientific standpoint, and I believe it has much to offer, I do not think it is a practical strategy for adding to our knowledge and understanding of so complex a system as stress and emotion. The high costs of longitudinal systems research, which is what would be needed to fulfill Somerfield's program, and established institutional patterns with their well-entrenched professional reward systems, would inhibit researchers and supporting agencies from following his recommendations.

There are also too many antecedent, mediating, and outcome variables to deal with for an adequate test of this strategy. I believe the good idea of doing research within a systems theory framework is likely to fail. And restricting one's research to a modest number of variables to make it more practical reduces the value of systems thinking and research.

Still another reservation, which goes to the heart of my concerns about psychological science itself, is that systems theory research is dependent entirely on a traditional analytic science cause-and-effect framework, which in itself is incomplete as an approach to gaining knowledge (Lazarus, 1998). I have been at pains in chapter 1 to show that we should view what we are studying when looking for causal variables as part-whole relationships or as limited systems operating within larger systems. After we have broken a phenomenon down in a reductive, analytic search for causal components—that is, part processes—the whole phenomenon must still be resynthesized to what it is in nature. Traditional science does not, as a rule, put them back together again, and often treats the parts as if they were the whole.

As a result of my growing reservations about these issues, I became interested in a different approach to the emotions—one that adopts a narrative perspective. In Lazarus and Lazarus (1994) my wife and I came close to proposing such an approach, but we did not because that book was intended for nonprofessionals. I present such an approach in this chapter.

But before embarking on the narrative methodology for the study of the emotions, I want to be fair to the systems view, which I had previously espoused (*see* Lazarus, 1990), and whose logical virtues I can still appreciate. I also want to verbalize more fully and clearly some other reservations about systems research on stress and emotion. Allow me, therefore, to backtrack to a systems view of stress, coping, and the emotions, and to consider some of its problems in more detail, after which I try to formulate a narrative approach that could guide programmatic research.

A SYSTEMS THEORY APPROACH

In Lazarus and Folkman (1984), we presented several charts identifying the variables of a psychological stress and coping system as then conceptualized. One (p. 305) was a theoretical schematization of stress, coping, and adaptation. A second (p. 307) looked more closely at the portion of the first chart that dealt microanalytically with mediating processes over time and across diverse types of encounters. A third chart (p. 308) distinguished among types of variables and processes, including causal antecedents, mediating processes, and immediate effects, which were presented at three levels of analysis, the social, psychological, and physiological.

These charts portrayed what we believed then to be the most important variables of a systems approach to stress and coping, which interact to produce the state of mind and adaptational patterns that characterize a stressful transaction. The basic chart is reproduced again below in Figure 8.1a.

I have also added to and modified Figure 8.1a slightly to make it more complete in light of afterthoughts during the intervening years. The revision is shown in Figure 8.1b. A few more causal antecedents have been added in keeping with my present intention to integrate stress and emotion within the same analytic system. I have also added a new mediating appraisal construct—namely, benefit—which underlies positively toned emotions, the idea of core relational themes, and an outcome variable that consists of immediate and long-term emotions.

The original figures for the second and third charts in the 1984 book have again been reproduced in Figures 8.2 and 8.3.

To make the psychodynamics of Figure 8.1a fully comprehensible, one would need to set up separate figures representing different temporal moments and conditions for each process variable in the system—namely, appraisal, coping, and the relational theme for each emotion. I struggled for a long time to no avail to think of ways of putting the theory together in a single figure, or even a figure for each emotion, but this strategy became too complex and cumbersome.

If we are to do justice to all the important variables and their sites of influence, in addition to the multiplication of figures the system would need to have more than a two-dimensional space. All that one can do with most figures is to list the variables for each epistemic category—that is, antecedents, mediating processes, immediate, and long-term consequences—and to suggest, somewhat vaguely, the processual relationships with arrows.

Although I have used figures sparingly in previous writing, I have always been wary of them and the arrows employed to show the directional influences of the variables and their feedback loops. Figures like these, and those with boxes connected with multiple arrows, suggest much more knowledge and detailed conceptualizations than are available at present. They leave out crucial processes and relationships,

Causal Antecedents	→ Mediating Processes Time 1 ... T2 ... T3 ... Tn Encounter 1 ... 2 ... 3 ... n	→ Immediate Effects	→ Long-term Effects
Person variables Values-commitments Beliefs: Existential sense of control	Primary appraisal Secondary appraisal Reappraisal	Physiological changes Positive or negative feelings Quality of encounter outcome	Somatic health/illness Morale (well-being) Social functioning
Environment Situational demands, constraints Resources (e.g., social network) Ambiguity of harm Imminence of harm	Coping Problem focused Emotion focused Seeking, obtaining, and using social support		
	Resolutions of each stressful encounter		

FIGURE 8.1a   A theoretical schematization of stress, coping, and adaptation. From Lazarus & Folkman (1984), p. 305.

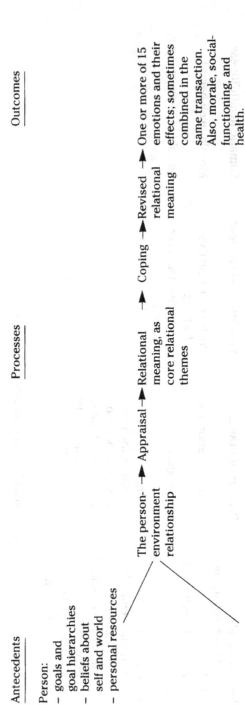

FIGURE 8.1b A revised model of stress and coping.

Mediating processes

Time 1	Time 2	Time 3	... Time N
encounter 1	Encounter 2	Encounter 3	... Encounter N

Appraisal-reappraisal

Coping
   Problem-focused
   Emotion-focused

Social support
   Emotional
   Tangible
   Informational

FIGURE 8.2   A transactional model: Ipsative-normative arrangement. From Lazarus & Folkman (1984), p. 307.

and they often obscure what one wants to communicate because the arrows are, at best, suggestive, and do not identify the diverse contexts so important to what happens in nature. I fear that what they do is to grossly oversimplify the system, and create only the illusion of understanding.

For example, appraising and coping processes influence just about everything in the system, but the specifics of this influence are not communicated by a generalized arrow or double arrow—the forms of influence are too complex and conditional to be adequately portrayed in such an oversimplified, schematic way. Similarly, there are so many different kinds of coping processes, and their influences are so complex and conditional, that a few arrows tell us little. In effect, for a broad theory the "right medicine" must lie in the details, and psychological scientists who present only simplifying principles, believing that they can be diagrammed neatly, may be fooling themselves and managing to undercut the richness and complexity inherent in the principles being portrayed.

Besides, the essence of an adaptational transaction is that the whole system changes from moment to moment and from one emotional context to another, sometimes as a result of a seemingly minor statement, action, or expressive gesture. This change, which may be profound as when there is a complete transformation of the emotional content, can be the result of a single antecedent variable, mediating process, or

	Causal Antecedents	Mediating Processes	Immediate Effects	Long-term Effects
SOCIAL	Socioeconomic status Cultural templates Institutional systems Group structures (e.g., role patterns) Social networks	Social supports as proffered Available social/institutional means of ameliorating problems	Social disturbances Government responses Sociopolitical pressures Group alienation	Social failure Revolution Social change Structural changes
PSYCHOLOGICAL	Person variables Values-commitments Beliefs-assumptions (e.g., personal control) Cognitive coping styles Environmental (Situational) variables Situational demands Imminence Timing Ambiguity Social and material resources	Vulnerabilities Appraisal-reappraisal Coping Problem focused Emotion focused Cultivating, seeking, and using social support Perceived social support Emotional Tangible Informational	Positive or negative feelings Quality of outcome of stressful encounters	Morale Functioning in the world
PHYSIOLOGICAL	Genetic or constitutional factors Physiological conditioning— Individual response Stereotype (e.g., Lacey) Illness risk factors (e.g., smoking)	Immune resources Species vulnerability Temporary vulnerability Acquired defects	Somatic changes (precursors of illness) Acute illness	Chronic illness Impaired physiological functioning Recovery from illness Longevity

FIGURE 8.3 Three levels of analysis. From Lazarus & Folkman (1984), p. 308.

outcome, yet lead to major reappraisals that profoundly change the relational meanings of the transaction for those engaged in it.

In Figure 8.2 in Lazarus and Folkman (1984), we tried to suggest temporal and condition-induced changes by representing them as mediating processes. In one row, we used the designations "$T1, T2, T3, Tn$" to represent time; a second row employed the designations "Encounter 1, 2, 3, n" to represent conditions. As I said, there seems to be no handy way to portray the multiple contents of these processual changes, except in a set of schematizing snapshots, like the separate frames of a motion picture. So we must not go overboard about the value of a few simplifying diagrams. They obscure as much as they clarify.

My reservations about systems theories, which provide merely general guidelines for research variables worthy of study, were strengthened by failure to find a workable diagrammatic formula nearly 15 years after the Lazarus-Folkman book appeared. The unsuccessful struggle to find one helped fuel my growing interest in narrative strategies. The main issues, however, are not diagrammatic, but lie in the assumptions we must make, which are addressed below.

One of the commentators on Somerfield's article, David Spiegel (1997), mentioned narrative analysis in his comments, which I found apt and instructive and compatible with my own outlook. I quote some of what he wrote below (p. 170), though I have broken up some of his longer statements into several paragraphs to increase clarity and sharpen the emphasis:

> Professor Somerfield asks us in his interesting article to re-examine the archetypal epistemological problem. We must to some extent impose our perceptions upon the world in order to perceive, organize and understand it, and yet we always do so at a price.
>
> Modern psychological science has been biased towards quantitative analysis of data, a rather Aristotelian viewpoint, but also toward the goal of platonic simplicity of theory. We are often caught in the dilemma that *our theories are either too elegant to be meaningful or too full of meaning to be elegant.*
>
> Coping is an important construct and yet it has become clear that it has a short life span—that we must ask the question "Coping by whom? At what time in response to what stressor? And in what context?"
>
> It is a healthy development in research that rigorous investigations are starting to utilize techniques that a decade ago would have been considered hopelessly messy, such as narrative analysis. Thus, researchers are beginning to address the common complaint of clinicians, that they fail to adequately take into account the existential reality of individuals in life threatening situations. Developments in cognitive psychology have been similarly helpful.

We have moved from an era of arid behaviorism in which the very brain that distinguishes human experience from that of all other animals was slighted as a black box and largely ignored, to one in which the perceptual, emotional and cognitive processing of information has become an interesting and important problem to be examined. (italics added)

When he says in the statement I have italicized that "our theories are either too elegant to be meaningful or too full of meaning to be elegant," Spiegel's phraseoloty is epigrammatically pure and absolutely delightful. I was so pleased by it that I wrote it down for later use, and trotted it out here in developing this argument.

In thinking about the contents of this quotation, by the way, the reader should remember that in my version of a systems analyses the antecedents consist of objective variables of the person and the environment, but it is the person's construal of these that counts—that is, what I have been calling appraisal and relational meaning. As Somerfield acknowledges in his author's response to the commentators, research can be variable centered or person centered, and which is chosen makes a vital difference in how one looks at the emotion process (*see also* Magnusson & Bergman, 1997).

Now, however, we must revisit the distinctions made in chapter 1 between objective and subjective and think them through more carefully. They are especially relevant to the variable- versus person-centered distinction, which seems not to have been as carefully drawn as it should be for maximal clarity.

REVISITING OBJECTIVE VERSUS SUBJECTIVE

This distinction really depends on whose perspective is being used to refer to the person and the environment in the person-environment relationship. When, for example, personality psychologists attempt to measure or describe the personality of an individual, or many individuals, their perspective is usually variable centered and objective. It does not matter what are the sources of data, personality tests, or clinical inferences. It is the professional or research observer who is making the assessment, and with the intention of describing persons as they really are, not as they think they are.

The same would apply if one attempted to describe the self or the environment on the basis of a consensus of observers. Even if one considers the perspective of a single individual, a person-centered approach can remain objective in that it is the observer who defines what the person is like and how that person views self and world. This contrasts with a person-centered perspective that is entirely subjective—that is, when the view of self and world is from an individual person's own perspective.

The tricky part of these two distinctions, person versus variable centered, and objective versus subjective, is that we tend to think of variable centered as objective and person centered as subjective. However, this association is not always an accurate rendition of the research possibilities and even less of the research realities. We must think of the permutations and combinations as a fourfold table, one with four cells—namely, variable centered and objective, variable centered and subjective, person centered and objective, and person centered and subjective, though they are not equally probable in all four cells.

Regardless of our biased impression, however, there is no reason variable and person centered could not be considered from *both* the objective and subjective frame of reference, though to do so may seem like a stretch and a bit awkward. It becomes evident that the objective versus subjective, and variable- versus person-centered distinctions can involve all sorts of permutations and combinations.

This reasoning must still be applied to the narrative approach in the study of the emotions. In doing so, it might be useful to draw on an analogy between biography and autobiography. In biography, it is someone else who is telling the life story. Biographers may use a mixture of objective and subjective sources of data, but the presumption is usually made that the biographer is searching for objective truth, not merely the truth as viewed by the subject of the biography. Autobiographers, conversely, are telling their own life story as conceived by the storyteller. It is usually written from a subjective frame of reference, even if the author maintains the illusion that this life is being described objectively.

It behooves us to keep this analogy in mind when we examine the narrative approach to the emotions. Although a narrative approach is usually viewed from a subjective frame of reference, if the preceding reasoning is sound, it could be made to reflect either an objective or a subjective frame of reference. This would depend, of course, on who is doing the assessment of self and world. Remember too that my own bias is that it is the person-environment relationship, as construed by the person, which is the best strategy for obtaining an adequate understanding of stress, emotion, and adaptation.

A different but related comment on Somerfield's thesis, which was made by Hannalore Weber (1997), emphasizes personal goals as the main organizing principle wherein meaning is achieved. Although she focuses on a person-centered perspective, her statement of this is not necessarily limited to the principle of methodological subjectivity. Personal goals as personality dispositions can be measured subjectively by asking the person about goals and goal hierarchies, or independently of the person's appraisal. This would highlight the difference between subjective and objective approaches, assuming that they are not highly correlated.

In so saying, allow me also to remind you that my kind of subjectivism presumes that a person always negotiates between the desire to know the truth and the desire to view the truth in the most positive light possible to preserve hope and sanguinity. In other words, because wish and reality both contribute to what is appraised, mine is a modified subjectivism; therefore, it must remain on friendly terms with objective, variable-centered research.

Returning now to the problems of systems theory research on stress and emotion, objective variables operate at a different level of analysis than relational meanings, which are strongly subjective, and often partly private until we try to make them public. I am somewhat uncertain about the wisdom of putting these levels of analysis together in the same schematization; doing so might conflate their roles and significance.

One good reason for putting them together, however, is for the unique purpose of testing whether the individual's subjective perspective conforms to the objective evidence, based on the judgments of observers. In doing this, we must be wary about presuming that if the two sources of knowledge disagree, the discrepancy implies psychopathology. Inevitably there is the question of which to base our inferences on, the subjective or the objective. My own hunch is, more often than not, that the subjective is closer to the truth, but others may take a different view.

Although it would be useful to compare the objective and subjective frames of reference, putting them together routinely in the same correlational matrix in garden-variety systems research on the variables that might account for stress, emotion, and adaptation carries a major analytic danger. It mixes apples and oranges, so to speak, especially if the relationship between them is weak or modest, which is an empirical question. Perhaps a transformation is needed, such as Block's (1961) Q-sort methodology for mixed types of data.

Given the preceding reasoning, I now offer what I believe is a viable commonsense alternative—namely, a narrative or storied approach to each emotion, whose time may have come. If my concerns about levels of analysis could be assuaged, then this approach might make it possible to combine variable- and person-centered, subjective and objective, and normative and individualistic perspectives within the same research designs without losing the special values of each.

If we want to study emotion narratives as science, we must combine the narratives of many individuals to see in what ways the stories are shared and reflect the collective experience of people in each of the emotions, and in what ways they diverge. It will be necessary to do this to determine the prototypical narrative for each emotion, and to consider subvarieties that deserve being treated as special categories—but more of this shortly.

EMOTION NARRATIVES

A narrative approach to persons and their lives is not new to psychology. It has gained considerable favor in recent years. The list of those who have drawn on it or made it central to their thinking is growing. A modest sampling, however, would include Bruner (1990), Cohler (1982), Coles (1989), Gergen and Gergen (1986), Josselson and Lieblich (1993), McAdams (1996, 1997), Polkinghorne (1988), Sarbin (1986), and from a psychoanalytic perspective, Schafer (1981) and Spence (1982).

It is notable that work of this kind thrived mostly in the 1980s and 1990s, the period during which interest in the emotions also burgeoned. The cognitivizing of psychology since the 1970s, which meant a firm rejection of radical behaviorism and the wider acceptance of a cognitive-mediational perspective, probably had much to do with this.

There has not been, as far as I know, a systematic portrayal of a narrative approach to the emotions, one that would also provide for programmatic research to fit a narrative conceptualization. Although appraisal theory often sounds like a narrative (e.g., Shaver, et al., 1987), and makes use of a similar perspective, no one at present seems to know exactly how to go about developing a narrative approach, so much of what is written below may seem to have a radical flavor.

What is an emotion narrative, and what is its structure? To use the imagery of Lazarus & Lazarus (1994), it is a dramatic plot or story that describes the provocation of the emotion and its background, which helps define what made some action, or lack of action when it is desired, provocative, and how it progressed and turned out. The drama begins with the provoking action and proceeds through the continuing transaction—usually interpersonal. The provocation is best viewed as the figure in a *figure-ground* relationship.

Generally, to understand the emotional reaction to a provocation requires more than an examination of the initial action. We need to know its *background,* which takes the form of a history of the relationship and the relevant personality variables (dispositions) that shape the emotional reactions of the persons who play a role in the ongoing transaction.

The important personality variables (see also chapter 3) consist of goals and goal hierarchies (in layperson's terms, what is important and unimportant to the person), beliefs about self and world, and personal resources. Goals and beliefs, and the mutual actions and reactions that occur, fuel *situational intentions* that are present either before or during the transaction. Beliefs include what the parties have learned to expect from each other, and in what ways they are motivationally important to each other.

These person-centered and environmental variables (most often what another person does) set the stage for appraisals by both parties—these might be similar or quite different—of the relational meaning of what is happening, which, in turn, shapes the emotions aroused and how they change over the course of the encounter. Appraisals and reappraisals generate coping processes, which are adaptationally relevant responses to complex demands, constraints, and opportunities, and are a key part of the emotion process. These cognitive-motivational-relational processes influence and change the *relational meanings* constructed from the chain of events that characterizes the emotional drama.

Unless we want to use only a snapshot of a single moment rather than a continuing motion picture, the narrative does not end with the emotional reaction of one or both participants. Emotional encounters proceed continuously over time, as in a drama or motion picture film, and when they end—if they ever do—it may be only temporarily, as the parties separate, resolve their conflict, or terminate the transaction or business.

We could, for example, define an ending as the close of a particular kind of business that is being transacted and the beginning of another, based on each person's goals and situational intentions. Depending on personal characteristics, and the depth and continuity of the relationship, the emotional transaction may not really end, however, until the departure or death of one or both of the participants; it may still continue to fester in the mind of a survivor.

Like the fiction writer of a dramatic story, the movie director who decides when to shut off the camera for dramatic effect, or because the conflict has been resolved, it is often arbitrary when we say the transaction has ended. In most relationships, each new transaction tends to repeat previous ones, though the details are likely to differ and new issues may emerge. Relationships do not usually remain static, but change over time, without old features necessarily being discarded.

As I said, the emotion process can be seen in figure-ground terms, the background in the form of a relational history. This background has as much to do with why what occurred was an emotional provocation, as does the figural act itself. Thus, Klos and Singer (1981) report that the arousal of anger in parent-child relationships they studied was influenced by the history of interpersonal stress even more than the provocative action itself, which is what most observers would be inclined to blame.

What occurred leads to several alternative short-term outcomes—for example, an impasse, partial resolution, full resolution, continuing emotional distress, deepening resentment, a parting of the ways, violence, and so forth, none of which is readily predictable without a full grasp of the figure and background of these events and what is in the minds of the two participants. What happens in this flow influences the emotional states and actions of the provocateur, as well as the recipient, and this recurrent feedback constitutes a kind of social dialogue in which the roles of provocateur and recipient can be reversed any number of times.

PROTOTYPICAL NARRATIVES

For a narrative approach to be useful, we need to generate a scenario for each of the emotions, one that can be regarded as a *prototype* for that emotion. Although each particular instance of an emotion varies in detail, depending on person characteristics (e.g., distinctive goals, goal hierarchies, belief systems, and personal resources), and on the social or physical environmental conditions that are confronted whether real or imagined, a prototypical version portrays how the emotion is typically aroused in most or all persons who experience the emotion as well as how it is coped with and expressed. Prototype means that there is a collective sharing of the basics of an emotion narrative for a particular emotion category.

To speak of a prototype is to make a theoretical construction. It requires making a selection of many possible emotional scenarios buttressed by observation. Even when similar in form and content, no two emotional transactions are ever exactly alike because the circumstances always differ, if only slightly.

Some features of the story are essential to the arousal of each emotion. Other features are mere details that do not affect the basics of the prototypical narrative, though they may influence the reaction in ways that are not essential. The prototypical relational meaning, or core relational theme for any given emotion, is its cognitive-motivational essence, which is shared by anyone experiencing that emotion. Other characteristics reflect either important or minor qualitative variations and so could represent the prototype or one of its variants.

Although there is quite a bit of agreement, not all appraisal theorists are likely to subscribe to exactly the same prototypical narrative. For example, my claim that the offense in prototypical anger is being slighted or demeaned is challenged by other theorists who view the plot for anger differently. In my version, an inconsiderate or a malicious act that is clearly a put-down is a necessary provocation for an appraisal that one has been demeaned (Lazarus, 1991). Others (Berkowitz, 1989), however, view the primary basis of anger as goal frustration, and the inference that it was unjustified or intentional—therefore, a put-down—as a nonessential feature.

There is also the interesting question of whether babies and young children are aroused to anger by exactly the same psychological processes as adults. The reason for the question is that it takes quite a bit of social understanding to sense the offensive meaning of being demeaned or belittled, and it is not clear that very young children have such understanding or when and how, developmentally, they attain it. It is possible, perhaps even likely, that babies, who certainly seem to be capable of a reaction that looks like anger, experience a different kind of anger. We might refer to anger in the very young child as a proto-anger, that is, an emotion that only begins to approach adult anger but which is not yet the same as that of an adult.

Perhaps we even need to consider the possibility of more than one core relational theme for anger, or for any proto-emotion that appears in early development. The resolution of such issues and the theoretical disagreements involved in these issues and resolutions must, in a large measure, be closely tied to empirical observation. However, obtaining suitable data is not easy because babies cannot say what they think, want, or feel, and past research on this subject, most of which dealt with aggression rather than the emotion of anger, remains ambiguous (Lazarus, 1991).

We must now consider more concretely what is meant by nonprototypical variants of an emotion. Consider, for example, the case of anger. We speak of many kinds of anger, such as chronic hostility, cold anger, righteous anger, indignation, irritation or annoyance, rage, gloating, pouting, disdain (or scorn, sarcasm, and contempt), inhibited anger, and chronic hostility. Some of these are distinctive variants of anger, and some are minor qualitative or quantitative details, yet share basic essentials of the prototypical anger narrative. Which it should be, prototype or variant, is a judgment call, a strategic decision based on theoretical utility.

Several variants of those listed previously are sufficiently different from the prototype to warrant a distinctive identity yet retained within the broad anger rubric. These distinctive variants include inhibited anger, pouting, and chronic hostility. I discuss them in chapter 9 when the emotion narrative for anger is examined.

The same strategic decision incidentally also applies to other overlapping but discrete emotions, such as anxiety, fright, guilt, and shame. The core relational theme for anxiety is an uncertain, existential threat. For guilt it is having transgressed a moral imperative. For shame it is having failed to live up to an ego ideal. Despite differences, a case could be made for treating them as variants of one generic form, anxiety. And so we might refer to them, respectively, as anticipatory anxiety, guilt anxiety, and shame anxiety. I favor treating them as more different than similar because their antecedents and behavioral outcomes are also different, which seems to be the way most appraisal theorists view them (Lazarus, 1991; H. B. Lewis, 1971; M. Lewis, Sullivan, Stanger, & Weiss, 1989; Tangney & Fischer, 1995).

In the same vein, we can see overlaps as well as contrasts between anxiety and fright. You will see in chapter 9 that I regard them as closely related but quite different emotional states, from the standpoint of both the provocations and their descriptive response qualities. So I hyphenate them, as anxiety-fright. The decision about prototype and variant must be made for a few emotions and is always a judgment call.

It is noteworthy that my narrative approach to emotion is heavily influenced by the way clinicians understand an individual's psychodynamics in the context of treatment. A story about the patient's life and emotional troubles, often referred to as a case history, is developed by means of essentially the same interview questions as I have been suggesting for an assessment of the person's social relationships, the relational meanings constructed for them, the emotions that are associated with these meanings, and the troubles and symptoms that led the person to seek professional help.

An important difference, however, between a scientific narrative approach and a purely clinical one is the programmatic effort by the seeking of knowledge to identify the prototypical plot or story line and its variants, as inferred from a variety of persons in contrast with the clinical need to understand a single individual. To make the effort a science, the focus cannot be solely on an individual person, or a set of environmental conditions, but on what is common as well as divergent in the narrative for each emotion.

Although the individual in which we are interested would be the primary clinical focus, the place of that individual in research on emotion prototypes, along with many other persons as research subjects, is to be a partial source of information about the normative relational meaning, and the factors that affect it. This combining of cases provides a database against which different narrative theories can be evaluated.

POTENTIAL RESEARCH ON EMOTION NARRATIVES

The premise of appraisal research is that each appraisal component expresses a different meaning-related evaluation that influences the emotion that is aroused. Research observation is needed to support or refute the role of these components in the choice of each emotion.

In a review and analysis of research on appraising, Lazarus and Smith (1988) identified several methods for linking appraisals with the emotions they presumably shape. Some methods identify similarities among the meanings of emotion words, such as anger, sadness, and anxiety, sometimes using priming tasks that point the research subject toward particular semantic properties. Some examine the reactions to experimenter-supplied emotional vignettes. Some ask subjects to state their own likely or imagined reactions to such vignettes by means of role playing techniques. Some seek retrospective memories about how subjects have thought, felt, and reacted in real-life emotional encounters. And some ask subjects to report current thoughts and feelings in an ongoing adaptational encounter.

One of the most common approaches requests subject-participants to report a recent emotional event and describe the appraisal they made as the event was occurring. This semi-naturalistic approach depends on the ability of the person to reconstruct the emotional event in the presence of the researcher. Though the reconstruction depends on memory, which can always be inadequate or falsified, and requires a careful use of a well-designed interview or questionnaire, this method provides a reasonable basis for understanding the way appraisals shape each of the emotions.

Nevertheless, some of the methodologies noted earlier seem more like abstract intellectual exercises that study cognition-emotion relations in the abstract sense rather than being explorations of real emotions. Others come closer to actual emotions. The more the method tries to get a person to relive an actual event, the more it would seem to address the emotion process, thereby producing a better fit with emotion narratives in nature (Lazarus & Smith, 1988).

By the same token, naturalistic developmental and clinical studies of ongoing mother-child transactions can make direct observations possible on which an examination of emotion narratives could also be based. That would obviate many of the problems with reconstructions of emotions in the past. Although her work was not formally directed at emotion narratives, research of this sort by Dunn (1988) and Dunn & Munn (1985), who watched the emotional interchanges of children at play, and their interactions with their mothers, serves as a ready example. This point could easily be extended to clinical studies of coping and emotion in any other special population, such as those who are aging (Lazarus, 1998).

Quasi-experiments, or combined experiments and naturalistic studies, can also be designed for the study of emotion narratives. As has sometimes been done (Carstensen, Graff, Levenson, & Gottman, 1996, which I described in chapter 7), one could bring married couples into the laboratory to discuss a contentious subject for a period, recording the behavior of the couple and reviewing with them what had happened. This would generate data for inferences about what they were thinking and feeling, thereby revealing the emotion process including how it was aroused via appraisal and coped with.

It is not difficult to videotape what happens during emotional transactions, and this could be done without greatly interfering with the natural process. An important step in such research is to bring each individual back to view the videotape and comment on what he or she was thinking and feeling at each stage of the encounter. In this way, the subject-participant can reveal some of the emotional and regulatory processes involved in the social transactions.

Participants in such studies can also be challenged to clarify and evaluate what had happened. For example, if the person reports feeling nothing, but the evidence from psychophysiological measurement or behavior during the videotaped session suggests otherwise (Weinstein, Averill, Opton, & Lazarus, 1968), the experimenter could point out the contradiction and explore it further to get nearer the truth.

A narrative approach can easily focus on both appraisals and emotion narratives, which depend on the process of appraising. It would take little change in standard procedures to transform appraisal-centered research into narrative studies having the aim of identifying the provocations and the background factors leading up to diverse emotions. One would want to explore all kinds of emotion with a view to matching narrative theory to each kind of prototypical emotion as well as the variations around each prototype.

It would be possible to collect many narratives related to anger, anxiety, guilt, or other emotions, and evaluate them deductively or inductively, while questioning at every step the empirical basis of the ideas of the participants about the processes involved in each emotion.

Independent data could also be obtained about the personalities of the subject-participants, for example, their goals and goal hierarchies, beliefs about self and world, and other personality traits to test our notions about these variables as background factors in the emotion process.

In so saying, I am emphasizing the programmatic use of the clinical method in psychology to study the emotion process, based on what is regularly done in treatment sessions, such as cognitive therapy. Researchers could build a database for a narrative approach to the emotions that combined a naturalistic methodology with a quasi-experimental approach. It could simultaneously employ behavioral and physiological measures to supplement self-reports, making it truly multimethod. Attention could be directed to broad theoretical targets—for example, the roles of appraisal, coping, and of any other features of the emotion narrative that might be of interest.

OBJECTIONS TO A NARRATIVE APPROACH TO THE EMOTIONS

Objections can be presented for any type of methodology in emotion research or for any type of psychological issue, and I doubt that anyone can foresee every one. Each research approach could be said to have advantages and disadvantages, but the best approach would be to take a broad rather than narrow view of methods, as long as the research strategy and measurement approach one chooses is as precise as can be made at our present stage of understanding and technical measurement abilities.

Probably the most common objection would be the narrative approach's heavy dependence on self-report, but other methods can be employed to supplement such reports. One would want to employ the best observational and inferential strategies of the clinical method for identifying conscious and unconscious motives, and ego-defenses that undoubtedly distort what is reported.

I counter this objection by saying that a limited subjectivism will allow us to get closer to the truth than the simplistic presumption that people respond solely to the objective conditions of their lives—in effect, their goals, beliefs, and strategies of coping have an impact on that response. In my modified subjectivism, which I wrote about briefly in Chapter 1, people do make a strong effort to identify the objective realities of their plight, but they also try to put a positive spin on that plight to preserve hope and sanguinity.

Why deny the latter part of the negotiation process involved in appraisal and approach things only from the objective perspective, which we clearly know is only part the story? We would be wiser to do our best to overcome the problems of self-report, allowing us to draw on the advantages of a subjective framework, without denying our equally powerful need to know the truth. We can gain much by allowing for both objectivity and wishful thinking in everything we do.

A second objection, which would apply to all retrospective accounts of past emotions, is that narrative accounts of previously experienced emotions depend on memory, which could be faulty. They also depend on the willingness and ability of the person to describe past experience accurately and honestly. Memories are always reconstructions of the past, which probably change throughout our lives, but they need not be distortions of the meaning that has been constructed about what happened. The solution is to do what we can to evaluate such memories and to maximize the conditions that favor accuracy.

An even more serious problem is that often what is reported and evaluated by the research subject-participant can be a post hoc rationalization rather than a valid psychological account of what happened. I have already responded to this objection in chapter 4, as raised in the critique of appraisal theory by Parkinson and Manstead, and I need not do so again.

A third objection, related to the second, has to do with whether or not what is reconstructed in the subject-participant's account has much emotional heat left in it, or is more of an intellectual exercise than the real thing. If the latter, then the question that must be answered is to what extent and how this distorts our understanding of the emotion process. It is possible that the emotion narrative will be less valid or useful if its recall fails to evoke the emotion. On the other hand, perhaps only the memory is enough for our research purposes, a possibility that might be studied empirically. My hunch is that the closer in time one does the reconstruction, and the more the subject-participant relives the emotional experience, the more ecological validity the narrative should have.

But the best answer is that problems like this provide the most important reason that multiple research methods are needed, such as the direct observation and analysis of videotaped emotional episodes in, say, an argument or any other adaptive interchange between clinician and patient, spouses, friends, lovers, or children. It is always better not to rely on a single methodology, narrative studies of emotion included (see the section dealing with my wish list for the research future at the end of chapter 10).

A fourth objection is really not so much an objection as a problem of measurement. Narratives are like interview data, often diffuse and difficult to quantify. So the researcher who chooses to work with emotion narratives must be willing to accept the challenge of coding the interviews, developing rating scales for the variables and processes to be identified in each story and, where possible, developing quantitive as well as qualitative measures.

The challenges of doing this, and judging the validity of inferences derived from qualitative data in the study of the psychodynamics of interpersonal transactions, troubles many scientists. There is also skepticism about the use of hermeneutic procedures on any verbal text as an approach to knowledge. The solutions require skill and fortitude but, as was illustrated in chapter 6 in discussions of chronic stress and spillover from work and family stress, the potential of such an effort to enhance our understanding of interpersonal transactions can make the challenge eminently worthwhile.

We need to remember that science depends on the willingness and skill with which we relate our theoretical analyses to observations, which are used to describe phenomena and to induce or deduce explanations of what is observed. The type of observation—that is, whether it is based on laboratory experiments that manipulate variables or naturalistic observation that involve description and, if possible, quantitative measurement, is less relevant than the serious effort to observe, measure, and think carefully about the meaning of what we observe.

It cannot be denied that advances in observation, from the microscope to the telescope and many breathtaking new methods available today, have transformed science throughout its history. Science is not an easy game to play, and measurement—however precise—which distorts nature or is not relevant to the psychodynamic problem at hand is a dead end. I think narratives offer a more useful approach to understanding than traditional psychological research methods, and they certainly come closer to the natural ways in which we construct meaning from our life experiences.

There is one further potential problem with the narrative approach as a research method. Even within prototypical examples of an emotion, such as anger, each person's story will be different in details and context from those of others, and even different within the same person's diverse anger experiences. To build a portrait of the general structure of anger, we must abstract what is essential from the dizzying array of variations in detail.

What must be done, therefore, is to seek the prototypical elements of these stories, perhaps using a checklist for the interviewer of what story aspects to look for. This is why what I said about the structure of the emotion narrative is so important, for example, the provocation and the background with its many variables that could each influence how the emotional event emerges and procedes. A theoretical structure, especially one that is supported by observation, directs our attantion to what to look for in emotion narratives. Identifying these variables, some of which have to do with the environmental influences and some having to do with person characteristics (both subjective and objective ones), is essential to the task of abstracting portraits of prototypical and variant emotion narratives.

By approaching the task in this way, we can combine variable-centered and person-centered research strategies, which are both essential for an understanding of our emotional lives. Because it was based on a modern but incomplete definition of what science should be, psychology in the past has been almost entirely devoted to variable-centered research. It is time we found ways of adding person-centered strategies, which allow us also to bring relational meaning into our conceptualizations and research strategies. Some researchers are already doing this, but these strategies could be improved, made more complete and practical, and used more widely.

Whether or not narratives will live up to my expectations concerning our understanding of the emotions, they offer a promising alternative to the ways we have studied our emotional lives in the past and should be tried programmatically. I am convinced we will learn much if we provisionally adopt this approach. I would like to have my hand in such a program, but I fear it is too late for me to undertake what is needed.

We are now ready to consider prototypical narrative accounts of the emotions (*see* Shaver, Schwartz, Kirson, & O'Connor, 1987, for an interesting account of emotions that suggests prototypical narratives). In chapter 9, the psychodynamics of each of 15 emotions are examined, with a narrative approach in mind. The reader can also explore accounts of these emotions as actual case histories and sometimes in more detail, in Lazarus & Lazarus (1994).

Narrative Vignettes for Each of 15 Emotions

This chapter deals with stress- or negatively-toned emotions, and the so-called positively-toned emotions. The account of the emotions begins with what can be called the nasty emotions (anger, envy, and jealousy), and I spend more time with anger and its variants than to any other in order to provide a detailed case study that illustrates narrative-type thinking.

The briefer accounts of the emotions proceed with the remainder of the 15 emotions examined, including the existential emotions (anxiety-fright, guilt, and shame), emotions provoked by unfavorable life conditions (relief, hope, sadness-depression), the empathic emotions (gratitude and compassion), and finally emotions provoked by favorable life conditions (happiness, pride, and love). Although this classification contains some problems, it is probably as good an alternative as any other.

I note in passing that it is not easy to say what a positively-toned emotion is. The decision depends on which of three considerations are taken as the criterion—namely, the conditions of arousal, the subjective quality of the experience, or social values, and each does not always lead to the same choice. In any case, I assume that happiness/joy, pride, and love have the strongest credentials for the designation positive.

THE NASTY EMOTIONS

ANGER

Of all the emotions, with the possible exception of anxiety, anger seems to have been studied and speculated about most, probably because of society's need to control destructive violence. During the ascendency of behaviorism, and because emotions are subjective concepts, anger was given short shrift in favor of aggression, which has to do with observable behaviors involving attack in word or deed.

Interest in anger, in contrast to aggression, has been revived in recent years by the research and writings of many scholars—for example, Averill (1982, 1983), Berkowitz (1969, 1989), Buss (1961), Toch (1969, 1983), Megargee and Hokanson (1970), and psychoanalytic and biological-evolutionary thinkers, such as, Carthy and Ebling, 1964; *see also* Lazarus (1991) and Lazarus and Lazarus (1994)—a full list is unnecessary. These writings provide a substantial literature, which has not changed much over recent years, except for the advent of sociobiology (Wilson, 1975).

The core relational theme for anger, especially when directed at another person rather than oneself, is a *demeaning offense against me and mine.* Anger depends heavily on the goal of preserving or enhancing self- or social-esteem. The two key appraisal-based meanings at the heart of anger consist of *harm* to the self and the assignment of *blame.* Blame for the offense to this goal can be directed at oneself or another. If one blames oneself, anger is turned inward; if one blames another, the anger is, accordingly, directed outwardly.

If an attack on the other person who deserves the blame can be accomplished without unreasonable danger, anger is the likely emotion. On the other hand, if we judge that that attack places us at serious risk, anxiety or fright may supersede or accompany anger, especially if the other person threatens to retaliate. If the threat of retaliation is too great to be tolerated, the expression of anger will either be mixed with anxiety and inhibited, or anxiety will be the dominant or sole emotion. There may also be oscillation between anger, fright, and anxiety, depending on what is going on. The impulse to attack, which is part of the anger, may be inhibited, and the conditions resulting in anger may get reappraised and, therefore, moderated or turned into something else.

An angry encounter in an adult is often, if not usually, provoked by an offensive act that gives evidence that the perpetrator intended a slight or put-down. The inference about a malevolent intention can also be supported by the impression that the perpetrator was capable of controlling the offensive action, but didn't. Sometimes, as in a direct verbal or physical attack, the malevolence is fairly obvious.

The inference that we have been slighted can also be encouraged by carelessness or irresponsibility when there has been an offensive action. Although in such an instance the intention is often ambiguous, carelessness can be readily construed as giving short-shrift to our rights and privileges, leading to the justifiable impression that we have been slighted; then we believe the offending person should have been more careful to give us the proper regard.

It is difficult to know whether and to what extent this analysis applies to anger in the young baby; one so immature cannot readily grasp the implicit idea of self-esteem or one's place in a social status hierarchy. Within a matter of months a baby can distinguish between self and other—though the developmental timing of this remains problematic—but this probably does not apply to a social slight or insight, which requires considerable experience and knowledge.

A baby might be able to recognize malevolence, however, especially when it experiences physical constraint (*see*, for example, Campos, Campos, & Barrett, 1989; Campos & Stenberg, 1989). But it is difficult to tell what is in the mind of a baby who is too young to tell us, so the issue of what a baby is reacting to when angered, or even whether the reaction is anger, remains unsettled.

If we look for a phylogenetic parallel to status in human social life, a large proportion of animal species engage in within-species dominance struggles, which play a powerful role in the social control of the survival-related functions of eating and mating. Most human social arrangements depend on a substantial degree of social status, so it is not far fetched that a very young child could become sensitive quite early to the status hierarchy, and be threatened by a put down. This is an empirical question that is difficult to settle at an early stage of life, which is likely to be without well-developed abstract concepts and speech.

The basis of a child's anger notwithstanding, a sensing of another person's intentions can provide the grounds for assigning blame. The attribution of blame might well be regarded as a key feature of anger, and essential to the appraisal leading to this emotion. Even when the evidence for a malicious intent is weak or non-existent, a less than impartial observer might suspect that the target of the action may be primed and ready to take offense when no offense was intended, on the basis of experience-honed personality traits. Above all, whatever was said or done to arouse anger must be viewed by the target as having assaulted the goal of enhancing or protecting his or her self-esteem, which is the main motivation lying behind the anger and the desire for revenge. Again we see an illustration of the importance of the person-environment relationship in emotion.

Below is one version of a narrative of mutual anger aroused in a married couple who are having a bitter argument (*see* Lazarus & Lazarus, 1994). It illustrates a number of themes indicated above, the most important of which is the ever-present, but often hidden relational background on which the provocation depends, and the flow of events in which coping alters the appraisal and the actions and reactions that flow from it, leading to a new relational meaning and, consequently, a changed emotional state.

It [the argument] began while the couple was making breakfast and getting ready to go to work. The husband usually has fresh orange juice squeezed by his wife. This morning she fills a glass with frozen juice.

The husband wonders out loud why she has not followed the usual routine. She responds testily that she must be at work early, and if he wanted freshly squeezed juice he should do it himself. He takes offense and sulks a bit making no response when she speaks. She says, "Well, it looks like sulking time. That's all you know how to do—sulk. You have no consideration for me, and I'm sick of doing everything as if you were a spoiled child." His anger is now rising too: "No, it's me you don't consider." Getting up from the table, he utters an insulting epithet and walks out.

The wife is now irate and she follows him into the bedroom, noting in an accusatory way that he had been uncommunicative last night when he got home from work. She also suggests that they have been failing to get along. The wife is now saying very harsh things to her husband, and she goes over a long list of character assassinations, most of which she has used in other arguments. The mutual anger escalates. "To hell with you," he shouts, hatefully. "And to hell with *you*," she rejoins in the same vein.

As the husband is putting on his coat to leave for work, he volunteers with evident distress that he learned at work yesterday that a number of employees had been let go and he would have to take a cut in pay. At this admission, the wife's behavior is suddenly transformed from attack to trying to make amends. She holds out her hand to keep him from leaving and apologizes for her outburst.

The anger has disappeared for the moment. She now feels guilt for what she has said, and anxiety too about his job and their economic plight, which she verbalizes. He sits down and says that he shares her anxiety, his anger also having mostly abated. She pulls him up to her and hugs him, and he responds in kind, but without much enthusiasm. She asks why he hadn't told her about this last night, but he shrugs his shoulders. Both seem relieved and even affectionate, though he is not as demonstrative as she, and was more wounded by the interchange. They begin to discuss their reactions to the job crisis, but have to stop talking to go to work, promising to speak about it again that evening.

I use this story in the discussion that follows as an illustration of the prototypical narrative of anger, and analyze it from the standpoint of appraisal theory. My objective is to indicate the way background variables and ongoing processes in the anger story help us understand the emotional flow. To grasp the cognitive-motivational basis of anger and the dramatic changes to the emotions of anxiety and affection, we need to know something of the background of the participants' relationship, their individual goals, which tell us what is important to them, their beliefs, and personal resources and liabilities. These goals and beliefs, and appraising and coping processes, along with relevant environmental events, provide most of the answers to questions about why these transactions happened as they did.

Superficially, what provoked the argument on the morning it took place was the failure of the wife to do what she usually does—that is, to squeeze the orange juice—which led the husband to respond by asking why. The immediate provocation is the wife's action, in this case an inaction that violated her husband's expectations, and his query, to which the wife responds testily, saying she must be at work early. Sensing that there is something more than meets the eye in what was happening, he gets annoyed and sulks, which potentiates in his wife an angry attack in which she berates him mercilessly.

This gets his goat and they are off and running, literally working themselves into a rage in which character assassination is prominent. Because the issue that began the argument seems so trivial, we can be reasonably confident that we need to look elsewhere for the deeper, less accessible causes of the marital spat. There is more to this argument than is obvious to the uninformed observer.

What is the significance of the husband's behavior that provoked the wife's need for retaliation? Her complaint that he is a person who sulks seems to be a major source of resentment. Why was she offended by his silence the night before? She seems to have been itching for a fight. From what she herself says, the silence was appraised as signifying indifference toward her. She felt she was being taken for granted and, therefore, belittled and perhaps unloved, which turned her longstanding, smoldering resentment into rage. This appraisal fueled her intention to repair her wounded self-esteem by bringing him down.

Retaliation often reflects the desperation and self-destructiveness so often inherent in an effort to exact vengeance, inasmuch as it may thwart other important goals. Lack of regard for other goals is what highlights the idea that emotions are irrational. In effect, assaulting her husband to get even with him could hardly be expected to make him more loving.

One could be a Monday morning quarterback here and speculate about what might have happened had the causal antecedents been different. Consider, for example, some of the variables that, if changed, might have made a difference. The wife's goal of feeling loved is chronically frustrated. This episode of anger might not have occurred if this frustrated goal had been of little importance to the wife or, if she had believed her husband cared for her. Whether or not such a belief was sound, the anger might have been mitigated or absent. If she had been more concerned with preserving the relationship, and less with her wounded ego, she might have tempered her anger so as not to do even more damage. And if she had she been able to make a more charitable appraisal of his behavior the night before, she might not have felt so offended. In other words, to draw a patently obvious conclusion, if she had been a different woman, things might have gone differently.

There is also the question of how the wife coped with the stressful relationship with her husband. The night before, when he was frustratingly silent, she might have tried to draw him out and, in doing so, discovered what was bothering him at work. Yet, in spite of her assaultiveness, she seems more vulnerable than in command of herself and her life situation. Though its premises were incomplete and, therefore, inadequate, her anger follows logically from the way she appraised the situation—that is, the personal meaning she constructed from her goals and beliefs about her marriage and what had been going on in the relationship.

What about the husband, about whom we know much less? He too might have been more concerned about the relationship, and had he acted on this concern earlier, he might have dampened the wife's ire. If he succeeded in getting the wife's attention the night before about what was going on at work and in their marriage, they might have addressed, and perhaps worked out, at least temporarily, some of their relationship problems.

Only very late in the game, when they both had to leave for work, and probably because what had happened at his job shamed him and added to his feelings of inadequacy, did he blurt out what was distressing him. What he said at that point transformed the immediate relationship. Had he been inclined and able to inhibit his angry retaliation for his wife's assault, he might have found excuses for her assaultiveness and overlooked it instead of retaliating. Only his plea about his job situation, which he offered after much anger had been exchanged, might have halted her diatribe. The job problem obviously threatened her security as well as his, and abruptly changed the dynamics of the transaction.

Luckily, but too late to abort the argument at the start, his move to tell his wife about the trouble he was in at work was precisely what was needed to turn the highly negative, assaultive situation toward a more benign denouement. The news that he might lose his job made his wife recognize the threat it presented to her as well as him. She then became anxious about the danger to their economic well-being. In an instant, the relational meaning of the encounter, and her anger, changed to guilt when she recognized she had been unfair to her husband, and had hurt him without justification.

At that moment, her sense of being demeaned by his indifference was set aside in the face of the new, graver threat. She clearly didn't want to abandon the marriage. Her sense of danger made it easier to empathize with her husband's plight. Her effort to reach out to him with a hug transformed the immediate relationship from one of anger to one of affection, to which he responded appropriately, even if without much enthusiasm.

The antecedent variables in this angry encounter are classic. They consisted of an open verbal assault and a troubled relational history. The wife's thwarted goals and beliefs, and her subjective definition of her marital problem, help fuel her anger. Their immature coping processes escalated the anger until the husband acknowledged that he is in danger of losing his job (I interpret this as a plea for support, as well as an expression of his distress). Change the meaning of what is going on, and voilà, the emotion also changes. We have been watching, so to speak, an emotional drama the main characteristics of which, despite variations in detail, are legion, and prototypical of anger.

VARIANTS OF PROTOTYPICAL ANGER

We are now ready to explore the main variants of prototypical anger and explore the variables and processes that lead to these variants. Below I examine some common variations, inhibited anger, righteous anger, pouting, and hostility. In my view, only inhibited anger, pouting, and hostility, are distinct enough forms of anger to make a claim to a special status. Pouting is as much a mode of coping as an emotion, per se. Other variants, such as irritation, annoyance, and rage reflect different anger intensities, so they should *not* be granted the status of distinct types of anger. And, as will be seen shortly, hostility is a sentiment or disposition to get angry, rather than the actual emotion of anger.

Before going any further, I should first comment on the problem of *cold anger,* which some readers might suppose should be treated as a distinct type. The classic literary document that provides a good model for so-called cold anger is Alexandre Dumas' story of Edmund Dantes, who became *The Count of Monte Cristo* (1844–1845) after being falsely imprisoned in the Chateau D'If for ten years. With the help of a priest who was imprisoned in a neighboring cell, Dantes escapes and finds a treasure, which he uses in a deliberate and planful fashion—as opposed to hot and impulsive—to destroy, one by one over a period of years, those who treacherously and corruptly had him imprisoned.

Cold anger appears to be the wrong metaphor for an emotional pattern one seldom sees. The person who appears to manifest cold anger may be smoldering with hot anger, yet managing to conceal it in a calculating and deceptive process of planned revenge, whether or not the revenge is ever acted out. We might presume that, in private, the anger in that person's mind could be florid with fantasies and schemes to gratify the urge for revenge—in effect, there might be ample, though hidden, moments of hot anger. The anger, if one can recognize it, only looks cold because its expression is suppressed. There is no cold anger, only suppressed anger, which is discussed below as inhibited anger, though it might be leaked inadvertently, and sometimes even intentionally, to perceptive observers.

Inhibited Anger

Because of the violence and social destructiveness connected with anger, the control of anger and aggression has been of interest at least since the days of Seneca, the Roman philosopher, who wrote extensively about the problem (Toch, 1983). Today this concern is widespread in our country and centers on television and movie violence and its influence on violent crime in young people.

In the heyday of psychoanalysis, suppression of anger was considered harmful, based on a view of mind that draws on an analogy to a steam boiler. If an emotion, such as anger, becomes too strong and the person cannot "let off steam" by expressing it, the pressure was said to build until there is either an explosion, say, a mental breakdown, or the transformation of the unreleased energy into symptoms of illness, as in so-called psychosomatic disorders. Today, most psychologists reject the boiler analogy and its implication that unexpressed anger is dangerous. Instead, the modern view is that the effects of bottling up anger, or expressing it, depend on the consequences for the social relationship that provoked it rather than the failure to let off steam.

If, for example, the expression of anger results in working out the interpersonal bases of the anger, thereby preserving what is valuable in the relationship and even a sense of mutual trust, the anger dissipates and is no longer in place psychologically to poison that relationship. If, on the other hand, the anger cannot be worked out, and the relationship has been irreconcilably poisoned, the interpersonal outcome may be festering anger, distancing, or a termination of the relationship. And if the resentment is unexpressed, the relationship problem may become chronic, with damaging interpersonal consequences. In other words, the positive or negative value of inhibiting anger expression or expressing it depends largely on what it produces in the way of long term relational outcomes, any health or illness effects notwithstanding.

I remember participating in a foolish and naive game young teenagers used to play called "Truth," and perhaps still do. The game was to ask each youth to speak an unflattering and unspoken truth about each of the other persons in the group. As you might guess, sometimes the truth was a very unpalatable one, which shamed the person about whom it was spoken. In addition to the immediate distress, it often poisoned the relationship between that person and his or her accuser, sometimes even destroying the social group. Although people often think that good relationships usually depend on absolute candor, this is quite naive. Usually, social groups maintain a tacit social understanding that certain truths may not be expressed because of the relational harm they can do.

This very common emotional state, which it is reasonable to call inhibited or controlled anger, can be brought about by strong negative values about anger and its expression when anger is aroused, or as a result of fear of retaliation. The person does his or her best not to express the anger visibly. An important issue raised by this form of anger has to do with individual differences in the capacity to control the expression of felt anger—that is, whether or not a person is capable of suppressing it. Some who try, fail, or unintentionally leak the presence of anger to others despite the effort to suppress it. Block & Block, (1980) have referred to this process of suppression as *ego control,* which can take three forms: undercontrol, overcontrol, and resilient or healthy control.

A second important issue is whether there are health-related costs of suppressing anger or, perhaps, benefits from expressing it. There is evidence, for example, that expressing an emotion rather than suppressing it completely can have health-related benefits. For example, Pennebaker and his colleagues, have published extensive research showing that verbalizing traumatic experiences, as when students write home about homesickness and particular anxieties at college (*see,* for example, Pennebaker, Colder, & Sharp,1990), leads to fewer visits to physicians for illness. Though statistically significant, the strength of this effect seems rather modest, and the traumatic situations seem a bit too mild to take very seriously, which has always made me wonder about the demonstration of the principle in this research.

A popular book by Tavris (1984) advises the suppression of anger (by counting to 10), which also illustrates the continuing interest in this problem. Tavris adopts a stance totally opposite to that of Pennebaker et al. (1989), advising everyone that suppression is desirable and not personally damaging. I shall have more to say about the health-related consequences of emotions and coping in chapter 10.

Righteous Anger

The focus of this kind of anger is self-justification, with an emphasis on the sanctity of our own goals and the impropriety of the actions of the person who offend us. Variants include indignation and outrage, which, in a display of self-righteousness, creates the impression that one is appalled at what has happened and may make the manipulation of others easier.

Indignation and outrage are both shaped by a belief in one's own probity, or the desire to believe in it even when it is not true, perhaps as a denial because it is not true. Though indignation can be strong, the term is ambiguous because it can imply a milder emotion, as in a partly inhibited expression of anger. Outrage clearly betokens a more intense, full-blooded rejection of another person or of a sociopolitical condition. Righteousness justifies our anger and provides an excuse for its high intensity, even to the point of rage because we have right on our side.

In all likelihood, the greater the self-righteousness, the more intense the anger is apt to be—in a sense, it contains a heavy does of self-presentation (*see* Weber & Laux, 1993). Shame about one's behavior often serves as a provocation to self-righteous anger; one does not want to be observed being engaged in wrongdoing, especially if this will be regarded as a characterological defect.

I vividly remember a personal incident in a crowded restaurant parking lot, where I caught someone parking illegally in the last available place, where, as a customer, I was privileged to park. Having caught her in the wrongful act, and remonstrating with her, I have never been responded to in more nasty fashion, as if I had been the person in the wrong. I acted offensively in her eyes by observing her impropriety, and she let me have it with all the force and invective of which she was capable. I had also acted self-righteously about her usurpation of a parking space to which I felt entitled.

Righteous anger allows us to externalize blame we should properly accept as our own, and it feels better than having to own up to one's shameful behavior. Some people, perhaps most of us, find it easy to transform a wrong we have committed into a right. Humans are superbly talented in justifying their evil doing, whether it is greed, lying, violating a trust, ostracism, prejudice, discrimination, murder, or genocide.

The righteousness of anger may be a quality of all anger. In this view, I am strongly influenced by Solomon's (1980) picturesque treatment of the righteous feelings in anger, in which case it should not be distinguished from prototypical anger. The psychodynamics are interesting and, I think, recognizable, making his statement worth quoting. Solomon (1980, pp. 274–275) writes:

> Anger is to be an analyzed in terms of a quasi-courtroom scenario, in which one takes the role of judge, jury, prosecuting attorney and, on occasion, executioner. The object of anger is the accused, the crime is an offense, the overall scenario is one of judgmental self-righteousness. (One might add that the court is almost always of the kangaroo variety, with self-esteem taking clear priority over justice).

This righteousness has two common sources: The first is the social provocation itself. It is easier to feel and act angry when the reasons for it are impeccable. If we are treated differently from what is considered fair play—for example, when we are singled out for criticism, though being no more deserving than anyone else, it is easier to view the criticism as malevolent—hence, a demeaning offense that threatens our self- and social-esteem.

An obvious injustice provides a good excuse for anger, which is directed at something or someone else, but we sometimes use the injustice as self-justification. A strong sense of justice (Lerner, 1980) is conducive to characterological righteousness. All the better if it is a shared community belief that has been violated. For some people, perhaps out of a religious commitment, just the appearance of being righteous is what is important.

So, we see that righteousness may be forged defensively, as when our own behavior violates the rules, but we are bound and determined to demonstrate the opposite—in effect, that we are honest and righteous. This can also lead to an excessive concern about lack of righteousness in others as a way of demonstrating it in ourselves, a form of defense that psychoanalysts have long called projection. Defensive anger is very difficult for others to deal with. When we cannot acknowledge our ego-sustaining hidden agenda, there may be no room for compromise.

A second source of righteousness is social and personal vulnerability; if one is not very secure about one's own probity or if we believe we are not generally well treated by others, we are likely to externalize the blame and attack other victims. An offense occurring against helpless others with whom we identify, or on whom we project our own vulnerability, may also generate anger and a sense of outrage.

A vulnerable person whose social and self-esteem are at stake in an encounter has many potential ways of coping with this vulnerability. One is to use a minor provocation as an excuse for the anger. We may, for example, feel a smoldering anger about a slight but are unable to express it because it will seem too trivial to warrant making much of. The wife in the illustration of anger that began this chapter displayed this kind of process. She feels keenly that she deserves better from her husband, and this fuels her tendency to feel anger toward him.

Pouting

Pouting is a special form of anger, a distinct variant of the anger proto-type, which deserves its own special category. It can best be charac-terized as insecure anger, and it verifies the rule that we need to believe we are capable of overcoming another who might retaliate to feel anger without anxiety. The person who pouts is engaging in a soft attack, a mild reproach that implies the other person does not care enough, which can almost seem more akin to disappointment than open anger. The reaction suggests dependence on the other person's attentions and good will. The pouter does not dare make a strong attack lest the other person became totally alienated and the relation-ship endangered or lost. Pouting presents a picture of neediness, inad-equacy, and even childishness.

To bring the point home, pouting should be contrasted with gloat-ing. *Gloating* is not a separate type of anger though it has some distinc-tive qualities, such as what is referred to in the unique German word, *schadenfreude*—that is, the open enjoyment of the other person's comeuppance. What best characterizes gloating is the sense of securi-ty with which anger can be felt and expressed. It is usually public, sug-gesting that the gloater feels comfortable with the anger.

If the intensity of the gloating, with its implication of anger, is very strong, this implies that gloaters believe they are responding to sub-stantial personal harm. A mild retaliation is not enough to assuage the person who has been severely injured. Conversely, if the revenge is severer than the original harm warrants, then guilt may be added to or take the place of the anger, even if some person or force other than the vengeful victim arranged the revenge rather than the angry gloater. But if it contained much guilt, it would no longer be gloating.

Because we feel it is justified, open gloating can draw on all the forms of put-down, which vividly, and sometimes cleverly, express the anger and sense of revenge—disdain (scorn), sarcasm, and contempt come to mind. Some psychologists, such as Ekman & Friesen (1988), regard contempt as a separate emotion, but I treat it as very close to proto-typical anger because it seems to describe basically an attempt to repair a wounded self-esteem, with open contempt for the perpetrator. It could also be a defensive or a form of self-promotion.

The background variables I have considered in previous discussions play an important role in the distinction between pouting and gloating. These include the status of the relationship, the nature of the attack, and person variables. A key dispositional variable that contributes to pouting should be a vulnerable or low self-esteem. The more dependent and inadequate the person, the more likely there will be pouting, and the less likely will there be gloating.

Hostility

There are important differences between anger and hostility, though they are often treated as synonymous. Hostility, or hatred, is not a reaction or state but is, rather, a sentiment or disposition. We say a person is hostile to another person, but that does not mean that person is actually experiencing the emotion of anger. Anger occurs only when the hostile person is in the presence of the hated person, or when he or she thinks about that person. Otherwise, the anger is latent, rather than aroused, yet always ready to arise in the presence or at the thought of the other.

Anger directed at someone toward whom we are not usually hostile can be aroused by a provocation, but when it dissipates and the transaction is concluded, there need be no residual hostility. As Averill (1983) points out, most anger is directed toward persons we love, or are close to psychologically—that is, family members or intimates rather than strangers. Closeness or intimacy implies the other person is important to us, which increases the likelihood that that person will create frustration or threaten one's personal commitments.

But persons toward whom one harbors hostility may arouse anger at just the sight or thought of them as well as their active physical presence. So, although the two concepts are closely related, we should reserve the term hostility, or hatred, for the sentiment—that is, the disposition to become angry, but retain the concept of anger for the hot or emotional state when it is aroused.

ENVY AND JEALOUSY

Envy and jealousy are usually discussed together because they are closely related yet different. Recent and informative works dealing with envy and jealousy have been published by Hupka (1981), Salovey (1990), Stearns (1989), White (1981), and White & Mullen (1989), among others.

People are often confused about the similarities and differences between these two emotions, often saying, for example, that they are jealous when they mean envious. Envy is the simpler of these two emotions because it is a two-person relationship in which we desire (the biblical word is covet) what someone else has and believe we are deprived of it unfairly because we are just as worthy. Jealousy, conversely, is a three-person relationship in which we blame a third party for a loss, or threat of loss, of what we cherish.

For example, we may feel jealous when another person gains a job, a prize, or promotion, and so on, in competitive situation when we too are also seeking it. When a loss or threat of loss to another involves a loved one's interest and affection, we speak of romantic jealousy, which may be the most common form.

ENVY

The core relational theme for envy is wanting what someone else has. Superficially, this seems to make envy a very simple emotion, provoked by the sight or thought that someone else has what we crave. In garden-variety envy, we see something that another person possesses, for example, wonderful or promising children, success, wealth, fame, popularity, beauty, a fine automobile or home—obviously elusive sources of happiness—and we long for them.

But like most other emotions, much more is involved in envy than meets the eye. Though we are all quite capable of moments or periods of envy, few of us often or constantly experience envy. The feeling of deprivation, of being cheated is an essential feature of the agony and pathology of envy. Social psychologists speak of this as downward social comparison—that is, comparing ourselves unfavorably with others.

A common way of coping with this deprivation is to try to rationalize, ignore, minimize, or deny that we feel deprived. "Look," we say to ourselves, "with all (his, her, or their) wealth, they are still unhappy," or "they suffer from numerous ailments or handicaps. In reality, and on the whole, I am much better off." Social psychologists speak of this form of coping as upward social comparison—that is, comparing ourselves favorably with others. One thinks, for example, "I have a serious cancer, but (this or that other person) is much worse off than I" (Taylor, Lichtman, & Wood, 1984).

This is why we gossip about celebrities when there is the suggestion that they are unhappy or have suffered some tragedy. Remember those great stars of entertainment, Judy Garland and Marilyn Monroe, wonderfully favored by beauty, talent, talent, success, and wealth, yet unhappy and suicidal. To see them as worse off than we, or as tragic figures, combats envy and may make us feel better about our own modest circumstances. It is as if they are being punished for their good fortune, and we may take pleasure in their misery, which is similar to gloating.

Another way to cope with deprivation is to moralize about envy as one of the seven deadly sins (Schimmel, 1992). Schimmel retells the biblical story of King Solomon and the two women who both claim to be the mother of the same child. Forced to adjudicate the dispute, the king threatens to cut the baby in two to give half to each of the mothers. In a celebrated act of wisdom, Solomon sees that one of the mothers agrees, whereas the other is horrified and cannot allow the child to be killed. He understands that the true mother must be the one who would rather save her child even if that means letting the other mother have it. The story also points up the potential cruelty and destructiveness of envy as well as its moral overtones. Moralizing about the evils of envy may helps some to avoid being eaten up by this emotion.

We also cope with envy by coming to believe that the things we want, such as wealth, fame, and the like, are not really sources of happiness. We try to put the things most people strive for into philosophical perspective, as the Greek stoics and Indian Buddhists did when they argued that mental grace, peace of mind, or Nirvana are achieved only by renouncing what most people seem to want in life.

A major complication of envy (jealousy too) is that, although it is sometimes an emotional state that comes and goes depending on the circumstances, like all emotions it can also be a personality trait. We speak of envious persons, people who are consumed with the envy of another or others—perhaps anyone who seems to be better off. Or they foolishly judge everyone else as better off than they. Such persons have probably struggled all their lives with envy and resentment over others being prettier or more handsome, popular, smart, or financially better off.

Psychoanalytic theorists have attempted to explain the trait of envy, especially its pathological and pathogenic qualities, by reference to the early childhood experience of sibling rivalry when, for example, a second child arrives in the family. Siblings are often rivals for parental attention and succor. Indeed, in nursing mammals, such as monkeys and dogs, one or several siblings even die because there is not a sufficient supply of milk or more vigorous siblings hog the supply.

Some readers might remember what the entertainer, Tommy Smothers, said repeatedly in the 1960s on camera to his brother Dick. "Mother loved you best," he often would say. That statement was both funny and poignant because most of us can resonate with the painful experience of competition with childhood siblings, in which greed and deprivation—associated with envy, jealousy, fear, and anger—are closely connected in the mind with being the loser in the earliest form of competition in life.

Those who suffer from the trait of envy are unhappy people, always envious of others, certain that the fates dealt them a poor hand, complaining, resentful, and unable to accept and find pleasure in their own life circumstances. Describing one such person whom he saw in treatment, clinical psychologist, James Bugenthal (1990) suggested that envy has become a lifestyle on which the patient depended for security and comfort. Such people may refuse to give up their misery. They are more threatened to be without this coping crutch than by continuing to live with a form of misery they know and understand, and so they resist venturing into a strange and forbidding psychological territory without envy as a way of seeing and presenting themselves socially.

JEALOUSY

Many of the things I said about envy also apply to jealousy, but as I noted, the two emotions are also different in important respects, the most important difference being that jealousy is always a three-person game, in which the jealous person believes he or she has a rival for something that is valued, most commonly the love or affection of another. To put it formally, the core relational theme for jealousy is resenting a third party for loss or threat of loss of another's bounty or affection.

The anger inherent in the romantic jealousy of a love triangle is based on the sense that we have been dealt with treacherously by our lover or by the person who has stolen our lover. Indeed, one of the most common bases of jealousy is sexual infidelity. This theme is portrayed dramatically in the Shakespearean tragedy, Othello, which led to murder and suicide.

The emotion of jealousy may have an objective provocation, as in the case of actual infidelity or solid evidence of the loss of interest on the part of a lover. However, much jealousy might be called neurotic because the provocation is only imagined. This kind of jealousy expresses a personality flaw in which a person is prone to jealousy, which is not justified by the reality. The misery and violence that can stem from it, more than any other themes, is what makes jealousy both fascinating, frightening, and potentially tragic.

What is the personal problem that makes a person prone to jealousy? One answer is that the meaning underlying much jealousy is an exaggerated need for love to be reassured about our personal identity and adequacy. This need leads the person to be ever on the lookout lest love be withdrawn and redirected to a rival. The message is, in effect, that the loved one should pay more attention. Like pouting, it can often be regarded as a cry for help: "Don't desert me" (Klein, 1946–1963; Tov Ruach, 1980).

Although we often think of the jealous person as angry and vengeful, we need to see that jealousy is as much an expression of a fear of loss by a self-centered, often pathetic person, who is needy. As Freud (1922) noted, jealousy not only involves a narcissistic wound making this emotion subject to the same relational meaning that underlies anger—namely, the effort to bolster one's ego and protect against ego-wounds—but also the fear of loss of love.

This suggests a psychological overlap between dispositional envy and jealousy, which, as we saw, can both stem from childhood sibling rivalries. And this is probably the reason why anger is so prominent in envy and jealousy, especially the latter, and why anger, envy, and jealousy deserve the label, the nasty emotions. As with all emotions, anger, envy, and jealousy are relational—that is, they are dependent on both environmental and person characteristics, and on the personal meanings an individual constructs out of the ongoing and changing person-environment relationship.

EXISTENTIAL EMOTIONS

Existential emotions are reactions to threats to our identity as persons in the societies in which we live; they concern who we are, what we stand for, and our fate in life. They are, of course, stress emotions. The most obvious existential emotions are anxiety-fright, guilt, and shame. This does not mean that other emotions, such as anger and hope, do not contain existential issues; they do. The existential side of most of our emotions, all or most of which have existential aspects, is under-emphasized in emotion theory. These aspects also define the difference between acute emotions and moods (Lazarus, 1991a).

What is threatened in each of the existential emotions differs. *Anxiety-fright* centers on personal security, our place in the world, and issues of life and death, which make anxiety, especially, quite broad in scope. In *guilt,* the defining issue is our concept of morality and our commitment to it. Its threat to our social identity occurs when we engage in actions that involve moral lapses. In *shame,* the core issue is a failure to live up to ego ideals, which can impugn our basic character as a person (*see* Piers & Singer, 1971, among others who have made this distinction; e.g., H. B. Lewis, 1971).

Guilt and shame are always social because they deal with how we are viewed by others. A guilty or ashamed person might say, "I could see my mother staring at me in disapproval or disgust." However, both emotions require that disapproval be internalized, which leads us to become our own worst critics. Self-blame, which originally required disapproval of a parent, an important caretaker, or our peer group, ultimately becomes crucial for both emotions.

So the physical presence of someone else is not necessary to arouse guilt or shame because, in addition to what others might think, we have internalized many of the same social standards, and know full well that we have violated one or more of these standards. But in addition to the silent, punitive voice within us, which we refer to as conscience and ego ideal, just the thought that what we have done would be regarded as reprehensible by persons from the past can arouse guilt or shame, even if they are no longer alive, as long as we believe they would have disapproved.

Guilt and shame, and other closely related emotions, such as embarrassment and pride, are referred to by many psychologists as the *self-conscious* emotions. Recent and revealing discussions of them have been published in Lewis & Haviland (1993); Lewis, Sullivan, Stanger, & Weiss (1989); Tangney & Fischer (1995); and others.

One of the important issues about all emotions, as well as the self-conscious emotions, consists of how and when in childhood or adulthood these emotions develop. In what I consider a *tour de force* Mascolo and Fischer (1995) have made a splendid analysis of the childhood development of pride, shame, and guilt, which shows the power of the appraisal concept to fuel productive and rational ideas about this development. They define pride as the appraisal that one is responsible for socially valued outcomes.

Beginning with pride as a prototype for the developmental steps involved in these emotions, these authors (1995, p. 69) emphasize the dynamic skills that evolve in early childhood, which they regard as a "tool kit for mapping self-evaluative emotional development." Skills refer to the power to act in ways that affect the environment (including other persons). They evolve on the basis of what the child learns at different periods of its development about the contingencies between its own actions and the physical and social environment.

About this they write (1995, p. 70):

Skills develop through four basic tiers, which first emerge at different age periods. Each tier is defined in terms of a different skill unit: "reflexes" (beginning at birth), "sensorimotor actions" (beginning at about 3–4 months) "representations" (beginning at about 18–24 months), and "abstractions" or generalizations about how one is compared with others (beginning at about 10–12 years). Each tier builds upon the preceding one in the sense that skills at a later tier emerge from hierarchical reorganizations of skills at the prior tier, with complex systems at one tier producing a new unit of behavior at the next tier.

Drawing on research observations of their own and those of many others, they suggest that in step 1, the child connects a simple act to a goal-related positive outcome, as in experiencing enjoyment at dropping a toy block and seeing it fall to the floor. In step 2, the child connects its actions with goal-related positive outcomes, including the reactions of others. There is a big jump from step 2 to step 3 when the child begins to attribute the result of its actions to the self, and when later on it senses that this is to be regarded as good; when the infant throws a block, sees it fly through the air, and hears mother or father react approvingly, it comes to understand that it has been responsible for a positive social value and feels proud.

Ultimately, the child recognizes these performances as indicating a positive trait (I'm good at this, or whatever), and is able to manipulate such ideas about self and others abstractly. What I called the *tour de force* is the extension of the idea of appraisal to a detailed examination of what is being appraised and how it changes as the self-conscious emotions develop step by step into adult pride, guilt, and shame. For readers who want to see appraisal in concrete, developmental terms, I commend them to this thoughtful, logical, and potentially useful analysis of these three emotions. Parallel developmental analyses could be made for all other emotions as well.

All three emotions—anxiety, guilt, and shame—could be said to be characterized by different kinds of anxiety, each having a different provocation. Nonbeing or *death anxiety* is the underlying concern of anxiety-fright. *Guilt anxiety* is concerned with moral lapses, and *shame anxiety* is concerned with the failure to live up to an ego ideal. There seems to be no problem differentiating anxiety from both guilt and shame, but guilt and shame have important overlaps that tend to obscure the distinction between them. Let us explore each of the three existential emotions in turn.

ANXIETY-FRIGHT

We have three conceptual choices for anxiety and fright. One is to treat them as separate and to some extent different emotions; a second is to regard them as one emotion with two subvarieties; a third is to overlook their differences and treat them as one. On the basis of substantial differences, it is a mistake to view them as the same and sensible to emphasize their substantive differences. This is the purpose of the hyphen between them, so we can see their close connections and, at the same time, see their substantial differences.

Let us begin with fright, which is by far the simpler of the two emotions. The core relational theme for fright is facing a sudden and overwhelming concrete physical danger. Here are some common examples: The airplane in which we are traveling suddenly blows up, dives toward the ground, or springs a fire in the midst of a flight; still alive, we are confronted with the strong possibility, or perhaps near certainty, of imminent death. A tornado is heading directly toward one's residence and is too close to adequately prepare for it. Someone is firing an automatic weapon into a crowd in which we are present.

Well, you get the idea. We are in immediate danger of being seriously injured or killed by a life-threatening emergency. Our emotional experience is likely to be fright or panic, along with exceedingly strong physiological mobilization. The imminent disaster dominates our perceptions as we struggle to assess what is happening and what, if anything, might be done about it. Fright is sudden and usually short-lived; the danger either passes, or we are injured or killed.

In contrast, anxiety is quite a different experience. The synonyms of the emotion, such as apprehension, unease, concern, and worry, suggest this. It is usually slow and vague, a diffuse, continuing, anticipatory state of unease. The concrete danger being faced in anxiety may be that we shall not get the job for which we are applying, fail to pass the test, do poorly in an interview or other performance, fail to cover one's debts, be unable to pay the rent, raise one's children, or discover that we are seriously ill with a life-threatening disease, perhaps dying slowly from cancer or suffering from chest pain and breathing difficulties, which suggest the presence of a serious cardiovascular disease. If we seem to be undergoing an acute heart attack, the chronic or recurrent anxiety about our well-being may turn into fright.

Concrete dangers, however, usually carry a further momentous implication. They express dangers to our ego identity, that is, who we are, where we are headed, and the ultimate loss of our ego identity in death, which is why anxiety is referred to as the existential emotion par excellence. The core relational theme of anxiety is, therefore, facing an uncertain, existential threat (Lazarus & Averill, 1972).

It is not just the immediate, concrete dangers with which we must deal—that is, the difficult examination, poor performance, or the life-threatening disease. Even more important, they express our concern about dying and ultimate nonbeing. The fact that we cannot say what dying or death will be like, or when it will occur, adds to the existential burden from which all humankind has always suffered and which has been a major theme of great literature. And it is the uncertainty connected with the threat being faced that is distinctive of anxiety.

Anxiety is ubiquitous yet unique as an emotion in the lives of sentient creatures—that is, those who are conscious of their experience and can sense, if not verbalize, the future. The uncertainty mobilizes much of what we do in life but often interferes with our constructive efforts. For these and other reasons, anxiety was once regarded by psychologists as the central emotion in human adaptation and psychopathology. Much of *abnormal psychology*—a common term for psychopathology during the 1930s and in several later decades—was centered on anxiety as the drive or motivation for pathogenic modes of coping, such as neurosis and psychosis.

In later years, however, psychology began to broaden its view of psychopathology to include other emotions, such as anger, guilt, shame, and depression, but with one important difference—namely, there was no monopolistic assumption that any one of these emotions was the psychological touchstone of psychopathology. All our emotions, both negatively and positively toned, reflect basic human dilemmas, conflicts, and sources of pleasure and joy; they are capable of indicating, if not fomenting, distress and dysfunction. Failure to cope adequately with our emotions and the conditions that bring them about is an important basis of psychopathology. In recent years, our analyses have increasingly emphasized the coping process in the search for understanding about the sources of dysfunction.

There has also been a major change in how we look at the emotions themselves. In the 1930s through the early 1960s, the focus was on emotions as independent variables—that is, how they affected adaptive thought and problem solving. A surfeit of studies showed that anxiety impaired human functioning, and a great deal of debate occurred about how this worked. The dominant theory has been that anxiety displaced other drive concerns and interfered with the thought process (Easterbrook, 1959).

Later, however, with the advent of the so-called cognitive revolution in the 1960s and 1970s, emotions came to be viewed as dependent variables too (Lazarus, 1968)—that is, research interest turned to the antecedent (causal) conditions resulting in the emotions. Cognitive and motivational psychological activity were said to play a causal role in the arousal of each of the emotions, reversing the previous emphasis that emotions impaired thought. Both ways of thinking are correct, but each represents only part the story about how the three main constructs of mind—cognition, motivation, and emotion—were interrelated. These changes played a part in the early stirring of appraisal theory.

GUILT

The core relational theme, and the provocation of guilt is having transgressed a moral imperative. If we have harmed someone, this adds to the pangs of guilt. But feeling guilt is a very complex matter. There are apt to be great individual differences, and how each of us is affected by guilt depends on our distinctive personalities and social relationships.

On the input side, for guilt to be aroused, most psychologists agree that there has to have been a moral transgression, either imagined or in reality. On the response side, guilt motivates a desire to atone, and even to be punished, whereas shame motivates an effort to hide one's failing, or to cope by externalizing the blame. So anger can be a way of coping with shame, which also points to the psychic interdependence of the emotions, a theme often missed in the way the dynamics of emotion are commonly described. Though we can make educated guesses, we know little about the kinds of circumstances or types of person that shape the process of externalizing blame.

A moral transgression can often be expiated by apology or making amends, leading to the weakening or elimination of the feeling of guilt (Ohbushi, Kameda, & Agarie, 1989). Religious variants for managing guilt include the Day of Atonement (Rosh Hashanah) in Judaism and in the Catholic ritual of confession. Their role in our psychological economy is an interesting question. The human capacity to assign blame or rationalize actions is also a self-serving limitation of our cultural systems of morality.

In early Christianity, the concept of original sin led to the urge for self-inflicted punishment, as manifested in the cult of self-flagellation during the bubonic plague in the 14th century, which was known as the "black death" because of changes in the skin color of the victims. Groups of Christians paraded in the streets, whipping themselves and each other, presumably trying to mollify God, just as many ancient peoples did through human sacrifice because they interpreted their society's misfortunes as a result of their deity's anger.

Guilt can refer to a specific, limited act that does not necessarily impugn one's character; one can feel guilty about it while remaining a good person. It can, however, extend to one's overall character, in which case we see ourselves as immoral or bad persons. This can apply to both guilt and shame, and we speak of such persons as guilt or shame ridden, and this overlap makes the differentiation of these emotions even more difficult.

Psychology has long assumed that guilt safeguards the moral values of a society. It does so by preventing offending actions, which presumably protects us from the psychological pain of guilt. Yet, as Freud pointed out in distinguishing between subjective guilt and legal guilt, there is, at best, only a modest correlation between feeling guilty and actually being guilty (cf., however, Mowrer's, 1976 dissenting voice on this). Some people feel guilty even though their lives have been led with strict probity, and others seem not to be much influenced in their actions by guilt feelings. Thus, the assumption about guilt as an emotion that protects moral social standards is more variable and complex than once thought.

Considering the psychological issues it is associated with, guilt is an extremely rich topic, and degree of interest in particular questions varies among social scientists. Some emphasize what makes us feel guilty. Is it, for example, that people feel guilty when they wish for something that is morally reprehensible even when they do not act on the wish? Or is this limited to certain kinds of people?

Other important questions have to do with the social and developmental origins of guilt (Zahn-Waxler & Kochanska, 1990), the role of learning and innate influences, the extent to which guilt is a trait as well as a state, the personal and social consequences of violations of social standards (Wicklund, 1975), the role of empathy in guilt (Hoffman, 1982), the contrast between the idea of universals and cultural sources of variation in the experience of guilt and the actions influenced by it (Shweder, 1993), and the extent to which it is more useful to emphasize behavioral, emotional, or cognitive components in the exploration of guilt; surely to consider all three makes the most sense.

SHAME

Like guilt, shame arises from a personal failure, most commonly in the presence of another person who disapproves of one's action or outlook. I noted earlier that this presence need not be literal, but can be fantasized or remembered, and there must be an internalized acceptance of the social proscription. So, like guilt, shame is a social emotion in that another person, whether present, imagined, or just remembered, can witness one's failure and criticize.

Because the disapproved action is apt to be regarded as a characterological failure, shame is one of the most distressing, devastating, and painful of all the emotions, and the most difficult emotion with which to cope. It is not the shame-provoking act per se that is devastating, but the implication that we deserve to be disgraced or humiliated. When a moral lapse is interpreted as a characterological failure, guilt can seem just as bad. So we must distinguish between two meanings of guilt and shame: one that is the result of a limited situational action that deserves disapproval and the other that is a hallmark of a reprehensible character.

The reader might remember that the red letter A in Hawthorne's classic novel, *The Scarlet Letter,* which Hester Pringle was forced to wear because of her acknowledged sexual infidelity, stamped her as a contemptible person and was a source of humiliation and shame. The implication of being a pariah also explains why the yellow stars forcibly worn by Jews in Germany by edict of the Nazis, were psychologically so offensive, undoubtedly a humiliation intended by the Nazi authorities, designed perhaps to induce helplessness and passivity (Frankl, 1959).

In the case of our African-American population, also facing a long history of prejudice and discrimination, the effort to convince themselves that Black is beautiful is a way of rejecting feelings of shame. The refusal to accept a negative, color-based social designation, and the weaker commitment to avoid giving a higher social standing to lighter-skinned Blacks, announces this rejection. This psychological process is apt to lead to resentment and anger rather than shame; blame is externalized rather than internalized. If we can feel pride in ourselves, despite public denigration, we are not experiencing shame, which requires collaboration between the person and the public view.

The core relational theme of shame is failure to live up to an ego ideal, which helps us distinguish shame from guilt. Shame is a discrepancy between what the person wants to be and the way that person is identified socially, whereas guilt is a moral lapse. The identity issue of shame, however, has nothing to do with a moral standard, but concerns one's ideal identity, which is usually derived from childhood influences that have been internalized. In a neo-Freudian analysis by H. B. Lewis (1971), the childhood roots of shame are said to be the threat of rejection or abandonment as a result of parental criticisms of a child's failure to live up to adult standards, this concern being unconscious.

For example, if our ego ideal is to be a sharp trader, a successful manipulator of people, or whatever positive values have been acquired during childhood, when such an ideal has been abrogated by our actions, the emotion is shame not guilt. Thus, to be a clever manipulator who is successful in a self-serving confidence game might be the ego ideal of some, though this does not fit the Judeo-Christian commitment to being honest and above-board.

Highly successful entrepreneurs might be ashamed to be taken in by a swindle, but might also subscribe to conventional morality and regard hurting people in the course of their acquisitive and power goals as unsavory (consider, for example, the case of J. C. Penny, the multimillionaire founder of a major retail chain). Thus, shame and guilt are the result of quite different kinds of social values: one focused on diverse traits that should be admired and the other centered on conventional ideas about morality. This input-based distinction between guilt and shame can often be subtle, which makes for considerable confusion about the differences between the two emotions.

The unconscious origins of shame, and its devastating implications, also mean that it is much more difficult to cope with the conditions bringing this emotion about than guilt. Guilt-ridden persons want to cry out publicly about their moral crime and gain forgiveness. Those who seek suffering for their sins are sometimes referred to as masochists. Shame-ridden persons, in contrast, want desperately to absolve themselves of the opprobrium of shame, to blame someone else if they can rather than accept their characterological defect.

Shame-ridden persons may be more prone to suicide, which is a common mode of coping in Japan when one's actions are condemned. This is a theme expressed poetically in the suicide of Madame Butterfly in Puccini's operatic masterpiece. After desertion by her American lover, Lieutenant Pinkerton returns to take away her illicit male child so he can be raised by Pinkerton and his new American wife. This places Butterfly in a hopeless position of loss of face. There is nothing left for her to live for, so she kills herself by the ritual of Sepuchre by disemboweling herself with a sword.

EMOTIONS PROVOKED BY UNFAVORABLE LIFE CONDITIONS

These include relief, hope, and sadness-depression, each of which is examined in turn.

RELIEF

This is the simplest of all emotions, cognitively speaking. It begins with a frustrating or threatening life condition, one from which we would all be glad to be freed. It is called relief because the negative condition, an important threat, has either not materialized or has changed for the better. I resist equating relief with happiness, which is, in itself, a positive state of mind, which is brought about by something desirable rather than merely a cessation of misery or anxiety.

Consider a loved one who has been medically diagnosed as having a life-threatening or incapacitating ailment. The loved one and, of course, the ill person, are greatly worried about what will happen. They await word about a biopsy, which will reveal what must be faced. Relief comes suddenly from the doctor's statement that the condition is not serious, the symptoms being readily treatable and certain to disappear. This information brings a sudden change in the emotional state of both persons from anxiety or dread to relief.

Relief can follow any stress emotion, such as guilt or shame over what we have done as well as anxiety, anger, and jealousy, if and when its consequences turn out to be less damaging than we had feared. The concern may have existed for quite a while, but the relief is virtually instantaneous once we learn that whatever was of concern has eased or gone away. We are freed from the previous distress and can turn our attention to other agendas.

Some might question whether relief is really an emotion. After all, it constitutes a reduction or cessation of emotional distress rather than an increase in emotional arousal. This is an ambiguity, however, only if we define an emotion as an increase in arousal. It would be better to say that relief is an emotional state because, after the good news, there is a change to a less distressing frame of mind. The emphasis here is on change rather than the direction of change, which also allows us to treat sadness as an emotion. Because it refers to a situation in which nothing can be done to restore what has been lost, sadness involves lowered rather than raised arousal.

HOPE

As in the case of relief, hope is a state of mind in which a positive outcome has not yet occurred but is sought, most often under an unfavorable situation. It is not clear whether hope is more often linked to negative life conditions than to positive ones. Elsewhere (Lazarus, 1991), I identified the core relational theme of hope as fearing the worst but yearning for better. The provocation for hope is a threatening but uncertain condition. Uncertainty permits hope to occur because, if all favorable options are foreclosed, this yearning state of mind is difficult to bring about. Hope is also an anticipatory emotion, its focus being the future, whereas relief is an outcome emotion because it occurs after a distressing problem has abated or gone away.

At different times and in different cultures (e.g., in Ancient Greece), hope was considered more of a bane than a boon, whereas in modern Christian lore, hope is one of the virtues, as in faith, hope, and charity. The ambivalence comes, in part, from the dilemma about the origins of hope and from the modern clinical impression that hope is certainly better than despair. There are probably great individual differences in the disposition to hope, as expressed in the aphorism about people whose cup is always half full (the optimist) or half-empty (the pessimist). But optimism refers to positive expectations whenever there is uncertainty, which is seldom the main connotation of hope.

As in the cases of relief and sadness, we can raise the question of whether hope is truly an emotion. A logical option is to treat it a coping process rather than an emotion. Recent evidence (Folkman, Chesney, & Christopher-Richards, 1994; Stein, Folkman, Trabasso, & Richards, 1997), which I discussed in chapter 6 under the topic of chronic stress, suggests that victims of severe, unrelenting stress can only draw on small pleasures that may give them some joy despite being depressed, presumably keeping hope alive in an effort to cope. Such persons—for example, those caring for a partner dying of AIDS (Lazarus, Kanner, & Folkman,1980)—make more of small sources of pleasure than others more favorably situated to sustain themselves. In such a situation, hope could be considered a mode of coping.

As people are dying or facing the death of a loved one, hope of recovery may wane. But it is not necessarily abandoned altogether, though it seems to narrow in scope. Thus, when a lengthy remission of symptoms is no longer credible, one hopes to have just another good day, or a few hours in which to be without pain and able to communicate clearly to loved ones. We cling to a very modest benefit to avoid despair and perhaps even to remain sanguine.

SADNESS-DEPRESSION

Like anxiety-fright, sadness and depression are also hyphenated to indicate both their close relationship and important differences. Sadness is an emotion whose core relational theme is experiencing an irrevocable loss.

Depression is often theorized to be the result of a sense of hopelessness about restoring a worthwhile life following major loss. While being emotional, it is not a single emotion but a complex emotional state, a mixture of several emotions that come and go depending on where one is in the process of grieving and what has happened to produce the loss. The emotions of depression consist of anxiety, anger, guilt and shame. These are the emotions of struggle against one's fate because we have not yet given up on changing it. In the early stages of grieving, there is sometimes a compelling fantasy that what was lost will be returned; for example, the dead spouse is not dead but will suddenly reappear, perhaps at the door as in the past at the end of a day's work. The person is not yet ready to accept the finality of the loss, though he or she is often despairing, which is what depression usually means.

The anxiety of depression occurs because the loss threatens our longstanding identity and betokens uncertainty about how we will live in the future. Anger occurs because we resent the failure of doctors or others, perhaps even ourselves, to care more adequately for the lost person. Or, paradoxically, we are angry at the dead person who deserted us. Guilt arises from the impression that our role in the death was negative, from the failure to have properly appreciated the dead one when he or she was alive, from our anger in life toward the deceased loved one, or from having survived when the loved one did not, which we refer to as survivor guilt. Shame arises from the sense that our role in the past or in the loss reflects badly on our character.

In sadness, there is no longer any hope of restoring what has been lost. For wistful sadness rather than depression to be our state of mind, the loss must be accepted as irrevocable—that is, we know that what has been lost cannot be restored. In other words, after a major loss, psychological work must be done to view it in a relatively benign way, in which past, present, and future are somehow reconciled. This, and the absence of coping actions, makes sadness different from other emotions. The mood in sadness is also not despairing.

Only when the loss has been accepted, or one is reconciled to it, can we get on with our life. Sociologists and anthropologists point out that the rituals of death—for example, viewing the body at the funeral and, in the Jewish religion, going to the cemetery a year later, help us to realize the person is gone and allow us to celebrate our connection with the dead person who is now at peace or whom we might have previously felt we did not fully appreciate while alive. This is what the struggle of grief is all about, which is not an emotion, but an emotional coping process. Depending on what has happened in the past and present, and how it is construed, not everyone has such an intense and difficult emotional struggle.

EMPATHIC EMOTIONS

These emotions include gratitude and compassion, both of which require the capacity for empathy, which means to place ourselves emotionally in the shoes of a suffering person. Although this capacity is often assumed to be universal in humans, it seems to vary for reasons that remain obscure, perhaps some combination of genetic influences or life experiences. Sociopaths—that is, persons who manipulate others in a self-centered way—are a case in point. They can be charming and effective, so they must have a solid intellectual, if not emotional, understanding of other people's emotions. But they do not display the humane spark of empathy.

GRATITUDE

In what way might the emotion of gratitude depend on empathy? Is not the gift giver the one who must have empathy in recognizing and responding to another's need by bestowing an altruistic gift? Making a big show of a gift can be clumsy and hurtful under certain circumstances, which makes the problem of the recipient psychologically more difficult.

Actually, however, the one who receives a gift too must be sensitive about this because giving and receiving is always a two-way relationship between a donor and a recipient, and often a far more complex one than appears on the surface. The complexity is telegraphed to the recipient in the expression, an altruistic gift, which I used earlier. If the recipient of the gift views the donor as self-serving—for example, if the gift is designed to obligate the recipient in a quid pro quo arrangement, to show superiority, to earn gratitude, to make the recipient feel bad, or to demonstrate generosity to the world—the recipient may resist the gift and become offended and angry rather than grateful. Then, any spoken thank you is apt to be grudging.

The whole process of gift giving and receiving, and the gratitude that may follow it, depends on a complex pattern of subtle social meanings that shape the emotions experienced in either role. It is not always easy for the donor to disguise the venal intent behind the gift giving, in which case the recipient does not feel gratitude, though it may be disingenuously affected because evidence of gratitude is expected. The core relational theme for gratitude is appreciating an altruistic gift that provides personal benefit.

The donor and recipient may or may not view gratitude in the same way. For example, the donor may believe, incorrectly, that he or she has only the well-being of the recipient in mind, but the recipient may know better. And the recipient may believe, incorrectly, that the gift is altruistic. Or, both partners in the exchange may be deceived in either respect.

One of the interesting variations in this mutual dance of giving and receiving is that doing something for another is also the job of certain professions, such as a nurse, physician, or public employer. Then we do not normally feel grateful unless the person has gone out of his way to help. Conversely, if we expect poor treatment from people in these professions, we may feel grateful simply for the good grace or integrity with which the job has been done.

Needs of a recipient are an important basis for the motivation for giving and for accepting the gift. On the surface, one would think from this that the more needy a person, the greater the feeling of gratitude. The reverse often turns out to be true, however, especially when recipients believe their needs are unjust or a source of shame. In such a case, the donor may be resented, and the recipient may feel entitled to what is given. One of the bitter political struggles of our times is the conservative political effort to eliminate entitlements, such as welfare payments or unemployment insurance, and the liberal effort to resist such a trend, mainly in the interest of preserving the pride and integrity of needy persons.

COMPASSION

This too is an emotion that is based on empathy and may well be uniquely human (Hoffman, 1982). In compassion, we are in tune with the other person's suffering or joy, though the term is usually used in connection with unhappy conditions of life. Another word is pity, but this seems to convey a condescending or disdainful message. The Spanish word, *simpatico,* seems to get the idea right.

Compassion is not simply duplicating or mirroring what the other person feels, but is an emotion of its own that a person who is compassionate feels about a suffering other. Our own version of suffering can never be identical in detail and depth with another person's. The meaning of compassion is that we understand something of what the other person is going through and want to help if possible. In Lazarus (1991), the core relational theme of compassion was defined as being moved by another's suffering and wanting to help, which seems to capture the meaning.

The goal of compassion in a relative, lover, or friend is easy to understand. We are committed to the well-being of those we love, so our goal is to see them secure and happy, and we become distressed to see things go badly for them. But if we are not distressed or are ambivalent because of rivalry, we feel guilt or shame as well as perhaps compassion.

Compassion for strangers is more complicated, however. What explains it? Why do we place ourselves figuratively in the shoes of the one who suffers? One good explanation is that we could experience their plight, so we are attracted to it to understand it better and perhaps protect ourselves on the basis of what we learn.

Another good answer comes from Lerner's (1980) ideas about the need to believe in a world that is just, even when it is not. If innocent people and children who are usually the worst victims of human depredation and war suffer needlessly, justice is violated, and we are made anxious lest the world must be viewed as chaotic, making us seem subject to the same dismal fate. So we make a psychic commitment to a just world and are threatened if our view of it is undermined. Thus, suffering in someone else, even a stranger, is distressing, and we want to make things right. One way of coping with injustice is to blame the victim. In that way we explain the bad fate of victims as just—in effect, we see them as having brought the disaster on themselves, and, therefore, they deserve to suffer.

Compassion is, however, a double-edged sword. If we are too compassionate, and suffer too much, we can be seen as having abandoned our own interests. So we must protect ourselves against unbridled compassion. Too much compassion, paradoxically, can impair our ability to help. To help, we must steel ourselves so as not to fall apart in the face of another's tragic distress.

To cope effectively, and help those who suffer, we must learn how to distance ourselves emotionally from the emotional significance of their suffering, so it does not overwhelm us. Yet in doing so we must not turn away too far from our humanitarian instincts, lest we appear cold and unsympathetic. Doctors, nurses, those who do psychotherapy, and emergency and disaster teams, do this all the time, and could not do their jobs if they failed to learn how to distance to protect themselves from burnout, while still observing with care and handling things to employ their skills effectively.

An impressive lesson about this comes from the experiences of disaster teams immediately after the Loma Prieta earthquake in Oakland, California, on October 17, 1989. Somewhat less than a mile of the Cypress Street viaduct of the Interstate 880 Freeway collapsed during rush hour, which killed and buried 42 people and injured 108. Forty-seven male workers were charged with cleaning up the mess, which meant recovering the dead and maimed bodies from their buried cars.

A fascinating study by Stuhlmiller (1996) throws light on the emotional experience of these men and how they coped with it. One of them described an attempt to reassure himself that the victims died without suffering. He provides a graphic account of the distressing task and his struggle to handle the situation without falling apart. You can see in the subsequent description, which pulls together a number of different statements that are not always in logical order, how he ruminates about whether the people died quickly enough not to have experienced prolonged suffering, which he appears to need to believe. You can see that the workman is struggling with his tendency to identify with the victims, which means to imagine himself in the same situation.

> We pulled other bodies out that night. Looking at it, trying to analyze it in my mind, it was easy to see, again, trying to make myself comfortable with it from the standpoint that he died on impact, he died quick. He probably saw it coming, but he died awful quick. The woman, I always had some grave reservations as to whether or not she died right away. Again, in the back of my mind, it bothered me that if these people didn't die right away. At the time I remember thinking, my God, should we have gotten to them quicker, could we have saved their lives?
>
> She was positioned in the seat almost as if she rebounded that way, fine. If she didn't rebound in it, she was kind of turned sideways looking toward the driver. So I really had a gut feeling, my God, she didn't die right away, she was still conscious and she was trying to talk to her boyfriend, husband, brother, whoever the guy was, and yet you know he died right away because nobody could take a chest blow like that and take out the entire steering column and live through it. So that bothered me for a long time. I'm better with it now (pp. 155–156).

Throughout the interviews, Stuhlmiller shows us how the awful smell of decay, torn bodies, and the ugly task of cutting body parts to free the victims from their entombment in the wreckage, created a scene that was difficult to cope with emotionally. The sights and smells communicated a terrible meaning about the nature of a violent death. Most of the men coped by distancing, by means of which they tried not to assimilate fully the emotional significance of what they were seeing, while doing the work appropriately, which meant looking carefully at the scene to free the mangled bodies. Their distress seems palpable, and you can almost feel them struggle not to be overwhelmed by it.

I have been portraying distancing as an asset, a necessary way to do what one must in dealing with tragedy. However, in a fascinating set of speculations during the Vietnam War, distancing is treated as a form of inhumanity, as when we use it to keep from feeling compassion for the enemy by dehumanizing them (Bernard, Ottenberg, & Redl, 1965). If the enemy can be viewed as less than human, we can avoid identifying with their suffering or fate, so that it need not be taken seriously nor felt as their own. In so doing, we could watch some of the war being fought on television, and become habituated to evil, a price society pays for our ability to protect ourselves in this way.

EMOTIONS PROVOKED BY FAVORABLE
LIFE CONDITIONS

I turn now to three so-called positively toned emotions: happiness-joy, pride, and love. We saw earlier that even these emotions are not necessarily free of stress, sometimes arising directly from stress or negative conditions of life, as in the case of relief and hope, sometimes provoking stress, as in the fear of getting sandbagged by a happy event, being turned against by others because of unseemly pride, or becoming sensitive to the idea one's loved one does not return the feeling of love sufficiently. Nevertheless, these emotions are considered to be positively toned because much of the time the conditions that arouse them make us feel good.

HAPPINESS-JOY

With respect to its provocation, we speak, perhaps sardonically, of happiness as buying a new car, having the love of a good man or woman, engaging in productive work, and getting what one wants. Happiness is often treated in this way, superficially, making it center on shallow objectives and trivialities, which contributes to the widespread misunderstanding of this emotion.

This state of mind really has two meanings, reflected in the two hyphenated words in the heading: happiness, which is a calm sentiment—or perhaps it should be called a positive assessment of one's general well-being (Diener, 1984)—and joy, which is a strong emotional state provoked by events that show one's life is going well. Joy, which centers on a desirable occurrence, is also characterized by psychophysiological excitement (deRivera, Possell, Verette, & Weiner, 1989) rather than merely a tempered (or cool) but positive assessment of one's well-being.

The two meanings create much confusion because it is not always easy to tell which the writer or speaker means, the tempered sentiment or the strong emotion. As a sentiment, being happy refers to a positive assessment of one's life, though the sentiment may also serve as a disposition to react to a provocation with the feeling of joy when something positive has happened in our life.

If we were to put words in the mouth of the person reporting this intellectual kind of happiness, it might be expressed in a cool, detached tone, such as "I am better off than most," or by making a judgment on a scale designed to measure well-being. One uses such descriptively mild words as cheerful, gay, glad, and playful, which describe calm, positive satisfaction about one's life.

The emotion of joy is a different kettle of fish, as expressed in its synonyms—for example, gleeful, delighted, jubilant, exultant, euphoric, and elated. The person says with enthusiasm, "I feel happy or joyful," emphasizing the emotion rather than the more intellectual assessment of one's overall well-being. Persons in such a state may be so excited about what gives them joy that they are totally distracted from what is going on about them.

Oddly enough, although most people would say that one of their life objectives is to be happy, we know relatively little about the causation of happiness or joy. It is not fruitful to speak of this as a goal of life because there is no consistent way to pursue it, given the vagueness of what it means to be happy and the elusiveness of what brings such a state about (*see*, for example, Veenhoven, 1990, for an examination of different ideologies and attitudes about happiness).

Anyway, what is often said about this seems quite wrong. For example, the notion that happiness or joy comes from getting what one wants seems especially shallow when we look carefully at what actually happens when an important goal is sought, then attained, say, an advanced degree on which we are working, an award signifying success in our main occupation, marriage with the person (man or woman) we have been courting, and so on. Commonly there is joy, or at least great pleasure, and a sense of contentment for a short time, perhaps days, sometimes a few months, but joy from such an attainment ends early as the realities of living set in.

We cannot live in the past, but need an encore, so to speak, and we must get on with the next task or stage of life. An advanced degree is not the end of striving, but we soon discover it is a beginning, a preparation for a job that we must seek, or an opportunity for an entry point into the professional life it makes possible. The same applies to an award, which is certainly a most positive experience, but we are usually able to bask in it for only a little while before we proceed to further goals, perhaps to justify others' faith in us.

The same can be said for the positive result of courting. We all know that viewing marriage as an ending in which the couple lived happily ever after is movie fantasy. The most important tasks follow marriage rather then precede it, and even a good marriage has its ups and downs as well as, sometimes, tragedy. Those who believe the happily-ever-after fiction are likely to be shocked and dismayed at what follows. Besides, getting what we think we want is not always a source of pleasure or joy.

Having been saying this for years, and rarely seeing it discussed, imagine my surprise when I saw a recent *New York Times* article by Fran Bruni (1998). Bruni uses several stories of sports figures, such as Greg Louganis, who won a silver medal in the 1976 Olympics, two golds in 1984, and another two in 1988. Diving could be said to be his life. In looking back, he says he mainly misses the training. For some time he wondered what he would do next, finding a new goal that would replace the Olympic gold. We appear to need a sense of purpose, but it is not the achievement that counts in the long run but striving toward it.

Perhaps this is why Aristotle viewed happiness as the fullest use of one's physical and mental resources—as a process rather than an outcome. Treating happiness-joy as an outcome is justified in only a temporary sense, but it is not sufficient in the long run. The ways we should measure the two meanings of happiness must also be different to reflect their conceptual differences.

The distinction between outcome and process is the main reason I define the core relational theme of happiness-joy as making reasonable progress toward the realization of a goal. This theme emphasizes the process of living and doing more than the attainment of goals, which is often disappointing. This outlook tends to trivialize the provocation for happiness as an event or a transaction compared with the continuing engagement in striving and doing. If we say, as Aristotle does, of happiness as living, doing, and using one's intellectual and bodily resources to the fullest, the provocation for happiness or joy becomes less an event or occasion, and more a continuing process. This is a difficult but important lesson to learn as early as possible in life.

PRIDE

On the surface, pride appears to overlap considerably with happiness, but they are quite different in relational meaning. The core relational theme of pride is enhancing one's self or ego identity by taking credit for a valued object or achievement, either our own or that of someone or group with whom we identify. Notice that what this relational meaning does is to emphasize taking credit, an opposite state of mind from accepting blame.

This distinctive meaning is a product of David Hume's (1957) famous analysis of the differences between happiness and pride. Pride is not only the result of a positive event or condition that makes us feel happy—for example, a beautiful home, an achievement, evidence of knowledge or wealth, a contribution to society, bravery, or fortitude—it is also a transaction that enhances our sense of personal worth or adds to our social position. The achievement may be our own, that of our child, or a group or team with which we identify.

When the San Francisco 49er football team wins in the superbowl, it is a victory for many people who merely reside in that city, even those who contributed nothing to the team or the game. Each views it is his own team and feels proud, thereby implicitly taking credit for its success. They feel expansive about the victory, some expressing this with celebrations long into the night of the game, or applauding the victorious team as they come home.

But pride is not unequivocally a positively toned emotion; it can also produce social opprobrium. The negative side of pride is expressed in numerous aphorisms that warn of overweening pride (which can be called hubris), deprecate a proud person as having a swelled head, or as in the biblical incantation, "pride goethe before a fall." Thus, in our society, a person should not brag or boast too much because it can be taken as a put-down of others.

In the American song, "You're a Grand Old Flag," one of its lines proudly boasts that we are "the land of the free and the home of the brave, but another line says, "with never a boast or a brag," to present ourselves as properly humble. The two opposing ideas suggest the ambivalence we have about pride. This is also implied by the fact that our value system also welcomes humility, while at the same time applauding those who thrust themselves forward aggressively. Japanese show this ambivalence too. In Japan if one's child or spouse is complimented, the parent is apt to shrug off the praise, as if to deny the compliment, though this is probably to avoid an unseemly display of pride even though the parent still feels proud inwardly.

The ambivalence about the morality or propriety of pride is also illustrated in our society when celebrities must be careful not to seem too arrogant or prideful about their favorable social position. The public admires them greatly but, at the same time, feels envious. So to avoid alienating people whose approbation is, after all, the basis of their often fragile fame, celebrities often make displays of humility to ward off disapproval, sometimes even pointing to the pathos of their lives in public interviews, presumably to gain sympathy and to deter envy and hostility.

Another great social harm that can stem from feeling unduly proud of self, country, race, ethnicity, or religion—the latter four versions are spoken of ethnocentrism, or in my generation, gingoism—is making negative evaluations of other groups. This is a state of mind in which we devalue outgroups, even to the point of suspicion, contempt, and hatred. It is one thing to feel pride in country, race, ethnicity, or religion, but still another to insult or humiliate other groups, a practice that is widespread and that, not uncommonly, leads to cruel and destructive wars and genocide. Pride is a double-edged sword that must be managed with subtlety and care.

LOVE

When people are asked to mention emotions, love is usually high on their list. Most people think of love as a highly positive emotional state. Yet this surely depends on the circumstances and person. Love can be exhilarating, wonderful, and a unique state of mind. Most people also want to love and to be loved.

Under unfavorable circumstances, however, and in the hands of people who do not know what to do with it, love can also be a source of misery. For example, if you love someone who does not love you in return, or what is called unrequited love (Baumeister & Wotman, 1992), this condition of life can be pure misery. Not only is your own love frustrated, but the rejection may also be taken as an assault on your self-esteem. Somerset Maugham's novel, *Of Human Bondage,* graphically depicts the love of an insecure man with a club foot who becomes an emotional slave of a shallow and thoughtless women who does not reciprocate his feelings.

Love often involves uncertainties about whether one is loved in return, even if the uncertainty is based on self-doubts rather than actual evidence of indifference on the part of the loved one. In such cases, there will be times of great distress. So love, which is so often idealized in literature, is seldom a simple or long-sustained emotional state of mind involving only happiness-joy (Kemper, 1978).

As with other states of mind, such as happiness or hostility, love is both a sentiment and an emotional state. When two people are in love, even if the early stage of courtship and affirmation involves both yearning and actualization, the lovers have to deal with the ordinary, mundane life demands and struggles, which occupy their attention while they are lovers. One's business or profession, the care of children, schooling, and dealing with parents and friends, all focus the attention of both partners on the relationship, each exacting its own special sources of stress as well as producing happiness-joy.

It is not as though love is the only emotion experienced in a love relationship, but that love as an emotion must take its turn in the total adaptational process required in an intimate relationship. The typical pattern of love consists of many emotions as the relationship shifts from one life context and issue to another, leading to occasions of anger, anxiety, guilt, shame, relief, hope, gratitude, compassion, joy, and pride—in fact, the entire gamut of the emotions—each a product of the struggle of two people to attain their individual and joint goals. Love is not always at the center of the two minds, so we can speak of love as a general sentiment that disposes both parties to experience feelings of love but in which there are many other emotional agendas, not all of them positively toned.

Several different kinds of love have been distinguished. For a rich analysis of eight types of love, see Sternberg (1986, 1987), whose theory of love involves three components, intimacy, passion, and decision-commitment (*see also* Hendrick & Hendrick, 1989, for criticisms). The types of love described by Sternberg include infatuation, liking, empty love (without intimacy and passion), fatuous love (a combination of passion and decision-commitment without intimacy), consummate love (in which decision-commitment combine with passion and intimacy), companionate love, which can be further divided into maternal and paternal—that is, the love between parent and child—and love of friends.

Companionate love is different from romantic love, especially in that the love of parent and child, or of friends, is usually desexualized, although child sexual abuse does occur, and not infrequently, and the child's feelings about a parent can also have a sexual overtone or yearning, often unconscious, as in the Freudian Oedipus complex so richly described in D. H. Lawrence in the novel *Sons and Lovers.*

The core relational theme for love in the general sense is desiring or participating in affection, usually but not necessarily reciprocated. The provocation for romantic love is a meeting of lovers, whether heterosexual or homosexual, and mutual behavior that suggest interest in one or both parties, which is followed up in what we call courtship. This is fueled, in part, by sexual maturation in teenagers, and the influence of hormones at all ages.

Fehr (1988) has attempted a prototypical analysis of the concepts of love and commitment, and performed several studies designed to test it. Her approach to prototype, however, is quite different from my narrative version. Her research was designed to determine whether love and commitment are necessarily conjoined in the popular or lay conception. In other words, love is not treated as a story about an ongoing relationship, but consists of a set of analytic components, the research task being to identify what those components are.

Aron and Westbay (1996) adopt a similar view of the attempt to define love and assess how it is seen by ordinary people. These authors are also concerned with the components of passion, intimacy, and commitment, which are studied by asking people to identify what they consider the central features of love. Their research confirms this three-factor concept of the love prototype. Like Fehr's, it is a structural approach, whereas a narrative approach is always process centered in that it offers a dynamic portrait of the ongoing process of loving, including falling in love as well as a prototypical storyline and its main variations.

As Aron and Westbay (1996, p. 548) put it:

> in these studies we found that the basic three-dimensional structure applies to both how one thinks about love in general (its prototype structure) and how one experiences love (how one describes one's own, actual love relationship).

Along with the prototypical structure, one also finds great individual differences in the answers to these questions. I submit, however, that a narrative portrait of love, which can also display individual variation as well as different varieties of love, comes closer to the dynamics of diverse love relationships, and is easier to understand, because it relates to the fluctuating experience of a love relationship, which most of us have experienced.

Love is also tangled up with cultural values and our outlook toward it has changed greatly over the centuries, which complicates the work of researchers such as Fehr, and Aron and Westbay. Love was at one time in Western history not considered relevant to marriage, which was arranged entirely as a business matter. However, the desire for loving and supportive relationships has probably always been a focus of humanity, even when marriages were arranged and love de-emphasized.

This desire led to the emergence of romantic relationships, which were emphasized in ancient Romanesque literature and later in Western society from the early Middle Ages on, especially in English fiction in the 13th century, as exemplified in the stories of King Arthur's Knights of the Round Table. In the Arthur mythology, it was the infidelity of Guinevere, his wife, and Lancelot, a knight of the Round Table, that helped destroy Camelot.

A 20th century example of an arranged marriage that is portrayed romantically is the relationship between Tevye and Golde in *Fiddler on the Roof,* the successful musical about the life in, and ultimate fate of, a

Jewish Shtetl in Russia during the period of anti-Jewish pogroms. Tevye and Golde sing the song, "Do You Love Me?," somewhat uncertainly—or perhaps reluctantly (depending on how one interprets what he sings)—acknowledging a love that had grown with time, though never before verbalized as such.

PART V

Clinical Issues

In chapter 10, the problem of demonstrating the role of stress and emotion in health is discussed, especially in infectious illnesses, which depend heavily on the immune function. The chapter also examines clinical interventions in stress management and treatment. The book closes with my wish list for psychology in the future, predicated on my strong dissatisfaction, and that of numerous other social scientists and psychologists, about the direction psychology has been heading, and my hopes.

C H A P T E R   T E N

Health, Clinical Intervention, and the Future

T hree topics are taken up in this, the final chapter, in the following order: Stress and health, clinical intervention with mental health problems, and at the end of the chapter I offer a vision for the future of this field of research and ideas, and for psychology as a whole.

By far the most difficult and unresolved issue for the field of stress, emotion, and coping has to do with their effects on adaptational outcomes. The conviction that such effects are substantial, both among professionals and laypersons, is what fuels much of the interest in these multidisciplinary topics. The case for a causal relationship, and the details about how this might work, need to be strengthened considerably to make it more than a controversial belief.

This does not mean that stress, emotion, and coping, which are the products of life's adaptational struggles, are the main or only causes of health and illness. There are much more powerful causes including genetic programming, microbes, and poor health practices. It is more likely that stress, emotion, and coping exacerbate these causes rather than directly affecting health and illness.

One of the essential requirements for demonstrating a causal relationship is to decide which adaptational outcomes are important and how they should be measured. For most researchers and theoreticians, there are three main outcome categories, morale (or subjective well-being), social and work functioning, and somatic health. Relationships between them are complex and in many respects obscure. Lazarus & Folkman (1984) dealt with all three, but because little has changed with respect to the first two, and because newer possibilities are particularly promising, such as the growing knowledge of the functions of the immune system, I center most of my attention here on the narrower topic of physical health.

259

STRESS AND HEALTH

The potential link between these two complex sets of variables has become more important than ever for many people because we are living much longer than was typical 50 or more years ago. As we age, chronic illnesses, such as cancer, heart disease, and acute infectious illnesses, will end up killing most of us.

With respect to microbial infection, not long ago those concerned with health and illness assumed that antibiotics and vaccines had eliminated this threat to life. Now, however, as a result of increasing microbial resistance to antibiotics as a result of overuse, uncertainty about our ability to control infection has been growing once again. We may not yet have conquered one of the four horsemen of the apocalypse—namely, pestilence. Table 10.1 presents some historical data on pestilence.

Anyway, more than ever, our vital concern with health and illness has gained continuous media attention in our postindustrial world. University sponsored newsletters dealing with health issues have proliferated. They focus on diet, exercise, and all sorts of health-related fads and fashions, such as the presumed anticancer values of wine, vitamins, and herbal medicines, driving many of us up the wall with proscriptions and prescriptions for a long, healthy life, all in search of the modern fountain of youth.

A whole new field of psychology has emerged from this concern, which is referred to as health psychology. Its substance is the psychophysiology of health and illness, the causation of illness, and the promotion of health. A relatively new division of the American Psychological Association, named Health Psychology, is now one of the larger subfields of psychology and publishes its own scientific journal.

The American Psychosomatic Society is an interdisciplinary group with both a medical and nonmedical membership, which, for a long time, has been publishing a scientific journal named *Psychosomatic Medicine,* which deals with the interface between psychology and physical health. There have also been important books published on this topic, such as one by Lipowski, Lipsitt, and Whybrow (1976), and by Ader (1981) on psychoneuroimmunology as well as many others. And there is a journal specializing in alternative forms of medicine called *Advances, The Journal of Mind-Body Health.*

College textbooks on health psychology, and related topics, have proliferated. An incomplete list would include Gatchel & Baum (1983); Feist & Brannon (1988); Rice (1998); and Taylor (1986); not to speak of impressive, more detailed compendia and handbooks, such as Gentry

TABLE 10.1   The Deadly Past

Though less widely known, the 1918–1919 influenza pandemic was among history's most deadly events. Here are some of the most important others

	Deaths in millions
Influenza (1918–1919)	20–40
Black Death (1348–1350)	20–25
World War II (1939–1945)[1]	15.9
AIDS (through 1997)	11.7
World War I (1914–1918)[2]	9.2

[1] Military deaths
[2] Includes Japanese deaths from 1937
Sources: U.N., World Book Encyclopedia. From *New York Times International,* p. A6, Friday, August 21, 1998.

(1984); Matarazzo, Weiss, Herd, Miller, and Weiss (1984); Mechanic (1983); and Stone, Cohen, and Adler (1979). It would take several more pages of text to list most of the relevant books and journals in this burgeoning field, and to discuss the several scholarly and clinical disciplines identified with it.

What is striking is that virtually all such books and journals treat stress and coping as central constructs. When push comes to shove, an important role is accorded to stress, emotions, and coping by the subdiscipline of health psychology. Other relevant topics include stress physiology, environmental hazards, nutrition, obesity and dieting, exercise, smoking, drugs, and alcohol.

One of the chapters in Lazarus & Folkman (1984) dealt extensively with the broad topic of stress and health. Now, even 15 years later, it still remains a reasonable and well-documented account. Since then there has been a tremendous increase in research and sophistication about the immune process, which is said to be involved not only in infectious illness, but in such disorders as cancer and heart disease.

In a recent article that presents an approach to positive health, in contrast with the long-standing tendency to define health as the opposite of illness, Ryff and Singer (1998) complain that there has been too much emphasis on stress and too little on positive states of mind and the things we do to transcend the threats and hardships of modern life. Their main objective was to influence thought about positive mental health. On this, however, they received mixed reviews. Though I thought the article was timely, commentaries by other specialists in this arena presented numerous qualifications and criticisms, and questioned whether it had said anything new.

One of the issues bothering some critics had to do with the nature of happiness, which must be seen as a byproduct of a good life rather than something to be sought directly. Some questioned whether the concept of happiness had a clear meaning or was even relevant to health. The debate among these scholars connects well with what I wrote in chapter 9 about happiness-joy.

In this chapter I intend to comment on where, in general, we stand today with respect to the role of stress and the emotional life in physical health and illness. When it comes to details and implications, this area of research and theory remains controversial, as I indicate in the broad question raised in the next major heading:

HAVE WE DEMONSTRATED WHETHER AND HOW STRESS AND EMOTION INFLUENCE HEALTH?

A substantial degree of what might be called scientific politics troubles this area of research and theory. Perhaps because of the high stake professionals and laypersons alike have in the issue, and the strong prejudices it elicits, to suggest that there is any doubt about what almost everyone wants to believe—namely, that this question should answered in the affirmative—is to invite heavy criticism.

I say this because a brief comment of mine along these lines was published recently in the journal called *Advances* (subtitled *The Journal of Mind-Body Health* (Lazarus, 1992). This journal thoughtfully and sanguinely explores what we know and the problems of methodology and metatheory. There is a surprising amount of involvement on the part of very substantial and well-known health scientists and practitioners. A later issue of *Advances* addressed some of the issues of alternative medicine, which is also a controversial subject, including interesting articles by Russek & Schwartz (1996), and comments on it by Cunningham (1996), Dafter (1996), and others on the role of the self in cancer.

Anyway, my comment was titled, "Four reasons why it is difficult to demonstrate psychosocial influences on health." It had originally been published as a commentary in Snyder and Forsyth's (1991, p. 798) *Handbook of Social and Clinical Psychology.* Needham Heights, MA: Allyn & Bacon. I present this commentary almost exactly as it appeared after minor editing by the *Advances* journal editor (Lazarus, 1992, pp. 6–7):

> I would like to offer four reasons—essentially methodological—why it is difficult to demonstrate unequivocally that there are important psychosocial influences on health even though we all tend to believe that they exist.

First, health is affected by a great many factors over which we have little or no control, but which are probably very powerful influences nonetheless. These include genetic-constitutional factors, accidents, environmental toxins, and long-term life-styles, which involved using harmful agents as in drinking and smoking, and which are undoubtedly of transcendent importance, especially in vulnerable persons. After the influence on health variance that is played by these factors, and probably a host of others of which researchers are only dimly aware, has been taken into account, there may be only modest amounts of variance left to show the operation of psychosocial factors like stress.

Second, health is usually very stable and does not change rapidly, except under special circumstances, such as aging or rapidly progressing illnesses. In our research we have found the correlation over a year—with admittedly poor measures—to be about .70. To demonstrate causal influence requires that one show that psychosocial factors produce changes in health, but because of this stability, doing this is very difficult (*see* Kasl, 1983). The reduction of variance makes the demonstration more uncertain despite the fact that this degree of correlation still leaves half the total variance for diverse influences to affect.

Third, to show that stress and coping affects long-term health requires that we measure stable patterns during the time interval in which we make our observations. Except for short-lived infections, for illnesses such as heart disease and cancer, which take decades to develop, it is not what happens in a single stressful transaction that is important, but what happens consistently over time. The only solution is either to find processes that are stable or representative of the person—a rather unlikely state of affairs—or to monitor what happens in the time interval of interest. This means sampling what is going on repeatedly, rather than making only a single pre- and post-assessment.

In one response to the problem, several researchers, (for example, Caspi, Bolger, & Eckenrode, 1987; Eckenrode, 1984; Stone and Neale, 1984) have begun to realize that monitoring a relatively short time interval for stress, coping, and illness symptoms offers a more practical strategy for doing this than trying to study the problem over years of longitudinal research. Along these lines, DeLongis, Folkman, and I (1988), in research using an intra- as well as inter-individual design, showed that certain personality traits, such as negative self-esteem and the perception of poor social support, predicted a rise in illness symptoms following increased daily stress.

Fourth, I believe we will never effectively study the relationship between stress, coping, and health unless we have some conceptual guidelines for what we mean by health, which are not now in evidence. As I have noted elsewhere (Lazarus, 1990), if longevity is the criterion of health, then one condition, mucous colitis, seems to have little or no bearing on the outcome variable, but another condition, hypertension, does; however, if social functioning is the criterion of health, then hypertension has no bearing—especially when it remains untreated by distressing drugs—but colitis does. This example is only one of many that highlights the need for a workable theory of health that would be useful in helping us create a sound measurement strategy for epidemiological and clinical research.

My reason for offering this relatively pessimistic account of our prospects for adequately supporting the contention that psychosocial factors such as stress and coping are important influences on health is not to discourage clinical, social, and personality psychologists interested in health. One hates to be a spoilsport. Rather, it seems to me that these methodological issues are so important that professionals always need to keep them in mind lest they fail to understand what is really known and not known about behavior and health, how to go about getting valid answers, and that they may be mistaken about the prescriptions they offer for intervention and self-help. Only sophistication about our knowledge base will help us avoid making outrageous claims that only uninformed laypersons and physicians—who undoubtedly want to believe—would be willing to accept.

Although many of the commentators on what I wrote were respectful and, in the main, supportive, others were offended, believed I overstated the research problems, and felt I had been too pessimistic, and even simplistic. To a considerable extent, I think they were defensive about the basic proposition—certainly not open minded—as if I had maligned a sacred cow, and in some cases they distorted my message. In raising the questions I did, I had certainly brought out the troops.

Fundamental issues remain about how stress and emotion, which include coping, affect health outcomes. For example, since Selye's (1974) distinction between eustress and distress—that is, constructive or good stress and destructive or bad stress—we have been entertaining the assumption that positive emotional states, such as joy, love, and positive striving (as in the case of challenge), facilitate health and protect against illness, whereas negative emotional states, such as anger, envy, and jealousy, damage health.

Not much research has effectively explored this topic. One recent study (Kaplan, Manuck, Williams, & Strawn, 1993) has produced indirect evidence with monkeys that frequent and prolonged cardiovascular reactivity under conditions of negative emotions, resulting from disruptions of dominance hierarchies, impairs cardiovascular health by leading to advanced coronary disease. Solid, programmatic research to evaluate whether positive emotional states improve physical health is, by and large, lacking.

Nor is there an organized scientific accounting to help us identify constructive or destructive stress and emotions, though we know it is inappropriate to regard stress as having only a negative influence on our lives. Life would be dull and unsatisfying without some degree of stress, and boredom is stressful too. Besides, experience with some degree of stress is probably necessary to condition us to deal effectively with the inevitable threats, harms, and losses characteristic of life. In other words, under certain conditions people grow from stress, whereas under others they are traumatized and grievously impaired (see chapter 6).

We have also made little progress in determining whether stress results in illness as a result of a general mechanism or, alternatively, that particular illnesses are tied to a specific psychodynamic process. The generality position states, as Selye (1956/1976) had proposed, that stress of any kind increases susceptibility to all illness. If this is so, then a possible mechanism to explain individual differences in illness patterns is the existence of vulnerable organ systems, with stress resulting in symptoms on the basis of existing vulnerabilities in different people.

The specificity position arose from the psychoanalytic doctrine that particular conflicts or emotions produce their own specific diseases— in other words, a different conflict or emotion underlies each illness. Although the psychoanalytic version of specificity went out of fashion in the 1940s, other versions are still taken seriously today—for example, that hostility, or the way it is dealt with, disposes a person to heart disease, and that inhibiting one's own identity in order to be acceptable to others disposes us to cancer.

This view presumes that there is, in effect, a special cardiovascular disease or cancer personality. Such an approach is comparable to Type A theory, which postulated that living under constant time pressure disposes one to heart disease, a stance mostly discredited today in favor of the hostility hypothesis (*see,* for example, Spielberger, Krasner, & Solomon, 1988; Spielberger & Sydeman, 1994; and Williams & Williams, 1993, for accounts of research on this idea). Still another version is that hopelessness disposes a person to cancer (Jenkins, 1996).

For the reader who wishes to pursue this line of thought further, Friedman (1990) has presented a good review of theories, hypotheses, and research that link stress to chronic illnesses. And Epstein (1989) has published a fascinating personal account of a cancer-inducing lifestyle that, she claims, was transformed by psychotherapy, and which accounts for her seemingly miraculous recovery. Lazarus & Folkman (1984), Lazarus & Lazarus (1994), and most up-to-date books on health psychology also discuss evidence in favor or against this line of thought.

Without regard to detail, how might stress, emotions, and coping create their presumed effects on health? In Lazarus & Folkman (1984), we examined three main kinds of influence, which I have condensed subsequently to two: Stress and coping affect health by (a) changing the neurochemistry of the body, and (b) generating dangerous or damaging transactions with environmental conditions. Thus, in proposition (a) we fail to regulate emotional distress with its somatic effects; in proposition (b) we adopt a lifestyle that represents physically harmful ways of coping with stress, as in smoking, drinking, drug abuse, or taking excessive physical risks.

These alternative routes to illness increase the odds of recurrent or consistent bodily disturbances under stress, which should lead to tissue damage, as suggested in Selye's GAS (see chapter 2) and allow our health to be placed at risk by imprudent volitional actions.

STRESS AND INFECTIOUS ILLNESS

What has changed most since Lazarus & Folkman (1984) is the tremendous growth of interest in and research on biochemical reactions to stress, especially the immune process (see, for example, Jemmott & Locke, 1984; also Glaser, Kiecolt-Glaser, Bonneau, Malarkey, Kennedy, & Hughes, 1992). One need only pick up any recent issue of *Psychosomatic Medicine* to find numerous studies of biochemical changes under stress, including those involved in the immune process. I restrict myself below to a modest number of examples to make a coordinated case for the effects of stress on illness, and indicate how these effects might work.

The *immune process* is now recognized to be extremely complex, involving as it does many different kinds of antibodies, each of which combats foreign proteins (including germs) in a different way, but presumably defend against foreign agents in a coordinated fashion. We still understand poorly, however, the specific changes that lead to diseases like heart disease or cancer, or to increased or reduced protection against them. There is much still to be learned about how the immune process works in a living organism, especially in one so complex as a person, who's mind must be organized to manage diverse environmental demands and social influences and to gratify its own biological and psychological needs.

I have chosen to discuss only infectious illness because I believe the case for stress emotions as important factors in them is one of the strongest. What must be spelled out in research about the stress-somatic illness relationship is to accomplish three fundamental objectives within the same study: (a) measure stress adequately and identify the conditions that cause it. This is probably one of the main weak links in the study of stress, emotion, and illness—especially in light of ubiquitous individual differences; (b) show that stress increases the risk of infectious illness; and (c) demonstrate that stress weakens the immune system, probably by hormones that stress produces. These three types of findings must be combined within the same research design to see clearly their interconnections, and to identify the immune agents that apply to each disease, whether infectious or otherwise (as in cancer and heart disease, which require many years to emerge).

With respect to the first point about the immune agent, a Swedish study by Bergman & Magnusson (1979) demonstrated that stress in high school can be produced by a combination of high achievement striving and poor performance on exams, which results in hormonal changes that could impair the functioning of the immune system, thereby weakening the body's defense against germs. However, direct evidence that it did was not sought in this study.

High school students were rated by their teachers with respect to how ambitious they were academically. Then they were exposed to an exam. The ambitious boys secreted more adrenaline, an adrenal stress hormone, on the exam, but boys who did not seem to care about academic success secreted less than those rated as ambitious. We can see in this instance that when a strong academic motivation (goal commitment) was threatened (by a school exam) stress was aroused, which led to the secretion of powerful hormones that are capable of weakening the immune system.

The second point, which concerns evidence about the susceptibility to illness as a result of stress, was explored in a study by Kasl, Evans, & Niederman (1979) with West Point cadets who had contracted infectious mononucleosis, often referred to as the student's disease, because anecdotally it is so common in competitive student life. Students who became ill showed a distinctive combination of high academic achievement motivation and poor academic performance compared with those who did not become ill. So here we see evidence, which supplements the study by Bergmann and Magnusson, that stress increases the risk of infectious illness.

A recent study that has generated great interest in both medicine and psychology was recently published by Cohen, Tyrrell, & Smith (1991) on stress and susceptibility to the common cold. This study also addresses the second point dealing with the effects of stress on susceptibility to illness. This is the same Cohen who did the study of stressful social relationships in monkeys, which weakened the T-cell function of the immune process. Because most colds are not very serious, this question could be studied experimentally in the laboratory without seriously endangering the long-term health of participating human subjects.

Cohen et al. demonstrated that stress emotions can weaken the immune process and increase susceptibility to rhinoviral infections. They did this by inserting a cold virus into the nasal passages of volunteer subjects. They then compared its effects on two experimental subgroups, one that reported high stress during the past year and the other low stress. Subjects who had previously suffered from high stress got infected more readily than those with low stress. The more the stress, the more likely were those who received the cold virus to contract the common cold. The research also demonstrated that stress increased susceptibility to the virus by weakening the immune system, as observed in the loss of T-cell function. It did not, however, measure any of the hormones that might be the physiological mediators of the stress effect.

Thus, Cohen, Tyrrell, and Smith's (1991) research dealt with two of the three points that must be shown in the same study if we want to establish the interconnected processes whereby stress causes illness. It dealt both with the second point that stress-induced changes in the immune process increases the likelihood of infectious illness and the third point that stress does this by weakening the immune process.

The third point about a weakened immune process was also addressed in a study by Cohen, Kaplan, Cunnick, Manuck, & Rabin (1992). The social behavior of monkeys was observed for 26 months, with a focus on the initiation of social relationships, and the extent to which these relationships were stable and relaxed or unsettled and stressful. The unstable relationships, which typically involved the stress of social rejection, were found to be associated with suppressed T-cell immune activity, one of the major agents of the immune system. T cells metabolize bits of invading germs; they then become sensitized to these germs as the body's enemy, and subsequently kill and eat the invaders.

This study showed, therefore, that social stress suppressed one aspect of immune activity, which is important in defending against an invasion of the body by germs. In addition, Stone, Cox, Valdimarsdottir, & Jandorf (1987), and Stone, Neale, Cox, & Napoli (1994) have also obtained positive within-subject correlations between positive mood and immune system functioning, a relatively rare study that connected a positive emotional state to immune changes that favor health.

A recent study has appeared after this chapter was written that is remarkable in several ways and worth mentioning in the context of evidence that stress is a powerful factor in physical health as a result of its impact on the immune process. Marucha, Kiecolt-Glaser, & Favagehi (1998) reported a combination field and laboratory study in which the dependent variable was how rapidly two carefully designed experimental wounds 3.5 mm in size, made by the researchers on the hard palate of 11 dental students, healed under conditions of low and high stress.

The first wound was made to coincide in time with the academic summer vacation, presumably a low-stress period. The second was placed on the other side of the palate 3 days before the first major examination of the term, presumably a high-stress period. The authors employed a powerful research design in which each student served as his own control, which tends to limit individual differences in the comparison between the healing of the two wounds. Healing was assessed by daily photographs and a foaming response to hydrogen peroxide.

During the stressful examination period, it took an average of 3 days longer for the wound to completely heal (i.e., 40% longer) compared with the healing time of wounds made at the time of the nonstressful vacation period. Interleukin and messenger RNA also declined by 68% during the examination period, suggesting that these features of the immune process played a key role in the difference in healing rates. It is difficult not to see these findings as strong evidence for the role of stress, and the immune process, in the body's process of healing.

Unfortunately, the first point remains a major sticking point because there is little consensus about how stress is brought about and how to measure it. Most of the experimental procedures employed for this depend on stimuli whose influence on the subjects is undoubtedly variable (often because of motivational and belief differences) rather than defining stress as Bergmann and Magnusson (1979), cited above, did— namely, by a particular kind of person-environment relationship, characterized by high motivation coupled with a threat to that motivation.

In the case of the Marucha et al. study, however, the normative difference between a vacation and an important exam was apparently striking enough to transcend individual differences in stress arousal, resulting in a major contrast in the effects of the putative stress and no stress condition on wound healing. The same implication also helps us understand the strong, positive findings in the Cohen et al. study on the effects of stress on the susceptibility to colds, also via the role of the immune process.

The three fundamental findings required to make a firm case for the theory that stress causes infectious illness have not thus far been combined in the same study, insofar as I am aware. This leaves the proposition about stress and physical health less certain, and certainly less detailed than most scientists and practitioners want it to be, or that it should be. Still, all things considered, it must, nevertheless, be regarded as quite a strong case.

Going beyond infectious illness, however, when I am asked about the relationship between stress emotions and long-term diseases, such as cancer and heart disease, my answer is that the hypothesized connection between stress, emotion, and coping is eminently plausible, though at this juncture we do not know enough about the psychological and physiological details. The case has clearly not been well supported, much less proved, for chronic diseases, nor have the details been pinned down (*see also* Lazarus & Lazarus, 1994, for an account of this issue).

The preceding paragraph provides the rationale for the caution I showed in the statement printed in *Advances,* with which I began this section. We are making substantial progress, and future research on this problem can be regarded as extremely promising, but there is a long way to go.

STRESS MANAGEMENT AND TREATMENT

I touched on this topic in chapter 6 in my discussion of crisis intervention, and very slightly in the section on post-traumatic stress disorders. A fairly elaborate treatment of it was presented in Lazarus & Folkman (1984). Little has changed since that time except for a modern search for common ground on the part of therapists of different theoretical schools who, only a few decades ago, were at loggerheads.

What I plan to do first is to talk about three special issues: (a) tying stress management and treatment to the type of clinical problem being dealt with (it should be added that a therapeutic program needs to be consistent with one's theoretical approach); (b) dysfunction as a state or trait; and (c) how psychological change is brought about, which is the most important issue, as I see it.

1. *Tying treatment to the type of clinical problem.* People experience adaptational problems for a great many reasons, some of which can be corrected by training them to have better information and skills. Lazarus & Folkman (1984) cited the problems of men and women who must now live alone after having suffered from divorce or the death of a spouse. In most such cases, new stressful demands must be dealt

with which, in the past, had been managed mainly or solely by the now absent spouse, such as the care of children, housekeeping, handling money and credit, traveling, and maintaining the car as well as the chronic sources of stress that result from loneliness, dating, and sexual frustrations. Often the men and women exposed to this kind of loss feel whelmed—if not overwhelmed—by the new demands because they do not know how to handle them. Their morale is often poor, and their functioning inadequate.

They probably do not need psychotherapy but would profit from information about, and experience with, managing the new demands—in effect, they need good advice. Psychic conflicts or neuroticism is not what is troubling them, but lack of information and skills is, and it is possible that simply talking with a friend or reading books written for these persons would be enough to put them on the right track. Then, over time, life tasks that were originally stressful could become second nature.

However, the seeds of dysfunction and distress often lie, partly at least, within persons, especially if they have been struggling unsuccessfully with chronic stress for a long time, which suggests a neurotic contribution to their problems; they have failed after a considerable time to learn the necessary adaptive solutions. The lack of capacity to obtain and use necessary information and skills, and to learn what needs to be done to manage alone, is often a tip-off to the presence of internal conflicts, defense mechanisms, and ineffective coping. In such persons, psychotherapy is appropriate. The neurotic person is likely to be unaware of the origins of the problems and what could be done to improve things.

The first issue for the management of stress, therefore, is to make a clinical judgment about whether we are dealing with a temporary trauma-induced crisis, a straightforward problem of insufficient information or skill and/or a mild or severe form of psychopathology for which clinical intervention is needed. Because the person in trouble seldom can make an accurate diagnostic judgment about this, it must come from the professional clinician.

2. *Dysfunction as a state or trait.* I have been at pains to contrast structure and process in chapter I, and to compensate for the modern tendency in psychology, especially in the field of personality, to overemphasize stability and structure instead of process. Once we turn to the treatment of neurotic dysfunction, however, the emphasis tends to shift to stable psychological structures or personality traits (Lazarus, 1989b).

This is because clinicians who deal with long-term maladaptation assume, with good reason, that the problem presented by a person in trouble is a stable defect in ongoing person-environment relationships. Most probably, the person who sought treatment is vulnerable in some way, which leads chronically to a faulty appraisal pattern about what is happening, inept coping, and probably both. This state of affairs undoubtedly has a long personal history. Thus, clinicians see the need to change personality traits, which are viewed as the proximal causes of psychopathology.

We need to remember that it is rarely a single transaction that produces a crisis of dysfunction and distress, but the presence of a recurrent or chronic problem of living, which is the most probable source of the trouble. When a single traumatic event results in a crisis, the problem is apt to be temporary, which is why crisis theory and management is more process centered than traditional therapy, focused as it is on aiding the patient to survive the crisis and move forward, a type of intervention that was referred to as secondary prevention in chapter 6.

The person who comes for help at a particular time of life often does so because something has precipitated the decision to do so, and this is usually worth knowing in assessing the nature of the person's vulnerability. In addition to environmental pressures, something about that person is contributing to the dysfunction and distress. The task of clinical intervention is to identify what this is, to develop an understanding of it, and to help the person to change. It is the stable dysfunction and distress that must be dealt with if the patient is to improve.

As the reader will see shortly, cognitive therapists, such as (Beck, 1976; Beck & Emery, 1985; Ellis, 1962, Ellis & Bernard, 1985; Meichenbaum, 1977; and Meichenbaum & Jaremko, 1983) assume that the patient is viewing things inappropriately, perhaps as a result of defenses that operate as personality traits, or habits of thought that distort the realities being appraised and the inept coping process this appraisal generates. The task of therapy is to discover these stable cognitive-motivational-relational tendencies, observe how they work, and try to change them for the better. (For more recent references on psychotherapy and the emotions, see Freeman, Simon, Beutler, & Arkowitz, 1989; and Safran & Greenberg, 1991).

3. *How change is brought about.* Influenced by Plato and Aristotle's tripartite conception of the structure of mind (cognition, motivation, and emotion), which are supplemented by two other important variables—namely, conditions of the environment and the choice of actions—Lazarus & Folkman (1984) contrasted four different themes concerning how change is produced in clinical work with patients. These themes express different conceptions of the most useful targets of therapy.

They have to do with ideas about the main variables and processes that influence adaptation and maladaptation. In much of therapeutic practice, including traditional psychodynamic insight and cognitive therapy, these variables are juggled together in various ways, each combination representing a loose theoretical formulation about how clinical change occurs.

There are four conceptual formulations: (a) emotions shape thought and action; (b) actions shape thought and emotion; (c) the environment shapes thought, emotion, and action; and (d) thoughts shape emotions and action. They are useful to remember when one considers how change in appraisal and coping tendencies might be brought about. The main theoretical differences have to do with the different ways cognition, motivation, emotion, the environment, and action are said to be organized in the mind. The difficulty of bringing any of these targeted changes about should also be noted in passing. Ultimately, it is the patient who must be motivated to engage in a struggle to change.

When the environment is conceived to be the prime factor in what we want, feel, think, and how we act, then it must be changed so that the other variables and processes change accordingly because they are all interdependent. If the main instigators of maladaptation are motivation (or drives) and emotions, then changing them is the focus of therapy. If behavior or actions are said to be the prime villains in psychopathology, the person must be encouraged to adopt better ways of coping (acting), in which case the other variables will fall into place. And if, as the cognitivists believe, it is how you appraise stressful events and, therefore, cope with them, then changing appraisal and coping become the keys to the therapeutic strategy.

One of the striking features of modern psychotherapy is that, increasingly of late, protagonists of divergent theoretical approaches—for example, psychodynamic or psychoanalytic, behavior therapy, and cognitive therapy—seem to agree that all five variables—thought, motivation, emotion, the environment, and coping (action)—combine or interact in the process of change, whether the change is to more psychopathology or better mental health.

This more recent outlook avoids either-or thinking about the causes of adaptational problems. There is, in effect, something wrong meta-theoretically with the view, which was widely accepted for many years, that only one of the five variables is the sole key to the complicated process of change. Instead of focusing on one or another of them as separate variables, there is a growing conviction that mental health depends on the unity or integration of mind, and that disunity or disintegration constitutes psychopathology.

To divide the mind into separate, warring functions, is to visualize persons who cannot move consistently down a life pathway. They cannot seem to do otherwise but react to whatever conditions they are facing at the moment. That is, they do not hold to a sustained plan. Such persons seem out of touch with (or lack control over) their feelings, the environment, what they want, and how they think or act. They suffer from what might be called disconnection.

It is one thing to say that separation of the components of mind is possible, as in distancing, isolation, depersonalization, repression, or dissociation, all of which are tantamount to psychopathology, but another thing to say this is the normal of healthy condition. Nevertheless, dissociations are relative rather than absolute, and one function may "know" somehow what the other is up to. As Fischer and Pipp (1984, p. 89) put it:

> With development, the capacity for integrating components of thought and behavior grows, and at the same time, the capacity for active fractionation increases (e.g., dissociation and repression). The mind is, therefore both fractionated and integrated; there is neither a unitary conscious system nor a unitary unconscious one, but there are conscious and unconscious components that can be coordinated or kept separate.

In a mentally healthy person, it is tempting to think that a single, central organizational process—say, the ego or self—is in charge, choosing what course to follow, what values and goals to pursue, how to feel, how to govern one's actions, and so on. To separate motivation, cognition, and emotion, action, and the environment, is to conceive of the mind, which is usually coordinated and directed, as an unintegrated or dissociated system in which each function operates on its own. However, for sound mental health—that is, to experience integration or harmony—one must want what fits one's emotions and thoughts, and what makes a good fit with the environment in which one lives, and the actions in which one engages (see Lazarus, 1989c).

Consider, for example, the simple situation in which we are dining in a restaurant, and there are three items on the menu that are tremendously appealing, making it very difficult to choose. Despite the difficulty, however, we do not remain locked in indecision for long, but make the best choice we can and act on it. Without some agency of mind that acts analogously to a company chief executive, we would be unable to act because numerous conflicts are typical in our lives.

Most conflicts among our motives and pressures to act are far more significant for well-being than the choice of what to eat. Yet we act on them if we are mentally healthy and pursue consistent, sometimes lengthy, paths throughout much of our lives, sometimes changing our choice because it turns out that we made a mistake. This is the only way we can experience integrity and coherence in our lives.

Others have also argued for the unity and coherence of the main constructs of our minds, a position that has been applied to perception (or cognition) and action. For example, about this von Hofsten (1985, p. 95), has written:

> It has been argued in the present chapter that perception and action are functionally inseparable. The function of perception is to guide action in setting goals as well as supporting movements. This is done by making knowledge about critical task-related properties of the world (i.e., affordances) immediately available to the action system.

In the same edited book from which the quote from von Hofsten was drawn, Neisser (1985, p. 97) wrote:

> under normal circumstances perception and action are simultaneous and well-coordinated. The links between them are very close. Indeed, [he quotes from] von Hofsten (1985, p. 8) [as finding] them all but inseparable. "It is difficult to speak of one of these two aspects of biological functioning without referring to the other." But unfortunately it is *not* difficult; we have doing it for a century.

Psychotherapy for stress disorders must overcome the disconnection of the components of the mind that leads to dysfunction. Permit me to quote from three well-known cognitive therapists on the interdependence of these components, then from a pair of behavior therapists, on the interdependence of cognition, emotion, and motivation in therapeutic change.

Meichenbaum and Cameron (1983, p. 141) wrote as follows about their stress-innoculation training procedure in which people who have trouble dealing with expectable occupational stresses rehearse positive self-statements in an effort to psych themselves up before and during a stressful encounter:

> It is important to understand that [self-statements] are not offered as catch-phrases or as verbal palliatives to be repeated mindlessly. There is a difference between encouraging the use of a formula or psychological litany that tends to lead to rote repetition and emotionless patter versus problem-solving thinking that is the object of stress inoculation training. Formula-oriented thoughts that are exclusively general tend to prove ineffective.

Such routine and emotionless litanies are reminiscent of the discredited therapeutic approach of Emile Coué, a French psychotherapist who practiced in the early years of the 20th Century. Coué became famous worldwide for the following self-statement, which he urged patients to repeat often: "Every day in every way I'm getting better and better." For the reason wisely articulated by Meichenbaum and Cameron above, this approach never took hold.

Albert Ellis (1984, p. 216), an early forerunner of cognitive therapies and the founder of what he called rational-emotive therapy (RET), wrote the following about the unity of cognition, motivation, and emotion:

> RET assumes that human thinking and emotion are not two disparate or different processes, but that they significantly overlap and are in some respects, for all practical purposes, essentially the same thing. Like the two other basic life processes, sensing and moving [acting], they are integrally integrated and never can be seen wholly apart from each other. Instead then of saying that "Smith thinks about this problem," we should more accurately say that "Smith senses-moves-feels-THINKS about this problem."

Finally, Aaron T. Beck, progenitor of another version of cognitive therapy, tells us that affect (emotion) is not enough to create therapeutic change without cognitive processing and the working through of insights about what ails the person. He states (1987, pp. 161–162):

> some type of intellectual framework is important if the cathartic, flooding, or emotional experience is to have a therapeutic effect. It is apparent that people go through catharses and abreactions continuously throughout their lives—without any benefit. What seems to be offered within a therapeutic milieu is the patient's ability to experience simultaneously the "hot cognitions" and to step back, as it were, and to observe this experience objectively. When therapy is effective, the essential components are the production of "hot cognitions" and affect within a therapeutic structure and the opportunity to reality-test these cognitions—whether the therapist is employing psychoanalysis, behavior therapy, cognitive therapy, or one of the experiential therapies.

Cognitive therapies, like psychoanalysis, emphasize the need for insight about the meaning of one's adaptational struggles. But insight that is entirely cognitive, is not sufficient. There must be what Wachtel (1977), who tried to reconcile psychoanalytic thinking with behavior therapy, referred to as emotional insight, which is what Beck, in the quote above, meant by hot cognitions. Working through, a concept originating in psychoanalysis, refers to using the insights that one has gained in therapy in real-life transactions outside the therapist's office, as the patient struggles to apply them to recurrent or chronic dysfunctional and distressing experiences.

One of the best examples I encountered when engaged in clinical work was a 25-year-old women—let us call her Ruth—who struggled to deal effectively with an overpowering mother who dominated and overprotected her (*see* Lazarus & Lazarus, 1994, pp. 267–271, for a fuller account of this case). Whenever this kind of struggle occurred, she felt guilty and anxious about undermining her mother's wishes, lest it seem like rejection and, perhaps, lead to retaliation, which the young woman feared.

> After her marriage, Ruth became pregnant, and her mother said she wanted to stay with her at the time of the delivery and when the baby came home. This endangered Ruth's strong desire for autonomy; she and her husband wanted to take care of the baby, and the presence of her bossy mother seemed to be threatening.
>
> Ruth had been in extensive treatment and had come to understand quite well what her problems were in her relationship with her mother. But this insight would be for naught if she couldn't firmly confront her mother and prevent her from coming. Each time the mother phoned and broached the subject, the young woman became terribly distressed, and would give in to her mother's wishes. The mother's hostile attitude increased her anxiety and guilt greatly, and she seemed helpless to take control of the situation. Her husband was supportive, and he also wanted them to be left alone to deal with the newborn.
>
> Each time on the phone, Ruth tried sensitively to state how she felt about the visit, having rehearsed what she would say, but on each occasion her mother would respond with anger and grief, and Ruth would fail to hold firm. After many tries, she finally did, and unlike previous occasions, stuck to her guns, leaving no door open for the mother to override her decision. Never before confronted with such firmness, the mother ultimately backed down.
>
> The daughter, Ruth, invited her mother to visit six months after the baby arrived. It was a difficult visit emotionally, but she felt she had finally made some progress, and was able to restore some good will and harmony with her mother. Thus, just having insight about one's needs and problems doesn't guarantee that a person will change the coping behavior so that the emotional distress previously associated with troubled relationships and transactions could abate.

Working through a neurotic problem is often a difficult and distressing struggle of trying to apply what one has learned in treatment. We can refer to this as emotional insight, which involves both distress about one's awareness of what was once a hidden, unconscious conflict, and the will to apply the insight effectively. Without emotional insight—that is, the new, emotionalized understanding of how to deal with previously negative emotional relationships, the intellectual knowledge is of little therapeutic value. When the knowledge involved in the insight is cold and vacuous, it also lacks conviction. All the therapists quoted above end up emphasizing, or at least accepting, the principle of the interdependence of cognition (understanding or insight) and emotion.

Behavior therapy had its origins as a protest against psychoanalysis with its concern with deep, unconscious structures and processes of the mind, such as ego defenses, which prevented people from recognizing what caused their neurotic anxieties and handicapped them from coping effectively. In the early days, the psychoanalytic ideas of catharsis and insight were roundly rejected.

Today, however, among psychotherapists there appears to be considerable reconciliation. Behaviorists are suggesting, though not necessarily in these exact words, that to cope more effectively patients must learn that their expectations about their vulnerability to harm are wrong. They must stop avoiding what they fear and act in ways that make the discovery of the positive reality possible—in effect, they must confront what they fear and learn from it. Let us see what two modern behavior therapists, Foa and Kozak, who, citing Lang (1977, 1979) call "the principle of exposure," say about this. They write (Foa & Kozak, 1986, p. 20):

> Anxiety disorders are continuous attempts to avoid confrontation with fear-evoking cues. Indeed, if neurotics are avoiders who fail to recognize and/or retrieve discomfort-evoking information about themselves or their environment, psychotherapy might be construed as providing a setting in which confrontation with such information is promoted so that changes in affect can occur.

Although behaviorists do not usually speak of meaning, to learn what is necessary from the confrontation with what threatens us requires that we discover that what we fear will not materialize or harm us, so we no longer have to defend against it as we did in the past. This involves a changed expectation and implies we have gained a new meaning about the environment and our relationship with it. Even the clinical procedures employed by different therapeutic schools overlap substantially, if not in precise detail, then in analogous ways. Regardless of how the new meaning comes about, learning is essential for change to take place.

SUMMING UP

A cognitive-motivational-relational theory of emotion points us toward the adaptational trials and errors that are made in our continuing efforts to deal with harm, threat, challenge, and benefit. The theory, centered on appraisal and coping, rests on the five conceptual horsemen of appraisal theory, cognition, motivation, emotion, input from the environment, and actions.

Regardless of the words one uses to describe these variables and process, they are more and more viewed as united in the meanings constructed from them (Lazarus, 1991d). Whether the adaptational problem is minor or severe, or takes place in a work or family setting, and whether the clinical approach is preventive or treatment oriented, the essential psychological ingredients of an analysis of adaptation and maladaptation always involves the same five psychological sets of variables.

Thus, unless one adopts a very radical metatheoretical outlook, the main psychodynamic ingredients remain the same regardless of the theoretical approach one employs, and for mental health these ingredients must be coordinated and in reasonable harmony. The diverse approaches to treatment distinguish themselves by the language they use to describe what is happening and by organizing the five sets of variables a bit differently. These same variables also operate whether one is describing what is happening in narrative terms, or in a systems theory formulation, which identifies multiple variables as causal factors in adaptational outcomes, as I suggested in chapter 8.

There seems to be more compatibility today among therapeutic systems than argument. There is less reason to argue competitively about the structures and processes of adaptation and maladaptation than we had assumed to be necessary throughout the history of our field. The current rapprochement among diverse schools of therapy attests to this. I hope that even more effort to see common themes will, in the future, create a modern golden age of discovery about issues that have previously been contentious.

FUTURE PERSPECTIVE

Throughout this book, the reader has surely sensed my dissatisfaction with the restrictive way in which psychology approaches theory and research. From the beginnings of psychology as a formal discipline, psychologists felt they had to demonstrate the comparability of their research to the physical sciences. By adopting a natural science approach that involved strict determinism, psychologists became precious and narrow-minded about how knowledge must be acquired.

Aided and abetted by behaviorism, and its philosophical correlate, positivism, too many psychologists regard the best way of doing research as the laboratory experiment and the large sample epidemiological survey. Psychological research was conceived as a way mainly of proving or disproving hypotheses about structural aspects of mind and human behavior. There was little room for description and the study of process.

What followed has been a proliferation of research that doesn't much advance our knowledge of how we adapt to and expand our personal horizons. Few psychologists pay attention to the ever-increasing data being collected and reported in scientific journals. Social scientists in general, as well as psychologists in particular, are increasingly expressing dissatisfaction with what we are learning about people and their social relationships. Some, such as Richard Jessor (1996), have been calling for more openness about theory and research methods as the postpositivist wave of the future, and expressing optimism about this.

Whenever I have given voice to my dissatisfaction, I have also felt it necessary to add that this is not a call for carelessness about our interpretations of observations, or for sloppiness in our measurement of constructs on which we depend for understanding. Each of the methods we employ in psychological research needs to be as precise as we can make it as well as appropriately interpreted.

When we use in-depth interviewing to obtain self-report data, the methods of interviewing, and the self-reports themselves, should be of the highest quality. And when we use inventories to measure psychological traits and processes, these should be constructed carefully and with due regard to validation and to the qualities and processes of mind that are important in how we adapt to our life conditions. Our assessment procedures should never be constructed in a casual or slap-dash fashion, though if we are looking at process and change, the psychometric principles must be different from those designed to study stable traits.

I favor more openness and diversity about kinds of method. Method must follow from and be consistent with the conceptualizations from which research is derived. When I suggested that multimethod sources of data, which include self-report, observations of behavior, and psychophysiological data be used as much as possible, it was to increase the quality of psychodynamic inferences but not to favor one method over another.

All three basic sources of data require inferences to make sense of the observed data, and we strengthen the substantive case for these inferences by using, if possible, more than one source of data. There are problems in making inferences from self-report data, just as there are problems with direct observations of behavior, and with psychophysiological data. By itself, one data source is not more or less vulnerable to error than any other, or more likely to yield the best interpretation.

However, we must also be wary about another issue—namely, that to use more than one data source in an effort to increase the validity of our interpretations is more tricky than previously recognized or acknowledged. When more than one source of data is used in research, disagreements are likely to occur among them. This happens so often as to be perplexing. It leads us to feel a widespread concern about method variance—that is, doubt that interpretative validity is apt to be found within a single data source.

In clinical work we assume that such disagreements suggest that our patients are dissimulating or defensive and are lacking in a valid understanding of their motives. However, there is another possible explanation, to wit, that each source of data, operating at different levels of analysis—that is, behavior, subjective reports of thoughts, desires, emotions, and psychophysiological measurements—has its own particular causes.

Conversely, there is a widespread but unfortunate belief that a single response measure, say, facial expressions, constitutes the gold standard of objective measurement of emotional states, on the overstated premise that it is closely determined by species genetics and evolution. If you feel angry, this will be expressed somehow in the face, even if suppressed, because it will inevitably leak to the perceptive observer, and a camera.

This position is seriously mistaken because, at best, it is a half-truth. The problem is that there are other determinants of expression as well as the emotion itself, such as the need to deceive to survive in a hostile environment (Fridlund, 1991, 1994). The same could be said about autonomic nervous system or hormonal measurements, which must reflect the energetics of the body. Thus, in the regulation of an emotion, such as anger, suppression has been found to result in more autonomic arousal than reappraising the meaning of a situation (Gross, 1998).

The point is that each sources of response data is influenced by more than one variable. Therefore, we should not expect the different levels of analysis to show very high agreement—some agreement, yes, though how much is an empirical question that has not been adequately studied. Before we use multimethod sources of data to check on our inferences, we had better know the rules about how they are affected by our complicated and diverse patterns of adaptation. This puts a crimp in the recommendation to depend on more than one source. Each data source has its own special interpretative implications.

Some years ago my colleagues and I showed that the degree of correlation within the autonomic nervous system between heart rate and skin conductance depended on whether we used interindividual or intraindividual correlational methods. It was near zero in the former arrangement, but almost .5 when intraindividual correlational methods were employed (Lazarus, Speisman, & Mordkoff, 1963). So one's method of answering the question about agreement and disagreement among data sources can make a large difference.

Little attention has been given to the problem of the correlations among response measures. I have recently seen a draft of a paper by Rainer Reisenzein (in preparation), from the University of Bielefeld in Bielefeld, Germany, which is being prepared for publication. There, the author examines the degree of relationship among the components of emotion syndromes in the case of the emotional state of surprise.

Reisenzein carefully examines and metatheoretical and methodological issues involved and provides substantial data from an extremely careful and complex study suggesting that the relationship is generally modest in strength. The data also support the findings of Lazarus, Speisman, and Mordkoff (1963) that an intraindividual methodology produces stronger relationships than an interindividual methodology. Anyone having an interest in this issues should write the author, or seek out the article when it is published.

Consistent with what I said in chapter 1, I now offer four themes that represent a vision for the future of psychology. I presented a similar line of reasoning in a different form at the end of Lazarus (1998a), but I do it much more briefly here.

First, we should abandon our reluctance to think of mind in subjective terms, which is the premise of the concept of appraisal. My subjectivity, however, is not the same as traditional phenomenology. As I noted in chapter 1, and repeat it here for emphasis, I think of appraising as a continuing process of negotiation between our need to know the realities of our transactions and, at the same time, to make the most sanguine assessment we can, based on our needs and hopes. The human species, and most individuals within our species, would have failed to survive and flourish if both of these stances were not integrated into the appraising process.

Second, we should stop defining research solely as a search for normative principles, thereby treating our field as having only to do with people in general. Rather, we should take individual and group variation seriously, spelling it out in detail. Description is just as essential in science as causal analysis. Our focus on normative data, even in personality psychology, deprives us of a sense of the whole person as a complex individual, with an individual history and life trajectory.

There is a universalistic as well as individualistic side to this issue. When I was just coming into this field, I remember hearing an aphorism about universality and individuality that I liked very much, because it seemed to say so much so tersely. Its basic theme was that in some ways we are like everyone else, but in other ways we are like no other person.

Shore (1996), a cultural anthropologist, suggests that anthropology has had to struggle throughout its history between a concept of universal mind and a recognition that cultures differ in how they formally understand life. But, without solid evidence of how the people think and feel, we must not presume that the formally stated cultural outlook is internalized (or in the minds) of everyone or even most of the people in that society.

Each of us can be said to constitute a culture of one, although this statement seems to assault the idea of culture as a collective phenomenon. In any case, at the same time that we acknowledge individual differences, we need also to identify the ways of thinking we share with others living within our culture, and with all the other humans on the earth. This is a tricky issue that, as Shore points out, cultural and psychological anthropologists, have not dealt with successfully in the past.

Third, in contradistinction to the stimulus-response psychology of the past, we need to develop a language of relationships between persons in any given transaction and over time. This also means we must take a more contextual view of ourselves, in contrast with the focus of the past solely on universal mechanisms.

And just as important, we must become comfortable thinking about the *relational meanings* that shape how we act and react. These meanings depend on feedback loops, the same loops we utilize in digital computers but cast as meanings that each of us constructs about what is happening. As I said much earlier, though meaning depends on it, information is not meaning. I don't believe there is any other suitable way of understanding stress, emotions, and coping. Proceeding in this way is not a luxury; it is an absolute necessity if we are to create a truly effective research psychology.

And we should be bold enough to consider that traditional causal analysis is not enough to produce the understanding we want, because it reduces what we learn to separate variables that in nature operate in a *part-whole* relationship. To truly understand, the parts have to be synthesized back into nature's whole. But to take proper advantage of cause-and-effect understanding, we must focus on *longitudinal research* methods, or at least prospective or repeated measurement research designs rather than cross-sectional ones that give us no adequate way to think causally. We should also draw a portrait of each of our research participants rather than settling for statistical means or medians.

What I have been saying implies that causal analysis is not the only way to understand ourselves and the world. Without synthesis, reductive analysis is, in the end, inadequate as science. As Aristotle pointed out, there are several different ways to think of cause. I am thinking especially of logical causation rather than synthetic causation, in which patterns of appraisal logically imply particular emotions without there being any causal ascription. In other words, relational meanings and emotion can be thought of as different aspects of the same process, one implying the other (see, for example, Shweder, 1993b). For the interested reader, I have also dealt in somewhat greater detail with issues like this in Lazarus (1991a, and 1998a).

All of science consists of part-whole relationships—for example, between cells and organs, organs and persons, persons and other persons, and between persons and their larger worlds, such as groups, nations, and global ecologies. This brings us to a form of field theory. There were some bold theorists years ago who saw this clearly (Murphy, 1947/1966). We need to rediscover their ideas, which our field ignores at its peril.

I do not know whether any of this will eventuate in the future. We are such a contentious discipline that it is difficult for any radical departure to get a respectful hearing, much less to lead to programmatic changes. Some of our problems lie in the reward structure of academe, wherein rapid publication, rather than programmatic research and replication, is the coin of the realm.

I ended another recent monograph (Lazarus, 1998a) with a fortune cookie message that seems to me to make a lot of dour sense for our discipline, while seeming hopeful. It read: "Discontent is the first step in the progress of man or a nation." There are signs that discontent with psychology's direction and progress is growing. If we remain smug and believe, like Anatole France's Dr. Pangloss, that what we have is the best of all possible worlds, none of my thoughts about the future of stress, coping, and emotion, much less for psychology as a whole, are likely to come to pass.

Though it is undoubtedly impossible, I wish I could be around to see such a positive outcome in our long-standing efforts to understand the human mind and its role in the struggle to adapt to the stressful conditions under which we live. I would like to believe we are heading toward a new golden age, though as an elderly person, I doubt I will experience the next chapter. I hope you, the reader, will not regard it as too arrogant of me to suggest in a final comment that upcoming generations must try to change the way psychology goes about the task of trying to understanding ourselves, so in the future, the job will be done better.

References

Abella, R., & Heslin, R. (1989). Appraisal processes, coping, and the regulation of stress-related emotions in a college examination. *Basic and Applied Social Psychology, 10,* 311–327.

Ader, R. (1981). (Ed.). *Psychoneuroimmunology.* New York: Academic Press.

Ahlström, G. (1994). *Consequences of muscular dystrophy: Impairment, disability, coping, and quality of life.* Doctoral Dissertation. Acta Universitatis Upsaliensis, Uppsala.

Ainsworth, M. D. S. (1979). Infant-mother attachment. *American Psychologist, 34,* 932–937.

Albee, G. W. (1998). Is the bible the only source of truth? *Contemporary Psychology, 43,* 571–572.

Aldwin, C. M. (1994). *Stress, coping, and development: An integrative perspective.* New York: Guilford.

Aldwin, C. M., & Brustrom, J. (1997). Theories of coping with chronic stress: Illustrations from the health psychology and aging literatures. In B. H. Gottlieb (Ed.), *Coping with chronic stress* (pp. 75–103). New York: Plenum.

Aldwin, C. M., & Revenson, T. A. (1987). Does coping help? A reexamination of the relation between coping and mental health. *Journal of Personality and Social Psychology, 53,* 337–348.

Al-Issa, I., & Tousignant, M. (1997). (Eds.). *Ethnicity, immigration, and psychopathology.* New York: Plenum.

Allport, G. W. (1937). *Personality: A psychological interpretation.* New York: Holt, Rinehart, & Winston.

Allport, G. W., & Vernon, P. E. (1933). *Studies in expressive movement.* New York: Macmillan.

American Psychiatric Association (1980). *Diagnostic and statistical manual of mental disorders* (3rd Ed., rev.) Washington, DC: Author.

American Psychiatric Association (1994). *Diagnostic and statistical manual of mental disorders* (4th ed.). Washington, DC: Author.

Antonovsky, A. (1987). *Unraveling the mystery of health: How people manage stress and stay well.* San Francisco: Jossey-Bass.

Aristotle. (1941). Rhetoric. In R. McKeon (Ed.), *The basic works of Aristotle.* New York: Random House.

Arnold, M. B. (1960). *Emotion and personality* (2 vols.), New York: Columbia University Press.

Aron, A., & Westbay, L. (1996). Dimensions of the prototype of love. *Journal of Personality and Social Psychology, 70,* 535–551.

Asch, S. E. (1952). *Social psychology.* Upper Saddle River, NJ: Prentice Hall.

Auerbach, S. M. (1989). Stress management and coping research in the health care setting: An overview and methodological commentary, *Journal of Consulting and Clinical Psychology, 57,* 388–395.

Averill, J. R. (1982). *Anger and aggression: An essay on emotion.* New York: Springer-Verlag.

Averill, J. R. (1983). Studies on anger and aggression: Implications for a theory of emotion. *American Psychologist, 38,* 1145–1160.

Babrow, A. S., Kasch, C. R., & Ford, L. A. (in press). The many meanings of "uncertainty" in illness: Toward a systematic accounting. *Health Communication.*

Baker, G. W., & Chapman, D. W. (Eds.). (1962). *Man and society in disaster.* New York: Basic Books.

Baltes, P. B., & Baltes, M. M. (1990). Psychological perspectives on successful aging: The model of selective optimization with compensation. In P. B. Baltes, & M. M. Baltes (Eds.), *Successful aging: Perspectives from the behavioral sciences* (pp. 1–34). New York: Cambridge University Press.

Baltes, P. B., & Carstenson, L. L. (1996). The process of successful ageing. *Aging and Society, 16,* 397–422.

Bandura, A. (1982). Self-efficacy mechanism in human agency. *American Psychologist, 37,* 122–147.

Bandura, A. (1997). *Self-efficacy: The exercise of control.* New York: Freeman.

Bargh, J. A. (1990). Auto-motives: Preconscious determinants of social interaction. In E. T. Higgins & R. M. Sorrentino (Eds.), *Handbook of motivation and cognition* (Vol. 2, pp. 93–130). New York: Guilford.

Baron, R. M., & Boudreau, L. A. (1987). an ecological perspective on integrating personality and social psychology. *Journal of Personality and Social Psychology, 53,* 1222–1228.

Barone, D. F. (1991). Developing a transactional psychology of work stress. In P. L. Perewé (Ed.), *Handbook of job stress.* Special issue of the *Journal of Social Behavior and Personality, 6,* 31–38.

Barrera, M. (1981). Social support in the adjustment of pregnant adolescents: Assessment issues. In B. H. Gottlieb (Ed.), *Social networks and social support* (pp. 69–96). Beverly Hills, CA: Sage.

Baumeister, R. F., & Wotman, S. R. (1992). *Breaking hearts: The two sides of unrequited love.* New York: Guilford.

Beck, A. T. (1976). *Cognitive therapy and the emotional disorders.* New York: International Universities Press.

Beck, A. T. (1987). Cognitive therapy. In J. Zeig (Ed.), *Evolution of psychotherapy.* New York: Brunner/Mazel.

Beck, A. T., & Emery, G. (1985). *Anxiety disorders and phobias: A cognitive perspective.* New York: Basic Books.

Ben-Zur, H. (in press). Dimensions and patterns in decision making models and the controlled/automatic distinction in human information processing. *European Journal of Cognitive Psychology.*

Ben-Zur, H., & Wardi, N. (1994). Type A behavior pattern and decision making strategies. *Personality and Individual Differences, 17,* 323–334.

Bergman, L. R., & Magnusson, D. (1979). Overachievement and catacholamine excretion in an achievement-demanding situation. *Psychosomatic Medicine, 41,* 181–188.

Berkman, L., & Syme, S. L. (1979). Social networks, host resistance, and mortality: A nine-year follow-up study of Alameda County residences. *American Journal of Epidemiology, 109,* 186–204.

Berkowitz, L. (1962). *Aggression.* New York: McGraw-Hill.

Berkowitz, L. (1989). Frustration-aggression hypothesis: Examination and reformulation. *Psychological Bulletin, 106,* 59–73.

Bernard, V. W., Ottenberg, P., & Redl, F. (1965). Dehumanization: A composite psychological defense in relation to modern war (pp. 64–82). In M. Schwebel (Ed.), *Behavioral science and behavior books.* Palo Alto: Science and Behavior Books.

Berry, J. W. & Commentators (1997). Immigration, acculturation, and adaptation. *Applied Psychology: An International Review, 46,* 5–68.

Blascovich, J., & Tomaka, J. (1996). The biopsychosocial model of arousal regulation. *Advances in Experimental Social Psychology, 28,* 1–51.

Block, J. (1961). *The Q-sort method in personality assessment and psychiatric research.* Springfield, IL: Charles. C. Thomas.

Block, J. H., & Block, J. (1980). The role of ego control and ego resiliency in the organization of behavior. In W. A. Collins (Ed.), *Development of cognition, affect, and social relations: The Minnesota symposium in child psychology* (pp. 39–101). Hillsdale, NJ: Erlbaum.

Bolger, N. (1990). Coping as a personality process: A prospective study. *Journal of Personality and Social Psychology, 59,* 525–537.

Bolger, N., Foster, M., Vinokur, A. D., & Ng, R. (1996). Close relationships and adjustment to a life crisis: The case of breast cancer. *Journal of Personality and Social Psychology, 70,* 283–294.

Bolles, R. C. (1974). Cognition and motivation: Some historical trends. In B. Weiner (Ed.), *Cognitive views of human motivation* (pp. 1–20). New York: Academic Press.

Bombadier, C. H., D'Amico, C., & Jordan, J. S. (1990). The relationship of appraisal and coping to chronic illness adjustment. *Behavior Research and Therapy, 28,* 297–304.

Bond, M. H., & Smith, P. B. (1996). Cross-cultural social and organizational psychology. *Annual Review of Psychology, 47,* 205–235.

Bowers, K. S. (1987). Revisioning the unconscious. *Canadian Psychology/ Psychologie Canadienne, 28,* 93–132.

Bowlby, J. (1969). *Attachment and loss: Vol. I. Attachment.* New York: Basic Books.

Bowlby, J. (1973). *Attachment and loss: Vol. 2. Separation: Anxiety and anger.* New York: Basic Books.

Bowlby, J. (1980). *Attachment and loss: Vol. 3. Loss: Sadness and depression.* New York: Basic Books.

Bramsen, I., Bleiker, E. M. A., Mattanja Triemstra, A. H., Van Rossum, S. M. G., & Van Der Ploeg, H. M. (1995). *Anxiety, Stress, and Coping, 8,* 337–352.

Brewin, C. R. (1989). Cognitive change processes in psychotherapy. *Psychological Review, 96,* 379–394.

Brewin, C. R., Dalgleish, T., & Joseph, S. (1996). A dual representation theory of posttraumatic stress disorder. *Psychological Review, 103,* 670–686.

Brewin, C. R., MacCarthy, B., & Furnham, A. (1989). Social support in the face of adversity: The role of cognitive appraisal. *Journal of Research in Personality, 23,* 354–372.

Brief, A. P., & George, J. M. (1991). Psychological stress in the workplace: A brief comment on Lazarus' outlook. In P. L. Perewé (Ed.), *Handbook of job stress.* Special issue of the *Journal of Social Behavior and Personality, 6,* 15–20.

Brody, N. (Ed.). (1987). The unconscious. *Personality and Social Psychology Bulletin, Special issue, 13.*

Bronfenbrenner, R. (1986). Ecology of the family as a context for human development. *Developmental Psychology, 22,* 723–742.

Brown, D. E. (1991). *Human universals.* New York: McGraw-Hill.

Bruner, J. S. (1990). *Acts of meaning.* Cambridge, MA: Harvard University Press.

Bruner, J. S., & Goodman, C. D. (1947). Value and need as organizing factors in perception. *Journal of Abnormal and Social Psychology, 42,* 33–44.

Bruni, F. (1998). At the end of the rainbow, ennui in the pot of gold. *New York Times,* March 1, Section 4, pp. 1–4.

Buck, R. (1985). Prime theory: An integrated view of motivation and emotion. *Psychological Review, 92,* 389–413.

Bugental, J. F. T. (1990). *Intimate journeys: Stories from life-changing therapy.* San Francisco: Jossey-Bass.

Buss, A. (1961). *The psychology of aggression.* New York: Wiley.

Byrne, D. (1964). Repression-sensitization as a dimension of personality. In B. A. Maher (Ed.), *Progress in experimental personality research* (Vol. 1, pp. 169–220). New York: Academic Press.

Cacioppo, J. T., & Berntson, G. G. (1992). Social psychological contributions to the decade of the brain: Doctrine of multilevel analysis. *American Psychologist, 47,* 1019–1028.

Calhoun, C., & Solomon, R. S. (1984). (Eds.). *What is an emotion?: Classic readings in philosophical psychology.* New York: Oxford University Press.

Campos, J. J., Campos, R. G., & Barrett, K. C. (1989). Emergent themes in the study of emotional development and emotion regulation. *Developmental Psychology, 25,* 394–402.

Campos, J., Mumme, D., Kermoian, R., & Campos, R. (1994). A functionalist perspective on the nature of emotion. In N. Fox (Ed.), The development of emotional regulation: Biological and behavioral considerations. *Monographs of the Society for Research in Child Development,* Vol. 59 (2/3, Serial No. 240).

Campos, J. J., & Stenberg, C. (1981). Perception, appraisal, and emotion: The onset of social referencing. In M. E. Lamb & L. R. Sherrod (Eds.), *Infant social cognition: Empirical and theoretical considerations.* Hillsdale: NJ: Erlbaum.

Cannon, W. B. (1932). *The wisdom of the body* (2nd ed.). New York: Norton.

Caplan, G. (1964). *Principles of preventive psychiatry.* New York: Basic Books.

Caputo, J. L., Rudolph, D. L., & Morgan, D. W. (1998). Influence of positive life events on blood pressure in adolescents. *Journal of Behavioral Medicine, 21,* 115–129.

Carlson, R. (1971). Where is the person in personality research? *Psychological Bulletin, 75,* 203–219.

Carstensen, L. L., Graff, J., Levenson, R. W., & Gottman, J. M. (1996). Affect in intimate relationships: The developmental course of marriage. In C. Magai & S. H. McFadden (Eds.), *Handbook of emotion, adult development, and aging* (pp. 227–247). San Diego: Academic Press.

Carthy, J. D., & Ebling, F. J. (1964). *The natural history of aggression.* London: Academic Press.

Carver, C. S. (1996). Foreword. In M. Zeidner & N. S. Endler (Eds.), *Handbook of coping: Theory, research, applications* (pp. xi–xiii). New York: Wiley.

Caspi, A., Bolger, N., & Eckenrode, J. (1987). Linking person and context in the daily stress process. *Journal of Personality and Social Psychology, 52,* 184–195.

Cassel, J. (1976). The contribution of the social environment to host resistance. *American Journal of Epidemiology, 104,* 107–123.

Ceslowitz, S. B. (1989). Burnout and coping strategies among hospital staff nurses. *Journal of Advanced Nursing, 14,* 553–557.

Chang, E. C. (1998). Dispositional optimism and primary and secondary appraisal of a stressor: Controlling for confounding influences and relations to coping and psychological and physical adjustment. *Journal of Personality and Social Psychology, 74,* 1109–1120.

Cignac, M. A. M., & Gottlieb, B. H. (1997). Changes in coping with chronic stress: The role of caregivers' appraisals of coping efficacy. In B. H. Gottlieb (Ed.), *Coping with chronic stress* (pp. 245–267). New York: Plenum.

Cobb, S. (1976). Social support as a moderator of life stress. *Psychosomatic Medicine, 38,* 300–314.

Coelho, G. V. (Ed.). (1972). *Mental health and social change: An annotated bibliography.* Rockville, Md: National Institute of Mental Health.

Coelho, G. V., & Irving, R. I. (Eds.). (1981). *Coping and adaptation: An annotated bibliography and study guide.* Rockville, MD: National Institute of Mental Health.

Cofer, C. N. & Appley, M. H. (1964). *Motivation: Theory and research.* New York: Wiley.

Cohen, F., & Lazarus, R. S. (1973). Active coping processes, coping dispositions, and recovery from surgery. *Psychosomatic Medicine, 35,* 375–398.

Cohen, F., Reese, L. B., Kaplan, G. A., & Riggio, R. E. (1986). Coping with the stresses of arthritis. In R. W. Moskowitz & M. R. Haug (Eds.), *Arthritis and the elderly.* New York: Springer.

Cohen, S., Kaplan, J. R., Cunnick, J. E., Manuck, S. B., & Rabin, B. S. (1992). Chronic social stress, affiliation, and cellular immune response in nonhuman primates. *Psychological Science, 3,* 301–304.

Cohen, S., Kessler, R. C., & Gordon, L. U. *Measuring stress.* New York: Oxford, 1995.

Cohen, S., Tyrrell, D. A. J., & Smith, A. P. (1991). Psychological stress and susceptibility to the common cold. *New England Journal of Medicine, 325,* 606–612.

Cohler, B. J. (1982). Personal narrative and the life course. In P. Baltes & O. G. Brim Jr. (Eds.), *Life span development and behavior* (Vol. 4, pp. 205–241). New York: Academic Press.

Coles, R. (1989). *The call to stories.* Boston: Houghton Mifflin.

Collins, D. L., Baum, A., & Singer, J. E. (1983). Coping with chronic stress at Three Mile Island. *Health Psychology, 2,* 149–166.

Compas, B. E. (1987). Coping with stress during childhood and adolescence. *Psychological Bulletin, 101,* 393–403.

Compas, B. E., Connor, J., Osowiecki, D., & Welch, A. (1997). Effortful and involuntary responses to stress: Implications for coping with chronic stress (pp. 105–130). In B. H. Gottlieb (Ed)., *Coping with chronic stress.* New York: Plenum.

Compas, B. E., Davis, G. E., Forsythe, C. J., & Wagner, B. M. (1987). Assessment of major and daily stressful events during adolescence: The adolescent perceived events scale. *Journal of Consulting and Clinical Psychology, 55,* 534–541.

Compas, B. E., Malcarne, V. L., & Fondacaro, K. M. (1988). Coping with stressful events in older children and young adolescents. *Journal of Consulting and Clinical Psychology, 56,* 405–411.

Compas, B. E., Worsham, N. L., & Ey, S. (1992). Conceptual and developmental issues in children's coping with stress. In A. M. La Greca, L. J. Siegel, J. L. Wallander, & C. E. Walker (Eds.), *Stress and coping in child health* (pp. 7–24). New York: Guilford.

Conway, M. A., & Bekerian, D. A. (1987). Situational knowledge and emotions. *Cognition and Emotion, 1,* 145–191.

Cooper, C. L., & Payne, R. (1980). *Current concerns in occcupational stress.* Chichester, England: Wiley.

Cooper, C. L., & Payne, R. (1991). *Personality and stress: Individual differences in the stress process.* Chichester, England: Wiley.

Corlett, E. N., & Richardson, J. (1981). *Stress, work design, and productivity.* Chichester, England: Wiley.

Costa, P. T., Somerfield, M. R., and McCrae, R. R. (1996). In M. Zeidner & N. S. Endler (Eds.). *Handbook of coping: Theory, research, applications* (pp. 44–61). New York: Wiley.

Covington, M. V., & Omelich, C. L. (1987). "I knew it was cold before the exam": A test of the anxiety-blockage hypothesis. *Journal of Educational Psychology, 79,* 393–400.

Crocker, P., & Bouffard, M. (1990, Nov-Dec). Coping and participation of physically disabled adults in physical activity. *Journal de L'AC-SEPL.*

Croog, S. (1970). The family as a source of stress. In S. Levine & N. A. Scotch (Eds). *Social stress.* Chicago: Aldine.

Croyle, R. T. (in press). Appraisal of health threats: Cognition, motivation, and social comparison [Special issue]. *Cognitive therapy and research: Cognitive perspectives in Health Psychology.*

Croyle, R. T., Sun, Yi-Chun, & Louie, D. H. (1993). Psychological minimization of cholesterol test results: Moderators of appraisal in college students and community residents. *Health Psychology, 12,* 503–507.

Cunningham, A. J. (1996). Can the self affect the course of cancer? *Advances, 12,* 58–62.

Dafter, R. E. (1996). Shifts of core emotional self-experience: Can they influence cancer outcomes? *Advances, 12,* 63–71.

Dalkvist, J., & Rollenhagen, C. (1989). *On the cognitive aspects of emotions: A review and a model* (No. 703). Department of Psychology, University of Stockholm.

Deary, I. J., Blenkin, H., Agius, R. M., Endler, N. S., Zealley, H., & Wood, R. (1996). Models of job-related stress and personal achievement among consultant doctors. *British Journal of Psychology, 93,* 222–230.

DeLongis, A., Coyne, J. C., Dakof, G., Folkman, S., & Lazarus, R. S. (1982). Relationship of daily hassles, uplifts, and major life events to health status. *Health Psychology, 1,* 119–136.

DeLongis, A., Folkman, S., & Lazarus, R. S. (1988). Hassles, health, and mood: Psychological and social resources as mediators. *Journal of Personality and Social Psychology, 54,* 486–495.

De Ridder, D. T. D. (1995). Social status and coping: An exploration of the mediating role of beliefs. *Anxiety, Stress, and Coping, 8,* 311–324.

de Rivera, J. (1977). A structural theory of the emotions, Monograph 40. *Psychological Issues, 10,* 9–169.

de Rivera, J., Possell, L., Verette, J. A., & Weiner, B. (1989). Distinguishing elation, gladness, and joy. *Journal of Personality and Social Psychology, 57,* 1015–1023.

de Sousa, R. (1995). Consciousness and rationality: How not to reinvent the wheel. *Psychological Inquiry, 6,* 208–212.

Dewe, P. J. (1987). New Zealand ministers of religion: Identifying sources of stress and coping strategies. *Work & Stress, 1,* 351–363.

Dewe, P. J. (1989). Examining the nature of work stress: Individual evaluations of stressful experiences and coping. *Human Relations, 42,* 993–1013.

Dewe, P. J. (1991a). Measuring work stressors: The role of frequency, duration, and demand. *Work & Stress, 5,* 77–91.

Dewe, P. J. (1991b). Primary appraisal, secondary appraisal and coping:

Their role in stressful work encounters. *Journal of Occupational Psychology, 64,* 331–351.

Dewe, P. J. (1992a). The appraisal process: Exploring the role of meaning, importance, control, and coping in work stress. *Anxiety, Stress, and Coping, 5,* 95–109.

Dewe, P. J. (1992b). Applying the concept of appraisal to work stressors: Some exploratory analysis. *Human Relations, 45,* 143–164.

Dewe, P. J., & Guest, D. E. (1990). Methods of coping with stress at work: A conceptual analysis and empirical study of measurement issues. *Journal of Organizational Behavior, 11,* 135–150.

Dewey, J. (1894). The theory of emotion. (1894). *The Psychological Review, I,* 553–569.

Dewey, J., & Bentley, A. E. (1949). *Knowing and the known.* Boston: Beacon Press.

Diener, E. (1984). Subjective well-being. *Psychological Bulletin, 95,* 542–575.

Dohrenwend, B. S., & Dohrenwend, B. P. (1974). *Stressful life events: Their nature and effects.* New York: Wiley.

Dohrenwend, B. S., Dohrenwend, B. P., Dodson, M., & Shrout, P. E. (1984). Symptoms, hassles, social supports and life events: The problem of confounded measures. *Journal of Abnormal Psychology, 93,* 222–230.

Dreikurs, R. (Ed.). (1967). *Psychodynamics, psychotherapy, and counseling.* Chicago: Alfred Adler Institute.

Duffy, E. (1962). *Activation and behavior.* New York: Wiley.

Dunahoo, C. L., Hobfoll, S. E., Monnier, J., Hulsizer, M. R., & Johnson, R. (1998). There's more than rugged individualism in coping: 1. Even the lone ranger had Tonto. *Anxiety, Stress, and Coping, 11,* 137–165.

Dunkel-Schetter, C., Feinstein, L. G., Taylor, S. E., & Falke, R. L. (1992). Patterns of coping with cancer. *Health Psychology, 11,* 79–87.

Dunn, J. (1988). *The beginnings of social understanding.* Cambridge, MA: Harvard University Press.

Dunn, J., & Munn, P. (1985). Becoming a family member: Family conflict and the development of social understanding in the second year. *Child Development, 56,* 480–492.

Durkheim, E. (1893). *De la division du travail social.* Paris: F. Alcan. (Not read.)

Dweck, C. S., & Licht, B. G. (1980). Learned helplessness and intellectual achievement. In J. Garber & M. E. P. Seligman (Eds.), *Human helplessness: Theory and applications* (pp. 197–221). New York: Academic Press.

Dweck, C. S., & Wortman, C. B. (1982). Learned helplessness, anxiety, and achievement motivation: Neglected parallels in cognitive, affective, and coping responses. In H. W. Krohne & L. Laux (Eds.), *Achievement, stress, and anxiety* (pp. 93–125). Washington, DC: Hemisphere.

D'Zurilla, T. J. (1986). *Problem-solving therapy: A social competence approach to clinical intervention.* New York: Springer.

D'Zurilla, T. J., & Goldfried, M. (1971). Problem solving and behavior modification. *Journal of Abnormal Psychology, 78,* 107–126.

D'Zurilla, T. J., & Nezu, A. (1982). Social problem solving in adults. In P. C. Kendall (Ed.), *Advances in cognitive-behavioral research and therapy* (Vol. 1). New York: Academic Press.

Easterbrook, J. A. (1959). The effect of emotion on cue utilization and the organization of behavior. *Psychological Review, 66,* 183–201.

Eckenrode, J. (1984). Impact of chronic and acute stressors on daily reports of mood. *Journal of Personality and Social Psychology, 46,* 907–918.

Eckenrode, J., & Gore, S. (1990). Stress and coping at the boundary of work and family (pp. 1–16). In J. Eckenrode, & S. Gore (Eds.), *Stress between work and family.* New York: PLenum.

Edwards, J. M., & Trimble, K. (1992). Anxiety, coping and academic performance. *Anxiety, Stress, and Coping, 5,* 337–350.

Ekman, P. (1985, 1992). *Telling lies: Clues to deceit in the marketplace, politics, and marriage.* New York: Norton.

Ekman, P., & Davidson, R. J. (Eds.). (1994). *The nature of emotion: Fundamental questions.* New York: Oxford University Press.

Ekman, P., & Friesen, W. V. (1988). Who knows about contempt: A reply to Izard and Haynes. *Motivation and Emotion, 12,* 17–22.

Elder, G. H., Jr. (1974). *The children of the Great Depression.* Chicago: University of Chicago Press.

Elliott, G. R., & Eisdorfer, C. (1982). (Eds.). *Stress and human health: Analysis and implications for research.* New York: Springer.

Ellis, A. (1962). *Reason and emotion in psychotherapy.* New York: Lyle Stuart.

Ellis, A. (1984). Is the unified-interaction approach to cognitive-behavior modification a reinvention of the wheel? *Clinical Psychology Review, 4,* 215–218.

Ellis, A., & Bernard, M. E. (1985). What is rational emotive therapy (RET)? In A. Ellis & M. E. Bernard (Eds.), *Clinical applications of rational-emotive therapy* (pp. 1–30). Monterey, CA: Brooks/Cole.

Epstein, A. H. (1989). *Mind, fantasy, and healing: One woman's journey from conflict and illness to wholeness and health.* New York: Delcorte Press.

Epstein, S. (1990). Cognitive experiential self-theory. In L. Pervin (Ed.), *Handbook of personality theory and research* (pp. 165–192). New York: Guilford.

Epstein, S., & Meier, P. (1989). Constructive thinking: A broad coping variable with specific components. *Journal of Personality and Social Psychology, 57,* 332–350.

Erdelyi, M. H. (1985). *Psychoanalysis: Freud's cognitive psychology.* New York: Freeman.

Erdelyi, M. H. (1992). Psychodynamics and the unconscious. *American Psychologist, 47,* 784–787.

Eriksen, C. W. (1960). Discrimination and learning without awareness: A methodological survey and evaluation: *Psychological Review, 67,* 379–400.

Eriksen, C. W. (1962). (Ed.). *Behavior and awareness—a symposium of research and interpretation* (pp. 3–26). Durham, NC: Duke University Press.

Eriksen, C. W., & Lazarus, R. S. (1952). Perceptual defense and projective tests. *Journal of Abnormal and Social Psychology, 47,* 302–308.]

Erikson, E. H. (1950/1963). *Childhood and society.* New York: Norton.

Etzion, D., Eden, D., & Lapidot, Y. (1998). Relief from job stressors and burnout: Reserve service as a respite. *Journal of Applied Psychology, 83,* 577–585.

Fairbank, J. A., Hansen, D. J., & Fitterling, J. M. (1991). Patterns of appraisal and coping across different stressor conditions among former prisoners of war with and without posttraumatic stress disorder. *Journal of Consulting and Clinical Psychology, 59,* 274–281.

Fehr, B. (1988). Prototype analysis of the concepts of love and commitment. *Journal of Personality and Social Psychology, 55,* 557–579.

Feist, J., & Brannon, L. (1988). *Health psychology: An introduction to behavior and health.* Belmont, CA: Wadsworth.

Felton, B. J., & Revenson, T. A. (1984) Coping with chronic illness: A study of illness controllability and the influence of coping strategies on psychological adjustment. *Journal of Consulting and Clinical Psychology, 52,* 343–353.

Fischer, K. W., & Pipp, S. L. (1984). Development of the structures of unconscious thought. In K. Bowers & D. Meichenbaum (Eds.), *The unconscious reconsidered* (pp. 88–148). New York: Wiley.

Fleishman, J. A., & Fogel, B. (1994). Coping and depressive symptoms among people with AIDS. *Health Psychology, 13,* 156–169.

Florian, V., Mikulincer, M., & Taubman, O. (1995). Does hardiness contribute to mental health during a stressful real-life situation? The roles of appraisal and coping. *Journal of Personality and Social Psychology, 68,* 687–695.

Foa, E., & Kozak, J. J. (1986). Emotional processing of fear: Exposure to corrective information. *Psychological Bulletin, 99,* 20–35.

Folkman, S. (1984). Personal control and stress and coping processes: A theoretical analysis. *Journal of Personality and Social Psychology, 46,* 839–852.

Folkman, S. (1997a). Introduction to the special section: Use of bereavement narratives to predict well-being in men whose partners died of AIDS- Four theoretical perspectives. *Journal of Personality and Social Psychology, 72,* 851–854.

Folkman, S. (1997b). Positive psychological states and coping with severe stress. *Social Science and Medicine, 45,* 1207–1221.

Folkman, S., Chesney, M. S., and Christopher-Richards, A. (1994). Stress and coping in caregiving partners of men with AIDS. *Psychiatric Clinics of North America, 17,* 35–53.

Folkman, S., Chesney, M., Collette, L., Boccellari, A., & Cooke, M. (1996). Postbereavement depressive mood and its prebereavement predictors in HIV+ and HIV-gay men. *Journal of Personality and Social Psychology, 70,* 336–348.

Folkman, S., & Lazarus, R. S. (1980). An analysis of coping in a middle-aged community sample. *Journal of Health and Social Behavior, 21,* 219–239.

Folkman, S., & Lazarus, R. S. (1985). If it changes it must be a process: Study of emotion and coping during three stages of a college examination. *Journal of Personality and Social Psychology, 48,* 150–170.

Folkman, S., and Lazarus, R. S. (1988a). Coping as a mediator of emotion. *Journal of Personality and Social Psychology, 54,* 466–475.

Folkman, S., & Lazarus, R. S. (1988b). *Manual for the Ways of Coping Questionnaire.* Palo Alto: Consulting Psychologists Press. Now published by MIND GARDEN.

Folkman, S., and Lazarus, R. S. (1988c). Coping and emotion. *Social Science in Medicine, 26,* 309–317.

Folkman, S., Lazarus, R. S., Dunkel-Schetter, C., DeLongis, A., & Gruen, R. (1986). The dynamics of a stressful encounter: Cognitive appraisal, coping, and encounter outcomes. *Journal of Personality and Social Psychology, 50,* 992–1003.

Folkman, S., Lazarus, R. S., Gruen, R., & DeLongis, A. (1986). Appraisal, coping, health status, and psychological symptoms. *Journal of Personality and Social Psychology, 50,* 572–597.

Folkman, S., Lazarus, R. S., Pimley, S., & Novacek, J. (1987). Age differences in stress and coping processes. *Psychology and Aging, 2,* 171–184.

Folkman, S., Moskowitz, J. T., Ozer, E. M., & Park, C. L. (1997). Positive meaningful events and coping in the context of HIV/AIDS. In B. H. Gottlieb (Ed.), *Coping with chronic stress* (pp. 293–314). New York: Plenum.

Folkman, S., & Stein, N. L. (1996). A goal-process approach to analyzing narrative memories for AIDS-related stressful events. In N. L. Stein, P. Ornstein, B. Tversky, & C. Brainerd (Eds.), *Memory for everyday and emotional events* (pp. 113–137). Hillsdale, NJ: Erlbaum.

Frankl, V. (1959). *Man's search for meaning.* Boston: Beacon.

Freeman, A., Simon, K. M., Beutler, L. E., & Arkowitz, H. (1989). *Comprehensive handbook of cognitive therapy.* New York: Plenum.

French, J. R. P., Jr., Caplan, R. B., & Van Harrison, R. (1982). *The mechanisms of job stress and strain.* Chichester, England: Wiley.

Frese, M., & Sabini, J. (Eds.). (1985). *Goal directed behavior: The concept of action in psychology.* Hillsdale, NJ: Erlbaum.

Freud, S. (1922). *Some neurotic mechanisms in jealousy, paranoia and homosexuality* (Vol. 18). London: Hogarth.

Fridlund, A. J. (1991). Evolution and facial action in reflex, social motive, and paralanguage. *Biological Psychology, 32,* 3–100.

Fridlund, A. J. (1994). *Human facial expression.* San Diego, CA: Academic Press.

Friedman, H. S. (1990). (Ed.). *Personality and disease.* New York: Wiley.

Frijda, N. H. (1986). *The emotions.* Cambridge: Cambridge University Press.

Frijda, N. H. (1988). The laws of emotion. *American Psychologist, 43,* 349–358.

Gardner, R. W., Holzman, P. S., Klein, G. S., Linton, H. B., & Spence, D. P. (1959). Cognitive control, a study of individual consistencies in cognitive behavior. *Psychological Issues, 1,* 1–186.

Garmezy, N. (1983). Stressors of childhood. In N. Garmezy & M. Rutter (Eds.), *Stress, coping and development in children* (pp. 43–84). New York: McGraw-Hill.

Garmezy, N., & Rutter, M. (1983). (Eds.), *Stress, coping and development in children.* New York: McGraw-Hill.

Gatchel, R. J., & Baum, A. (1983). *An introduction to health psychology.* Reading, MA: Addison-Wesley.

Gazzaniga, M. S. (1995). *The cognitive neurosciences.* Cambridge: MIT Press.

George, J. M., Scott, D. S., Turner, S. P., & Gregg, J. M. (1980). The effects of psychological factors and physical trauma on recovery from oral surgery. *Journal of Behavioral Medicine, 3,* 291–310.

Gentry, W. D. (1984). (Ed.). *Handbook of behavioral medicine.* New York: Guilford.

Gergen, K. J., & Gergen, M. M. (1986). Narrative form and the construction of psychological science. In T. R. Sarbin (Ed.), *Narrative psychology: The storied nature of human conduct* (pp. 22–44). New York: Praeger.

Gibson, J. J. (1966). *The senses considered as perceptual systems.* Boston: Houghton Mifflin.

Giorgi, A. (1970). *Psychology as a human science.* New York: Harper & Row.

Glaser, R., Kiecolt-Glaser, J. K., Bonneau, R. H., Malarkey, W., Kennedy, S., & Hughes, J. (1992). Stress-induced modulation of the immune response to recombinant hepatitis B. Vaccine. *Psychosomatic Medicine, 54,* 22–29.

Goffman, E. (1959). *The presentation of self in everyday life.* Garden City, NY: Doubleday.

Goffman, E. (1971). *Relations in public.* New York: Basic Books.

Goldstein, M. J. (1959). The relationship between coping and avoiding behavior and response to fear-arousing propaganda. *Journal or Abnormal and Social Psychology, 58,* 247–252.

Goldstein, M. J. (1973). Individual differences in response to stress. *American Journal of Community Psychology, 1,* 113–137.

Goleman, D. (1995). *Emotional intelligence: Why it can matter more than IQ.* New York: Bantam.

Gottlieb, B. H. (Ed.). (1997a). *Coping with chronic stress.* New York: Plenum.

Gottlieb, B. H. (1997b). Conceptual and measurement issues in the study of coping with chronic stress. In B. H. Gottlieb (Ed.), *Coping with chronic stress* (pp. 3–40). New York: Plenum.

Greenberg, J., Solomon, S., Pyszcynski, T., Rosenblatt, A., Burling, J., Lyon, D., Simon, L., & Pinel, E. (1992). Why do people need self-esteem? Converging evidence that self-esteem serves an anxiety-buffering function. *Journal of Personality and Social Psychology, 63,* 913–922.

Greenwald, A. G. (1992). New look: 3. Unconscious cognition reclaimed. *American Psychologist, 47,* 766–779.

Grinker, R. R. & Spiegel, J. P. (1945). *Men under stress.* New York: McGraw-Hill.

Gross, J. J. (1998). Antecedent- and response-focused emotion regulation: Divergent consequences for experience, expression, and physiology. *Journal of Personality and Social Psychology, 74,* 224–237.

Gruen, R. J., Folkman, S., & Lazarus, R. S. (1989). Centrality and individual differences in the meaning of daily hassles. *Journal of Personality, 56,* 743–762.

Haan, N. (1969). A tripartite model of ego-functioning: Values and clinical research applications. *Journal of Nervous and Mental Diseases, 148,* 14–30.

Haggerty, R. J., Sherrod, L. R., Garmezy, N., & Rutter, M. (1996). *Stress, risk, and resilience in children and adolescents.* New York: Cambridge University Press.

Hallberg, L. R.-M., & Carlsson, S. G. (1991). A qualitative study of strategies for managing a hearing impairment. *British Journal of Audiology, 25,* 201–211.

Hamburg, B. A. (1974). Early adolescence: A specific and stressful stage of the life cycle. In G. V. Coelho, D. A. Hamburg, & J. E. Adams (Eds.), *Coping and adaptation* (pp. 101–124). New York: Basic Books.

Hamilton, V. L., Hoffman, W. S., Broman, C. L., & Rauma, D. (1993). Unemployment, distress, and coping: A panel study of autoworkers. *Journal of Personality and Social Psychology, 65,* 234–247.

Harris, J. R. (1991). The utility of the transaction approach for occupational stress research. In P. L. Perrewé (Ed.), Handbook of job stress. Special issue of the *Journal of Social Behavior and Personality, 6,* 21–29.

Harlow, H. F. (1953). Mice, monkeys, men and motives. *Psychological Review, 60,* 23–32.

Hawthorne, N. (1883). *The scarlet letter.* Boston: Houghton Mifflin.

Heider, F. (1958). *The psychology of interpersonal relations.* New York: Wiley.

Heim, E. (1991). Coping and adaptation in cancer. In C. L. Cooper & M. Watson (Eds.). *Cancer and stress: Psychological, biological and coping studies* (pp. 197–235). London, England: Wiley.

Heim, E., Augustiny, K. F., Blaser, A., Bürki, C., Kühne, D., Rothenbühler, M., Schaffner, L., & Valach, L. (1987). Coping with breast cancer: A longitudinal prospective study. *Psychotherapy and Psychosomatics, 48,* 44–59.

Heim, E., Augustiny, K. F., Schaffner, L., & Valach, L. (1993). Coping with breast cancer over time and situation. *Journal of Psychosomatic Research, 37,* 523–542.

Heller, K. (Ed.). (1986). Disaggregating the process of social support. [Special series], *Journal of Consulting and Clinical Psychology, 54,* 387–470.

Hemenover, S. H., & Dienstbier, R. A. (1996a). Predication of stress appraisals from mastery, extraversion, neuroticism, and general appraisal tendencies. *Motivation and Emotion, 20,* 299–317.

Hemenover, S. H., & Dienstbier, R. A. (1996b). The effects of an appraisal manipulation: Affect, intrusive cognitions, and performance for two cognitive tasks. *Motivation and Emotion, 20,* 319–340.

Hendrick, C., & Hendrick, S. S. (1989). Research on love: Does it measure up? *Journal of Personality and Social Psychology, 56,* 784–794.

Hepburn, C. G., Loughlin, C. A., & Barling, J. (1997). Coping with chronic work stress. In B. H. Gottlieb (Ed.), *Coping with chronic stress* (pp. 343–366). New York: Plenum.

Hetherington, E. M. (1998). (Ed.). Applications of developmental science [Special issue]. *American Psychologist, 53,* 93–259.

Hetherington, E. M., & Blechman, E. A. (1996). *Stress, coping, and resiliency in children and families.* Mahwah, NJ: Erlbaum.

Hinkle, L. E. Jr. (1973). The concept of "stress" in the biological and social sciences. *Science, Medicine & Man, 1,* 31–48.

Hinkle, L. E. Jr. (1977). The concept of "stress" in the biological and social sciences. In Z. J. Lipowski, D. R. Lipsitt, & P. C. Whybrow (Eds.), *Psychosomatic medicine: Current trends and clinical implications.* New York: Oxford University Press.

Hobfoll, S. E., Schwarzer, R., and Chon, K-K. (1996). Disentangling the stress labyrinth: Interpreting the meaning of the term stress as it is studied. *Japanese Health Psychology, 4,* 1–22.

Hock, M., Krohne, H. W., & Kaiser, J. (1996). Coping dispositions and the processing of ambiguous stimuli. *Journal of Personality and Social Psychology, 70,* 1052–1066.

Hoffman, M. L. (1982). Development of prosocial motivation: Empathy and guilt. In N. Eisenberg (Ed.), *The development of prosocial behavior.* New York: Academic Press.

von Hofsten, C. (1985). Perception and action. In M. Frese & J. Sabini (Eds.), *Goal directed behavior: The concept of action in psychology* (pp. 80–96). Hillsdale, NJ: Erlbaum.

Holahan, C. J., & Moos, R. H. (1987). Personal and contextual determinants of coping strategies. *Journal of Personality and Social Psychology, 52,* 946–955.

Holahan, C. J., Moos, R. H., Holahan, C. K., & Brennan, P. L. (1995). Social support, coping, and depressive symptoms in a late-middle-aged sample of patients reporting cardiac illness. *Health Psychology, 14,* 152–163.

Hollingshead, A. B., & Redlich F. C. (1958). *Social class and mental illness.* New York: Wiley.

Holmes, T. H., & Rahe, R. H. (1967). The social readjustment rating scale. *Journal of Psychosomatic Research, 11,* 213–218.

Holzman, P. S., & Gardner, R. W. (1959). Leveling and repression. *Journal of Abnormal Psychology, 59,* 151–155.

Horowitz, M. J. (1976). *Stress response syndromes.* New York: Jason Aronson.

Horowtiz, M. J. (1982). Stress response syndromes and their treatment. In L. Goldberger & S. Breznitz (Eds.), *Handbook of stress* (pp. 711–732). New York: Free Press.

Horowitz, M. J. (1989). Relationship schema formulation: Role relationship models and intrapsychic conflict. *Psychiatry, 52,* 260–274.

House, J. S. (1981), Social structure and personality. In M. Rosenberg & R. H. Turner (Eds.), *Social psychology: Sociological perspectives* (pp. 525–561). New York: Basic Books.

Hume, D. (1957). *An inquiry concerning the principles of morals.* New York: Library of Liberal Arts.

Hunter, J. E. (1997). Special section, articles by Harris, R. J., Abelson, R. P., Scarr, S., & Estes, W. K. *Psychological Science, 8,* 1–20.

Hupka, R. B. (1981). Cultural determinants of jealousy. *Alternative Lifestyles, 4,* 310–356.

Jacobson, D. (1987). Models of stress and meanings of unemployment: Reactions to job loss among technical professionals. *Social Science in Medicine, 24,* 13–21.

Janis, I. L. (1951). *Air war and emotional stress.* New York: McGraw-Hill.

Janis, I. L. (1958). *Psychological stress: Psychoanalytic and behavioral studies of surgical patients.* New York: Wiley.

Janis, I. L. (1962). Psychological effects of warnings. In G. W. Baker & D. W. Chapman (Eds.), *Man and society in disaster* (pp. 55–92). New York: Basic Books.

Janis, I. L. (1968). Attitude change via role playing. In R. Abelson, E. Aronson, E. J. McGuire, et al. (Eds.), *Theories of cognitive consistency: A sourcebook.* Chicago: Rand McNally.

Janis, I. L., & Mann, L. (1977). *Decision making.* New York: Free Press.

Janoff-Bulman, R. (1989). Assumptive worlds and the stress of traumatic effects. *Social Cognition, 7,* 113–136.

Janoff-Bulman, R. (1992). *Shattered assumptions: Toward a new psychology of trauma.* New York: Free Press.

Jemmott, J. B., & Locke, S. E. (1984). Psychosocial factors, immunological mediation, and human susceptibility to infectious diseases: How much do we know? *Psychological Bulletin, 95,* 78–108.

Jenkins, C. D. (1996). "While there's hope, there's life." Editorial comment. *Psychosomatic Medicine, 58,* 122–124.

Jerusalem, M., & Schwarzer, R. (1989). Anxiety and self-concept as antecedents of stress and coping: A longitudinal study with German and Turkish adolescents. *Personality and Individual Differences, 10,* 785–792.

Jessor, R. (1981). The perceived environment in psychological theory and research. In D. Magnusson (Ed.), *Toward a psychology of situations: An interactional perspective* (pp. 297–317). Hillsdale, NJ: Erlbaum.

Jessor, R. (1996). Ethnographic methods in contemporary perspective. In R. Jessor, A. Colby, & R. A. Shweder (Eds.). *Ethnography and human development: Context and meaning in social inquiry* (pp. 3–14). Chicago: University of Chicago Press.

Josselson, R., & Lieblich, A. (Eds.). (1993). *The narrative study of lives.* Newbury Park, CA: Sage.

Kâgitçibasi, C., & Berry, J. W. (1989). Cross-cultural psychology: current research and trends. *Annual Review of Psychology, 40,* 493–531.

Kahana, B., Kahana, E., Harel, Z., Kelly, K., Monaghan, P., & Holland, L. (1997). A framework for understanding the chronic stress of holocaust survivors. In. B. H. Gottlieb (Ed.), *Coping with chronic stress.* (pp. 315–342). New York: Plenum.

Kahn, R. L., Wolfe, D. M., Quinn, R. P., Snoek, J. D., & Rosenthal, R. A. (1964). *Organizational stress: Studies in role conflict and ambiguity.* New York: Wiley.

Kanner, A., Coyne, J. C., Schaefer, C., & Lazarus, R. S. (1981). Comparison of two modes of stress measurement: Daily hassles and uplifts versus major life events. *Journal of Behavioral Medicine, 4,* 1–39.

Kaplan, B. H., Cassel, J. C., & Gore, S. (1977). Social support and health. *Medical Care, 15,* 47–58.

Kaplan, J. R., Manuck, S. B., Williams, J. K., & Strawn, W. (1993). Psychosocial influences on atherosclerosis: Evidence for effects and mechanisms in nonhuman primates. In J. Blascovich & E. Katkin (Eds.), *Cardiovascular reactivity to psychological stress and disease* (pp. 3–26). Washington, DC: American Psychological Association.

Kardiner, A. (1939). *The individual in his society.* New York: Columbia University Press.

Kasl, S. V. (1983). Pursuing the link between stressful life experiences and disease: A time for reappraisal. In C. L. Cooper (Ed.), *Stress research* (pp. 79–102). New York: Wiley.

Kasl, S. V., Evans, A. S., & Niederman, J. C. (1979). Psychosocial risk factors in the development of infectious mononucleosis. *Psychosomatic Medicine, 41,* 445–466.

Kelly, G. A. (1955). *The psychology of personal constructs.* New York: Norton.

Kelman, H. C. (1961). Processes of opinion change. *Public Opinion Quarterly, 25,* 57–58.

Kemper, T. D. (1978). *A social interaction theory of emotions.* New York: Wiley.

Kihlstrom, J. F. (1987). The cognitive unconscious. *Science, 237,* 1445–1452.

Kihlstrom, J. F. (1990). The psychological unconscious. In L. A. Pervin (Ed.), *Handbook of personality: Theory and research* (pp. 445–464). New York: Guilford.

Kihlstrom, J. F., Barnhardt, T. M., & Tataryn, D. J. (1992). The psychological unconscious: Found, lost, and regained. *American Psychologist, 47,* 788–791.

Kim, U., Triandis, H. C., Kâgitçibasi, C., Choi, S-C. & Yoon, G. (Eds.). (1994). *Individualism and collectivism: Theory, method, and applications.* Thousand Oaks, CA: Sage

Kitayama, S., & Marcus, H. R. (Eds.). (1994). *Emotion and culture: Empirical studies of mutual influence.* Washington, DC: American Psychological Association.

Kitayama, S., Marcus, H. R., & Matsumoto, H. (1995). Culture, self, and emotion: A cultural perspective on "self-conscious" emotions. In J. P. Tangney & K. W. Fischer (Eds.), *Self-conscious emotions: The psychology of shame, guilt, embarrassment, and pride* (pp. 439–464). New York: Guilford.

Kitayama, S., & Masuda, T. (1995). Reappraising cognitive appraisal from a cultural perspective. *Psychological Inquiry, 6,* 217–223.

Kleber, R. J., Figley, C. R., & Gersons, B. P. R. (1995). *Beyond trauma: Cultural and societal dynamics.* New York: Plenum.

Klein, G. S. (1958). Cognitive control and motivation. In G. Lindzey (Ed.), *Assessment of motives.* New York: Holt, Rinehart & Winston.

Klein, G. S. (1964). Need and regulation. In M. R. Jones, (Ed.). *Nebraska Symposium on Motivation.* Lincoln: University of Nebraska Press.

Klein, M. (1946–1963). *Envy and gratitude and other works.* London: Hogarth Press.

Klinger, E. (1975). Consequences of commitments to and disengagement from incentives. *Psychological Review, 82,* 1–25.

Klos, D. S., & Singer, J. L. (1981). Determinants of the adolescent's ongoing thought following simulated parental confrontations. *Journal of Personality and Social Psychology, 41,* 975–987.

Kohlmann, C. W. (1993). Rigid and flexible modes of coping: Related to coping style? *Anxiety, Stress, and Coping, 6,* 107–123.

Krohne, H. W. (1978). Individual differences in coping with stress and anxiety. In C. D. Spielberger & I. G. Sarason (Eds.), *Stress and anxiety* (Vol. 5, pp. 233–260). Washington, DC: Hemisphere.

Krohne, H. W. (1993). Vigilance and cognitive avoidance as concepts in coping research. In H. W. Krohne (Ed.), *Attention and avoidance: Strategies in coping with aversiveness* (pp. 19–50). Toronto: Hogrefe & Huber.

Krohne, H. W. (1996). Individual differences in coping. In M. Zeidner & N. S. Endler (Eds.), *Handbook of coping: Theory, research, applications* (pp. 381–409). New York: Wiley.

Krohne, H. W., & Egloff, B. (in press). Vigilant and avoidant coping: Theory and measurement. In C. D. Spielberger & I. G. Sarason (Eds.), *Stress and emotion* (Vol. 17). Washington, DC: Taylor & Francis.

Krohne, H. W., & Rogner, J. (1982). Repression-sensitization as a central construct in coping research. In H. W. Krohne & L. Laux (Eds.), *Achievement, stress, and anxiety* (pp. 167–193). Washington, DC: Hemisphere.

Krohne, H. W., Slangen, K., & Kleemann, P. P. (1996). Coping variables as predictors of perioperative emotional states and adjustment. *Psychology and Health, 11,* 315–330.

Krupnick, J. L., and Horowitz, M. J. (1981). Stress response syndromes: Recurrent themes. *Archives of General Psychiatry, 38,* 428–435.

Kühlmann, T. M. (1990). Coping with occupational stress among urban bus and tram drivers. *Journal of Occupational Psychology, 63,* 89–96.

Kuhn, T. S. (1970). *The structure of scientific revolutions* (2nd ed.). Chicago: University of Chicago Press.

Landreville, P., Dubé, M., Lalande, G., & Alain, M. (1994). Appraisal, coping, and depressive symptoms in older adults with reduced mobility. *Journal of Social Behavior and Personality: Special issue. Psychosocial perspectives on disability, 9,* 269–286).

Landreville, P., & Vezina, J. (1994). Differences in appraisal and coping between elderly coronary artery disease patients high and low in depressive symptoms. *Journal of Mental Health, 3,* 79–89.

Lang, P. J. (1977). Imagery in therapy: An information processing analysis of fear. *Behavior Therapy, 8,* 862–886.

Lang, P. J. (1979). A bio-informational theory of emotional imagery. *Psychophysiology, 16,* 495–512.

Langston, C. A. (1994). Capitalizing on and coping with daily-life events: Expressive responses to positive events. *Journal of Personality and Social Psychology, 67,* 1112–1125.

Larrson, G. (1989). Personality, appraisal and cognitive coping processes, and performance during various conditions of stress. *Military Psychology, 1,* 167–182.

Larrson, G., Kempe, C., & Starrin, B. (1988). Appraisal and coping processes in acute time-limited stressful situations: A study of police officers. *European Journal of Personality, 2,* 259–276.

Laux, L., & Weber, H. (1991). Presentations of self in coping with anger and anxiety: An intentional approach. *Anxiety Research, 3,* 233–255.

Lavallee, L. F., & Campbell, J. D. (1995). Impact of personal goals on self-regulation processes elicited by daily negative events, *Journal of Personality and Social Psychology, 69,* 341–352.

Law, A., Logan, H., & Baron, R. S. (1994). Desire for control, felt control, and stress inoculation training during dental treatment. *Journal of Personality and Social Psychology, 67,* 926–936.

Lazarus, R. S. (1964). A laboratory approach to the dynamics of psychological stress. *American Psychologist, 19,* 400–411.

Lazarus, R. S. (1966). *Psychological stress and the coping process.* New York: McGraw-Hill.

Lazarus, R. S. (1968). Emotions and adaptation: Conceptual and empirical relations. In W. J. Arnold (Ed.), *Nebraska Symposium on Motivation* (pp. 175–266). Lincoln: University of Nebraska Press.

Lazarus, R. S. (1981). The stress and coping paradigm. In C. Eisdorfer, D. Cohen, A. Kleinman, & P. Maxim (Eds.). *Models for clinical psychopathology* (pp. 177–214). New York: Spectrum.

Lazarus, R. S. (1982). Thoughts on the relations between emotion and cognition. *American Psychologist, 37,* 1019–1024.

Lazarus, R. S. (1983). The costs and benefits of denial. In S. Breznitz (Ed.), *The denial of stress* (pp. 1–30). New York: International Universities Press.

Lazarus, R. S. (1984a). On the primacy of cognition. *American Psychologist, 39,* 124–129.

Lazarus, R. S. (1984b). Puzzles in the study of daily hassles. *Journal of Behavioral Medicine, 7,* 375–389.

Lazarus, R. S. (1985). The trivialization of distress. In J. C. Rosen & L. J. Solomon (Eds.), *Preventing health risk behaviors and promoting coping with illness* (Vol. 8, Vermont Conference on the primary prevention of psychopathology (pp. 279–298). Hanover, NH: University Press of New England. Reprinted in Hammonds, B. L. & Scheirer, C. J. (Eds.). The Master Lecture Series, 1983 (Vol. 3, pp. 121–144. Washington, DCP: American Psychological Association.

Lazarus, R. S. (1989a). Constructs of the mind in mental health and psychotherapy. In A. Freeman, H. Arkowitz, K. M. Simon, L. E. Beutler, & H. Arkowitz (Eds.), *Comprehensive Handbook of Cognitive Therapy* (pp. 99–121). New York: Plenum.

Lazarus, R. S. (1989b). Cognition and emotion from the RET viewpoint. *Journal of Rational-Emotive & Cognitive-Behavior Therapy, 13,* 29–54.

Lazarus, R. S. (1989c). Constructs of the mind in mental health and psychotherapy. In A. Freeman, K. M. Simon, L. E. Butler, & A. Arkowitz (Eds.), *Comprehensive handbook of cognitive therapy*. (pp. 99–121). New York: Plenum.

Lazarus, R. S., & Commentators (1990). Theory-based stress measurement. *Psychological Inquiry, 1,* 3–51.

Lazarus, R. S. (1991a). *Emotion and adaptation*. New York: Oxford University Press.

Lazarus, R. S. (1991b). Cognition and motivation in emotion. *American Psychologist, 46,* 352–367.

Lazarus, R. S. (1991c). Psychological stress in the workplace. In P. L. Perrewé (Ed.), Handbook of job stress. Special Issue of the *Journal of Social Behavioral and Personality, 6,* 1–13.

Lazarus, R. S. (1991d). Emotion theory and psychotherapy. In J. D. Safran & L. S. Greenberg (Eds.), *Affective change events in psychotherapy* (pp. 290–301). New York: Academic Press.

Lazarus, R. S. (1991e). Progress on a cognitive-motivational-relational theory of emotion. *American Psychologist, 46,* 819–834.

Lazarus, R. S. (1991f). Commentary 6: Evaluating Psychosocial Factors in Health. In C. R. Snyder & D. R. Forsyth (Eds.). *Handbook of social and clinical psychology* (p. 798). Needham Heights, MA: Allyn & Bacon.

Lazarus, R. S. (1992). Four reasons why it is difficult to demonstrate psychosocial influences on health. *Advances: The Journal of Mind-body Health, 8,* 6–7.

Lazarus, R. S. (1993a). Coping theory and research: Past, present, and future. *Psychosomatic Medicine, 55,* 234–247.

Lazarus, R. S. (1993b). From psychological stress to the emotions: A history of changing outlooks. In *Annual review of psychology, 1993* (pp. 1–21). Palo Alto: Annual Reviews.

Lazarus, R. S. (1996). The role of coping in the emotions and how coping changes over the life course. In C. Magai & S. H. McFadden (Eds), *Handbook of emotion, adult development, and aging* (pp. 289–306). New York: Academic Press.

Lazarus, R. S. (1997). How we cope with stress. *Mental Health Research,* Vol. 16, pp. 1–24. Seoul, Korea: Hangyang University.

Lazarus, R. S. (1998a). *Fifty years of research and theory by R. S. Lazarus: Perennial historical issues.* Mahwah, NJ: Erlbaum.

Lazarus, R. S. (1998b). Coping with aging: Individuality as a key to understanding. In I. H. Nordhus, G. VandenBos, S. Berg, & P. Fromholt (Eds.), *Clinical Geropsychology* (pp.109–127). Washington, DC: American Psychological Association.

Lazarus, R. S. (1998). Coping from the perspective of personality. *Zeitschrift für Differentielle und Diagnostische Psychologie, 19,* 213–231

Lazarus, R. S., & Alfert, E. (1964). The short-circuiting of threat by experimentally altering cognitive appraisal. *Journal of Abnormal and Social Psychology, 69,* 195–205.

Lazarus. R. S., & Averill, J. R. (1972). Emotion and cognition: With special reference to anxiety. In C. D. Spielberger (Ed.), *Anxiety and behavior* (2nd ed., pp. 242–283). New York: Academic Press.

Lazarus, R. S., Averill, J. R., & Opton, E. M. Jr. (1970). Toward a cognitive theory of emotions. In M. Arnold (Ed.), *Feelings and emotions* (pp. 207–232). New York: Academic Press.

Lazarus, R. S., Averill, J. R., & Opton, E. M. Jr. (1974). The psychology of coping: Issues of research and assessment. In G. V. Coelho, D. A. Hamburg, & J. F. Adams (Eds.), *Coping and adaptation* (pp. 249–315). New York: Basic Books.

Lazarus, R. S., & Baker, R. W. (1956a). Personality and psychological stress: A theoretical and methodological framework. *Psychological Newsletter, 8,* 21–32.

Lazarus, R. S., & Baker, R. W. (1956b). Psychology. *Progress in Neurology and Psychiatry, 11,* 253–271.

Lazarus, R. S., and commentators. (1990). Theory-based stress measurement. *Psychological Inquiry, 1,* 3–51.

Lazarus, R. S., & commentators. (1992). Can we demonstrate important psychosocial influences on health? *Advances, 8,* 5–45.

Lazarus, R. S., & commentators. (1993). Book review essays by Shweder, R. A., Trabasso, T., Stein, N.; Panksepp, J., & author's response. *Psychological Inquiry, 4,* 322–342.

Lazarus, R. S., & commentators. (1995). Vexing research problems inherent in cognitive-mediational theories of emotion, and some solutions. *Psychological Inquiry, 6,* 183–265.

Lazarus, R. S., Coyne, J. C., & Folkman, S. (1982). Cognition, emotion and motivation: The doctoring of Humpty-Dumpty. In R. W. J. Neufeld (Ed.), *Psychological stress and psychopathology* (pp. 218–239). New York: McGraw-Hill.

Lazarus, R. S., & DeLongis, A. (1983). Psyschological stress and coping in aging. *American Psychologist, 38,* 245–254.

Lazarus, R. S., DeLongis, A., Folkman, S., & Gruen, R. (1985). Stress and adaptational outcomes: The problem of confounded measures. *American Psychologist, 40,* 770–779.

Lazarus, R. S., Deese, J., & Osler, S. F. (1952). The effects of psychological stress upon performance. *Psychological Bulletin, 49,* 293–317.

Lazarus, R. S., & Eriksen, C. W. (1952). Effects of failure stress upon skilled performance. *Journal of Experimental Psychology, 43,* 100–105.

Lazarus, R. S., Eriksen, C. W., & Fonda, C. P. (1951). Personality dynamics and auditory perceptual recognition. *Journal of Personality, 19,* 471–482.

Lazarus, R. S. & Folkman, S. (1984). *Stress, appraisal, and coping.* New York: Springer.

Lazarus, R. S., & Folkman, S. (1987). Transactional theory and research on emotions and coping. In L. Laux & G. Vossel (Eds.), Personality in biographical stress and coping research. *European Journal of Personality, 1,* 141–169.

Lazarus, R. S., & Folkman, S. (1989). *Manual for the hassles and uplifts scales.* Palo Alto: Consulting Psychologists Press.

Lazarus, R. S., Kanner, A, & Folkman, S. (1980). Emotions: A cognitive-phenomenological analysis. In R. Plutchik & H. Kellerman (Eds.), *Theories of emotion* (pp. 189–217). New York: Academic Press.

Lazarus, R. S., & Launier, R. (1978). Stress-related transactions between person and environment. In L. A. Pervin & M. Lewis (Eds.), *Perspectives in interactional psychology* (pp. 287–327). New York: Plenum.

Lazarus, R. S., & Lazarus, B. N. (1994). *Passion and reason: Making sense of our emotions.* New York: Oxford University Press.

Lazarus, R. S., & Longo, N. (1953). The consistency of psychological defenses against threat. *Journal of Abnormal and Social Psychology, 48,* 495–499.

Lazarus, R. S., & Smith, C. A. (1988). Knowledge and appraisal in the cognition-emotion relationship. *Cognition and Emotion, 2,* 281–300.

Lazarus, R. S., Speisman, J. C., & Mordkoff, A. M. (1963). The relationships between autonomic indicators of psychological stress: Heart rate and skin conductance. *Psychosomatic Medicine, 25,* 19–21.

Le Doux, J. W. (1989). Cognitive-emotional interactions in the brain. *Cognition and Emotion, 3,* 267–289.

Leeper, R. W. (1948). A motivational theory of emotion to replace "emotion as a disorganized response." *Psychological Review, 55,* 5–21.

Lepore, S. J. (1997). Social-environmental influences on the chronic stress process. In B. H. Gottlieb (Ed.), *Coping with chronic stress* (pp. 133–160). New York: Plenum.

Lerner, M. J. (1980). *The belief in a just world: A fundamental delusion.* New York: Plenum.

Leventhal, H. (1984). A perceptual motor theory of emotion. In K. R. Scherer & P. Ekman (Eds.), *Approaches to emotion* (pp. 271–291). Hillsdale, NJ: Erlbaum.

Levine, L. J. (1996). The anatomy of disappointment: A natural test of appraisal models of sadness, anger, and hope. *Cognition and Emotion, 10,* 337–359.

Lewicki, P., Hill, T., & Cyzewska, M. (1992). Nonconscious acquisition of information. *American Psychologist, 47,* 796–801.

Lewin, K. A. (1935). *A dynamic theory of personality* (K. E. Zener & D. K. Adams, Trans.). New York: McGraw-Hill.

Lewin, K. A. (1946). Behavior and development as a function of the total situation. In L. Carmichael (Ed.), *Manual of Child Psychology* (pp. 918–970). New York: Wiley.

Lewis, H. B. (1971). *Shame and guilt in neurosis.* New York: International Universities Press.

Lewis, M., & Haviland, J. M. (Eds.). (1993). *Handbook of emotions.* New York: Guilford.

Lewis, M., Sullivan, W. W., Stanger, C., and Weiss, M. (1989). Self-development and self-conscious emotions. *Child Development, 60,* 146–156.

Liebert, R. M., & Morris, L. W. (1967). Cognitive and emotional components of test anxiety: A distinction and some initial data. *Psychological Reports, 20,* 975–978.

Lindemann, E. (1944). Symptomatology and management of acute grief. *American Journal of Psychiatry, 101,* 141–148.

Lipowski, Z. J., Lipsitt, D. R., & Whybrow, P. C. (1977). (Eds.). *Psychosomatic medicine: Current trends and clinical applications.* New York: Oxford University Press.

Locke, E. A., and Taylor, M. S. (1990). Stress, coping, and the meaning of work. In W. Nord, & A. Brief (Eds.), *The Meaning of work.* New York: D.C Heath.

Loevinger, J. (1976). *Ego development: Conceptions and theories.* San Francisco: Jossey-Bass.

Loftus, E. F., & Klinger, M. R. (1992). Is the unconscious smart or dumb? *American Psychologist, 47,* 761–765.

Long, B. C., Kahn, S. E., & Schutz, R. W. (1992). Causal model of stress and coping: Women in management. *Journal of Counseling Psychology, 39,* 227–239.

Lucas, R. S. (1969). *Men in crisis.* New York: Basic Books.

Lumsden, D. P. (1981). Is the concept of "stress" of any use, anymore? In D. Randall (Ed.), *Contributions to primary prevention in mental health: working papers.* Toronto: Toronto National Office of the Canadian Mental Health Association.

Lutz, C., & White, G. M. (1986). The anthropology of emotions. *Annual Review of Anthropology, 15,* 405–436.

Maddi, S. R., & Kobasa, S. C. (1984). *The hardy executive: Health under stress.* Pacific Grove, CA: Brooks/Cole.

Maes, S., Leventhal, H., & de Ridder, D. T. D. (1996). Coping with chronic diseases. In M. Zeidner & N. S. Endler (Eds.), *Handbook of Coping: Theory, research, applications* (pp. 221–251). New York: Wiley.

Magai, C., & McFadden, S. H. (1996). (Eds.). *Handbook of emotion, adult development, and aging.* New York: Academic Press.

Magnusson, D., & Bergman, L. R. (1997). Individual development and adaptation: The IDA Program. *Reports from the Department of Psychology.* Stockholm, Sweden: Stockholm University.

Mandler, G. (1984). *Mind and body: Psychology of emotion and stress.* New York: Norton.

Manne, S. L., Sabblioni, M., & Bovbjerg, D. H. (1994). Coping with chemotherapy for breast cancer. *Journal of Behavioral Medicine, 17,* 41–55.

Manne, S. L., & Sandler, I. (1984). Coping and adjustment to genital herpes. *Journal of Behavioral Medicine, 7,* 391–410.

Manne, S. L., Taylor, K. L., Dougherty, J., & Kemeny, N. (1997), Supportive and negative responses in the partner relationship: Their association with psychological adjustment among individuals with cancer. *Journal of Behavioral Medicine, 20,* 101–125.

Mantovani, G. (1996). *New communication environments: From everyday to virtual.* London: Taylor & Francis.

Marcus, H. R., & Kitayama, S. (1991). Culture and the self: Implications for cognition, emotion, and motivation. *Psychological Review, 98,* 224–253.

Martelli, M. F., Auerbach, S. M., Alexander, J., & Mercuri, L. G. (1987). Stress management in the health care setting: Matching interventions with patient coping styles. *Journal of Consulting and Clinical Psychology, 55,* 201–207.

Marucha, P. T., Kiecolt-Glaser, J. K., & Favagehi, M. (1998). Mucosal wound healing is impaired by examination stress. *Psychosomatic Medicine, 60,* 362–365.

Mascolo, M. F., & Fischer, K. W. (1995). Developmental transformations in appraisals for pride, shame, and guilt. In J. P. Tangney, & K. W. Fischer (Eds.), *Self-conscious emotions: The psychology of shame, guilt embarrassment, and pride* (pp. 64–113). New York: Guilford.

Masel, C. N., Terry, D. J., & Gribble, M. (1996). The effects of coping on adjustment: Re-examining the goodness of fit model of coping effectiveness. *Anxiety, Stress, and Coping, 9,* 279–300.

Maslach, C. (1982). *Burnout: The cost of caring.* Englewood Cliffs, NJ: Prentice-Hall.

Maslow, A. H. (1964). Synergy in the society and the individual. *Journal of Individual Psychology, 20,* 153–164.

Mason, J. W., Maher, J. T., Hartley, L. H., Mougey, E., Perlow, M. J., & Jones, L. G. (1976). Selectivity of corticosteroid and catecholamine response to various natural stimuli. In G. Serban (Ed.), *Psychopathology of human adaptation.* New York: Plenum.

Mason, M. A., Skolnick, A., and Sugarman, S. D. (in press). *All our families. New policies for a new century.* New York: Oxford University Press.

Matarazzo, J. D., Weiss, S. M., Herd, J. A., Miller, N. E., & Weiss, S. M. (1984). (Eds.), *Behavioral health: A handbook of health enhancement and disease prevention.* New York: Wiley.

Mathews, K. A. (1981). "At a relatively early age the habit of working the machine to its maximum capacity:" Antecedents of the Type A coronary-prone behavior pattern. In S. S. Brehm, S. M. Kassin, & F. X. Gibbons (Eds.), *Developmental social psychology* (pp. 235–248). New York: Oxford University Press.

Maugham, S. (1915). *Of human bondage.* London: Heinemann.

Mauro, R., Sato, K., & Tucker, J. (1992). The role of appraisal in human emotions: A cross-cultural study. *Journal of Personality and Social Psychology, 62,* 301–317.

McAdams, D. P. (1996). Personality, modernity, and the storied self: A contemporary framework for studying persons. *Psychological Inquiry, 7,* 295–321.

McAdams, D. P. (1997). *The stories we live by: Personal myths and the making of the self.* New York: Guilford.

McClelland, D. C. (1951). *Personality.* New York: Sloane.

McClelland, D. C., Atkinson, J. W., Clark, R. A., & Lowell, E. L. (1953). *The achievement motive.* New York: Appleton-Century-Crofts.

McCrae, R. R., & Costa, P. T., Jr. (1986). Personality, coping, and coping effectiveness in an adult sample. *Journal of Personality, 54,* 385–405.

McFarlane, A. C. (1995). The severity of the trauma: Issues about its role in posttraumatic stress disorder. In R. J. Kleber, C. R. Figley, & Gersons, B. P. R. (Eds). *Beyond trauma: Cultural and societal dynamics* (pp. 31–54). New York: Plenum.

McQueeney, D. A., Stanton, A. L., & Sigmon, S. (1997). Efficacy of emotion-focused and problem-focused group therapies for women with fertility problems. *Journal of Behavioral Medicine, 20,* 313–331.

McReynolds, P. (1956). A restricted conceptualization of human anxiety and motivation. *Psychological Reports, Monograph Supplements, 6,* 293–312.

Mechanic, D. (1962/1978). *Students under stress: A study in the social psychology of adaptation.* New York: The Free Press. Reprinted in 1978 by the University of Wisconsin Press.

Mechanic, D. (1983). (Ed.). *Handbook of health, health care, and the health professions.* New York: The Free Press.

Megargee, E. I., & Hokanson, J. E. (1970). (Eds.). *The dynamics of aggression.* New York: Harper & Row.

Meichenbaum, D. (1977). *Cognitive-behavior modification: An integrative approach.* New York: Plenum.

Meichenbaum, D., & Cameron, R. (1983). Stress innoculation training: Toward a general paradigm for training coping skills. In D. Meichenbaum & J. E. Jaremko (Eds.), *Stress reduction and prevention* (pp. 115–154). New York: Plenum.

Meichenbaum, D., & Jaremko, M. E. (1983). *Stress reduction and prevention.* New York: Plenum.

Menninger, K. (1954). Regulatory devices of the ego under major stress. *International Journal of Psychoanalysis, 35,* 412–420.

Merikle, P. M. (1992). Perception without awareness. *American Psychologist, 47,* 792–795.

Merleau-Ponty, M. (1962). *Phenomenology of perception* (C. Smith, Trans.). London: Routledge & Kegan Paul.

Mesquita, B., & Frijda, N. H. (1992). Cultural variations in emotion. *Psychological Bulletin, 112,* 179–204.

Mill, J. S. (1949). *A system of logic.* London: Longmans, Green. (First published in 1843).

Miller, P., & Sperry, L. L. (1987). The socialization of anger and aggression. *Merrill-Palmer Quarterly, 33,* 1–31.

Miller, D. R., & Swanson, G. E. (1960). *Inner conflict and defense.* New York: Holt, Rinehart, & Winston.

Miller, S. M. (1981). Predictability and human stress: Toward clarification of evidence and theory. In L. Berkowitz (Ed.), *Advances in experimental social psychology* (Vol. 14, pp. 203–255). New York: Academic Press.

Miller, S. M. (1987). Monitoring and blunting: Validation of a questionnaire to assess styles of information seeking under threat. *Journal of Personality and Social Psychology, 52,* 345–353.

Miller, S. M., & Green, M. L. (1984). Coping with stress and frustration: Origins, nature, and development. In M. Lewis & I. C. Saarni (Eds.), *The socialization of emotions.* New York: Plenum.

Modell, A. H. (1993). *The private self.* Cambridge: Harvard University Press.

Moos, R. H., Brennan, P. L., Fondacara, M. R., & Moos, B. S. (1990). Approach and avoidance coping responses among older problem and nonproblem drinkers. *Psychology and Aging, 5,* 31–40.

Mowrer, O. H. (1976). From the dynamics of conscience to contract psychology: Clinical theory and practice in transition. In G. Serban (Ed.), *Psychopathology of human adaptation* (pp. 211–230). New York: Plenum.

Murphy, G. (1947/1966). *Personality: A biosocial approach to origins and structure.* New York: Basic Books.

Murphy, L. B., & Associates. (1962). *The widening world of childhood: Paths toward mastery.* New York: Basic Books.

Murphy, L. B., & Moriarty, A. E. (1976). *Vulnerability, coping, and growth: From infancy to adolescence.* New Haven, CT: Yale University Press.

Murray, H. A. (1938). *Explorations in personality.* New York: Oxford University Press.

Mechanic, D. (1962/1978). *Students under stress: A study in the social psychology of adaptation.* New York: The Free Press. Reprinted in 1978 by the University of Wisconsin Press.

Neisser, U. (1985). The role of invariant structures in the control of movement. In M. Frese & J. Sabini (Eds.), *Goal-directed behavior: The concept of action in psychology* (pp. 97–108). Hilldale, NJ: Erlbaum.

Nolen-Hoeksema, S. (1991). Responses to depression and their effects on the duration of depressive episodes. *Journal of Abnormal Psychology, 100,* 569–582.

Nolen-Hoeksema, S., & Morrow, J. (1991). A prospective study of depression and posttraumatic stress symptoms after a natural disaster: The 1989 Loma Prieta earthquake. *Journal of Personality and Social Psychology, 61,* 115–121.

Nolen-Hoeksema, S., Parker, L. E., & Larson, J. (1994). Ruminative coping with depressed mood following loss. *Journal of Personality and Social Psychology, 67,* 92–104.

Noojin, A., B., & Wallander, J. L. Perceived problem-solving ability, stress, and coping in mothers of children with physical disabilities: Potential cognitive influences on adjustment. *International Journal of Behavioral Medicine, 4,* 415–432.

Nuckolls, K. B., Cassel, J., & Kaplan, B. H. (1972). Psychological assets, life crisis, and the progress of pregnancy. *American Journal of Epidemiology, 95,* 431–441.

Nyamathi, A., Wayment, H. A., & Dunkel-Schetter, C. (1993). Psychosocial correlates of emotional distress and risk behavior in African-American women at risk for HIV infection. *Anxiety, Stress, and Coping, 6,* 133–148.

Oates, J. M. (1988). *Acquisition of esophageal speech following laryngectomy.* Doctoral Dissertation. La Trobe University, Bundoora, Australia.

Oatley, K., & Johnson-Laird, P. N. (1987). Towards a cognitive theory of emotions. *Cognition and Emotion, 1,* 29–50.

O'Brien, T. B., & DeLongis, A. (1997). Coping with chronic stress: An interpersonal perspective. In B. H. Gottlieb (Ed.), *Coping with chronic stress* (pp. 161–190). New York: Plenum.

Ohbushi, K., Kameda, M., & Agarie, N. (1989). Apology as an aggression control: Its role in mediating appraisal of and response to harm. *Journal of Personality and Social Psychology, 56,* 219–227.

Olff, M., Brosschot, J. F., Godaert, G., Benschop, R. J., Ballieux, R. E., Heijnen, C. J., de Smet, M. B. M., & Ursin, H. (1995). Modulatory effects of defense and coping on stress-induced changes in endocrine and immune parameters. *International Journal of Behavioral Medicine, 2,* 85–103.

Opton, E. M., Jr., Rankin, N., Nomikos, M., & Lazarus, R. S. (1965). The principle of short-circuiting of threat: Further evidence. *Journal of Personality, 33,* 622–635.

Orr, E., & Westman, M. (1990). Does hardiness moderate stress, and how?: A review. In M. Rosenbaum (Ed.), *Learned resourcefulness: On coping skills, self-control, and adaptive behavior* (pp. 64–94). New York: Springer.

Ortony, A., Clore, G. L., & Collins, A. (1988). *The cognitive structure of emotions.* New York: Cambridge University Press.

Panksepp, J. (1991). Affective neuroscience: A conceptual framework for the neurobiological study of emotions. In K. Strongman (Ed.), *International reviews of studies in emotions* (Vol. 1, pp. 59–99). New York: Wiley.

Panksepp, J. (1993). Where, when, and how does an appraisal become an emotion: "The times they are a changing." *Psychological Inquiry, 4,* 334–342.

Parker, J. D. A., & Endler, N. S. (1996). Coping and defense: A historical overview. In M. Zeidner, & N. S. Endler (1996). *Handbook of coping: Theory, research, applications* (pp. 3–23). New York: Wiley.

Parkes, K. R. (1984). Locus of control, cognitive appraisal, and coping in stressful episodes. *Journal of Personality and Social Psychology, 46,* 655–668.

Parkinson, B., & Manstead, A. S. R. (1992). Appraisal as a cause of emotion. In M. Clark (Ed.), *Emotion. Review of Personality and Social Psychology, 13,* 122–149.

Paterson, R. J., & Neufeld, R. W. J. (1987). Clear danger: Situational determinants of the appraisal of threat. *Psychological Bulletin, 101,* 404–416.

Pearlin, L. I., & McCall, M. E. (1990). Occupational stress and marital support: A description of microprocesses (pp. 39–60). In J. Eckenrode & S. Gore (Eds.), *Stress between work and family*. New York: Plenum.

Peeters, M. C. W., Buunk, B. P., & Schaufeli, W. B. (1995). A microanalytic exploration of the cognitive appraisal of daily stressful events at work: The role of controllability. *Anxiety, Stress, and Coping, 8,* 127–139.

Peeters, M. C. W., Schaufeli, W. B., & Buunk, B. P. (1995). The role of attributions in the cognitive appraisal of work-related stressful events: an event-recording approach. *Work & Stress, 9,* 463–474.

Pennebaker, J. W., Colder, M., & Sharp, L. K. (1990). Accelerating the coping process. *Journal of Personality and Social Psychology, 58,* 528–537.

Perrewé, P. L. (1991). *Job stress*. Corte Madera, CA: Select Press.

Peterson, K. C., Prout, M. F., & Schwarz, R. A. (1991). *Posttraumatic stress disorder: A clinician's guide*. New York: Plenum.

Piers, G., & Singer, M. B. (1971). *Shame and guilt*. New York: Norton.

Pines, A., Aronson, E. with Kaffry, D. (1981). *Burnout: From tedium to personal growth*. New York: The Free Press.

Polanyi, M. (1966). *The tacit dimension*. Garden City, NY: Doubleday.

Polkinghorne, D. (1988). *Narrative knowing and the human sciences*. Albany: State University of New York Press.

Pretzlik, U. (1997). *Children coping with a serious illness: A study exploring coping and distress in children with leukemia or aplastic anemia*. Amsterdam: Kohnstamm Institute: University of Amsterdam.

Pruchno, R. A., & Resch, N. L. (1989). Mental health of caregiving spouses: Coping as mediator, moderator, or main effect? *Psychology and Aging, 4,* 454–463.

Radloff, L. S. (1977). The CES-D scale: A self-report depression scale for research in the general population. *Applied Psychology Measurement, 1,* 385–401.

Reber, A. S. (1993). *Implicit learning and tacit knowledge: An essay on the cognitive unconscious*. New York: Oxford University Press.

Reisenzein, R. (1995). On appraisal as causes of emotions. *Psychological Inquiry, 6,* 233–237.

Reisenzein, R. (in press). A theory of emotional feelings as metarepresentational states of mind. In J. Laird (Ed.), *Feeling and thinking*.

Reisenzein, R. (in preparation). *Exploring the strength of association between the components of emotion syndromes: The case of surprise*.

Reisenzein, R., & Hofmann, T. (1993). Discriminating emotions from appraisal-relevant situational information: Baseline data for structural models of cognitive appraisals. *Cognition and Emotion, 7,* 271–293.

Repetti, R. L. (1987). Individual and common components of the social environment at work and psychological well-being. *Journal of Personality and Social Psychology, 52,* 710–720.

Repetti, R. L., & Wood, J. V. (1997). Families accommodating to chronic stress: Unintended and unnoticed processes. In B. H. Gottlieb (Ed.), *Coping with chronic stress* (pp. 191–220). New York: Plenum.

Rice, P. L. (1998). *Health Psychology.* Pacific Grove, CA: Brooks/Cole.

Roseman, I. J. (1984). Cognitive determinants of emotion: A structural theory. In P. Shaver (Ed.), *Review of personality and social psychology: Vol. 5. Emotions, relationships, and health* (pp. 11–36). Beverly Hills: Sage.

Rosenbaum, M. (1990). (Ed.) *Learned resourcefulness: On coping skills, self-control, and adaptive behavior.* New York: Springer.

Roskies, E. (1983). Stress management: Averting the evil eye. *Contemporary Psychology, 28,* 542–544.

Rotter, J. B. (1954). *Social learning and clinical psychology.* Upper Saddle River, NJ: Prentice Hall.

Russek, L. G., & Schwartz, G. E. (1996). Energy cardiology: A dynamical energy systems approach for integrating conventional and alternative medicine. *Advances, 12,* 4–24.

Rusting, C. L., & Nolen-Hoeksema, S. (1998). Regulating responses to anger: Effects of rumination and distraction on angry mood. *Journal of Personality and Social Psychology, 74,* 790–803.

Rutter, M. (Ed.). (1980). *Scientific foundations of developmental psychiatry.* London: Heinemann Medical.

Ryff, C. D., & Singer, B., & Commentators. (1998). The contours of positive human health. *Psychological Inquiry, 9,* 1–85.

Safran, J. D., & Greenberg, L. S. (1991). *Emotion, psychotherapy, & change.* New York: Guilford.

Salovey, P. (Ed.). (1990). *The psychology of jealousy and envy.* New York: Guilford.

Sarbin, T. (Ed.). (1986). *Narrative psychology: The storied nature of human conduct.* New York: Praeger.

Schafer, R. (1981). Narration in psychoanalytic dialogue. In W. J. J. Mitchell (Ed.), *On narrative* (pp. 25–49). Chicago: University of Chicago Press.

Scheier, M. F., & Carver, C. S. (1987). Dispositional optimism and physical well-being: The influence of generalized outcome expectancies on health. *Journal of Personality, 55,* 169–210.

Scherer, K. R. (1984). On the nature and function of emotion: A component process approach. In K. R. Scherer & P. Ekman (Eds.), *Approaches to emotion* (pp. 293–317). Hillsdale, NJ: Erlbaum.

Scherer, K. R., Wallbott, H. G., & Summerfield, A. R. (Eds.). (1986). *Experiencing emotion: A cross-cultural study.* Cambridge, England: Cambridge University Press.

Schimmel, S. (1992). *The seven deadly sins: Jewish, Christian, and classical reflections on human nature.* New York: The Free Press.

Schneider, K. J. (1998). Toward a science of the heart: Romanticism and the revival of psychology. *American Psychologist, 53,* 277–289.

Schore, A. N. (1994). *Affect regulation and the origin of the self: The neurobiology of emotional development.* Hillsdale, NJ: Erlbaum.

Schore, A. N. (1997). A century after Freud's Project: is a rapprochement between psychoanalysis and neurobiology at hand? *Journal of the American Psychoanalytic Association, 45,* 807–840.

Schore, A. N. (1998). The experience-dependent maturation of an evaluative system in the cortex. In K. H. Pribram (Ed.), *Brain and values: Is a biological science of values possible* (pp. 337–358). Mahwah, NJ: Erlbaum.

Schuldberg, D., & Karwacki, S. B. (1996). Stress, coping, and social support in hypothetically psychosis-prone subjects. *Psychological Reports, 78,* 1267–1283.

Schuldberg, D., Karwacki, S. B., & Burns, G. L. (1996). Stress, coping, and social support in hypothetically psychosis-prone subjects. *Psycho-logical Reports, 78,* 1267–1283.

Seiffge-Krenke, I. (1995). *Stress, coping, and relationships in adolescence.* Mahway, NJ: Erlbaum.

Sellers, R. M. (1995). Situational differences in the coping processes of student-athletes. *Anxiety, Stress, and Coping, 8,* 325–336.

Selye, H. (1956/1976). *The stress of life.* New York: McGraw-Hill.

Selye, H. (1974). *Stress without distress.* Philadelphia: Lippincott.

Shaver, P., Schwartz, J., Kirson, D., & O'Connor, C. (1987). Emotion knowledge: Further exploration of a prototype approach. *Journal of Personality and Social Psychology, 52,* 1061–1086.

Shedler, J., Mayman, M., & Manis, M. (1993). The illusion of mental health. *American Psychologist, 48,* 1117–1131.

Shedler, J., Mayman, M., & Manis, M. (1994). More illusion. *American Psychologist, 49,* 974–976.

Shepard, R. N. (1984). Ecological constraints on internal representation: Resonant kinematics of perceiving, imagining, thinking, and dreaming. *Psychological Review, 91,* 417–447.

Sherif, M. (1935). A study of some social factors in perception. *Archives of Psychology, 27,* 187.

Shore, B. (1996). *Culture in mind: Cognition, culture, and the problem of meaning.* New York: Oxford University Press.

Shweder, R. A. (1991). *Thinking through cultures: Expeditions in cultural psychology.* Cambridge, MA: Harvard University Press.

Shweder, R. A. (1993a). The cultural psychology of the emotions. In M. Lewis & J. Haviland (Eds.), *The handbook of emotions* (pp. 417–431). New York: Guilford.

Shweder, R. A., & author's response (1993b). Everything you ever wanted to know about cognitive appraisal theory without being conscious of it. *Psychological Inquiry, 4,* 322–342.

Shweder, R. A., & LeVine, R. S. (1984). *Cultural theory: Essays on mind, self, and emotion.* Cambridge, England: Cambridge University Press.

Silver, R. L., Boon, C., & Stones, M. H. (1983). Searching for meaning in misfortune: Making sense of incest. *Journal of Social Issues, 39,* 81–102.

Silver, R. L., & Wortman, C. (1980). Coping with undesirable life events. In J. Garber & M. E. P. Seligman (Eds.), *Human helplessness: Theory and applications* (pp. 279–340). New York: Academic Press.

Skinner, B. F. (1983). Intellectual self-management in old age. *American Psychologist, 38,* 239–244.

Slaikeu, K. A. (1984). *Crisis intervention: a handbook for practice and research.* Newton, MA: Allyn & Bacon. (Original work published 1944)

Smelser, N. J. (1963). *Theory of collective behavior.* New York: The Free press.

Smith, C. A. & Ellsworth, P. C. (1985). Patterns of cognitive appraisal in emotion. *Journal of Personality and Social Psychology, 48,* 813–838.

Smith, C. A., & Ellsworth, P. C. (1987). Patterns of appraisal and emotion related to taking an exam. *Journal of Personality and Social Psychology, 52,* 475–488.

Snyder, C. R., & Forsyth, D. R. (1991). (Eds.), *Handbook of social and clinical psychology.* Needham Heights, MA: Allyn & Bacon.

Snyder, C. R., Harris, C., Anderson, J. R., Holleran, S. A., Irving, L. M., Sigmon, S. T., Yoshinobu, L., Gibb, J., Langelle, C., & Harney, P. (1991). The will and the ways: Development and validation of an individual difference measure of hope. *Journal of Personality and Social Psychology, 60,* 570–585.

Solomon, R. C. (1976). *The passions. The myth and nature of human emotion.* Garden City, NY: Doubleday.

Solomon, R. C. (1980). Emotions and choice. In A. O. Rorty (Ed.), *Explaining emotions* (pp. 251–281). Berkeley: University of California Press.

Solomon, Z., Mikulincer, & Avitzur, E. (1988). Coping, locus of control, social support, and combat-related posttraumatic stress disorder: A prospective study. *Journal of Personality and Social Psychology, 55*, 279–285.

Solomon, Z., Mikulincer, M., & Hobfoll, S. E. (1987). Objective versus subjective measurement of stress and social support: Combat-related reactions. *Journal of Consulting and Clinical Psychology, 55*, 577–583.

Solomon, Z, Mikulincer, M., & Flum, H. (1988). Negative life events, coping responses, and combat-related psychopathology: A prospective study. *Journal of Abnormal Psychology, 97*, 302–307.

Somerfield, M. R., & commentators (1997). The utility of systems models of stress and coping for applied research: The case of cancer adaptation. *Journal of Health Psychology, 2*, 133–172.

Spence, D. (1982). *Narrative truth and historical truth*. New York: Norton.

Spiegel, D. (1997). Understanding risk assessment by cancer patients: A commentary on Somerfield. *Journal of Health Psychology, 2*, 170–171.

Spielberger, C. D., Gorsuch, R. L., & Lushene, R. E. (1970). *Manual for the State-Trait Anxiety Inventory*. Palo Alto, CA: Consulting Psychologists Press.

Spielberger, C. D, Krasner, S. S., & Solomon, E. P. (1988). The experience and control of anger. In M. P. Janisse (Ed.), *Health psychology: Individual differences and stress* (pp. 89–108). New York: Springer-Verlag.

Spielberger, C. D., & Sydeman, S. J. (1994). State-trait anxiety inventory and state-trait anger expression inventory. In M. E. Maruish (Ed.), *The use of psychological tests for treatment planning and outcome assessment* (pp. 292–321). Hillsdale, NJ: Erlbaum.

Speisman, J. C., Lazarus, R. S., Mordkoff, A. M., & Davison, L. A. (1964). The experimental reduction of stress based on ego-defense theory. *Journal of Abnormal and Social Psychology, 68*, 367–380.

Spivack, G., & Shure, M. B. (1982). The cognition of social adjustment: Interpersonal cognitive-problem-solving-thinking. In B. B. Lahey & A. E. Kazdin (Eds.), *Advances in clinical child psychology* (Vol. 5, pp. 323–372). New York: Plenum.

Spivack, G., & Shure, M. B. (1985). ICPS and beyond: Centripetal and centifugal forces. *American Journal of Community Psychology, 13*, 226–243.

Stanton, A. L., & Snider, P. R. (1993). Coping with a breast cancer diagnosis: A prospective study. *Health Psychology, 12*, 16–23.

Stanton, A. L., Tennen, H., Afleck, G., & Mendola, R. (1992). Coping and adjustment to infertility. *Journal of Social and Clinical Psychology, 11*, 1–13.

Staudenmeyer, H., Kinsman, R. S., Dirks, J. F., Spector, S. L., & Wangaard, C. (1979). Medical outcome in asthmatic patients. Effects of airways hyperactivity and symptom-focused anxiety. *Psychosomatic Medicine, 41,* 109–118.

Stearns, P. N. (1989). *Jealousy: The evolution of an emotion in American history.* New York: New York University Press.

Stein, N., Folkman, S., Trabasso, T., & Christopher-Richards, T. A. (1997). Appraisal and goal processes as predictors of psychological well-being in bereaved caregivers. *Journal of Personality and Social Psychology, 72,* 872–884.

Stein, N. L., Leventhal, B., & Trabasso, T. (Eds.). (1990). *Psychological and biological approaches to emotion.* Hillsdale, NJ: Erlbaum.

Stein, N. L., Liwag, M. D., & Wade, E. (1996). A goal-based approach to memory for emotional events: Implications for theories of understanding and socialization. In R. D. Kavanaugh, B. Zimmerberg, & S. Fein (Eds.), *Emotion: Interdisciplinary perspectives* (pp. 91–118). Mahway, NJ: Erlbaum.

Stephens, M. A., & Clark. S. L. (1997). Reciprocity in the expression of emotional support among later-life couples coping with stroke. In G. H. Gottlieb (Ed.), *Coping with chronic stress* (pp. 221–242). New York: Plenum.

Stern, W. (1930). Autobiography. In C. Murchison (Ed.), *A history of psychology in autobiography* (pp. 335–388), Worcester, MA: Clark University Press. (S. Langer, Trans.)

Sternberg, R. J. (1986). A triangular theory of love. *Psychological Review, 93,* 119–135.

Sternberg, R. J. (1987). Liking versus loving: A comparative evaluation of theories. *Psychological Bulletin, 102,* 331–345.

Stone, G. C., Cohen, F., & Adler, N. E. (1979). (Eds.). *Health psychology.* San Francisco: Jossey-Bass.

Stone, A. A., Cox, D. S., Valdimarsdottir, H., & Jandorf, L. (1987). Evidence that secretory IgA antibody is associated with daily mood. *Journal of Personality and Social Psychology, 52,* 988–993.

Stone, A. A., & Neale, J. M. (1984). The effects of severe daily events on mood. *Journal of Personality and Social Psychology, 46,* 137–144.

Stone, A. A., Neale, J. M., Cox, D. S., & Napoli, A. (1994). Daily events are associated with a secretory immune response to an oral antigen in men. *Health Psychology, 13,* 404–418.

Strentz, T., & Auerbach, S. M. (1988). Adjustment to the stress of simulated captivity: Effects of emotion-focused versus problem-focused preparation on hostages differing in locus of control. *Journal of Personality and Social Psychology, 55,* 652–660.

Stuhlmiller, C. M. (1996). *Rescuers of Cypress: Learning from disaster.* New York: Peter Lang.

Symington, T., Currie, A. R., Curran, R. C., & Davidson, J. N. (1955). The reaction of the adrenal cortex in conditions of stress. In Ciba Foundation Colloquia on Endocrinology. *The human adrenal cortex* (Vol. 8, pp. 70–91). Boston: Little, Brown.

Tait, R., & Silver, R. C. (1989). Coming to terms with major negative life events. In J. S. Uleman & J. A. Bargh (Eds.), *Unintended thought.* New York: Guilford.

Tangney, J. P., & Fischer, K. W. (1995). *Self-conscious emotions: The psychology of shame, guilt, embarrassment, and pride.* New York: Guilford.

Tavris, C. (1984). On the wisdom of counting to ten: Personal and social dangers of anger expression. In P. Shaver (Ed.), *Review of personality and social psychology. Emotions, relationships, and health* (pp. 170–191). Beverly Hills, CA: Sage.

Taylor, G. (1980). Pride. In A. O. Rorty (Ed.), *Explaining emotions* (pp. 385–402). Berkeley: University of California Press.

Taylor, S. E. (1986). *Health psychology.* New York: Random House.

Taylor, S. E., Lichtman, R. R., & Wood, J. V. (1984). Attributions, beliefs about control, and adjustment to breast cancer. *Journal of Personality and Social Psychology, 46,* 489–502.

Terry, D. J. (1994). Determinants of coping: The role of stable and situational factors. *Journal of Personality and Social Psychology, 66,* 895–910.

Terry, D. J., Tonge, L., & Callan, V. J. (1995). Employee adjustment to stress: The role of coping resources, situational factors, and coping responses. *Anxiety, Stress, and Coping, 8,* 1–24.

Thoits, P. A. (1982). Conceptual, methodological, and theoretical problems in studying social support as a buffer against life stress. *Journal of Health and Social Behavior, 23,* 145–159.

Thoits, P. A. (1986). Social support as coping assistance. *Journal of Consulting and Clinical Psychology, 54,* 416–423.

Toch, H. (1969). *Violent men.* Chicago: Aldine.

Toch, H. (1983). The management of hostile aggression: Seneca as applied social psychologist. *American Psychologist, 38,* 1022–1025.

Tolman, E. C. (1932). *Purposive behavior in animals and men.* New York: Appleton.

Tomaka, J., & Blascovich, J. (1994). Effects of justice beliefs on cognitive appraisal of and subjective, physiological, and behavioral responses to potential stress. *Journal of Personality and Social Psychology, 67,* 732–740.

Tomaka, J., Blascovich, J., Kelsey, R. M., & Leitten, C. L. (1993). Subjective, physiological, and behavioral effects of threat and challenge appraisal. *Journal of Personality and Social Psychology, 65*, 248–260.

Tomaka, J., Blascovich, J., Kibler, J., & Ernst, J. M. (1997). Cognitive and physiological antecedents of threat and challenge appraisal. *Journal of Personality and Social Psychology, 73*, 63–72.

Tomkins, J. (1989, March). Fighting words. *Harpers Magazine*, pp. 33–35.

Tomkins, S. S. (1962). *Affect, imagery, consciousness: Vol. I: The positive affects*. New York: Springer.

Tomkins, S. S. (1963). *Affect, imagery, consciousness: Vol. 2: The negative affects*. New York: Springer.

Tomkins, S. S. (1991). *Affect, imagery, consciousness: The negative affects, anger, and fear (Vol. 3)*. New York: Springer.

Tomkins, S. S. (1992). *Affect, imagery, consciousness: Cognition duplication and transformation of information (Vol. 4)*. New York: Springer.

Tompkins, V. H. Stress in aviation. (1959). In J. Hambling (ed.), *The nature of stress disorder* (pp. 73–80). Springfield, Il: Charles C. Thomas.

Tooby, J., & Cosmides, L. (1990). The past explains the present: Emotional adaptations and the structure of ancestral environments. *Ethology and Sociobiology, 11*, 375–424.

Tov-Ruach, L., (1980). Jealousy, attention, and loss. In A. O. Rorty (Ed.), *Explaining emotions* (pp. 465–488). Berkeley: University of California Press.

Troop, N. A. (1998). Theoretical note: When is a coping strategy not a coping strategy? *Anxiety, Stress, and Coping, 11*, 81–87.

Turner, J. A., Clancy, S., & Vitaliano, P. P. (1987). Relationships of stress, appraisal and coping, to chronic low back pain. Special Issue: Chronic pain. *Behavior Research and Therapy, 25*, 281–288.

Uleman, J. S., & Bargh, J. A. (Eds.). (1989). *Unintended thought*. New York: Guilford.

Vallacher, R. R., & Nowak, A. (1997). The emergence of dynamical social psychology. *Psychological Inquiry, 8*, 73–99.

Van Heck, G. L., Vingerhoets, J. J. M., & Van Hout, G. C. M. (1991). Coping and extreme response tendency in duodenal ulcer patients. *Psychosomatic Medicine, 53*, 566–575.

Veenhoven, R. (1990). (Ed.), *How harmful is happiness?* Rotterdam: Universitaire Per Rotterdam.

Vitaliano, P. P., DeWolfe, D. J., Maiuro, R. D., Russo, J., & Katon, W. (1990). Appraised changeability of a stressor as a modifier of the relationship between coping and depression: A test of the hypothesis of fit. *Journal of Personality and Social Psychology, 59,* 582–592.

Vitaliano, P. P., Russo, J., & Maiuro, R. D. (1987). Locus of control, type of stressor, and appraisal within a cognitive-phenomenological model of stress. *Journal of Research in Personality, 21,* 224–237.

Wachtel, P. L. (1977). *Psychonalysis and behavior therapy: Toward an integration.* New York: Basic Books.

Wallbott, H. G., & Scherer, K. R. Cultural determinants in experiencing shame and guilt. In J. P. Tangney & K. W. Fischer (Eds.), *Self-conscious emotions: The psychology of shame, guilt, embarrassment, and pride* (pp. 465–487). New York: Guilford.

Weber, H. (1997). Sometimes more complex, sometimes more simple: A commentary on Somerfield. *Journal of Health Psychology, 2,* 171–172.

Weber, H., & Laux, L. (1993). Presention of emotion. In G. Heck, P. L. van Bonaiuto, I. J. Deary, & W. Nowack (Eds.), *Personality psychology in Europe* (Vol. 4, pp. 235–255). Tilburg, The Netherlands: Tilburg University Press.

Weinberger, D. A., Schwartz, G. E., & Davidson, R. J. (1979). Low-anxious, high-anxious, and repressive coping styles: Psychometric patterns and behavioral and physiological responses to stress. *Journal of Abnormal Psychology, 88,* 369–380.

Weiner, B. (1986). *An attributional theory of motivation and emotion.* New York: Springer.

Weinstein, J., Averill, J. R., Opton, E. M., Jr., & Lazarus, R. S. (1968). Defensive style and discrepancy between self-report and physiological indexes of stress. *Journal of Personality and Social Psychology, 10,* 406–413.

Weisenberg, M., Schwarzwald, J., Waysman, M., Solomon, Z., & Klingman, A. (1993). Coping of school-age children in the sealed room during scud missile bombardment and postwar stress reactions. *Journal of Personality and Social Psychology, 61,* 462–467.

Weiss, P. A. (1939). *Principles of development: A text in experimental biology.* New York: Holt.

Weiss, R. S. (1990). Bringing work stress home. In J. Eckenrode & S. Gore (Eds.), *Stress between work and family* (pp. 17–37). New York: Plenum.

Wells, A., & Matthews, G. (1994). Self-consciousness and cognitive failures as predictors of coping in stressful episodes. *Cognition and Emotion, 8,* 279–295.

Westman, M., & Etzion, D. (1995). Crossover of stress, strain and resources from one spouse to another. *Journal of Organizational Behavior, 16, 169–181.*

Westman, M., & Shirom, A. (1995). Dimensions of coping behavior: A proposed conceptual framework. *Anxiety, Stress, and Coping, 8,* 87–100.

Wheaton, B. (1994). Sampling the stress universe. In W. R. Avison & I. H. Gotlib (Eds.). *Stress and mental health* (pp. 77–223). New York: Plenum.

White, G. L. (1981). A model of romantic jealousy. *Motivation and Emotion, 5,* 295–310.

White, G. L., & Mullen, P. W. (1989). *Jealousy: Theory, research, and clinical strategies.* New York: Guilford.

White, G. M., and Lutz, C. (1986). The anthropology of emotions. *Annual review of anthropology, 15,* 405–436.

White, P. A. (1990). Ideas about causation in philosophy and psychology. *American Psychologist, 108,* 3–18.

White, R. W. (1959). Motivation reconsidered: The concept of competence. *Psychological Review, 66,* 297–333.

Wicklund, R. A. (1975). Objective self-awareness. In L. Berkowitz (Ed.), *Advances in experimental social psychology* (Vol. 7). New York: Academic Press.

Williams, R., & Williams, V. (1993). *Anger kills: 17 strategies for controlling the hostility that can harm your health.* New York: Time Books/ Random House.

Wilson, E. O. (1975). *Sociobiology: The new synthesis.* Cambridge: Harvard University Press.

Witkin, H. A. (1965). Psychological differentiation and forms of pathology. *Journal of Abnormal and Social Psychology, 70,* 317–336.

Witkin, H. A., Lewis, H. B., Machover, K., Meissner, P. B., & Wapner, S. (1954). *Personality through perception.* New York: Harper & Row.

Witkin, H. A., Dyk, R. B., Faterson, H. F., Goodenough, D. R., & Karp, S. A. (1962). *Psychological differentiation.* New York: Wiley.

Wolf, T. M., Heller, S. S., Camp, C. J., & Faucett, J. M. (1995). The process of coping with a gross anatomy exam during the first year of medical school. *British Journal of Medical Psychology, 68,* 85–87.

Wortman, C. B., & Lehman, D. R. (1985). Reactions to victims of life crises: Social support attempts that fail. In I. G. Sarason, & B. R. Sarason (Eds.), *Social support: Theory, research and applications.* Dordrecht, The Netherlands: Martinus Nijhoff.

Wright, J. C., & Mischel, W. (1987). A conditional approach to dispositional constructs: The local predictability of social behavior [Special issue]. *Journal of Personality and Social Psychology, 53,* 1159–1177.

Wundt, W. (1905). *Grundriss der psychology* (7th rev. ed.). Leipzig: Engelman (not read).

Zahn-Waxler, C., & Kochanska, G. (1990). The origins of guilt. In R. S. Thompson (Ed.), *Nebraska Symposium on Motivation, 1988.* Lincoln: University of Nebraska Press.

Zajonc, R. B. (1980). Feeling and thinking: Preferences need no inferences. *American Psychologist, 35,* 151–175.

Zajonc, R. B. (1984). On the primacy of affect. *American Psychologist, 39,* 117–123.

Zautra, A. J., & Wrabetz, A. B. (1991). Coping success and its relationship to psychological distress for older adults. *Journal of Personality and Social Psychology, 61,* 801–810.

Zeidner, M., & Ben-Zur, H. (1994). Individual differences in anxiety, coping, and post-traumatic stress in the aftermath of the Persian Gulf war. *Personality and Individual Differences, 16,* 459–476.

Zeidner, M., & Endler, N. S. (1996). (Eds.). *Handbook of coping: Theory, research, applications.* New York: Wiley.

Subject Index

Name Index